PENOLOGY

PENOLOGY

Theory, Policy and Practice

Karen Harrison

First published 2020 by
RED GLOBE PRESS

Red Globe Press in the UK is an imprint of Springer Nature Limited, registered in England, company number 785998, of 4 Crinan Street, London, N1 9XW.

Red Globe Press® is a registered trademark in the United States, the United Kingdom, Europe and other countries.

ISBN 978-1-137-60784-3 hardback
ISBN 978-1-137-60783-6 paperback

This book is printed on paper suitable for recycling and made from fully managed and sustained forest sources. Logging, pulping and manufacturing processes are expected to conform to the environmental regulations of the country of origin.

A catalogue record for this book is available from the British Library.

A catalog record for this book is available from the Library of Congress.

Contents

List of Figures

List of Tables

List of Boxes

SPOTLIGHT COUNTRIES

PRISON CASE STUDIES

Abbreviations

ABD	Application for a Benefit Deduction
AEO	Attachment of Earnings Order
AP	Approved Premises
ASB	Anti-Social Behaviour
ASBO	Anti-Social Behaviour Order
BAME	Black, Asian and Minority Ethnic
BCST	Basic Custody Screening Tool
CA	Court of Appeal
CJA	Criminal Justice Act
CJIA	Criminal Justice and Immigration Act
CNA	Certified Normal Accommodation
CoSA	Circles of Support and Accountability
CPA	Contract Package Area
CPS	Crown Prosecution Service
CRs	Community Resolutions
CRC	Community Rehabilitation Company
CSCs	Close Supervision Centres
CSODS	Child Sexual Offender Disclosure Scheme
DIRF	Discrimination Incident Reporting Form
DTO	Detention and Training Order
ECHR	European Convention on Human Rights
ECtHR	European Court of Human Rights
FGC	Family Group Conferencing
FIU	Family Intervention Unit
FNO	Foreign National Offender
HDC	Home Detention Scheme
HMCTS	Her Majesty's Courts & Tribunal Service
HMIP	Her Majesty's Inspectorate of Prisons
HMPPS	Her Majesty's Prison & Probation Service
ID	Intellectually Disabled
IEP	Incentive & Earned Privileges
IMB	Independent Monitoring Board
IPP	Imprisonment for Public Protection
IRC	Immigration Removal Centre
LASPOA	Legal Aid, Sentencing and Punishment of Offenders Act
MBU	Mother and Baby Unit
MAPPA	Multi-Agency Public Protection Arrangements
MLAA	Madaripur Legal Aid Association
MMPR	Minimising and Managing Physical Restraint
NOMS	National Offender Management Service

NPS	National Probation Service
OBPs	Offending Behaviour Programmes
OOCDs	Out Of Court Disposals
ORA	Offender Rehabilitation Act
OVP	The Venezuelan Observatory for Prison
PbR	Payment by Results
PCSO	Police Community Support Officer
PFI	Private Finance Initiative
PIPE	Psychologically Informed Planned Environment
PNC	Police National Computer
PND	Penalty Notice for Disorder
PND-E	Penalty Notice for Disorder-Education
PSR	Pre-Sentence Report
PTSD	Post Traumatic Stress Disorder
RMDT	Random Mandatory Drug Testing
RPI	Restrictive Physical Intervention
ROM	Regional Offender Manager
ROTL	Release on Temporary License
SCH	Secure Children's Home
SDS	Standard Determinate Sentence
SED	Sentence Expiry Date
SFO	Serious Further Offence
SLED	Sentence and License Expiry Date
SOA	Sexual Offences Act
SOTP	Sex Offender Treatment Programme
SSO	Suspended Sentence Order
SSRIs	Selective Serotonin Reuptake Inhibitors
STC	Secure Training Centre
TC	Therapeutic Community
TR	Transforming Rehabilitation
TTG	Through-the-Gate
TUSED	Top-Up Supervision End Date
TWP	Together Women Project
UK	United Kingdom
UN	United Nations
US	United States of America
ViSOR	Violent and Sex Offender Register
VORPs	Victim Offender Reconciliation Programmes
YCS	Youth Custodial Service
YJB	Youth Justice Board
YJS	Youth Justice System
YOI	Young Offender Institution
YOP	Youth Offending Panel
YOT	Youth Offending Team
YRO	Youth Rehabilitation Order

1 Introduction

DEFINING PENOLOGY

A book which bears the title *Penology* should really begin with a definition of what its subject matter is and while you might think that this would be a simple task, the definition you use will determine how broad or narrow your understanding of penology is. Looked at in its simplest form, penology is made up of two separate words: the Latin *poena* (meaning punishment) and the Greek suffix *logia* (meaning the study of), making it the study of punishment. This is similar to the dictionary definition, which broadens it a little by stating that it is 'the study of the punishment of crime and of prison management' (Oxford Dictionaries Online, 2015). Key in both is the word 'punishment', which is defined as the 'infliction or imposition of a penalty as retribution for an offence' (Oxford Dictionaries Online, 2015). While both of these definitions, from the *Oxford Dictionary of English*, are useful, they are narrow in coverage. Looking at punishment first, the definition above is fairly simplistic in the sense that it limits its purpose to retribution. There are, however, a number of other reasons why a penalty might be inflicted, including as a way to deter or prevent others from behaving in a similar manner. Penalties may also be imposed for the benefit of the victim; such as compensating them for their losses, to keep the dangerous away from their communities or in order to rehabilitate the offender so that the public are safe. Detailed in Chapter 2, punishment is therefore much more than retribution alone.

Penology is also more than just prison management, with a better definition stating that it is the study of punishment (in all its guises) and the penal system. Part of the wider Criminal Justice System, which is also made up of the Police, the Crown Prosecution Service (CPS) and the Courts (see Sanders, et al., 2010; Harding, et al., 2017), the penal system is the collection of agencies and organisations which carry out the sentence of the court. In England and Wales while this does include the Prison Service, there is also the National Probation Service (NPS), Community Rehabilitation Companies (CRCs) and the Youth Custody Service (YCS). Taken at its broadest definition it could also include those organisations which enforce financial penalties, charities which provide rehabilitative programmes for offenders and supervisors who supervise unpaid work within the community. Furthermore, it could also comprise of those agencies whose task it is to monitor the work of prison and probation. This would include HM Inspectorate of Prisons (HMIP), HM Inspectorate of Probation and Independent Monitoring Boards (IMBs). A more encompassing definition of what penology is, is therefore provided by the Encyclopaedia Britannica:

> Penology, also called Penal Science, [is] the division of criminology that concerns itself with the philosophy and practice of society in its efforts to repress criminal activities. As the term signifies (from Latin *poena*, 'pain,' or

'suffering'), penology has stood in the past and, for the most part, still stands for the policy of inflicting punishment on the offender as a consequence of his wrongdoing; but it may reasonably be extended to cover other policies, not punitive in character, such as probation, medical treatment, and education, aimed at the cure or rehabilitation of the offender; and this is, in fact, the accepted present sense of the term. (Encyclopaedia Britannica, 2019)

SCOPE OF THE BOOK

This 'present sense of the term' (Encyclopaedia Britannica, 2019) is the one which is used for this book. Consequently, this isn't just another prisons book, but is one which encompasses all of the penal system, including penal theory, sentencing policy and the practice of how offenders are managed within both prisons and the community. While it is accepted that financial penalties may not be as thrilling as prisons, on the basis that they make up more than three quarters of all of the sentences of the court it is important that they are included and the key issues surrounding their use discussed. This likewise applies to out of court disposals and community penalties. Continuing with this broadness, the book will also cover a range of specific offenders rather than just focusing on White adult men. In addition to sex offenders, the book will also cover women offenders, children and young people, and Black, Asian and minority ethnic (BAME) groups.

It is important to state that the book is generally focused on the penal system in England and Wales. Despite this specificity the broader discussions on penal theory and policy will be relevant to other countries, and to increase interest and allow for comparison, eight spotlight countries have also been included. These are there to provoke discussion about differing practices around the World and provide examples of best and 'interesting' practice. There has been an attempt to include a broad representation of countries including Scotland from the United Kingdom, Finland and Spain from Europe, Kenya from Africa, the United States of America (US) and Venezuela from the Americas, New Zealand from Oceania and Bangladesh from Asia. Countries were also chosen based on their penal policies with the spectrum ranging from the most punitive (the US) to the more welfare and restorative justice orientated (Finland and New Zealand). Where appropriate, other countries have also been referred to. Whether England and Wales can learn anything from these jurisdictions is one of the key discussions of the book.

In addition to covering the academic literature, it is essential for a book that purports to be about penology practice, that actual practice is included. This has been largely achieved in two ways: first through speaking to a number of people who currently work either within or for agencies associated with the penal system and second, through prison visits. In total 16 people were interviewed for this book. While the majority of these worked within prisons, including governors, deputy governors, treatment providers and wing officers, two people working for the NPS, two police officers, two restorative justice practitioners and one charity worker were also included. Informal conversations were also had with practitioners that were encountered during the prison visits.

In addition to these interviews, eight prisons were visited. This was so the book could provide an accurate account of current prison life including, the daily regime, available activities and, importantly, the challenges which prisons in England and Wales are currently facing. Similar to the spotlight countries is was thought important to include a broad range of establishments and so the visits included a maximum-security prison (HMP Full Sutton), a local prison (HMP Wandsworth), a training prison (HMP Lindholme) and an open prison (HMP Springhill). To supplement this, visits were also made to a sex offender only prison (HMP Whatton), a prison operating a therapeutic community (HMP Grendon), a private prison (HMP Parc) and a Young Offender Institution (HMYOI Feltham). Each visited prison has been written up as a case study and then dispersed in relevant places throughout the book. Both the interviews and the prison visits have provided rich detail to the book, which is not available in one volume elsewhere. It is therefore appropriate that sincere gratitude is expressed to those who agreed to be interviewed, those who arranged access into the prisons, those who conducted the prison tours and those who were frank about their views and experiences. The book would be nothing without you.

STRUCTURE OF THE BOOK

Following the title, the structure of the book is divided into three main parts: theory, policy and practice. The first section, theory, encompasses Chapters 2 and 3, with Chapter 2 looking at the meaning of punishment and the foundations of penal theory. As outlined above we punish not just for retributivist reasons and so this chapter looks at the penal theories of deterrence, incapacitation and rehabilitation. Furthermore, it attempts to set these theories into some context by looking at some of the criminological schools of thought including the classical school and positivism. Sociological explanations of punishment are also briefly included in an attempt to strengthen this context and to help answer the question of why we punish. Acknowledging that there are problems with all of the theories cited above, Chapter 3 focuses on restorative justice as an alternative to our traditional criminal justice system. Looking at current restorative practices, including practice in Bangladesh, the chapter makes the argument that rather than relying on retribution or rehabilitation alone the new third way of managing offenders and reducing crime would be through a combination of retribution, rehabilitation and restorative justice.

The book then moves on to look at sentencing policy, with this covered in Chapter 4. In addition to looking at the infrastructure of the criminal courts, including an overview of the Magistrates' Court and the Crown Court the chapter details how sentencing decisions are made and outlines the guidelines which sentencers in England and Wales must follow. With reference to judicial discretion and the use of guidelines, the US is used as an example of a country where judicial discretion has been virtually eroded. The chapter then moves to consider the life sentence and uses this as an example when discussing the tensions between the executive (the government) and the judiciary (the courts) in sentence decisions.

While under the legal doctrine known as the separation of powers, the executive should not interfere with judicial decisions, the chapter shows how this is not always the case.

Chapters 5–9 then consider the sentences of the court with Chapter 5 covering out of court disposals and the fine. With these making up a significant proportion of all criminal justice outcomes, it was thought essential that these were included in the book, as they reflect the reality of punishment in England and Wales today. With reference to fines, the chapter considers how we should go about setting the level of the penalty and equally important, what we should do with those who do not pay. In this chapter Finland is used as an example of a country which has a day-fine system. This is then followed by a chapter on community sentencing with coverage of both the community order with requirements and the suspended sentence order. Much of this chapter, however, is focused on the organisation of offender management and the agencies who have been tasked with this role since the introduction of Transforming Rehabilitation. This saw the privatisation of a significant proportion of probation with nigh on disastrous effect. The fundamental question in this chapter is whether probation is dead, dying or just poorly. Scotland is the spotlight country here, with questions asked as to why with similar social and economic factors community sentencing has increased there while it has significantly decreased in England and Wales.

The prisons chapters start with Chapter 7, with this acting as an introduction to Chapters 8 and 9. Focusing on the structure of the prison estate and the different types of prison establishments which exist, five prisons are presented in the form of case studies. The chapter ends with a discussion of prison privatisation and asks the fundamental question of whether companies should make money out of locking people up. Chapter 8 is then devoted to the prison experience. These pains of imprisonment are looked at predominantly from the view of the prisoner, but towards the end the experiences of prison staff and also prison visitors are considered. Relying on information from prison visits, in addition to inspection reports and the academic literature, a worrying picture of prison is presented. One, perhaps tongue-in-cheek, suggestion is presented through the use of Venezuela as the spotlight country, where inmate governance is common in some of its jails. The final prisons chapter, Chapter 9 looks at release, recall and reintegration. Focusing initially on the legislation which governs automatic release, there is then a discussion on the Parole Board and the issues which it currently faces, including its lack of independence from the Ministry of Justice. The comparator country is Spain, where, when compared to England and Wales, significantly more prisoners are held in open regimes and parole and recall decisions are made by prison judges. Current problems with recall and how well offenders are supported when they return to their communities is also evaluated.

Leaving the sentences of the court behind, Chapters 10–12 look at specific groups of offenders with Chapter 10 focusing on those who are assessed as dangerous. While this can include all violent, sexual and terrorist offenders, the chapter deals predominantly with violent and more specifically with high-risk sex offenders. Rather than looking at a spotlight country, the chapter focuses on the prison regimes at HMP Whatton and HMP Grendon, both of which have been found to be useful with dangerous offenders. Acknowledging that most prisoners will one day be released into the community, the chapter also considers how high-risk offenders are managed in the community and assesses treatment programmes based on psychological and pharmacological interventions. Finally, Chapters 11 and 12 look at factors defined as protected characteristics under the Equality Act 2010, with Chapter 11 looking at how the penal system deals with children and young people. This has both a prison case study (HMYOI Feltham) and a spotlight country (New Zealand) with them representing the two ends of the spectrum in terms of how young people could be treated. Focusing on issues such as suicide, self-harm, control and restraint, the serious problems evidenced in the adult custodial estate in Chapter 8 also appear to be present in youth custody. To close is Chapter 12, which continues with the focus on protected characteristics and covers both women offenders and BAME groups. Research is used to show how both women and BAME offenders are discriminated against and suffer additional pains of imprisonment when compared to White men. A consideration of how women in Kenya are punished is included as is a brief discussion of the mass imprisonment of young Black men in the US.

AIMS OF THE BOOK

The book is designed to be used by a variety of audiences. For those new to the penal system in England and Wales it will serve as an introduction and can be used as a bridge to more specific academic and practice based sources. It can also be used as a text to support undergraduate and postgraduate study, whether this is on a criminology or a law programme. Throughout, the fundamental aim of the book is to encourage discussion and thought, with discussion questions being a prominent feature in all chapters. Each chapter additionally contains suggestions for further reading, with links to relevant films, radio programmes, lectures, media reports and presentations included. Finally there are points for you to consider, either on your own or in small groups. Some involve you thinking about designing your own prison and deciding on what regime you would have, others ask you to consider whether current policy and practice is fit for purpose, while others ask you to think about what changes are needed to ensure that our penal system is transparent, just and fair.

Penal policy and practice sits within a fast changing world with there being constant alterations to policy and resulting practice. At the time of writing, this was particularly true for probation practice, with the Ministry of Justice announcing the demise of CRCs just days before this book was completed. It is therefore worth noting that the book is up-to-date to May 2019.

2 Punishment and the Foundations of Penal Theory

INTRODUCTION

The most logical starting point for a book that considers penal policy and practice is penal theory. Penal theory seeks answers to the questions of whether, and if so on what grounds, we are justified in punishing offenders and to what ends, this punishment should be used. When somebody has committed behaviour that breaches the criminal law, there is a belief that that person should suffer something unpleasant. Punishment in this sense is therefore a penalty that is imposed in response to proven criminal behaviour. Duff (1998) argues that it is a communicative act, which informs the offender that what they have done is wrong. In England and Wales, as in other countries, punishment is carried out in a formalised way, a process that is administered through the criminal courts on behalf of the state (although see Chapter 5 for a discussion of out of court disposals and Chapter 11 for a brief consideration of civil orders). This includes ensuring that first, if the defendant pleads not guilty, they have had a fair trial and then second, that published sentencing policies and principles are adhered to (see Chapter 4). Due to the fact that the deliberate infliction of harm can be regarded as an evil and may, out of a sentencing context, be considered to be a breach of the criminal law, for it to be seen as a necessary evil, it must be warranted. To this end, punishment must have a justifying aim or function, because to punish merely because a harm has been committed may be considered by some as reprehensible as the original behaviour.

What that justification should be is the more difficult and controversial question, although in general the main sentencing theories can be divided into those which are forward-looking and those which are backward-looking (Brooks, 2015) (Hudson, 2003). Forward-looking accounts see punishment as a way in which some future benefit can be achieved, usually with the end goal being to limit future crime. Backward-looking approaches, on the other hand, view punishment as a method of correctional justice. People are punished because they are responsible for a moral wrong and therefore deserve to be punished. In this sense, the punishment is for punishments sake and while there may be some future benefit to it; this is not how its infliction is rationalised. Those who argue for forward-looking justifications of punishment are often referred to as 'instrumentalists' or 'reductionists', while those who favour the backward-looking approach are known as 'retributivists' (Bennett, 2008). In addition to looking at the key penal theories, this chapter will also briefly look at the main schools of criminological thought and some of the sociological explanations of punishment. This will help to explain how these theories have developed over time and the role that crime and punishment plays in society.

FORWARD-LOOKING APPROACHES

Forward-looking stances focus on the benefits that can be achieved through the infliction of punishment. Punishment in this sense is seen as a 'technique for solving a social problem' (Bennett, 2008, p. 14), such as the fear and harm caused by the commission of crime. Methods of punishment are therefore justified on the basis that they work to limit and/or prevent future crime, with it being argued that spending money on forward-looking approaches is much easier to rationalise because of these long-term benefits (Bennett, 2008). Such an argument does, however, rely on the fact that sentencing theories do work to this end and as outlined in more detail below 'the evidence on whether deterrence or rehabilitation are effective remains controversial and inconclusive at best' (Bennett, 2008, p. 15). The three main forward-looking approaches considered here are, deterrence, incapacitation and rehabilitation. Bentham (1998) argues that through all of them, crime can be limited: deterrence makes individuals too afraid to offend, incapacitation takes away their ability to offend and rehabilitation takes away their desire to offend. What these theories are and whether they work to reduce crime is considered below.

Deterrence

Ashworth (1998) defines deterrence as punishment, warranted by reference to its crime preventative consequences, with the foundations of the theory traceable to the work of two classical criminologists Cesare Beccaria and Jeremy Bentham. In 1764, Beccaria wrote an *Essay on Crimes and Punishment*, which questioned the standards that governed the use of criminal punishments in Italy. His argument, in relation to deterrence theory, was that 'individuals make decisions based on what will garner them pleasure and avoid pain, and unless deterred, they will pursue their own desires, even by committing crimes' (Tomlinson, 2016, p. 33). He further argued that deterring punishments needed to be certain, swift and proportionate to the committed crime and in addition needed to be public so that individuals knew what would happen to them if they breached the criminal law (Tomlinson, 2016). Emphasising this work and perhaps moving it forward, Bentham in *An Introduction to the Principles of Morals and Legislation*, in 1781, started to develop the idea of rational choice theory (Tomlinson, 2016). This views individuals as reasoning actors who will consider the means, ends, costs and benefits of any given action and then make a rational choice as to whether to proceed. The foundation of rational choice theory is behavioural choice, that is, we can all choose whether to act in a particular way. Proponents of deterrence hence argue that it is only deterrence theory, which is compatible with the idea that human beings have the ability to choose which actions they perform. Posner (1985) consequently argues that human beings are like calculators in that we continually assess whether the benefits or rewards of our actions outweigh the consequences. In this calculation, benefits include economic gain but also emotional responses to criminal behaviour such as revenge and satisfaction. Consequences include the expected punishment but also the cost of committing the crime and the offender's personal time (Posner, 1985). Deterrence theory in this way can only work if the negative consequences of criminal behaviour actually outweigh the perceived benefits. If this is achieved and somebody is dissuaded from criminal wrongdoing then deterrence is arguably the only theory that works to prevent people from entering the criminal justice system, rather than just dealing with them once they are there.

The theory has two main strands: individual and general deterrence. Individual deterrence, also known as special deterrence, deters a particular offender from offending or reoffending. This is highly individualised changing significantly between different people. A sentencing system using individual deterrence as its guiding theory would therefore need sufficient information about the offender before any sentencing decision was made. This would include previous convictions, character and the circumstances of the offence (Ashworth, 1998), but personal experiences and an individual's perceived risk of being caught in the future would also be important (Stafford & Warr, 1993). The severity of the punishment would increase as the list of previous convictions grew and because sentencing would become individualised there could be no consistency between offences (Ashworth, 1998). Unlike just deserts (discussed below), sentencing under deterrence would therefore need to be offender focused rather than offence focused.

Even though special deterrence is important, Ashworth (1998) and Bentham both argue that this is secondary to general deterrence, which 'ought to be the chief end of punishment' (Bentham, 1998, p. 54). Rather than focusing on the individual, general deterrence uses the sentence of an individual to deter those, with the inclination and opportunity to undertake an offence, from committing crime. Sentencing decisions under general deterrence are therefore based on what will deter the community at large, rather than what will deter the individual in question. Due to this aim, it can result in an individual offender being made an example of and receiving a more severe sentence than they otherwise might, with examples of this seen in sentencing practice following the English riots of 2011. From an individual's viewpoint, there is no way of predicting when this might happen and who might be picked, which makes the completion of Posner's (1985) economic and risk calculations difficult. The use of general deterrence is warranted, however, first because of its crime preventative effect but also on utilitarian grounds: the greater good of sparing future probable victims, is achieved for the greater number. The sacrifice of one individual is therefore a cost worth paying (Ashworth, 1998).

The English riots of 2011

On 4th August 2011, police shot and killed Mark Duggan on the Broadwater Farm estate, Tottenham, London, while attempting to arrest him for gun crime. Two days later, 300 people gathered outside Tottenham police station demanding justice for Mr Duggan and his family, with this ending in violent clashes between the crowd and police. During the night the violence continued, vehicles and shops were set alight and several people took the opportunity to steal items from shops. Overnight, the riots spread to other parts of London, including Enfield, Oxford Circus, Brixton, Waltham Forest, Hackney, Peckham, Clapham, Croydon, Ealing, Woolwich and Lewisham. Violence then erupted in Birmingham, Liverpool, Manchester, Nottingham and Bristol (BBC News, 2011a).

Despite the independence of the courts, several government ministers argued for severe sentences for those involved in the riots. Eric Pickles, the then Communities Secretary stated: 'We need to understand that people for a while thought that this was a crime without consequence – we cannot have people being frightened in their beds, frightened in their own homes for their public safety. That is why these kind of exemplary sentences are necessary' (BBC News, 2011b). Examples included:

- Two men jailed for four years for admitting using Facebook in an attempt to incite violence, even though no such disorder resulted.
- A 17 year old banned from using social media for 12 months and given a three-month overnight curfew for a similar offence.
- A man sentenced to 18 months in custody for having a stolen television in his car (BBC News, 2011b).

Of the 2710 people who appeared in court following the riots, 945 received immediate custodial sentences with an average length of 14.2 months. Compared to the previous year for similar offences this was a 400 per cent increase in length (Beckford, 2012).

Criticisms of deterrence

Doubts and debates about the use of deterrence in sentencing decisions have focused mainly on two areas: practicalities and severity. In terms of practical aspects, the theory requires a knowledge of what level of punishment will prevent individuals from undertaking criminal acts so that its deterrent effect is actually felt. This however is difficult to achieve, especially bearing in mind that different things will deter different people and it would be unjust to have vastly different sentences for similar criminal offences (Ashworth, 1998). While the threat of imprisonment, for example, may be a sufficient deterrent for one, another may view custody as a way of life. In a similar vein, it is usually impossible to accurately determine why a person has been deterred from offending. While it may be the threat of punishment, it could equally be other situational factors, such as social shaming, loss of family and friends and loss of employment. The theory additionally assumes that individuals do actually act as human calculators, constantly weighing up the perceived benefits and consequences of their actions, but we cannot assume that everyone is making these rational choices; especially when we take into account the number of offences committed under the influence of drugs or alcohol (Tomlinson, 2016).

Another criticism is that in order to create the necessary amount of fear, it is justifiable to either punish an innocent person or to hand out excessive exemplary sentences (Ashworth, 1998). As noted above, this is justified on utilitarian grounds, but it is questionable whether an individual should be used as a mere means to an end (Bennett, 2008). When weighing this up, we need to ask whether, for example, social control and order are more important than an individual's human rights. Deterrence may work to prevent some individuals from engaging in criminal behaviour but it is not possible to know when it works and for whom. Can we ever be sure therefore that the sacrifice of an individual will actually promote a greater good? Even if we could be sure that this greater good could be achieved surely this should never be justified if the use of the punishment is immoral.

Furthermore, recent research has suggested that instead of severity of punishment being the key influential factor in deterrence, it is actually the certainty of punishment that is more impactful (Tomlinson, 2016). It is therefore thought that the severity of a given punishment will only have a crime preventative effect where a person believes that there is a significant chance that they will actually be apprehended for their wrongdoing. If the risk of apprehension is thought to be minimal, then however severe the threatened punishment is, this will not prevent the commission of the crime (Wright, 2010). Webster and Doob (2012) also conclude that the threat of harsher sentences does not deter. So while life imprisonment and the death penalty may not always deter people from committing crimes of violence, increasing the number of police officers on the street potentially will. This additionally links in with other research, which states that the very existence of a punishment structure (i.e. police, courts and sentences) has a deterrent effect on human behaviour. This was evident in Melbourne, Australia, in 1918, Liverpool, England, in 1919 and Denmark in 1944 when these jurisdictions found themselves without a police force (Ashworth, 1998).

Discussion Questions

1. What would personally deter you from committing a criminal offence? Would it be the threat of punishment or something else?
2. What do you think of Posner's economic theory of deterrence?
3. Can the use of punishment be justified on the grounds that it will lead to a social benefit? Is this benefit enough to warrant punishing an innocent person?

Incapacitation

Incapacitation is when an offender is physically restrained or prevented from offending. The most obvious way of doing this is, in England and Wales, is through imprisonment, although incapacitation can also be achieved, to a lesser extent, with curfews, exclusion requirements (see Chapter 6) and through the removal of licenses (for e.g. driving, liquor and gaming). In other countries, such as China, Iran, Pakistan, Saudi Arabia, and parts of the United States of America (US), the ultimate form of restraint is through the death penalty. The idea of incapacitation goes as far back into history as rehabilitation (see below). Under a traditional rehabilitative ethos, those offenders assessed as treatable were cured, while those who were not were detained. Notwithstanding the fact that rehabilitation may be carried out within an incapacitative setting, the theory does not presuppose that physical restraint will result in any reformative change.

Incapacitation today is generally used as a sentencing rationale for dangerous offenders. Contrary to sentencing policy for 'normal' offenders, where the length of time in custody must be commensurate with the seriousness of the offence, dangerous offenders can be sentenced to disproportionate lengths of imprisonment (see Chapters 4 and 10). The rationale, public protection, has created a whole raft of preventative detention policies (such as mandatory life sentences, see Chapter 4), which are used against sexual, violent and terrorist offenders. Separate legislation also exists for those offenders classified as mentally disordered. In this sense, selective incapacitation is used to protect the public against the crimes of the most 'risky'.

Criticisms of selective incapacitation

The use of selective incapacitation can however be problematic because in order for it to be justified and equitable there needs to be a high level of certainty that those who are truly dangerous are accurately assessed. Assessments of risk in terms of reoffending and thus dangerousness are generally carried out in two ways: clinically, which involves a professional's opinion and actuarially, which involves the use of risk assessment tools. While it is generally accepted that the actuarial method provides greater predictor reliability over the clinical alternative, there are still problems with using risk assessment tools. This is largely because actuarial tools work by comparing similarities between the profile of an individual and aggregated knowledge of past events of a cohort of convicted offenders. For example, if a previous offender population of 250 armed robbers offended at a rate of 50 per cent, it is assumed that all other armed robbers will also reoffend at this rate. The method, therefore assumes that information from one offender population can be easily generalised and transferred to the individual placed under assessment, an issue commonly known as statistical fallacy (Dingwall, 1989). This, however, is rarely the case, and is problematic when an individual has different characteristics to the cohort data, especially evident when transferring data on White male offenders to either ethnic minorities or women offenders (Grubin & Wingate, 1996) (see Chapter 12 for a broader discussion on ethnic minorities and women offenders). There is also the problem of low base rates. The base rate is the 'known frequency of a behaviour occurring within the population as a whole' (Kemshall, 2002, p. 16) and is what any given offender is measured against to determine their risk. When the base rate in the general population for a particular offence is low, such as is the case for sexual offending, predicting behaviour on such low base rates can cause errors. Even if these base rates are artificially raised to try to compensate for this, there is then the risk of causing yet more errors. Pollock and colleagues (1989) therefore argue that in such cases the most accurate thing to do is to declare that no one is dangerous as this is just as likely as saying that some are. Such errors frequently cause false positives (where someone is assessed as dangerous but is not) and false negatives (where someone is assessed as low risk but is in fact dangerous). On this basis, some individuals will inevitably be incapacitated for disproportionate lengths of time for no justifiable reason.

Even if dangerousness and future criminal behaviour could be accurately predicted, it is still questionable whether it is right to detain somebody because of what they *might* do in the future rather than due to what they have done in the past. Linking in with rational choice theory, individuals should be treated as moral agents who have the capacity to decide whether they will act in a particular way. Labelling an individual as dangerous and thus initiating a separate sentencing policy against them means that we are treating individuals in a certain way because of what they are, rather than because of what they have done, again demanding the question of whether this is acceptable conduct.

Discussion Questions

1. Are there any crimes that deserve incapacitation for life? If yes, is that because this term is justified for past wrongdoing or because you also want to achieve public protection?
2. Should we, as Pollock and colleagues argue, assess no one as dangerous or is it better to ensure we incapacitate the dangerous by taking the chance that we may only be right in one out of three cases?

Rehabilitation

Traditional rehabilitation

Traditional rehabilitation is focused on a treatment model of working with offenders. Through treatment, the argument is that 'an offender's personality, outlook, habits, or opportunities [can be changed] so as to make him or her less inclined to commit crime' (von Hirsch, 1998, p. 1). The model takes the view that offending is best reduced by looking at factors that directly relate to the causes of crime, whether these be economic, social or personal. Furthermore, as not every member of society is equal it is believed that it is these inequalities which need to be treated so that a reduction in reoffending can be achieved (Hollin, 2004). Methods of treatment, in this sense, derive from a psychoanalytic tradition and include counselling, psychological assistance, training and other needed support (Hollin, 2004). The benefits of such treatment were thought to be two-fold. First, it would reform the offender and allow them to lead more fulfilling lives, but importantly it also had an instrumental goal in terms of social defence (Robinson, 2008).

For the first 60 years of the twentieth century, many considered rehabilitation to be the most important aim of the criminal justice system. Under this regime, decisions relating to sentence type and length were largely dominated by how best the offender could be treated. Seriousness of the offence, arguably the overriding factor used in today's sentencing decisions (see Chapter 4), was thus quite low on the sentencers list of priorities (von Hirsch, 1998). During this time, there was an assumption that therapists and counsellors knew what worked and that these forms of treatment were the means by which offenders would be rehabilitated. Optimism about the worth of rehabilitation lasted until the early 1970s, however, when a number of research findings concluded that nothing worked, academics such as Martinson (1974) in the US and Brody (1976) in the United Kingdom (UK) argued that no treatment programmes existed which were able to produce routine successes for the majority of offenders. Such depressing conclusions brought into question not just the effectiveness of rehabilitation, but also more significantly, whether it could continue to serve as the primary aim of sentencing. Allen, for example thought not, arguing, 'the deterrence of the great majority of the population from serious criminal activity is always the consideration of first importance'(Allen, 1998, pp. 18–19).

Criticisms of traditional rehabilitation

The theory of traditional rehabilitation works on the assumption that, "the offender is portrayed as a victim of circumstance, with some level of individual or social 'wrongness' or abnormality as the root cause of their behaviour" (Hollin, 2004, p. 6). According to this argument, crime is caused not through free choice but because of biological, psychological or social factors, which are beyond the individual's control (see Positivism below). It is therefore the role of rehabilitation to cure this wrongness or abnormality and turn the offender into a law-abiding citizen. While this viewpoint is idealistic, the assumption works heavily against the idea of a justice system based on offenders having free will to make their own choices. The blame for an offender's criminal act is thus placed on society and their environment, with none placed on the actual offender. While inequalities do exist in modern society, offending is not the only choice for those who suffer from these inequities with several disadvantaged people not resorting to crime in order to make their way through life.

In an attempt to defend the theory, however, Cullen and Gilbert (1982) argue that focusing on rehabilitation is the only way in which offenders can make a real pay-off to society. This is achieved, they claim, through turning the offender into a law-abiding citizen, who will no longer reoffend. They further contend that this can only be done with humane punishments and by compensating the offender for the social disadvantages that they have experienced in the past. Rehabilitation, they argue, is thus the only theory of criminal justice, which accepts the responsibility to do some good, while the others only work to inflict pain upon the offender and their family (Cullen & Gilbert, 1982).

Modern rehabilitation

Owing to 'Nothing Works', but also due to a change in political climate, where the rights of the victim were placed above the needs of the offender (see Chapter 6 for a further discussion on this in relation to probation practice), rehabilitation has had to evolve in order to survive (Robinson, 2008). This first transformation is sometimes referred to as 'Something Works', where programmes, based on cognitive-behavioural theory started to be used. In Wales, a probation programme known as STOP (Straight Thinking On Probation) was probably the first of this type in the UK (Raynor, 1998). It differed in two main ways to other probation practice: first, it was prescriptive, in that, probation officers had to stick to a manual and second it was systematic, in the sense that it employed a building block approach to skills learning (Raynor & Vanstone, 1997). Evaluations of the programme were positive (Raynor & Vanstone, 1997). While practitioners argued that, they never stopped working with offenders in a rehabilitatory way, this first evolution, which also included working with offenders in groups rather than as individuals, secured rehabilitations survival.

'Something Works' then gave way to 'What Works', with this initially referred to as the Effective Practice Initiative. Implemented into probation practice in 1998, the aim of the policy was to create a core curriculum of accredited offending behaviour programmes (OBPs) to be used with groups of offenders. Each programme was focused on the three principles of Risk (the higher the risk of reoffending the more intensive the programme), (offender) Need and Responsivity (where the offenders' and tutors' learning styles are matched) (Chapman & Hough, 1998), with the government investing heavily in them. Rehabilitation under 'What Works' therefore secured legitimacy on a utilitarian rationale, where the main beneficiaries of the programmes were viewed as victims and communities, rather than the offenders themselves (Robinson, 2008). More recently, the Good Lives Model (see Ward, 2002) has taken the Risk, Need, Responsivity model further, by building an offender's capacity to live a fulfilling and meaningful life. This reinvention of rehabilitation has meant that rehabilitation can be a priority in offender management but it is not an end in itself and is carefully balanced with the need for public protection.

The focus of rehabilitation has thus changed with an emphasis on education rather than on treatment. As highlighted above, traditional rehabilitation was based on a medical model, where the offender was treated and cured, in order for change to come about. Importance now, however, is placed on teaching the offender how to recognise situations, how to solve problems and how to cope with circumstances similar to those where they would previously have offended. Responsibility for the offender's behaviour under this new version of rehabilitation is shifted from society, offender management organisations and the state, and placed with the individual offender. Once techniques to control behaviour have been taught, it is then the offender's responsibility to turn this taught behaviour into practice and change their conduct. This non-treatment paradigm was first put forward by Bottoms and McWilliams (1979) who argued that while previously the casework relationship had been officer-centred, this new way of working was much more about providing the offender with help.

This self-responsibility can be highlighted by the way in which offenders are currently taught in OBPs (see Chapters 6 and 10). Different to traditional probation practice, accredited programmes encourage, perhaps even demand, that the offender is an active participant, rather than a mere passive recipient. In the past, treatment happened to offenders, while now, they are encouraged to engage with the programme and make it work for them. Programme content is also based much more on education than health, with an analogy easily made between offender management and the education system. Like the National Curriculum in schools, offenders like pupils are taught in the same way and are given the same opportunities and chance to 'graduate' at the end. The key focus is thus on teaching and learning rather than on treating and curing.

Using rehabilitation in a practical sense therefore means that something good can be achieved with the offender. Even if the principle sentencing aim is just deserts and the offender is imprisoned, a transformative effect can still be attained if time is taken to discover why the individual is offending. These are often referred to as criminogenic needs, defined as those 'attributes and/or dynamic risk factors of offenders which, if changed, are very likely to influence the probability of reoffending' (Clark, 2013, p. 74). Criminogenic needs are commonly categorised into two groups: static factors that will never change (e.g. offending history) and dynamic factors that can be altered (e.g. unemployment, drug addiction and poverty). On the basis that rehabilitation on its own may still be criticised, by some, as being too idealistic, the answer to modern day sentencing may therefore be to have a mixture of sentencing objectives. Von Hirsch and Maher (1998), for example, argue that just deserts and proportionality (see below) should have a limiting role and be used to set the upper and lower boundaries of quantum, while within these bounds, rehabilitation should be used to fine-tune and create the most just sentence (see Chapter 4 for examples on how this can work). This would therefore suggest a desert-determined amount of punishment, with a rehabilitative determined content (von Hirsch & Maher, 1998).

Criticisms of modern rehabilitation

Criticisms relating to rehabilitation focus on whether it can be said to work, especially when in the past it was claimed that nothing worked (Brody, 1976; Martinson, 1974). In order to determine accurately whether a programme is effective, it is important to undertake controlled experiments where treated offenders are matched on recidivism rates with an exact group of untreated offenders. By comparing the data, it is then possible to determine, what effect the treatment has had. There are, however, problems with this. First, it is unlikely that you will ever be able to find two exactly matched groups of offenders and second, even if you could, there is the ethical aspect of treating one group of offenders and making them 'safe' while leaving the other group untreated and potentially dangerous (Brown, 2010). Furthermore, similar to how deterrence can be criticised (see above) it cannot be assumed that just because an individual has stopped their criminal behaviour that it was due to some court-mandated intervention.

Perhaps due to these difficulties, academics today have moved from the language of whether rehabilitation works to talking about whether it can be said to help an offender 'go straight' (Ward & Maruna, 2007, p. 12). So while it is unlikely that a set programme will work for everyone, it can probably be said to help a person abstain from future criminal behaviour. Also, and linking in with the change to an educational model of rehabilitation, if someone is given help but still decides not to go straight then it is now considered to be that individual's fault rather than the helpers (Ward & Maruna, 2007). This has led some academics to go further and to talk about desistance rather than rehabilitation with McNeill arguing,

> Put simply, the implication is that offender management services need to think of themselves less as providers of correctional treatment (that belongs to the expert) and more as supporters of desistance processes (that belong to the desister). (McNeill, 2006, p. 46)

A relatively new term, desistance is 'the long-term abstinence of criminal behaviour among those for whom offending has become a pattern of behaviour' (McNeill, et al., 2012) and is viewed as an absence of offending rather than being an observable event (Rocque, et al., 2017). Over the last 30 years a body of research looking into why offenders cease from crime has developed, with studies looking at, for example, young adult men (Bottoms & Shapland, 2011), ethnic minorities (Calverley, 2012), and female street offenders (Sommers, et al., 1994). Factors said to contribute to desistance include age, marriage, parenthood, employment, education and family ties (Maruna, 2001; Farrall & Calverley, 2006). Desistance from crime will often require behavioural change and it is through OBPs that such change may be able to be effected.

Discussion Questions

1. Having considered the theories with a forward-looking approach, which theory or combination of theories do you think our sentencing system should be based upon?
2. Should this system prioritise the offender or the offence?
3. Which form of rehabilitation do you think is the most useful?
4. Rather than rehabilitation, should we instead be using the language of desistance?

BACKWARD-LOOKING APPROACHES

Backward-looking stances, as the name suggests look back to the crime and concentrate on meting out punishment in response to this behaviour. The infliction of punishment is therefore necessary because the offender deserves to be punished. Punishment in this sense is based on retribution, which is warranted in its own right, either to restore justice, avenge victims or express 'the justified outrage of reasonable people' (Bennett, 2008, p. 14). As highlighted above, there are problems with the theories which look forward, not least the fact that they do not respect the moral status of individuals and one way to ensure this is done is to favour a more retributivist approach. As explained by Bennett 'retributive punishment avoids these problems because it is directed towards the individual as a result of a failure for which she is responsible, not for the sake of some result she can be used to promote' (Bennett, 2008, p. 19). The penal theory most aligned to this approach is just deserts.

Just deserts

Just deserts theory, in its purest form, is based on the premise that the seriousness of the convicted crime is the sole determinant of the severity of the sentence. It is inextricably linked with retribution on the basis that it is not only the states right, but also its duty to punish those people who have breached the law (Moore, 1998). In this sense, a criminal offender deserves to be punished because they are morally blameworthy, with the task for the sentencer being to find a punishment that fits the crime. A key element of the theory is justice. It is therefore inequitable to hand out inappropriate punishments, such as those seen in general deterrence, as only those sentences that are commensurate with the severity of the crime are acceptable. This does not mean, however, that severe punishments cannot be used, nor that the offender cannot suffer from deprivations; just that such punishments have to be equal to the harm caused or risked being caused. In addition, because the theory is based on blameworthiness, culpability in committing the crime will also be taken into account (Frase, 2012). Correspondingly, it is also inappropriate not to punish someone who is deserving of it, as this too can amount to an injustice (Moore, 1998). Moore further argues that even where it would appear that no good has come of the punishment, the rendering of justice in itself is 'the good that justifies the harm' (Moore, 1998, p. 152). Due to this exclusive focus, pure just desert theorists do not concern themselves with any of the practical effects of punishment such as crime control or personal redemption. While these may indeed be by-products, they are not of prime importance.

Just deserts can also be referred to as moral deserts and works in a similar way to the issuing of monetary compensation in cases of contract disputes and civil negligence. The focus is on ensuring that the offender understands not only that they have committed a wrong, which will be met by some punishment but also that they are being treated as a wrongdoer. To illustrate this, von Hirsch uses the example of paying a fine as opposed to paying tax. While both involve the payment and loss of money, it is only the fine that comes with added disapproval or censure (von Hirsch, 2017). This has two aims: first, it recognises and acknowledges the infringed rights of the victim and second it appeals to the offender's sense of right and wrong by addressing the offender as a moral agent. It is therefore hoped that this communicative act of censure will lead to 'transparent persuasion' where the offender realises that their past behaviour is wrong and consequently modifies their future behaviour (Duff, 1998, p. 162). In this sense, both Duff and von Hirsch are more moderate in their understanding of the theory than perhaps is Moore (1998). Von Hirsch, for example, advocates that the punishment does not always need to be commensurate with the seriousness of the crime but rather that it should be proportionate. For him the key aspect of just deserts is attaching moral blameworthiness and therefore he sees no point in ascribing censure to an individual who is already repentant and taking steps to modify future behaviour. If, however, an individual does not respond to the moral appeal of the censure then it may be necessary to use the punishment for reasons of obedience, but even here, von Hirsch argues that this should be in addition to, rather than instead of, penal censure (von Hirsch, 2017).

How just deserts should work in sentencing practice has ignited some debate. One major point is whether the theory is used as a determining factor or as a limiting factor. In the former, and as noted above, just deserts is used as the sole determinant in deciding exactly what the sentence should be, while in the latter it provides some broad limits which ensure that the punishment is not so severe as to make it undeserved. In this second version just deserts is used to limit the upper and lower boundaries of a sentence, but it is not used for the fine-tuning or content (Morris, 1976). This modified model may be useful where proportionality is used to determine the type of sentence, for example a financial penalty or a community order, but other theories come into play to determine the amount of the fine or the precise package of requirements contained in the community order (see Chapter 4 for examples of how this works in practice). Moreover, it allows other theories to be taken into account in sentencing decisions where the sentencer is deciding between two sentences of equal severity such as a curfew or a programme requirement of a community order (see Chapter 6). If both have equal amounts of moral censure then they are both acceptable under just deserts and theorists who favour this approach do not need to object if the needs of incapacitation or treatment are then used to justify which of the two requirements is chosen.

Just deserts has a long history, with elements of it evident in early biblical teachings where it was thought appropriate to take 'an eye for an eye and a tooth for a tooth' (The Book of Exodus 21:24). Despite this long past, the theory as most understand it today, began in 1972, with *Struggle for Justice* (American Friends Service Committee, 1972), a Quaker-sponsored report on crime and punishment. The report recommended moderate, proportionate punishments and opposed deciding how severe a sentence should be using predictive or rehabilitative grounds. Coupled with a number of other reports, including *Doing Justice* (von Hirsch, 1976) and *Trials and Punishments* (Duff, 1986), just deserts became the 'central conception of justice in sentencing' (von Hirsch, 2017, p. 3), with numerical sentencing guidelines published and used in the US states of Minnesota and

Oregon (see Chapter 4 for the US federal sentencing guidelines). Not long after, the European countries of Finland, Sweden and then England and Wales followed suit, with Israel introducing a desert orientated sentencing system in 2012 (von Hirsch, 2017).

Sweden's Sentencing System

Drawing on two influential reports: *A New Penal System* and *Punishment and Justice* (von Hirsch, 2017), Sweden abolished indeterminate sentencing for young offenders and habitual offenders in 1979 and 1981 respectively, which had the effect of reducing the impact of deterrence and incapacitation in its sentencing system. Furthermore, in 1988 through the enactment of Chapters 29 and 30 of the country's Penal Code a new emphasis on proportionality was enshrined. The severity of any given sentence is now determined by looking at the seriousness of the offender's criminal behaviour. Such a task is aided by using aggravating and mitigating factors, with a list of these contained in the code (Swedish Penal Code Chapter 29, sections 2 and 3 respectively). This allows sentencers to individualise sentences taking into account precise details of both the offence and the offender to ensure, as far as possible, that a truly proportionate result is reached (von Hirsch, 2017).

Criticisms of just deserts

Just deserts in its purest form works on the premise that commensurate punishments are given through balancing the seriousness of the crime with the severity of the imposed sentence. How this is actually achieved in practice, however, can be problematic. While we know that seriousness is made up of harm caused or risked being caused plus the offender's culpability in committing the offence (see Chapter 4 for a fuller explanation on the meaning of seriousness), the key question is how these concepts are actually measured in real terms. Culpability can often be calculated by referring to the criminal law and distinguishing between behaviour that is intentional, reckless or negligent, but assessing how harmful an act is can be more difficult. To aid with this von Hirsch and Jareborg (1991) suggest that we concentrate on the victim's standard of living and assess how much the offence has reduced that standard. This can reflect both economic and non-economic interests so factors such as well-being, health and privacy can be taken into account. This they argue has a number of advantages including being able to consider cultural variations. For this to work each offence would need to be broken down into the kinds of interests which have potentially been infringed. This could include physical integrity, privacy, freedom from humiliation, material support and amenity. In a domestic burglary, for example, it may be that privacy and material amenity have been effected and so the task for the sentencer would be to determine to what extent the victim has been harmed. This they state could be further aided through using three categories of living standard – subsistence, minimal well-being and adequate well-being – where subsistence is seen as the most severe option. The more deprived a victim has been the more severe the punishment should be (von Hirsch & Jareborg, 1991).

Even if seriousness could be precisely determined, there is still the task of accurately determining what type of punishment that level of seriousness deserves, because as Hegel argues 'injustice is done if there is even one lash too many, or ... one week or one day in prison too many or too few' (Hegel, 1991, p. 245). Furthermore, we can never be sure that the suffering, hardship or inconvenience, which the offender endures, is truly commensurate with their wrongdoing because just deserts does not take the individual impact of the sentence into account. Sensitivity to penalties can therefore vary depending on determinants such as age, gender (Bentham, 1781), wealth or prison experience. For example, one person may prefer and suffer less from going to prison than from paying a fine, although traditionally we would view custody as a more severe sentencing option. This may be because the pains of imprisonment (see Chapter 8 for a discussion of these) for that person may be minimal, especially if they see imprisonment as an occupational hazard where they receive three meals a day and a roof over their head. For another, however, imprisonment may cause them to lose their job, home, family and self-respect. In this scenario, if both offenders were sentenced to custody because they had committed the same offence, it is unlikely that their punishments would be equal to each other and therefore just.

Another concern is the fact that even if a just punishment could be accurately measured, retributivists have never really justified why it is necessary to use punishment when responding to criminal behaviour. What is the actual justification for favouring punishment over, for example, a symbolic show of disapproval such as naming and shaming, or arguing with the wrongdoer or simply ignoring it? (Bennett, 2008) Until such questions can be answered, backward-looking approaches are arguably, just as problematic as forward-looking ones.

Discussion Points

1. Just deserts is the sentencing theory currently used in England and Wales. Is this the correct choice?
2. Should the theory be used as a determining factor or as a limiting factor?

SCHOOLS OF CRIMINOLOGY

To add some context to these theories it may be useful to explore in a little more detail how they were developed and their movement in and out of political favour. One way in which this can be achieved is through a brief consideration of the main schools of criminology. Outlined in Figure 2.1 the development of these schools of thought exemplify how criminal justice policies have shifted from deterrence to rehabilitation and finally to just deserts.

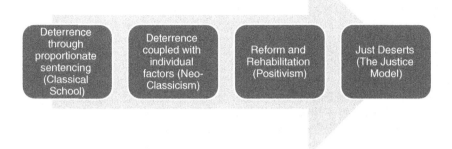

Figure 2.1 The evolution of penal theory

Classical school

The classical school of penal thought was linked with the European Enlightenment period of the eighteenth century and arguably was the beginning of criminology as a discipline. Previously, the State and the Church had absolute power, but the Enlightenment encouraged people to think for themselves, to analyse the problems of the day and importantly to come up with their own solutions. Important thinkers included John Locke, Isaac Newton and Voltaire, although arguably the two most influential Enlightenment theorists were Beccaria and Bentham (Williams, 2012). As highlighted above, Beccaria argued that everyone has free choice and that those who breach the criminal law should be punished because their interference with the rights of others merits such treatment. Punishments should not however be excessive, with the focus being on the offence rather than the offender. Beccaria therefore believed that an effective criminal justice system needed to provide four elements: a just and fair process, exactly the right amount of punishment, speedy justice, and certainty (Case, et al., 2017). Bentham likewise thought that punishments should be limited, although his reasoning was so that this would benefit the greatest number in society, that is utilitarianism. The use of excessive punishment in order to secure a general deterrent effect was therefore seen as warranted, because the greater good (i.e. the suppression of crime) was being achieved for the greater number (those who abided by the criminal law). Both men believed that the punishment should be just a little worse than the harm that the offence had caused, believing that this would be sufficient to deter criminal behaviour. The influence of the classical school can still be seen today: in order to prove a criminal offence you need to prove both a guilty mind (mens rea) and a guilty act (actus reus) and in many countries proportionality still plays a significant part in sentencing policy.

Neo-classicism

Neo-classicism highlights the fact that thinking does not stand still but will rather develop and build on traditional ideas, with this school of thought largely developing to remedy some of the problems which the classical school created. One of the main criticisms of the classical school is the fact that it saw all criminals as equal and thus ignored individual differences between them such as those based on age, mental capacity and previous behaviour (Williams, 2012). Neo-classicists still believe in free choice and rational choice theory but have introduced revisions to sentencing policy that account for the problems associated with the classical school. These include sentencing policies, which take into account aggravating and mitigating factors (see Chapter 4 for examples of these) mental capability, age (see Chapter 11) and mental disorders (Neese, 2017). Under neo-classicism, deterrence is still important, but accounting for individual factors opens the door to the use of reform and traditional rehabilitation.

Positivism

Positivist criminology developed in the nineteenth century with its focus on science rather than morals. Through collecting facts, positivism believes that the social world can be measured and explanations of behaviour gathered, with behaviour often attributed to biological, social or psychological influences. Opposite to the classical school, positivism focuses on the offender rather than the offence (Case, et al., 2017). According to positivism, crime is a product of heredity and social environment with it being these factors that determine whether an individual is predisposed to commit crime (Neese, 2017). In this sense, positivism believes that some individuals are just born criminal. One of the most famous early positivists was Cesare Lombroso who believed that because normal people would not commit crime, there had to be something pathologically different about those that did. Through *The Criminal Man* (1876) and *Crime, Its Causes and Remedies* (1899), Lombroso identified key characteristics based on skull size, bone structure and facial features which he claimed would identify a man as criminal.

Characteristics of thieves and murderers according to Lombroso

[T]heir expressive faces and manual dexterity, small wandering eyes that are often oblique in form, thick and close eyebrows, distorted or squashed noses, their beards and hair, sloping foreheads ... habitual murderers have a cold glassy stare and eyes that are sometimes bloodshot and filmy, the nose is often hawk-like and always large; the jaw is strong, the cheekbones broad; and their hair is dark, abundant, and crisply textured. Their beards are scanty, their canine teeth very developed, and their lips thin ... nearly all criminals have jug ears, thick hair, thin beards, pronounced sinuses, protruding chins and broad cheek bones. (Lombroso, 2006, p. 51)

Lombroso's findings have since been discredited, but what he is perhaps more famous for is the way in which he collected scientific data and then used this to either create or test theories. This is arguably the basis of modern day criminology. Neese therefore argues that:

> Positivism's focus on the individual may have been the greatest contribution to criminology and the criminal justice system. It led to classifications of offenders, such as habitual criminals, as well as categories between insanity and sanity. It also led to the use of psychology in studying offenders, opening the way for different kinds of sentences and treatments that fit the criminal and not the crime. (Neese, 2017)

Discussion Questions

1. What is your view of the classical school of criminology? Can we control crime by appealing to the morals of the majority or do we need to do more than this?
2. Should sentencing be primarily based on the offence or do we need to consider other factors as well?
3. What is your opinion of Lombroso's theory that some people are born criminal?

SOCIOLOGICAL EXPLANATIONS OF PUNISHMENT

Another way to look at the use of punishment is through a sociological perspective. Rather than focusing on justifying the use of punishment through theories based on retribution or crime reduction, sociology has traditionally looked at the role that crime and punishment play in society. Although there are a number of sociological explanations, the ones considered here derive from the work of Durkheim, Marx and Foucault. For a fuller explanation of all of these explanations, see (Case, et al., 2017).

Functionalism – Emile Durkheim (1858–1917)

By looking at the relationships that exist between crime, law and punishment, Durkheim, a French sociologist, argued that the primary role of punishment was to ensure social solidarity. One of his main contributions to sociology was the theory of functionalism, which argues that society and social order can only exist if each part of society is functioning properly. To help clarify this, Durkheim likened society to the human body explaining how for the body to function properly each component or organ needs to work together in partnership. If there is a crisis or malfunction in one component then this will effect the whole body. Like the human body, society is made up of several components or social institutions, with the main ones being the family, government, economy, media, education and religion (Durkheim, 2002). When something happens to cause imbalance in any of these institutions, such as criminal behaviour, it can lead to instability across all areas of society. The control of criminal behaviour through punishment is therefore thought of as important in terms of its contribution in maintaining social order, stability and productivity (Crossman, 2018).

Functionalist theory was at its most popular from the 1930s to the early 1960s. One of the most well-known functionalist sociologists at that time was Talcott Parsons, who looked at how different institutions ran, arguing that the smooth functioning of society could only be achieved when all of these institutions operated in harmony. This included institutions such as education and the military, but also extended to the family and religion (Parsons, 2013). Merton, however thought that this view was too simplistic, arguing that social structures were not always harmonious and could be dysfunctional for different types of people at different times in their lives. For example while schools worked to educate the young, they also created a separate youth culture, which could at times conflict with parental values (Merton, 1968). Further criticisms of functionalism, in relation to punishment, include the fact that some crimes are so dysfunctional (violence and sexual offences) that even for the functional purposes of maintaining order and ensuring social solidarity they should never be morally described as necessary. Furthermore, it is too simplistic to say that punishment benefits everyone in society, not only because we now live in diverse communities where there are no universal norms or values, but also because as, discussed below, it is often the poor who are punished for the benefit of the rich and powerful.

Conflict theory – Karl Marx (1818–1883)

Along with Durkheim, Marx is considered one of the founders of sociology, with his main contribution being that of conflict theory. Rather than assuming that social consensus and solidarity existed (see functionalism above), conflict theory focuses on the causes and consequences of class conflicts between the bourgeoisie (those who have the means of production such as factories) and the proletariat (those who have to sell their labour in order to survive). Writing at a time when capitalism was rising in Europe, Marx concentrated on the struggle over power, status and the allocation of resources, arguing that these were unfairly divided between the rich and the poor. Such imbalances in wealth and property would, he argued, worsen over time and would eventually lead to class consciousness and the development of trade unions and labour parties (Williams, 2012).

Marx never actually wrote about punishments, but a Marxian analysis of punishment as a social institution was carried out by Rusche and Kirchheimer in 1939. Their central argument had two main points: punishment is a function of economic conditions and the methods of punishment at any particular time will depend on the availability of the labour market. To explain this in more detail, the book is divided into three sections covering the early Middle Ages, the late Middle

Ages and the Enlightenment, or Modern period. At the end of the Middle Ages, when the economic conditions were poverty and insecurity due to a decrease in soil fertility and an increase in the population, punishments were needed to keep the lower classes in their place. Popular methods therefore included torture and execution, because at that time there was no need for their employment. This however changed in the nineteenth century, when through transportation much of the early White settlements in the US and Australia were built by convict labour (Rusche & Kirchheimer, 1939).

More recently, Wacquant (2009) has looked at how recent reforms in the US have led to the poor being punished in vastly disproportionate amounts when compared to the wealthy, predominantly White, middle classes (see Chapter 12 for a discussion on race and mass imprisonment in the US) (Wacquant, 2009). How society is run and what behaviour is classed as criminal is therefore determined not just by those in power but, also, for the benefit of those in power, often at the cost of the poor and working classes. Crimes carried out by the poor and especially those committed against the rich can often be prioritised over those committed by those in power. This can still be seen through the example of white collar and financial crimes. While offences of fraud, insider trading and environmental pollution can cause millions of pounds of damage, such offences are rarely prioritised over the street offences of shop lifting, robbery and criminal damage.

Social discipline – Michel Foucault (1926–1984)

The theme of power is also a focus of Foucault, especially in his book *Discipline and Punish* (Foucault, 1977). While this is presented as a historical account of the modern penal system, divided into the four sections of Torture, Punishment, Discipline and Prison, it is a structural analysis of how power is exercised (Garland, 1986). By looking at a number of historical examples of punishment, including public execution and corporeal punishment in the eighteenth century, Foucault argued that the way in which the powerful punished criminals, worked to re-establish the authority and power of the ruling classes. The form in which criminals were punished thus changed over time, largely due to society becoming more advanced, with the use of torture giving way to lighter punishments such as hard labour and chain gangs (Foucault, 1977). This focus on punishment then moved to discipline with the powerful turning the working classes into 'docile bodies' (Foucault, 1977, p. 135) who were trained in the ways of the powerful and punished if such ways were not followed. Such discipline now takes place in prisons, where offenders are sent to be corrected. The aim of a disciplinary society, Foucault argued, was to secure conformity and obedience through constant surveillance or through the uncertain belief that an individual was being monitored (Foucault, 1977). Punishment in this sense is viewed 'as a political tactic, situated within the general field of power relations' (Garland, 1986, p. 851), where the disobedient are made obedient generally through exerting influence on the soul (see Chapter 8 for a discussion on the psychological pains of imprisonment) rather than through physical forms of pain and torture. Punishment is still being inflicted, however, but in a more modern and technological way.

Discussion Questions

1. Functionalism argues that we need crime and the punishment of it in order for our society to function properly. What is your view on this?
2. How important is the role of power in crime and the control of it? How can we ensure that the 'proletariat' are treated fairly?
3. Can social discipline be achieved by turning citizens into docile bodies? Is such a proposal realistic on a practical level?

CONCLUSION

The fact that we must justify the use of punishment against those who have breached the criminal law is uncontroversial. How we go about doing this, however, is the more difficult task, with options including deterrence, incapacitation, rehabilitation and just deserts. As this chapter has tried to show, however, there are problems with all of these forward-looking and backward-looking approaches to penal theory. There is very little literature to prove that any of them work, and there are additional concerns about whether offenders are used as a means to an end, incapacitated for future rather than past deeds and whether the policies of the rich and powerful disproportionally effect the poor. It is also important to be honest about what we want achieved with those who commit crime. Do we want to punish for punishments sake or do we want to right the wrongs of what has happened and support the offender on a pathway of desistance. The current sentencing system in England and Wales is based on just deserts (retribution), but punishment that is truly equitable and worthwhile for both offenders and victims needs to be more than this. Sentencing therefore needs to take into account individual sensitivity to punishments, bring about reformative change, act as an effective deterrent but above all respect the rights of all those involved, including victims, offenders and the communities from which they come. This is no easy task and may well be one that our current retributive system is incapable of performing. Whether this is the case is the continuing subject matter of this book.

 Now read:

Canton, R. (2017) *Why Punish? An Introduction to the Philosophy of Punishment*. London: Red Globe Press.

Garland, D. (2018) *Punishment and Welfare: A History of Penal Strategies*. New Orleans: Quid Pro Books.

Maruna, S. (2001) *Making Good. How Ex-Convicts Reform and Rebuild their Lives*. Washington, DC: American Psychological Association.

von Hirsch, A. (2017) *Deserved Criminal Sentences*. Oxford: Hart Publishing.

Now watch:

Cambridge Law Faculty (2018) *Why Punish? Rob Canton* (21st Annual Bill McWilliams Memorial Lecture), available on YouTube at: https://www. youtube.com/watch?v=_X2VTNeLSaY.

Now consider:

Taking into account everything that you have read, what is the most appropriate theory or theories that we should be using to justify the punishment of offenders.

3 Rethinking Penal Theory

INTRODUCTION

The previous chapter; by focusing on the theories of deterrence, incapacitation, rehabilitation and just deserts; introduced the viewpoint that our criminal justice system, like many others around the world, is one based on retribution. Rehabilitation can also be argued to be a part of this conventional system because the vast majority of current rehabilitative programmes take place within the criminal justice settings of prison and probation and are, as such, a part of the court's sentence. This chapter, however, rethinks such norms by considering an alternative sentencing theory, namely restorative justice, and asks whether this could replace or at least play a much larger part in our current criminal justice system. What restorative justice is, its history and development, how it is currently used, whether it works, the criticisms made against its use and its scope for the future are all considered here. In short, the chapter argues that the best way forward for criminal justice is an amalgamation of retribution, rehabilitation and restorative justice.

THE DEVELOPMENT OF RESTORATIVE JUSTICE

Restorative justice as a theory and practice has a deep-rooted history. Based on ideas and principles taken from ancient societies, indigenous and native cultures and from a number of world religions, restorative justice is by no means a new concept (Maruna, 2014). In ancient societies, the goal of justice was not to punish offenders but rather to make reparation to the victim; with examples of early restorative practices including the Ifugao society in the Philippines, where a *monkalun*, or mediator would settle feuds, claims and counterclaims; and Eskimo villages, where a murderer would be expected to take on the widow and children of his victim (Gavrielides, 2011). During the Middle Ages (500–1500 AD) restorative practices began to change and by the end of the twelfth century they had been completely replaced by the criminal justice system with which we are now familiar (Gavrielides, 2011). This was largely due to the increase in the rights of the state, which first overshadowed and then totally supplanted the rights of the victim. With the rise of punishment, restitution was increasingly replaced with the more barbaric responses of whipping, the stocks, branding and capital punishment (Strong & Van Ness, 2015). Despite this change, reparative practices were still taking place in indigenous and other native cultures (Strong & Van Ness, 2015). The recent resurgence of restorative justice in Western cultures has arguably come about for three reasons: a loss in confidence in the ideals of rehabilitation and deterrence, a realisation that the victim is an important party in dispute resolution and the rise of interest in community justice. Such debate began in Westernised criminal justice settings in the 1970s and 1980s and has developed in momentum ever since.

Albert Eglash

Albert Eglash is often attributed with introducing the phrase 'restorative justice'. In a series of articles written in the late 1950s and another in 1977, he differentiated between three different models of justice, namely retributive justice (punishment), distributive justice (therapy) and restorative justice (restitution) (Eglash, 1977). The contribution that Eglash made to the development of restorative justice is often overlooked, largely because he seemed to focus more on offender benefits such as enhanced chances of community reintegration, rather than how it could work for victims. In 1977, for example, he stated that he never thought of victims and that 'any benefit to victims is a bonus, gravy, but not the meat and potatoes of the process' (Eglash, 1977, p. 99). Despite this, his work and ideas are still important and have contributed to the development of restorative practices (Maruna, 2014). For example, in 1957 he wrote about how an offender must offer some form of restitution in addition to punishment served, categorising compulsory punishment or reparation as 'the first mile' and creative restitution as the 'second mile' (Eglash, 1957, p. 620). It is only through this second mile that an offender can remedy the situation and make 'it good' (Eglash, 1957, p. 620). To illustrate this, he provides an example wherein a child who had damaged a mailbox, not only restored it to its previous condition but also made it more attractive (Eglash, 1977).

In creative or 'guided restitution' (Eglash, 1977, p. 93), the offender needs to make amends for what they have done, but is free to decide how this recompense will be made. To ensure that wholly insignificant gestures are not made, Eglash argues that the restitution must be an active effort that directly related to the criminal behaviour (Eglash, 1977). This had three distinct benefits: the offender actively sought to repair the harm, which enhanced relationships between the offender and the supervising authority and which also offered reconciliation between offender and victim (Eglash, 1959). Eglash's ideas were based on the Twelve Steps of Alcoholics Anonymous (Alcoholics Anonymous, 2016), which were established in 1939 and in particular on steps 8–10. These focus on making good the harm that the offender has caused and thus directly link with the later shared values and goals of restorative justice.

Randy Barnett

Following on from such thinking and believing that there was a crisis in the penal system, Randy Barnett, in 1977, introduced the idea of a new paradigm of criminal justice, which he argued could replace the existing model of punishment (Barnett, 1977). Coined as restitution rather than restorative justice, he felt that while a 'radical alternative' (Barnett, 1977, p. 280) it would be a far better way of dealing with both offenders and victims. Rather than viewing crime as an offence against the state, Barnett argued that restitution viewed crime 'as an offense by one individual against the rights of another. The victim has suffered a loss. Justice [therefore] consists of the culpable offender making good the loss he has caused' (Barnett, 1977, p. 287). The key point here is that the offender needs to 'make good' to the victim, not, as they previously would have done, to the state. 'His debt, therefore, is not to society, it is to the victim' (Barnett, 1977, p. 288). Barnett believed that this could be achieved either through punitive restitution or through a pure restitutional system. The first proposal, punitive restitution, is where restitution is added to the punishment paradigm, as an additional sentencing aim. In this scenario the offender is forced to compensate the victim by carrying out work, either inside or outside of prison, or by making a payment from his own pocket.

The more radical option was the pure system, where the goals of punishment and indeed the desire to punish an offender would be secondary to and would only occur if they were the result of reparations made to the victim. Under this model, it is not so much that the offender deserves to suffer, but that the victim needs to be compensated. This is therefore a complete overthrow of the punishment paradigm. If we take the example of a person who has been convicted of a crime in court and sentenced to make restitution, Barnett argued that a pure system could work as follows:

- If the person can make the restitution immediately then they can do so.
- If they cannot, but are trustworthy, a legal claim against future wages can be set up. Failure to pay would result in additional action.
- If they are unemployed or untrustworthy they would be confined to an employment project, an industrial enterprise where they would be employed and could earn money. Security levels would depend on the behaviour of the offender and as less secure facilities would be cheaper, offenders would benefit through higher wages. Room, board and restitution would be taken from wages. The offender could either keep the remainder or pay off the restitution quicker thereby shortening their time of confinement. If the offender refused to work then they would not be entitled to food and lodging and if they refused to pay restitution then they would not be entitled to release. (Barnett, 1977)

Such proposals are radical, especially as Barnett suggested that families could live with the offenders while they were in the employment projects. Arguing that such a system could be flexible, he also noted how it could be refined, including the introduction of victim crime insurance. This would allow the victim to receive payment in full, regardless of the offender's wealth, and would mean that the offender would owe the insurance company rather than the victim. He also argued that there could be a system of direct arbitration between the victim and the offender whereby the offender could negotiate a reduced amount of restitution in exchange for a guilty plea, thereby avoiding the costs and uncertainties of a contested trial. Furthermore, he mooted the idea of a system of sureties, where the restitution would be paid by a company or a responsible person and the offender would then be released under their supervision and/or possible employment. The offender would then owe the company or person and it would be their choice whether they enforced this or showed mercy (Barnett, 1977).

Barnett argued that this system would 'benefit the victim, the criminal and the taxpayer' (Barnett, 1977, p. 294) but there are objections to it, not least the fact that he is effectively creating one system for the rich and another for the poor. While it is appreciated that his priority is the availability of restitution for the victim, arguably, this should not be achieved without considering issues of equality or fair treatment. Other criticisms, acknowledged by Barnett, include the fact that crime offends not just individuals but also whole communities, that restitution does not always satisfy a victim's need for revenge (especially if it can be paid off easily), and that in some cases (again depending on ability to pay) monetary sanctions are not sufficient deterrents. In terms of the employment projects, the system assumes that people are willing and, more importantly have the skills to carry out purposeful work, and furthermore does not take into account mental frailty or other disability (Barnett, 1977). Restitution was thus an important step in the development of restorative justice but it was not the complete answer.

Nils Christie

In the same year, Nils Christie (1977) also published what was to become a seminal piece for the restorative justice movement, in which he argued that conflicts are property. Furthermore, they are property that should belong to those who are parties to the conflict and should not be stolen away by the state, which tends to muscle in on conflict and take over. In this sense Christie refers to lawyers as 'professional thieves' (Christie, 1977, p. 3) and states that they are 'particularly good at stealing conflicts' (Christie, 1977, p. 4). When this takes place, the conflicts then become the property of the lawyers. Christie argues that the consequence of the state taking over is that the victim loses the opportunity to get involved and have their say, often also losing out on compensation. This loss additionally applies to the community, who is also not allowed the opportunity to take part, and furthermore extends to the offender who rarely has the chance to apologise or explain why they have behaved in a particular way (Christie, 1977).

Christie believed the answer lay in the introduction of victim-oriented courts that would take place within neighbourhoods and communities. This would work in four stages as outlined in Figure 3.1. Christie's vision was that there would be an extreme degree of lay-orientation involved, allowing the conflict to be shared, rather than stolen from the victim and offender. Parties to the conflict and the community as a whole would be encouraged to work together to resolve the dispute and when this occurs, a judge is not needed (Christie, 1977). Christie openly acknowledged, however, that there may be problems with his suggestions, including 'a lack of neighbourhoods ... few too many victims [and] too many professionals' (Christie, 1977, p. 12), but these were, nevertheless, obstacles which could be overcome.

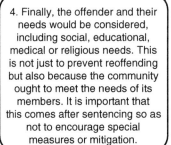

1. This would be similar to the current criminal justice system and would focus on the assessment of guilt. If lawyers were to be involved in this process at all, then this would be the only stage in which they were involved.

2. The court would then be told about the victim's situation including what could be done for them, not just by the offender which is first, but also by the local neighbourhood and the state. Only after this has passed – and this may take hours or days – is the punishment then decided upon.

4. Finally, the offender and their needs would be considered, including social, educational, medical or religious needs. This is not just to prevent reoffending but also because the community ought to meet the needs of its members. It is important that this comes after sentencing so as not to encourage special measures or mitigation.

3. Punishment would only be that which the judge found necessary to apply in addition to those "unintended constructive sufferings the offender would go through in his restitutive actions [with] the victim" (Christie, 1977, p. 10).

Figure 3.1 Christie's four stages of restorative justice

Howard Zehr

Next is Howard Zehr, an American criminologist who is attributed with directing the first victim–offender reconciliation programme in the United States of America (US) and is seen by many to be the first person to put forward a robust theory of restorative justice (Van Ness & Strong, 2010). Similar to Barnett, Zehr's priority is also to the victim, but in addition to their need to receive restitution he also argues that they need the opportunity to speak out about their feelings, experience justice and also forgiveness, have their questions answered, and, have their previous power restored (Zehr, 1985). Like Barnett, he also believes that the retributive system cannot achieve these aims, describing victims within it as 'mere footnotes in the process we call justice' (Zehr, 1985, p. 1), but he also thinks about the community and offenders. Offenders, Zehr believes, are also let down as they are not being held accountable for their actions, are not being given the opportunity to take responsibility for their deeds, nor the chance to make amends for their wrongs (Zehr, 1985). Likewise, community members also have needs which arise from criminal behaviour and which should additionally be met. The answer he believes is looking at the problem of crime through a new lens (Zehr, 2005), instead of using a retributive lens there is thus a need to introduce a 'restorative paradigm' (Zehr, 1985, p. 12).

The principles or philosophy of restorative justice as he sees it, is explained in *Changing Lenses* (Zehr, 2005) and the *Little Book of Restorative Justice* (Zehr, 2014). Emphasising the work of others he states how retributive justice focuses on giving offenders what they deserve, while restorative justice centres on what victims, communities and even offenders need (Zehr, 2014). When a crime takes place, it damages relationships: those between the offender and the victim, and those between the offender and the community. Violations such as these create obligations and the role of restorative justice is to ensure that the 'central obligation is to put right the wrongs' (Zehr, 2014, p. 24). This is achieved through the three pillars or central concepts of restorative justice, namely, harms and needs, obligations and engagement.

Harms and needs

The way in which restorative justice understands crime is that harm has been committed against both the victim and the wider community. The repair of this harm must therefore be the overriding aim of achieving justice, with the victim's needs at the heart of this, although the needs of the community and the offender are also taken into account (Zehr, 2014). The victim needs to feel vindicated, that someone else was to blame, that it will not happen again and that restitution can occur (Zehr, 2005). When the central focus is on victim needs, such practice allows justice to occur even where there is no identifiable offender (Zehr, 2014).

Obligations

Under a restorative justice model, breaches of the law result in obligations. As detailed above, these include repairing the harm caused, as well as ensuring that the offender is held accountable for their actions. Rather than this being evidenced through punishment, restorative justice strives to ensure that the offender understands what harms they have caused and what impact this harm has had on the victim and the wider community (Zehr, 2014). While this is the central focus, the community may well also have further obligations to both the victim and the offender. This could extend to limiting the causes of crime, achieved through plans that focus on both reparation and prevention (Zehr, 2014). Key to 'putting right' (Zehr, 2014, p. 32) is therefore not just addressing the harms that have been caused, but also the causes of this behaviour. This could be met by encouraging the offender to participate in constructive activities or educational programmes, and through helping the victim to feel secure in their home.

Engagement

In direct contrast to many current criminal justice practices, restorative justice ensures that all parties who have a stake in a criminal offence have the opportunity to participate in the justice process. As discussed below, restorative practices can vary and may not all involve direct contact between victim and offender, but all practices need to be inclusive and carried out with respect (Zehr, 2014).

John Braithwaite

Another important contributor to the development of restorative justice is John Braithwaite, who has written extensively about reintegrative shaming (Braithwaite, 1989). Braithwaite argues that the criminal justice system is largely a failure and that the reason why crime rates are so high is that too many societies stigmatise offenders rather than shaming them in a reintegrative way. In this sense 'stigmatisation is the kind of shaming which creates outcasts, it is disrespectful, humiliating' (Braithwaite, 2013, p. 59). It therefore treats criminals as evil people who have committed evil acts. It is disintegrative, and rather than helping a person to return to a community, it inhibits them from doing so. Putting more police on the street, who tend to treat offenders in this way and building more prisons which definitely treat offenders in this way, therefore increases rather than reduces crime (Braithwaite, 2013). Reintegrative shaming, on the other hand strongly disapproves of the evil act, but treats the person as essentially good and with respect. This separates the offender from their behaviour and gives them the opportunity to move on from past deeds. Even though Braithwaite used the phrase 'reintegrative shaming' in his seminal book (Braithwaite, 1989), he later said that he wished that he had actually called it 'restorative shaming' (Braithwaite, 2013, p. 59). This was based on the belief that neither punishment nor welfare had worked in corrections and that there was therefore a need for a third way. His belief was that this third way was restorative justice (Braithwaite, 2013).

> **Disintegrative shaming**: views the offender and the offence as one. The offender will always be judged on past deeds and classed as evil.
>
> **Reintegrative shaming**: separates the offender from their behaviour. Their past actions are stigmatised but the individual is not.

For Braithwaite, the importance of restorative justice in reducing crime and repairing harm is the positive role that it can play in restoration. For victims, he explains how they can often suffer a loss of dignity through criminal acts perpetrated against them, in addition to feeling disempowered and ignored, with the criminal justice system often compounding this disempowerment (Braithwaite, 2013). Restorative justice, however, can work to restore victims, offenders and communities. Such restoration can be done in a number of ways including restoring 'lost property, a sense of security, a sense of empowerment, social support, dignity, deliberative democracy, injury, and, harmony, based on a feeling that justice has been done' (Braithwaite, 2013, p. 60). As to offenders, while they may not have suffered the same types of losses as the victim, they may have suffered loss of dignity and this also needs repairing. Shame is caused by arrest and the trial, but also, for some, by the harm they have caused to others. Dignity can be restored by accepting this shame, taking responsibility for past actions and sincerely apologising. Depending on the offender's background and the circumstances of the offence, there may also be a need to restore empowerment and a sense of security for the offender. This could be tied up with employment, the feeling that there is a bright future and through the offender achieving some success whether that is in education, sport or work. It is also significant if the offender is forgiven not just by the victim but also by those whom the offender loves. It is therefore important to provide social support to the offender with such an approach leading to the restoring of a community (Braithwaite, 2013). Restorative justice is thus a system that repairs harm, restores relationships and consequently reduces crime (Braithwaite, 1989).

Discussion Questions

1. What are your initial thoughts about a criminal justice system that is based on restorative justice rather than on retribution? Is this something that you think is a) achievable and/or b) desirable?
2. How do you view the pure restitutional system as described by Barnett? What are its advantages and disadvantages and could you see it being effective in England and Wales today?
3. How much of a role do you think the victim and/or the community should have in sentencing?
4. Should restorative practices offer to help the offender or are they just for the victim?

DEFINITIONS OF RESTORATIVE JUSTICE

Before looking at how restorative justice is currently used within criminal justice and, importantly, how it could be used in the future, it may first be useful to define exactly what it is. Considering that the ideas of modern restorative justice have been with us for quite some time, it may be surprising that there is no agreed upon definition, with there being more consensus on what restorative justice is not rather than what it is. For example, Zehr (2014) argues that restorative justice is not primarily about reconciliation or forgiveness, is not limited to mediation, is not chiefly designed to reduce reoffending, is not a particular programme, is not predominantly intended for petty crimes or first-time offenders, and, may not be able to exist without a legal system (Zehr, 2014). Johnstone and Van Ness further argue that "the term 'restorative justice' appears to have no single clear and established meaning ... [rather it] means 'all things to all people'" (Johnstone & Van Ness, 2011, p. 6).

Despite such views, there have nevertheless been several attempts to define what it does encompass, with some of these presented in Figure 3.2. To add further confusion, others have used alternative terms when talking about practices that we might recognise as restorative justice. For example Morris refers to 'transformative justice', Burnside and Baker use 'relational justice' and Young describes such programmes as 'restorative community justice' (Strong & Van Ness, 2015).

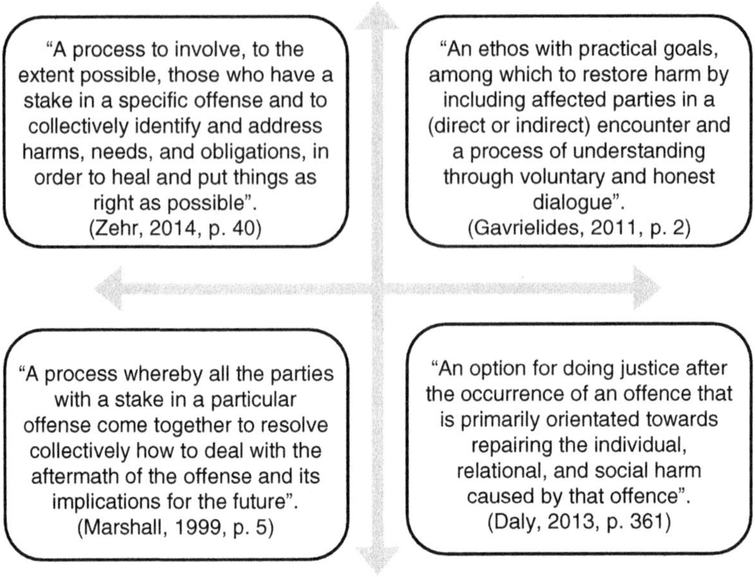

"A process to involve, to the extent possible, those who have a stake in a specific offense and to collectively identify and address harms, needs, and obligations, in order to heal and put things as right as possible". (Zehr, 2014, p. 40)	"An ethos with practical goals, among which to restore harm by including affected parties in a (direct or indirect) encounter and a process of understanding through voluntary and honest dialogue". (Gavrielides, 2011, p. 2)
"A process whereby all the parties with a stake in a particular offense come together to resolve collectively how to deal with the aftermath of the offense and its implications for the future". (Marshall, 1999, p. 5)	"An option for doing justice after the occurrence of an offence that is primarily orientated towards repairing the individual, relational, and social harm caused by that offence". (Daly, 2013, p. 361)

Figure 3.2 Definitions of restorative justice

In addition, Daly sets out four common elements:

1. Victims and offenders (who admit guilt) are active participants in a process which focuses on justice.
2. Criminal behaviour is addressed by the offender either through words or actions which positively affect the victim and the wider community.
3. Such activities repair the harm caused by the previous behaviour and thus restore relationships.
4. Discussions take place in informal settings where interaction, dialogue and engagement are emphasised. (Daly, 2013)

Johnstone contributes further by identifying five agendas of the restorative justice movement:

1. To promote the use of restorative processes within the social response to crime.
2. To encourage a new way of constructing crime and related problems and new conceptions of what constitutes a good solution to such problems.
3. To promote the use of restorative processes and principles in a variety of institutional settings as a way of handling deviant behaviour, conflict and 'under-performance'.
4. To promote restorative justice as part of the solution to the problem of achieving political reconciliation in the aftermath of mass violence and oppression.

5. To create a just society, defined as a society in which all human needs are met, and – as an aspect of this – to transform the way people understand their selves and their relation to the world around them. (Johnstone, 2008, p. 61)

The key ideas, as put forward by these agendas are that, in a change from traditional criminal justice processes, victims and members of the community are directly involved in not only holding the offender to account for their criminal behaviour but also in deciding what should be done. This allows far greater interaction between victim, offender and community, is focused on healing justice rather than punitive justice, and can be carried out in a culturally sensitive way. This consequently turns professionals into facilitators who guide the main actors through the process rather than themselves being centre stage. Such processes are not limited to criminal justice and can be used in schools and prisons and for workplace grievances and political reconciliation (Johnstone, 2008). While helpful, Daly argues that these five agendas show how wide-ranging in application and scope the term restorative justice has become. While she accepts that agendas one and three are concerned with justice practices, she argues that agenda four is concerned with 'transitional justice or truth-seeking mechanisms, and should not be called RJ' (Daly, 2016, p. 13). Likewise, she believes that agendas two and five, because they have no empirical focus, only relate to how one can think about, rather than actually practice crime and justice (Daly, 2016).

Due to this uncertainty over what restorative justice actually is, Braithwaite and Strong argue that rather than trying to define it, we should view both the processes and the values as a continuum which range from less restorative to more restorative (Suzuki & Hayes, 2016). Daly (2006), Johnstone and Van Ness (2011) have all acknowledged the difficulties of defining the concepts, although have agreed, until recently, that this is not fatalistic. Daly now asserts,

I have since changed my mind. My reasoning is that the research and development phase of restorative justice has now past, and it is time to assemble evidence, using a range of methods. Without a definition of RJ that can be applied and assessed empirically, we are bobbing on a raft in a sea of hopes and dreams. (Daly, 2016, p. 13)

Due to the importance of having this set, agreed upon definition, Daly now argues that restorative justice can be defined and that it is a 'justice mechanism' (Daly, 2016, p. 14), 'a justice response, process, activity measure or practice' (Daly, 2016, p. 18). Furthermore, she asserts that there are many justice mechanisms, with a continuum existing from conventional (criminal prosecutions, court trials and judicial sentencing) to innovative (problem-orientated courts, indigenous practice and truth-telling mechanisms). Restorative justice is thus one of a number of 'innovative justice' mechanisms (Daly, 2016, p. 17), and it is this term, innovative justice, that Daly argues we should now use. This, she states, allows restorative practice to be kept separate from other innovative justice mechanisms, which over the years have all been placed 'in the one basket of RJ' (Daly, 2016, p. 20). The definition, which Daly now puts forward, is:

> Restorative justice is a contemporary justice mechanism to address crime, disputes, and bounded community conflict. The mechanism is a meeting (or several meetings) of affected individuals, facilitated by one or more impartial people. Meetings can take place at all phases of the criminal process – pre-arrest, diversion from court, presentence, and post sentence – as well as for offending or conflicts not reported to the police. Specific practices will vary, depending on context, but are guided by rules and procedures that align with what is appropriate in the context of the crime, dispute, or bounded conflict. (Daly, 2016, p. 21)

Discussion Questions

1. How would you define restorative justice? Is it a theory, a way of thinking, or, a set of values?
2. Is it important that we have a set agreed upon definition? Which definition do you prefer?
3. How does restorative justice differ from conventional thinking about crime and justice?

RESTORATIVE JUSTICE IN PRACTICE

In Western society restorative justice as a means of dealing with criminal behaviour has traditionally been limited either to young offenders (see Chapters 5 and 11) or to relatively minor crimes. This has largely been due to the thought that less punitive options are only suitable for low levels of offending. This has changed, over the last few years, with it now being used to deal with more severe forms of violence such as death by dangerous driving, murder and rape, although this is still rare. Learning from its use in South Africa by the Truth and Reconciliation Commission, it has also been used for situations of mass violence (Zehr, 2014). To date, the vast majority of these practices have existed within a conventional criminal justice system and it is widely accepted, mainly for practical reasons, that this is currently the best way in which to widely implement restorative values and goals (Johnstone, 2011). There are generally three ways in which restorative justice can operate: victim offender reconciliation programmes, family group conferences and sentencing circles. These are not always mutually exclusive with blended models often used, or with one method used in order to prepare participants for another. While the aim of most practices is to facilitate face-to-face meetings this does not always occur and as outlined below victims and offenders are not always matched (see The Sycamore Tree project, page 40). This is an example of how practices have developed and do not always strictly adhere to the original aims of restorative justice; exemplifying why a continuum of practice is a useful concept. In all restorative practices, encounters are facilitated by trained individuals who ensure that all needs are met and that as far as possible harm is repaired.

Victim offender reconciliation programmes

The origins of contemporary victim offender reconciliation programmes (VORPs) are commonly traced to Mark Yantzi, a probation officer working in Ontario, Canada, who in 1974 came up with a 'pie-in-the-sky idea' (Zehr, 2005, p. 158) to deal with two young men who had vandalised 22 properties. Instead of using the usual criminal justice responses, Yantzi asked the Judge to sentence them to meeting their victims in the presence of him and one of his Mennonite (a protestant sect) colleagues (Johnstone, 2011). The Judge was initially reluctant but agreed to do so and the VORP became a condition of the men's probation order (Strong & Van Ness, 2015). The conference was so successful, particularly regarding the impact on the offenders in helping them to understand the consequences of their behaviour, that the Judge continued to make similar orders and the probation officer involved subsequently set up an organisation to support and run such meetings (Strong & Van Ness, 2015).

VORPs therefore typically involve the offender, their victim and a trained facilitator. The role of the facilitator is to encourage the parties to tell their stories, ask questions, explain the impact of the crime and work towards an agreement of restitution (Johnstone, 2011). Following on from this initial introduction in Canada, they have spread in use throughout much of the Western world. The first VORP took place in the US in 1978 and in 1981, Norway, the home country of Christie, piloted its first. By the end of the 1980s, almost 20 per cent of Norway's local governments were offering mediatory services (Strong & Van Ness, 2015). Similar programmes were first used in Finland and in England in 1983 and have since then spread throughout much of Europe (Strong & Van Ness, 2015).

Remedi

One organisation that facilitates VORPs in the North of England is Remedi, a charity that has been operating since 1996 (see www.remediuk.org). Its work began in Sheffield, predominantly with young offenders, but since then has expanded to adult services and now covers the full range of criminal offences including murder and sexual abuse. It works with victims and offenders both in the community and within prisons, facilitates both direct and indirect mediation and additionally offers training programmes (Remedi, 2016). To provide a flavour of their work, an example of one of their indirect mediation cases is outlined below.

A Remedi facilitated VORP

The female victim was 12 years old when the offender's sexual abuse started, with it resulting in the victim having children. Many years later, and via her victim liaison officer, she requested the opportunity to contact the offender to explain in detail, the impact that his abuse had had on her. She also wanted to know whether he had realised the extent of this impact and whether he was sorry. Previously she had been told that restorative justice was not appropriate in her case because it was felt that it would cause her more harm than good, but she persisted. Remedi carried out risk assessments and decided to take on the case.

The initial step was to meet with the victim to ascertain exactly what it was that she wanted to achieve. This was so Remedi could assess whether they could meet these expectations. They then went into prison to meet with the offender. Initially they did not mention that his victim had contacted them but just asked whether he would be interested in restorative justice. When he said yes, he was asked whether he would be willing to answer some questions from his victim. Significant amounts of time were taken in terms of preparing both parties with this culminating in questions and answers being passed between them via letters. On receiving a letter from the victim and finally realising the impact that he had caused, the perpetrator decided that he could no longer take part in the process. Even though he had previously completed a sex offender treatment programme (see Chapter 10) he had not fully comprehended the effect of his abuse. Although this was not direct contact and it did not end up with the parties 'hugging' (Remedi, 2016) it was nevertheless seen as a success as the victim felt that she had been heard. The practitioner involved stated that the time spent with the offender:

> had far more impact [on him] than anything else in the aftermath of what he went through in prison, and, even for those that want punishment, that was such a hard thing for him to have to go through, because he took responsibility and recognised the damage which he had done. (Remedi, 2016)

The Sycamore Tree Project

Another way in which VORPs are used is through the Sycamore Tree Project. Developed by Prison Fellowship International and borne out of a desire to facilitate reconciliation between victims and offenders, this prison-based programme has been used around the world since 1996 and now operates in 125 countries (Johnstone, 2016). In England and Wales, it has been operating since 1998 and to date has been used with over 22,000 offenders. It currently runs in over 40 prisons and young offender institutions (Parker, 2016). One of the main points to note regarding this programme, however, is that while it seeks to repair harm, offenders do not meet their own victims; rather they are matched with unconnected victims of crime. Parker, a Sycamore Tree tutor, explains how this can have two purposes: either it can be used for those offenders who will not get the opportunity to meet their actual victim or it can be used as a preparatory stage for those who will (Parker, 2016).

The programme works on a group-work basis with the size of the group being determined by the age of the participants: for adults, group sizes are usually limited to 20, for young adults it is 16 and for 15–18-year-olds smaller groups of 6–8 people are used (Parker, 2016). The programme is faith-based, with its origins in the story of Zacchaeus, the tax collector from the book of Luke in the New Testament, but it is not faith promoting and participants do not have to be believers of any faith (Johnstone, 2016). Participants do, however, have to accept their guilt and be willing to participate in group activities, including group discussions and homework exercises. The course consists of six, two and a half hour sessions and is delivered by one professional tutor and a number of trained volunteers. Sessions one and two look at the experiences of victims and ask offenders to think about their feelings and needs. Victims are then introduced into the programme at session three where they will tell their story including the impact that their crime had on them and their families. In cases of serious crime, the unconnected victims are often those who have lost family members either through murder or manslaughter (Parker, 2016).

The Sycamore Tree programme is slightly different to other VORPs in that there is no dialogue between the victim and offender (i.e. the offender does not share their story with the victim), although conversations do occur after the victim has spoken and sometimes there are 'elements of confession as some offenders choose to say a little about their own offending' (Parker, 2016, p. 18). As part of a homework exercise, participants are asked to write up the experience, including reflecting on the victim's feelings and how the experience made them feel. This is then used in later sessions to get them to think about the impact of their crimes on their own victims and on their families. In session six the 'victim' returns and is accompanied by invited members of the community. Offenders are then given the opportunity to make 'a symbolic act of restitution' (Parker, 2016, p. 19), with the session often including 'tears shed and emotion shared' (Parker, 2016, p. 19).

An important aspect of the programme is that it can be a useful tool in rebuilding relationships not just between the offender and their victim but also between the offender and their family. When an offender is punished by the courts, the pains of this punishment are often felt not just by the offender but also by their family (see Chapters 8 and 12). This may be because the family has less money, if the sentence is a financial penalty or the offender is no longer in the family home due to being incapacitated. Restorative practices can therefore be used to show the family that the offender is sorry for what they have done, that they take responsibility for these actions, that they understand the consequences and effects of this behaviour on the wider family and that they intend to take steps to prevent this from reoccurring in the future. While this is not traditionally the aim of such practices, such work could help more families stay connected when one member is in custody and may help when the time comes for this person to resettle back into the community (see Chapter 9).

Comments from offenders involved in the projects have been favourable. Feedback provided to a tutor spoken to for this book include 'the course has made me think about my crime and the effect of my crime on other people like my friends and family. I now have a greater understanding of victims of crime. I will never commit another crime and will not come to prison again' and from a victim participant 'I want you to know, that because of all your honesty [through the Sycamore Tree course] I am going to forgive those killers of my son. I am now free!' Another offender described it as the best programme that he had ever been on.

Family group conferences

Family group conferencing (FGC) is thought to derive from aboriginal practices, but in a modern context has been used in New Zealand since 1989 (see Chapter 11). Through the Children, Young Persons and Their Families Act 1989, the Youth Court was replaced with FGCs for most young offenders under the age of 17. The change in legislation was largely due to concerns from the Māori that too many of its young people were being brought into the juvenile justice system, rather than being dealt with through traditional Māori culture, which expects the family to work through problems and to make things right with both the victim and the victim's family (Strong & Van Ness, 2015). Instead of punishment, Māori culture focuses on healing and problem solving (MacRae & Zehr, 2004) and this form of intervention has been viewed as much more culturally relevant.

Similar to VORPs, FGC differs only in the sense that more people are involved in the process including family members, supporters of the victim and the offender and criminal justice workers (Johnstone, 2011). The result is not just a plan that includes restitution but also one that involves actions to prevent future offending. The ideal is that the conference will involve both the offender and the victim, although as FGC involves many more people than VORPs it is possible to have meaningful results even if the victim does not participate (Strong & Van Ness, 2015). In 1991, the model was slightly adapted and used by Australian police officers in Wagga Wagga, New South Wales, to divert young offenders from criminal charges and became known as restorative cautioning. Further examples include its use by Thames Valley Police in the England and the Royal Canadian Mounted Police (MacRae & Zehr, 2004). Both models have been adapted and used throughout the world for both juveniles and adults (Strong & Van Ness, 2015).

Sentencing circles

Sentencing circles are also thought to have indigenous roots, tracing their beginnings from the First Nations people in Canada. The first official sentencing circle is thought to have taken place in 1992 in the case of *R v Moses* in the Yukon Territory of Canada. The case involved a native Canadian whom it was thought the local community wanted sent to jail after he had harmed a police officer. The Judge invited interested members of the offender's community to participate in a sentencing circle, reviving the native way of dealing with criminal behaviour (Johnstone, 2011). Changing the layout of the court, 30 chairs were set out allowing court officials, police, First Nation members, probation, the victim and other interested parties to participate (Strong & Van Ness, 2015). Sentencing circles thus discuss what has happened, why such behaviour has occurred, what response should be made in relation to it and finally what can be done to prevent it from occurring in the future. A feather or talking stick is passed around and participants can only speak when they are in possession of this (Bazemore & Griffiths, 2003). Based on proposals made by the circle, the Judge then proceeds to sentence. In this first case, the Judge on the recommendations of the circle sentenced the offender to two years' probation (Johnstone, 2011) which included a programme of treatment that his family agreed to support him with (Strong & Van Ness, 2015).

As with the other restorative practices mentioned above, the key aim in sentencing circles is to listen and offer support to the victim, but they are arguably linked more closely to the conventional criminal justice system than the other aforementioned methods. The meeting will often begin with a prosecutor outlining the charge against the offender and will frequently conclude with a recommendation being taken back to a sentencing judge. It is however the role of the circle to make this recommendation and importantly to monitor and enforce the conditions of the sentence (Bazemore & Griffiths, 2003). In some cases, judges will suspend a decision on a custodial sentence so that they can see how the offender is complying with treatment, reparation and other responsibilities that have been passed down. Traditional healing and community building are therefore key aspects of this process (Bazemore & Griffiths, 2003).

Discussion Points

1. What do you think of these restorative practices? Are they methods of working which you could see taking centre stage in our criminal justice system?
2. Do you think that the same benefits of restorative justice can be achieved if a surrogate victim is used?
3. What are the disadvantages of such practices?

Population	167,838,318 (Worldometers, 2019a)
Prison population (including remand prisoners)	88,371 (Institute for Criminal Policy Research, 2019a)
Prison population per 100,000 of national population	53 (Institute for Criminal Policy Research, 2019a)
Remand prisoners	80.9% (Institute for Criminal Policy Research, 2019a)
Number of establishments	68 (Institute for Criminal Policy Research, 2019a)
Official capacity of prison service	40,664 (Institute for Criminal Policy Research, 2019a)
Occupancy level	217.3% (Institute for Criminal Policy Research, 2019a)

Brief Profile

Bangladesh is the eighth most populous country in the world. Formerly known as East Pakistan, it has only existed since 1971, when the two parts of Pakistan split. It spent 15 years under military rule in the 1970s and 80s and while democracy was restored in 1990, the political situation is still volatile. The country's capital is Dhaka, the main language spoken is Bengali and the major practised religions are Islam and Hinduism.

Criminal Justice

The country is divided into eight administrative divisions, which are further divided into 64 districts. These are divided into sub districts and then unions, which consist of multiple villages. Police stations operate on a union level. When a person is arrested by the police, (often because a fee has been paid by the complainant) they will initially be kept in a police cell, although these can be just holes in the floor. Suspects are often tortured in order that a confession is obtained and will then be moved to prison (Smith, K., 2016). Prisons are massively overcrowded with a large proportion of prisoners detained on a pre-trial basis. Bribery and corruption exists on many levels of the criminal justice system including the police, judges and prison officials (Smith, K., 2016).

Restorative Justice

In 2010, the Law Minister, decided that it was time for the country to comply with more Westernised ideas about restorative justice and consequently visited the United Kingdom (UK). Key aims were to reduce the prison population and to eradicate corruption. Taking into account existing traditional mediatory practices of village court elders (known as *Shalish*), UK practitioners have thus been instrumental in reviving restorative practices in Bangladesh. This began with the Madaripur Legal Aid Association, which introduced mediation as an alternative to going to court. The task of the UK practitioners was therefore to devise a community-based tool that could be used to solve problems, was respectful of traditional customs and which drew upon literature and findings from around the world.

Following the completion of a training manual, appropriate community volunteers were recruited and trained in 2011/12. Several focus groups were held to establish which practices were working and a training roadmap was created (Smith, K., 2016). Initially scripted conferencing was used, but in addition rehabilitation, reparation and crime prevention were built into the programme to provide longer-term support for the offender. The programme initially began in three districts and was available in 20 in 2016 (Smith, K., 2016). The programme is akin to FGC, where many members of the community are involved and can be quite large in scale, but it also has elements of a sentencing circle in terms of layout and turn taking (Smith, K., 2016). Harm is perceived as being experienced not just by the victim but also by the community. Balance does however need to be achieved, allowing all interested and effected parties to be involved, but without it turning into a public spectacle.

The programme is fairly prescribed, with the wrongdoer asked to speak first, explaining 'what happened; who do you think has been effected; how do you think they have been effected; what were your thoughts at the time and what have your thoughts been since' (Smith, K., 2016). The most harmed victim then speaks, covering the same questions but also 'what has been the hardest thing to deal with' (Smith, K., 2016). Additional victims, their supporters, relevant third parties and the offender's family (as secondary victims) then take turns to speak. The offender can then respond to what they have heard, often with a genuine expression of apology. The facilitator will then ask people to consider what they now want to happen, with the offender left until last (Smith, K., 2016). Some communities will draw up a contract and this is required if money exchanges hands, while others will accept a verbal agreement. Outcomes are then reported back to a central hub in Dhaka (Smith, K., 2016). If the matter is resolved the police are not usually involved, although there is nothing stopping a participant from additionally contacting the police.

Between October 2013 and October 2016, 2201 community conferences and 6162 mediatory meetings had taken place (Improvement of the Real Situation of Overcrowding in Prisons in Bangladesh, 2016). Restorative justice is now being used to solve land disputes, dowry issues, drug cases, gambling and petty crimes (Smith, K., 2016). Although it has not yet had any sizable impact on prison overcrowding, when the majority of those in prison are there for petty crimes, it is hoped that this will change in the future.

Discussion Points

1. What do you think to the way that restorative justice is developing and being used in Bangladesh?
2. Do you think that this national approach is an improvement to how we use restorative practices in England and Wales?
3. If someone agrees to have their case heard by the community, should this be instead of or in addition to the police also becoming involved?

DOES RESTORATIVE JUSTICE WORK?

As with all justice mechanisms, one of the main questions is whether it can be said to work. In the case of restorative justice, this means whether the practices being used can be said to repair the harm of the original offence, reduce reoffending and encourage the reintegration of the offender back into society. One of the main studies that has looked at the effectiveness of restorative practices is the reintegrative shaming experiments (RISE), which took place in Canberra, Australia, between 1995 and 2000. By comparing standard court proceedings with restorative focused diversionary conferences, the research found that in some situations the use of restorative conferences reduced reoffending (Sherman & Strang, 2007). Furthermore, those victims who participated in the conferences, when compared to those who went through the conventional court procedures, were found to be less fearful of the offenders, less angry about what had happened and more likely to receive a sincere apology (Strang, 2002). Similar findings were also found when looking at ten randomised trials of face-to-face restorative conferences. In terms of reconviction rates, the results suggested that the conferences were 'likely to reduce the future frequency of detected and prosecutable crimes' (Sherman, et al., 2015, p. 19), although it is worth noting that the authors felt that the conferences should be as a supplement rather than as a substitute for conventional justice.

Hoyle and Rosenblatt (2016), however, have cast some doubt over the effectiveness of restorative practices arguing that lessons in England and Wales have not been learnt and that the mistakes of the past are being repeated. Even though they acknowledge that there has been an increase in legislation and policies over the past few years, they conclude that

> a more strategic and coherent approach to the use of RJ is not likely unless those responsible for implementation make considerable progress in involving victims, broadening the circle to include more meaningful members of the community, educating the public about the principles and aims of RJ, and take seriously the need for reparation for victims and the wider communities affected by crime. (Hoyle & Rosenblatt, 2016, p. 45)

Interestingly, this increase in legislation, policy and international standards is seen by some as a problem. Gavrielides, for example, argues that the increase in European standards and directives, including the Victims Directive (Directive 2012/29/EU) has meant that restorative justice has lost its links with local communities, with such top-down regulatory controls threatening the development of innovative, unregistered, localised projects (Gavrielides, 2016).

CRITICISMS OF RESTORATIVE JUSTICE

In addition to the concerns mentioned above, another criticism of restorative justice focuses on its appropriateness for serious cases especially those involving sexual abuse, murder and domestic violence. One interesting article, which looks at this, traces the experiences of two women who were involved in a restorative meeting with one of the murderers of their brother (Walters, 2015). Even though the meeting took place 15 years after "John" had been killed, the sisters still had several unanswered questions and were still feeling the impact of their brother's death, including for one a near mental breakdown. They also had feelings of anger against one of the offenders who they felt had got off with a manslaughter charge because he had convinced the court that he had Asperger's syndrome. Through the meeting, the women were able to get answers to their questions but it also gave them an opportunity to explain to the offender the impact that their brother's death had had on them and what kind of man their brother was. To their surprise, the meeting also allowed them to see that the offender was normal and not the 'monster' that they had previously perceived, although one of the sisters stated how this realisation made her feel almost guilty that she no longer hated her brother's killer. The meeting concluded with a sincere apology from the offender and a promise that he would not return to his alcoholic past (Walters, 2015).

While this meeting was useful and worked to answer the victim's questions, it cannot repair the harm that the offence has caused. Such meetings are also not suitable for everyone, indeed two of "John's" sisters refused to take part because they were still too angry (Walters, 2015). Furthermore, it cannot always be assumed that the offender will consent to being part of a dialogue and in some situations, it may not be appropriate for the offender to be involved. This would therefore suggest that restorative meetings can only be offered in addition to conventional practices as it is unlikely that they could be undertaken in all cases. In all restorative meetings, but especially in cases where a serious crime has been committed, it is also essential that all parties are properly prepared for the experience. This includes ensuring that participants have realistic expectations, fully understand the emotional effects which the meeting may have on them and that they are facilitated by trained mediators who are skilled at conflict management.

Another criticism of modern restorative practices is that they are not as closely linked to indigenous roots as has been previously claimed. When looking at the use of FGC, in New Zealand (see Chapter 11), for example, Moyle and Tauri question how inclusive, to the Māori, modern day conferences actually are. Their findings suggest that not only have Māori participants found the processes to be 'Eurocentric, formulaic, and standardised' (Moyle & Tauri, 2016, p. 86), but many Māori elders were also treated disrespectfully by state officials and were side-lined in favour of state experts. The authors therefore conclude that either it needs to be acknowledged that FGC in New Zealand is not a 'Māori/Indigenous-inspired process' or the Māori need to be fully involved in the development and delivery of future conferencing practices so that the Māori are no longer marginalised (Moyle & Tauri, 2016, p. 102).

Other academics have focused on the widening definition of restorative justice and the fact that several projects that claim to be restorative, in its true sense are not. One example that Wood and Suzuki give is the Sycamore Tree Project (see above). While they accept that the programme uses restorative language in its goals, they contend that a project that does not involve the actual victim is offender focused, rather than being victim focused. They therefore conclude:

> To suggest that conferencing – a practice that involves primary stakeholders toward the goals of victim redress and offender accountability – and prison rehabilitation or compliance programs can both be subsumed under the banner of 'restorative justice' severely conflates the distinct aims and practices of each. (Wood & Suzuki, 2016, p. 152)

Similar criticisms are also made against the rebranding of some community orders as restorative and the thought that just because the offender is 'paying back' to the community that the harm is repaired (Wood & Suzuki, 2016). Linking in with the criticisms about the lack of definition by Daly (2016), Wood and Suzuki (2016) argue that we need to focus on restorative justice as an interaction between the main parties or its definition may drift further and become potentially meaningless. Further problems include the fact that the literature on restorative justice has not, outside indigenous cultures, really considered how it may work when taking into account factors such as ethnicity, social class, race and gender (Wood & Suzuki, 2016). The need for further research in all of these areas is therefore fundamental.

Discussion Points

1. Having considered some of the criticisms of restorative justice, have your views about it changed at all?
2. Are these problems insurmountable or is there still a future for restorative justice?
3. If you think that there is a future, what do you think this future looks like?

RETRIBUTION, REHABILITATION OR RESTORATIVE JUSTICE?

As previously, discussed, restorative justice exists on a continuum with programmes and interventions ranging from those that are fully restorative to those that are not. While there are some who argue that we could rid ourselves of our current conventional system, a system where retribution, rehabilitation and restorative justice exist together is the more realistic ambition. The key question therefore is whether conventional and innovative justice mechanisms can work together, especially when we could think of them as two diverse and conflicting principles of practice. Walgrave thinks yes, stating that rather than being at opposites on a spectrum, restoration and retribution are actually 'two sides of the same coin' (Walgrave, 2008, p. 62). He believes that the aim of both is the same, that is, the rebalancing of wrongful behaviour and that it is just how this rebalancing is done that sets the two principles apart. While retribution seeks to increase the harm by inflicting punishment on the offender, restoration looks to repair the harm and rebalance relationships (Walgrave, 2008). While he accepts that some obligations under restorative justice can be painful, he argues that they are not punishment because this is not the aim of those imposing the obligations (Walgrave, 2008). Zehr agrees with this view stating that while restorative practices may involve punishment it 'should not be normative and its uses and purposes should be carefully prescribed' (Zehr, 2005, p. 210). Differing slightly, London argues that restoration may need a punitive element in order that it can work properly, although he acknowledges that this is not the primary goal and should only be resorted to after the restorative conference. For him it is about restoring trust, both for the victim and the community and in some circumstances punishment may be an element of this process (Daly, 2013). Duff goes further, stating that you need punishment in order to have successful restoration. While he welcomes more enlightened responses to crime, such as restorative justice, he nevertheless believes that retribution is needed and that it is only through punishment that an offender can provide true restoration to the victim and the wider community (Daly, 2013). Despite the differences between these two mechanisms of justice there are, nevertheless, some similarities with the fundamental one being that they both want to 'right the balance' (Zehr, 2014, p. 59). As Walgrave (2008) argues, it is just how that balance is achieved which generally demarcates where on the continuum such a practice exists.

Restorative prisons

Rather than seeking to eradicate our current conventional criminal justice system, perhaps we should look to introduce a system, which has increasingly more restorative principles centrally embedded within it. One way in which this rebalancing of models could be usefully used is within the prison estate (see Chapters 7–12 for how prisons are currently run). The idea of a restorative prison has been with us for quite some time and even though there are some who do not believe that punishment and restorative justice can work in harmony, especially in a custodial environment (Guidoni, 2003), there are others who do (Edgar & Newell, 2013; Johnstone, 2014).

The idea of a fully restorative prison is admittedly a dream rather than a reality, but it is one which could work if there was the necessary will and commitment. Such a prison would run VORPs and FGC, so that relationships could be restored and other forms of harm repaired, but the vision would be far more than this. A restorative prison would thus have restorative values permeating throughout the whole system. For example, rather than induction and sentence planning being focused on punishment and hardship, prisoners would instead be encouraged to take active responsibility for their previous behaviour and to use their time in custody to make amends for their wrongs. Instead of being employed in meaningless work activity, prisoners would be encouraged to participate in constructive work which would benefit both the victims and the community that they have harmed (Johnstone, 2016). Such activities would enhance and repair relationships between the offender, their victim, their families and the community, would aid reintegration on release and would provide opportunities to make restoration, thus beneficial to all parties involved (Johnstone, 2016).

Restorative principles could also be applied to specific regimes in prisons and could even be used in close supervision centres and segregation units, often viewed as the most punitive side of prison life (see Chapter 7). Prisoners are often moved to segregation because they have harmed either property or other people and except time taken for small amounts of exercise, a shower and perhaps a phone call much of their time is spent locked up. Segregation units therefore often deal with the most difficult and dangerous of prisoners and it is common for prison officers working on such wings to experience aggression, cell damage, dirty protests and physical assaults (Edgar, 2016). On the basis that such prisoners do not engage in education or treatment programmes, no work is undertaken to confront their behaviour, their sentence is served passively and they are not asked to take any responsibility for their crimes. Such regimes should not be forgotten however, with Edgar (2016) showing that restorative principles can be used in segregation units. One example he cites was where a prisoner's exercise was cancelled but he was not informed and when he eventually found out 'he became abusive and threatened to harm anyone who opened his cell' (Edgar, 2016, p. 32). The Use of Force Coordinator started to get a team together, but while this was taking place a female prisoner officer started to talk to the prisoner. She heard what was wrong, agreed that he should have been informed, told him that making threats would not solve anything and suggested that he ask for his next exercise to be extended. She encouraged him to take responsibility for his actions and focus on solutions rather than the perceived wrongs. Within ten minutes the situation was back under control (Edgar, 2016).

The use of restorative justice in prison disciplinary proceedings has also been put forward by Butler and Maruna (2016). Grounded in empirical research conducted in four prisons in the UK, prisoners thought that current disciplinary proceedings lacked legitimacy. By dealing with the men using restorative principles, however, it is thought that serious crime will be better managed, and that it will allow for restorative values to 'extend well beyond the prison wall' (Butler & Maruna, 2016, p. 126).

Discussion Points

1. What do you think to the idea of a restorative prison? How do you think such an idea could be practically implemented?
2. Should restorative justice be used for serious crimes, or is it only ever suitable for young offenders and low level offending?
3. Can restorative justice survive on its own or would it work better if used in combination with retribution and rehabilitation?

CONCLUSION

As noted by Wood, even though restorative justice has been with us for some time and is arguably a 'new way of justice ... [its] impacts on the criminal justice system ... have been modest' (Wood, 2016, p. 2). While there is evidence of restorative practices in many countries around the world, it is only really New Zealand and certain Australian States (see the Young Offenders Act 1993 in Queensland) that have fully implemented it into their systems of justice. In England and Wales there has been significant investment in practices and training with £2 million allocated in 2013 and promises of another £30 million over the coming years (Hoyle & Rosenblatt, 2016) but restorative justice is still arguably very much on the fringes of criminal justice. As Greene argues, it is only the 'trivial offenders who would barely register on today's criminal justice radar (misdemeanants and nonviolent juveniles) [who] are front and centre in the restorative justice movement' (Greene, 2013, p. 380). The future for restorative justice is therefore uncertain, especially if lessons are not learnt from the past and national policies and European Directives take away community involvement and innovation. That said, there are many projects in England and Wales that are working well and many aspects of restorative justice that could be used more widely across the penal system. A combination of retribution, rehabilitation and restorative justice could therefore be the third new way of managing offenders and reducing crime, but if it is, the restorative justice element of this needs to be less piecemeal and more coordinated while not losing its invention and sense of community.

 Now read:

House of Commons Justice Committee (2016) *Restorative Justice*. London: House of Commons. This considers the effectiveness of and use of restorative justice in the UK.

Ward, T., Fox, K. and Garber, M. (2014) 'Restorative justice, offender rehabilitation and desistance', *Restorative Justice: An International Journal*, 2(1), 24–42.

Now watch:

BBC 3 (2014) *Can Criminals Say Sorry?* Available at: https://learning
onscreen.ac.uk/ondemand/index.php/prog/06E7568A?bcast=109246536
Dunne, J. (2016) *Transformative Justice*, Tedx Talks available on YouTube at:
https://www.youtube.com/watch?v=3oaPse7hXao

 Now consider:

Taking into account the problems in our current prison system (see Chapters
7–9) design a prison based on restorative rather than retributive principles.

4 Sentencing

INTRODUCTION

Sentencing is the task of deciding in what way and for how long an offender will be punished. It is defined as 'the allocation of criminal sanctions' (Padfield, et al., 2012, p. 955) and excluding the possibility of an appeal, will take place at the end of the criminal justice process, following either a guilty plea or a finding of guilt. As Johnson states, 'it is here that the criminal law is translated into criminal punishment' (Johnson, 2011, p. 696). Focusing on the phrase criminal sanctions differentiates sentencing from civil regulatory sanctions and civil preventative orders (Ashworth, 2015), although how the latter are used with young offenders and their parents is briefly discussed in Chapter 11. While the weightier, more serious sanctions are imposed by a criminal court, a courtroom is not always necessary for the allocation of criminal sanctions. As outlined in Chapter 5, including a discussion on the context and criticisms of them, there are a range of out of court disposals that can be administered by the police and Crown Prosecution Service. These include administrative fines and conditions on behaviour. Such sanctions have been found to be lawful because an individual has the right to take the matter to a court, if they reject the findings of the police (see *Ozturk v Germany* (1984) 6 EHRR 409) (Ashworth, 2015).

When allocating criminal sanctions it is imperative that sentencing decisions are fair, transparent and consistent. This is especially the case when referring to those made within a court setting, as it is these which often curtail an individual's freedoms (curfew, exclusion restrictions, attendance at certain programmes), liberties (custody) and rights to personal property (compensation, forfeiture and financial penalties) (Ashworth, 2015). How such decisions are made, who makes these decisions and what guidance is available is therefore key. Indeed when we talk of a sentencing system, we do so because there are guidelines introduced either through legislation, case law or policy, which regulate judicial discretion. If such a system were not in place then we would have 'lawlessness in sentencing' (Frankel, 1972, p. 1). It is also important to know who has responsibility for making sentencing decisions and in terms of a separation of powers, whether sentencing policy is controlled by the executive (government and parliament) or the judiciary. While it is commonly accepted that sentencing is a role carried out by the judiciary, the line between the two can at times become blurred, with the guidelines on minimum tariffs in life sentences an example of this.

Sentencing decisions also impact heavily on the penal system in the sense that they send offenders to already crowded prisons (see Chapters 7 and 8) and increase caseloads of already overworked offender managers (see Chapter 6). At a time when there has been an increase in the severity of custodial sentences even though overall recorded levels of crime have decreased, this additional impact on penal resources has become problematic. When governments have to make financial cuts and savings, these are often made from the penal system, before departments such as education and health are effected. Getting a sentencing decision right is thus crucial. This chapter will therefore explain who the sentencers are, how sentences are reached and what limits are placed on judicial discretion. The spotlight country is the United States of America (US). This is used to consider a system where judicial discretion has been virtually eradicated.

THE INFRASTRUCTURE OF SENTENCING

Leaving out of court disposals for Chapter 5, sentencing in England and Wales takes place in two levels of criminal courts: the Magistrates' Court and the Crown Court. Regardless of how serious an offence is, all criminal prosecutions in England and Wales will start in the Magistrates' Court. Where a case is heard and/or sentenced is dependent on what type of offence it is, with there being three categories of offence:

- Summary: minor offences including common assault and most driving offences.
- Triable either way: medium range offences including theft, burglary, handling stolen goods and fraud.
- Indictable: serious offences including murder, robbery and grievous bodily harm.

Summary cases are always tried in the Magistrates' Court. Triable either way can be dealt with in either court and indictable offences will always go to the Crown Court. If the magistrates believe that they have the expertise and sentencing powers to deal with a triable either way offence then they will keep it in the lower court. If they do not, they will commit the case to the higher court. This decision can, however, be overridden by the defendant if they elect to have their case heard by a Crown Court jury.

The Magistrates' Court

The Magistrates' Court is the workhouse of the criminal justice system dealing with approximately 95 per cent of all criminal cases (Courts and Tribunals Judicary, 2017b). Often known as summary justice, the aim of the Magistrates' Court is to provide a speedy procedure uncluttered with elaborate judicial rituals, making it far cheaper than the Crown Court. For example, a triable either way case heard in a Magistrates' Court would cost on average £900, which is increased to £3,900 if heard in a Crown Court. The difference in costs is more substantial when the defendant pleads not guilty (*The Economist*, 2013).

The Magistrates' Court is made up of a bench of three magistrates who are members of the community and who volunteer without pay. There are very few restrictions on who can be a magistrate, although the vast majority are white, middle class, middle aged (they have to retire at 70), ex professionals who have respect for the police and other criminal justice authorities. While magistrates are lay (non-legal), they will receive compulsory training of at least 18 hours or three full days (Gov.UK, 2016) and over time will pick up experience and knowledge of the law. Magistrates will sit either once a week, or once a fortnight although the minimum requirement is 13 days or 26 half days per year (Gov.UK, 2016). Establishing minimum requirements is necessary so that people can gain experience and provide a consistent service, but this often means that the vast majority of magistrates either do not work or are retired. Sitting in court on a regular basis means that magistrates might often see the same defendants in front of them, which can arguably prejudice their thinking on a particular defendant, consequentially influencing sentencing decisions. As magistrates are not legally qualified, they will be advised by a justice's clerk, who is either a solicitor or barrister with at least five years' experience. The clerk will advise on the law, procedure and sentencing. Decisions regarding fact are for the magistrates alone. They are also expected to assist unrepresented defendants in court and handle pre-trial proceedings in an attempt to reduce delays.

The current magistracy is arguably in crisis. Between April 2010 and December 2016, 8253 magistrates had resigned. This included 952 in the financial year of 2015/16 and 842 in the 8 months between 1 April and 5 December 2016 (HC Deb, 5 December 2016, cW). Bearing in mind that it is these individuals that deal with the vast majority of criminal cases it is therefore worrying that in 2006 there were 30,000 magistrates compared to 17,552 in April 2016 (Lord Chief Justice of England and Wales, 2018). Reasons cited for this mass departure include court closures, falling crime rates (which is positive) and an increase in the use of district judges. Malcolm Richardson, national chairman of the Magistrates' Association has gone further stating that factors such as 'budget cuts, court closures and a sense of being under-valued' have also been influential (Bowcott, 2016). Despite this level of departure, very few magistrates have been recruited since 2012. This has resulted in an aging population and a drop in morale, with magistrates 'interpret[ing] their shrinking numbers as a lack of governmental and judicial commitment to the magistracy' (Transform Justice, 2016, p. 3).

It may be worth looking at one of these reasons in more detail. Where a case is particularly complex, is likely to last for more than one day, or the court has a high caseload, cases can be heard by a district judge. These legally qualified individuals must have at least seven years' experience. They will sit on their own to hear cases and to sentence and so decide on both law and fact. Due to their legal knowledge and experience, it has been argued that they are much more efficient than magistrates and should therefore be used for all cases; although this obviously comes at a cost. Tensions between magistrates and district judges have been reported, where some magistrates feel that district judges are allocated the best cases and that their contribution to the justice system is valued above their own (Transform Justice, 2016). Partly due to such tensions and to test whether or not the magistracy should be retained, the Ministry of Justice, in 2013, commissioned research looking at the strengths and skills of the judiciary in the Magistrates' Court (Ministry of Justice & Ipsos MORI, 2013). The findings are summarised in Figure 4.1.

```
┌─ Magistrates ──────────────────────────────────────────┐
│                                                          │
│  • Greater connection with the local community so better placed to deliver │
│    local justice.                                        │
│  • A bench of three provides greater democracy, more likely to be open │
│    minded and less case hardened or fatigued.            │
│  • More cost effective -take longer than district judges but difference not │
│    enough to compensate for the higher costs of a judge. │
│                                                          │
└──────────────────────────────────────────────────────────┘
```

```
┌─ District Judges ──────────────────────────────────────┐
│                                                          │
│  • Speed in dealing with cases as no need to consult with others and less │
│    detailed arguments needed from prosecutors and defence solicitors as │
│    better understanding assumed.                         │
│  • Much better at case management.                       │
│  • Can deal with all types of cases irrelevant of how serious or complex. │
│                                                          │
└──────────────────────────────────────────────────────────┘
```

Figure 4.1 Strengths and skills of magistrates and district judges

While a number of observations were made about the Magistrates' Court, no recommendations were reached as to whether the magistracy should be retained, although the idea that magistrates were better able to deliver local justice was seen as a key strength. This claim however can be questioned, especially when the current makeup of the magistracy is evaluated in terms of whether they do truly represent their local communities. For example, in April 2018 while there was a pretty even split between men and women (55 per cent women) only four per cent of the 15,003 magistrates were under the age of 40, with 55 per cent aged over 60. Furthermore, only 12 per cent declared themselves as Black, Asian or Minority Ethnic (BAME) (Lord Chief Justice of England and Wales, 2018) (see Chapter 12 for how this lack of diversity can negatively affect sentencing decisions for women and BAME offenders). The reasons for a less diverse magistracy are varied and include as mentioned above an aging population partly because recruitment appears to have been put on hold. Low morale, which may have been communicated to potential applicants and insufficient resources to advertise opportunities to under-represented groups have also been cited (Transform Justice, 2016). Furthermore, it is thought that the terms and conditions of the role may no longer suit potential applicants. Magistrates have to sit a minimum of 13 days a year, but they are under pressure to sit more, in addition to attending training events and meetings, with some arguing they are not properly recompensed for income losses (Transform Justice, 2016). Despite such concerns, the magistracy is nevertheless likely to remain, largely because it is cheaper than replacing it with district judges.

An additional area of discussion is sentencing powers. Currently sentencers in the Magistrates' Court are limited to a maximum of six months in custody, if sentencing for a single offence. Where there is more than one offence this is raised to 12 months. Some have argued that such powers should be increased, with this arguably appropriate, bearing in mind that a magistrate in a Youth Court has the power to sentence up to two years imprisonment for a single offence. If sentencing powers were increased, it would mean that cases currently committed to the Crown Court, because the magistrates believe that the offence deserves a more severe sanction, could remain in the lower court. This would not only save money but would also reduce the burden on the Crown Court and thus speed up justice. If such an increase was ever to happen, it would be important that additional training was provided so that magistrates not only felt comfortable with these additional powers but that a sudden increase in custodial sentencing was prevented. This latter point is something, which has been raised by the Ministry of Justice, justices' clerks, governmental ministers and district judges; with some district judges believing that such extensions of power should only be extended to themselves (Transform Justice, 2016). The Magistrates' Association has stated that a rise in custodial sentencing would not occur, but until additional powers are given and trialled, it is unclear what the effect on sentencing would be. What is known, however, is that, convictions are generally higher in the Magistrates' Court than in the Crown Court, although this is not considerably different. In 2017/18, for example, the average conviction rate in the Magistrates' Court was 85.3 per cent as opposed to 79.9 per cent in the Crown Court (Crown Prosecution Service, 2018a). The difference may possibly be because magistrates are more likely to believe the police and prosecution, with a jury more likely to represent a broader spectrum of the defendant's peers and perhaps more willing to question those in authority.

Discussion Questions

1. What is your view of summary justice? List the advantages and disadvantages and consider whether the magistracy should be abolished and district judges used instead?
2. What level of sentencing powers do you think magistrates should have?

The Crown Court

The Crown Court deals with the remaining five per cent of criminal work (Courts and Tribunals Judiciary, 2017a), including all indictable offences and those triable either way offences where either the magistrates have committed the case or the offender has elected a jury trial. A Crown Court is made up of one Crown Court Judge and a jury, although as two thirds of the cases in the Crown Court involve a guilty plea the majority of cases are dealt with by a judge alone (Ashworth & Roberts, 2012). The jury is made up of 12 peers of the community taken from electoral rolls who listen to the evidence and decide on questions of facts. They will ultimately decide whether someone is guilty of the charged offence(s). Questions relating to the law and the summing up of the case are for the judge. The judge will also decide on sentence.

The main difference between judges and magistrates is that the former are legally qualified, with the vast majority gaining prior experience as barristers. Similar to magistrates however, they are drawn from a relatively small pool of people with little diversity evident. For example, in April 2018, there were 2978 court judges, of which only 29 per cent were female; seven per cent were from BAME backgrounds and 34 per cent were from non-barrister backgrounds (Lord Chief Justice of England and Wales, 2018). This lack of diversity has unsurprisingly attracted criticism. The Judicial Appointments Commission, senior judges and the legal profession have all expressed their dissatisfaction over the last few years, but very little has changed. Indeed in 1992, Lord Taylor, who was then the Lord Chief Justice of England and Wales stated: 'The present imbalance between male and female, white and black in the judiciary is obvious ... I have no doubt that the balance will be redressed in the next few years ... Within five years I would expect to see a substantial number of appointments from both of these groups' (House of Lords, Select Committee on the Constitution, 2012, p. 27). Twenty five years on, while there are more women and more from BAME backgrounds in the lower courts, the senior judiciary is still white and male (Justice, 2017b). Lord Neuberger has gone further stating that the judiciary is 'male, white, educated at public school and from the upper middle and middle classes' (Justice, 2017b). An example of this is the Supreme Court, where in 2019, of the 12 justices presiding, all were white and only three were female. This lack of gender diversity can be compared to other countries as seen in Table 4.1.

Table 4.1 International comparators on women judges in the most senior court (in descending order).

	Court	Women	Total number of judges	Women as % of court
New Zealand	Supreme Court	3	6	50%
Germany	Federal Constitutional Court	7	16	44%
Canada	Supreme Court	4	9	44%
Australia	High Court	3	7	43%
France	Constitutional Council	4	10	40%
	International Criminal Court	7	18	39%
Ireland	Supreme Court	4	11	36%
Norway	Supreme Court	7	20	35%
Denmark	Supreme Court	6	19	32%
USA	Supreme Court	3	9	33%
South Africa	Constitutional Court	3	9	33%
	European Court of Human Rights	15	47	32%
Sweden	Supreme Court	5	16	31%
Israel	Supreme Court	4	15	27%
UK	Supreme Court	3	12	25%
Italy	Constitutional Court	3	14	21%

Source: Data from Justice (2017a) *Increasing Judicial Diversity*. London: Justice, p. 17.

Lack of diversity can lead to the unfair administration of justice (see Chapter 12 for some examples of this). Diversity is therefore important for three key reasons:

1. To ensure legitimacy of the judiciary in the eyes of court users and the public.
2. To improve the quality of judgments through the benefit of a broader range of experiences and perspectives.
3. To ensure that judges are recruited through the fairest selection processes as possible which do not discriminate against any individual group of people. (Justice, 2017a, p. 5)

The key issue is therefore how judges should be appointed. Also relevant are the barriers, which prevent people from under-represented groups from entering into the judiciary. These include a lack of flexibility in working practices; perceptions that you need to be white, male and educated at public schools and/or Oxbridge; the need to visit other courts (which can be difficult for carers) and lack of any structured training, which favours those who have experience as barristers rather than as solicitors (Bindman & Monaghan, 2014). JUSTICE, an all-party law reform and human rights organisation (see https://justice.org.uk/), has made a number of key recommendations based around the themes of valuing difference, ensuring accountability, introducing fair and proactive recruitment, and creating attractive and inclusive career pathways and working conditions (Justice, 2017a). JUSTICE hope, that by taking this approach some change will be realised so that in the next five years not only will we see more women and BAME judges in more senior positions, but diversity will also be reflected in terms of disability, religious belief and sexual orientation (Justice, 2017a). At a time when judicial recruitment is at an all-time low (Jack, 2017) and it is expected that 41 per cent of judges from the Court of Appeal may leave the bench early, due to diminishing levels of morale and net earnings (Thomas, 2017), ensuring the fair and representative recruitment of our judiciary is paramount.

Discussion Questions

1. One of the differences between the Crown Court and the Magistrates' Court is how decisions relating to law and fact are separated. Which approach do you think is the more favourable?
2. How important is it that the judiciary (both magistrates and professional judges) represent the diverse communities in which we live? If you think this, is important, what can be done to ensure that we recruit and retain sentencers who more accurately represent our communities?

SENTENCING GUIDELINES

One of the perennial problems with sentencing and particularly prevalent with practice in the Magistrates' Court is consistency; with studies showing that while some magistrates' benches are more, probation-minded others are more custody-minded.

Research has shown, for example, that in some courts, BAME offenders are more likely to receive immediate imprisonment when compared to their white counterparts and women are more likely to be sentenced to community penalties (Ashworth & Roberts, 2012) (see Chapter 12 for more statistics and research findings on this). In an attempt to avoid these inequalities, sentencers in both Magistrates' and Crown Courts are restricted in their judicial discretion by both guidelines and legislation. Such limitations are collectively known as the sentencing system.

Judicial guidelines for sentencing were historically ad hoc, especially prior to the Crime and Disorder Act 1998. Before this time the only thing that really existed were a collection of Court of Appeal judgments passed over time and which were binding on all Magistrates' and Crown Court judges. The judgments cover a variety of offences and circumstances, but their main drawback was that they were not broad ranging enough and could only be initiated through appeal. Examples include *R v Saw* ([2009] EWCA Crim 1) which covers domestic burglary and *R v Billam* ((1986) 8 Cr App R (S) 48) which looks at rape. In response to such criticism, the Sentencing Advisory Panel was introduced by the Crime and Disorder Act 1998, which brought to an end 'long enjoyed wide discretion' (Roberts, 2013, p. 2). While it was felt that judicial discretion did need some control, 'US style sentencing grids [see below] were rejected by the Sentencing Commission Working Group as being inappropriately restrictive and contrary to the traditions of English sentencing' (Roberts, 2013, p. 3). The Panel's role was therefore to formulate guidelines on sentencing, which it initially submitted as advice to the Court of Appeal. The Court of Appeal would then consider the advice and decide whether to accept it. In 2003 an additional body, The Sentencing Guidelines Council was introduced. Its main function was to provide consistent sentencing guidelines for all Magistrates' and Crown Courts and was operational from February 2004. The Sentencing Advisory Panel continued to exist but gave their advice to the Sentencing Guidelines Council rather than to the Court of Appeal.

The Sentencing Council

There is now one body that produces sentencing guidelines. Known as the Sentencing Council, it was introduced in Part four, Chapter 1 of the Coroners and Justice Act 2009. Under the Act, the Council has a number of functions including consulting on and publishing definitive sentencing guidelines, monitoring the effect of these guidelines, promoting public confidence in sentencing and reporting about issues which are likely to affect sentencing. The aim of the Council is predominantly to ensure consistency and transparency in sentencing. To enable this, where an offence is committed after 6 April 2010, all courts must follow the guidelines and can only depart from them if to follow them would be contrary to the interests of justice (s. 125 Coroners and Justice Act 2009). If the offence is committed prior to this date then the court in question must have regard to the guidelines. The Sentencing Council is an independent public body, although as its members are appointed by the Lord Chancellor and the Lord Chief Justice, parliament does have an influence on sentencing decisions. The Council currently consists of the Lord Chief Justice and 14 other appointments. Members include representatives from the judiciary, probation, police, the Crown Prosecution Service, academics and victims' charities (Sentencing Council, 2017a).

The formulation of guidelines is quite prescriptive, with this beginning with a decision on what the guideline is focusing on. The Council will either decide on the topic itself, it may be required by legislation to produce a guideline or it may have received a proposal from the Lord Chancellor or the Court of Appeal. The Council will then conduct research and form a preliminary view. A consultation paper and a draft guideline are issued with a normal consultation period being 12 weeks. Taking into account the responses, the Council will then publish a definitive guideline, which becomes binding on all courts. The Council will continue to monitor the situation and if necessary will consider further amendments and developments.

Existing definitive guidelines are available on the Sentencing Council website (see www.sentencingcouncil.org.uk) and cover generalities such as the meaning of the term seriousness and how much reduction should be given for a guilty plea, as well as guidelines for specific offences. Examples include sexual offences, robbery, environmental offences and dangerous dog offences. Each guideline highlights factors that demonstrate high, medium and lesser culpability (A–C) and factors that help to determine whether the level of harm should be categorised as 1, 2 or 3. As explained in more detail below these help to decide how serious an offence is. A table for each offence is then provided which sets out a starting point for the offence and a category range. Aggravating factors will increase the starting point and personal mitigation will reduce it. Using such tables the court will arrive at a sentence that is commensurate or equal with the seriousness of the offence (see just deserts in Chapter 2). While the guidelines restrict judicial discretion in terms of starting point and sentencing range, the sentencer is able to decide where in that range the appropriate sentence should lie. An example of the starting points and category ranges available for street robbery under section 8(1) Theft Act 1968 is available in Table 4.2.

Table 4.2 Starting point and category ranges for street robbery.

	Culpability		
Harm	A	B	C
Category 1	Starting point 8 years' custody	Starting point 5 years' custody	Starting point 4 years' custody
	Category range 7–12 years' custody	Category range 4–8 years' custody	Category range 3–6 years' custody
Category 2	Starting point 5 years' custody	Starting point 4 years' custody	Starting point 2 years' custody
	Category range 4–8 years' custody	Category range 3–6 years' custody	Category range 1–4 years' custody
Category 3	Starting point 4 years' custody	Starting point 2 years' custody	Starting point 1 years' custody
	Category range 3–6 years' custody	Category range 1–4 years' custody	Category range High level community order–3 years' custody

Source: Sentencing Council (2016c) *Robbery Definitive Guideline*. London: Sentencing Council, p. 5.

Population	328,787,792 (Worldometers, 2019f)
Prison population (including remand prisoners)	2,121,600 (Institute for Criminal Policy Research, 2016)
Prison population per 100,000 of national population	655 (Institute for Criminal Policy Research, 2016)
Remand prisoners	21.6% (Institute for Criminal Policy Research, 2016)
Number of establishments	4455 (1292 state and federal facilities and 3163 local jails) (Institute for Criminal Policy Research, 2016)
Official capacity of prison service	2,140,321 (Institute for Criminal Policy Research, 2016)
Occupancy level	103.9% (Institute for Criminal Policy Research, 2016)

Brief Profile

The United States of America (US) is the third most populous country in the world. Despite there being a one billion-population difference when compared to China and India (Worldometers, 2019b), it still imprisons more people than any other country, having also the highest prison population rate per 100,000 of national population (Walmsley, 2018).

Sentencing Principles

Mass imprisonment in the US (see Chapter 12 for comments on this) is largely due to the country's sentencing regulations, which were introduced in 1987 to restrict judicial discretion and to enforce a tough law and order policy (Johnson, 2011). When making federal sentencing decisions, sentencers must refer to US Sentencing Commission guidelines (United States Sentencing Commission, 2016). These are in place to help judges determine not only which type of sentence to impose (probation, fine or imprisonment) but also sentence length, fine amount, probation conditions, whether or not imprisonment should be followed by supervision and also whether multiple sentences should run consecutively or concurrently (28 U.S. Code § 994). Separate State Guidelines also exist.

The guidelines cover every legislated offence. Sentencers are obliged to first find the relevant offence section and then follow a number of instructions. These are established to allow the judge to fine-tune the sentence so that it is appropriate for the individual crime. This can be illustrated by examining the offence of burglary (United States Sentencing Commission, 2016). The first step is to determine the base offence level, which for burglary of a residence is 17. The court must then include any specific offence characteristics, for example if there was more than minimal planning the offence level would be increased by two. The loss or harm caused by the crime will also increase the offence level with this being categorised in dollars; where a loss of more than $20,000 increases the level by two. If a controlled substance was taken another level is added and a further increase of two levels is given if the offender had a dangerous weapon at the time of the offence. If all of these factors were present then the offence level would be 24. Adjustments can then be made. These relate to both aggravating and mitigating factors, for example, if the offence was motivated by race, religion, ethnicity, gender or sexual orientation then a further three levels are added. If the victim was physically restrained the base level will increase by two. However, if the offender only played a minor part in the offence then the base level would decrease by two. Again assuming these characteristics this brings the example to an offence level of 27.

The court must then look at criminal history and criminal livelihood. Three points are added for each prior sentence of imprisonment, which exceeds one year and one month and two points are added if the offence was committed while on bail. Additional levels can also be added if the offender is classified as a career offender. If we assume 2 prior imprisonment terms of 14 months the criminal history points in this example are thus set at six. A sentencing grid then exists which must be used to determine the level of sentence in terms of months in custody or on probation. For our example, (see Table 4.3) the appropriate sentence would be a custodial range of between 87 and 108 months.

Table 4.3 US sentencing commission sentencing table 2016.

Offence Level	In months of imprisonment		
	Criminal History Category (Criminal History Points)		
	I (0 or 1)	II (2 or 3)	III (4, 5, 6)
27	70–87	79–97	87–108

Source: United States Sentencing Commission, 2016. *Guidelines Manual 2016*. Washington: United States Sentencing Commission, p. 419.

The sentencing table as a whole has 43 offence levels divided into 4 zones. Zone A incorporates levels 1–8; Zone B levels 9–11; Zone C levels 12–13 and Zone D levels 14–43. These Zones are used to determine the type of sentence with probation applicable for zones A and B offences only. With reference to probation, the guideline sets out a number of mandatory conditions applicable to all probation orders and some additional conditions that should be used depending on the circumstances of the offence and offender (United States Sentencing Commission, 2016).

The only time that a guideline-specified sentence can be departed from is when the court finds 'an aggravating or mitigating circumstance of a kind, or to a degree, not adequately taken into consideration by the Sentencing Commission' (18 U.S. Code § 3553(b)). While this creates a 'legal freedom' to depart from the guidelines, due to the detail of the guidelines, courts 'will not do so very often' (United States Sentencing Commission, 2016, p. 8). Essentially, therefore, the guidelines work to ensure that judicial sentencing discretion has been virtually eradicated. While this does offer certainty, equality and consistency, it also increases severity in sentencing. Other criticisms are that the guidelines are overly technical, abstract and complicated; restrict the use of sentencing considerations based around education, employment, family and community ties; and, increase the use of custody by decreasing the possibility of probation (Johnson, 2011). Tonry refers to them as the 'most controversial and disliked sentencing reform initiative in US history' (Tonry, 1996, p. 72).

Discussion Points

1. What are the advantages and disadvantages of the sentencing grid system used in the US?
2. Is this something which you would like to see introduced into England and Wales?

Although the sentencing systems in the US and England and Wales may appear similar, in the sense that both contain guidance on sentencing for individual offences, they are fundamentally different. The US, for example achieves consistency by providing a range of sentences and by discouraging departures from them (Roberts, 2013), whereas the system in England and Wales, as explained below, is more about the steps which must be followed in order to reach a sentencing decision. This therefore means that judges in England and Wales have many more opportunities, than their American counterparts, to exercise judicial discretion, after the initial starting point has been decided upon. As outlined below, this includes taking into consideration issues such as a guilty plea, aggravating and mitigating factors and whether the offender has aided the prosecution. The main difference between the two systems is therefore that the US wants consistency in outcome, whereas England and Wales favours a system which promotes consistency in approach.

Discussion Points

1. Do we need sentencing guidelines or should we just trust in judicial discretion?
2. From looking at the example of robbery and other offences from the Sentencing Council website, what do you think to these offence guidelines?
3. Which is the better approach to sentencing: consistency by outcome, or consistency in approach?

THE SENTENCING PROCESS

Five purposes of sentencing

Regardless of which court sentencing takes place in, there are a number of issues, which both magistrates and Crown Court judges must take into account when reaching their sentencing decisions. The first factor is the five purposes of sentencing (s.142 Criminal Justice Act (CJA) 2003), which are:

1. Punishment of offenders.
2. Reduction of crime (including its reduction by deterrence).
3. Reform and rehabilitation of offenders.
4. Protection of the public.
5. Making of reparation by offenders to persons affected by their offences.

These relate to the aims of the sentence and are essentially, what the sentencer is trying to achieve with the offender. They relate to penal theory (see Chapters 2 and 3) and can be achieved through imprisonment, offending behaviour programmes (OBPs) unpaid work, curfew, compensation and restorative justice.

There are, however, a number of problems with presenting the aims of sentencing in this fashion. The first relates to the fact that apart from reparation, the other aims are potentially conflicting and it is unclear in what circumstances, which aim, should be used or prioritised over another. Making this point, Ashworth and Roberts (2012), for example, question whether in the case of corporate offending the court should prioritise the aim of deterrence or whether it should be focused on some other aim as well. Furthermore, as stated by the Home Office in a sentencing review there is very little evidence to support the notion that deterrence, rehabilitation and public protection actually work as legitimate sentencing aims (Ashworth & Roberts, 2012). Despite these concerns, England and Wales are not alone in the listing of sentencing purposes, with similar aims used in Australia, Canada, Kenya (which also includes denunciation) and Russia with it being acknowledged that it would be difficult to present them in any other way.

Key decisions in the sentencing process

Another guiding principle, as mentioned above, is a regulated sentencing process (Sentencing Guidelines Council, 2008) (see Figure 4.2). While this must be followed in the Magistrates' Court, many of the steps also apply to Crown Court sentencing decisions.

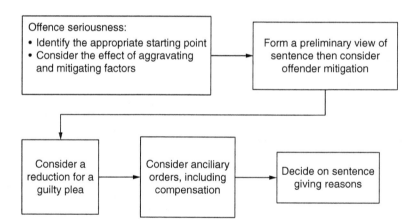

Figure 4.2 Key decisions in the sentencing process
Source: Sentencing Guidelines Council (2008) *Magistrates' Court Sentencing Guidelines*. London: Sentencing Guidelines Council.

Offence seriousness

Following this process, the first task for sentencers is to assess how serious a particular offence is. This is achieved by looking at the culpability of the offender in addition to the harm, which either the offence caused, or risked being caused. Guidelines on this exist within legislation (s. 143(1) CJA 2003) and a Sentencing

Council guideline: *Overarching Principles: Seriousness* (Sentencing Guidelines Council, 2004). This aims to guide sentencers in how they should determine when sentencing thresholds have been crossed, that is, when they should give a community or a custodial sentence. Similar to the definition in legislation, the guideline states that 'The seriousness of an offence is determined by two main parameters: the culpability of the offender and the harm caused or risked being caused by the offence' (Sentencing Guidelines Council, 2004, p. 3). A note clarifies the order of priority in terms of harm and culpability, stating that, while the level of harm caused is important, 'the culpability of the offender should be the initial factor in determining the seriousness of an offence' (Sentencing Guidelines Council, 2004, p. 5).

To enable sentencers to assess seriousness, the guideline identifies four levels of criminal culpability: intention, recklessness, knowledge and negligence. Intention, framed as the worst level, creates the greatest degree of culpability. The guideline also provides examples of factors that are indicative of higher culpability, such as the offence being religiously or racially aggravated. Likewise, factors that might suggest a lower level of culpability include mental illness and disability. Harm can be defined in terms of the effect that the crime has or may have on individual victims or the community (Sentencing Guidelines Council, 2004). This can also include other types of harm such as cruelty to animals on the basis that this can cause a human victim both psychological distress and financial loss (Sentencing Guidelines Council, 2004).

Once the seriousness of the offence is determined, the next step is to match the offence to a type and level of sentence. This exercise is assisted by the existence of both a custody threshold and a community sentence threshold test (s. 152(2) and s. 148(1) CJA 2003).

Section 152(2) CJA 2003 (custody threshold test): The court must not pass a custodial sentence unless it is of the opinion that the offence, or the combination of the offence and one or more offences associated with it, was so serious that neither a fine alone nor a community sentence can be justified for the offence.

Section 148(1) CJA 2003 (community threshold test): A court must not pass a community sentence on an offender unless it is of the opinion that the offence, or the combination of the offence and one or more offences associated with it, was serious enough to warrant such a sentence.

The approach that a court should take is to ask a number of questions including:

- Has the custody threshold been passed?
- If so, is it unavoidable that a custodial sentence be imposed?
- If so, can the sentence be suspended?
- If not, impose a sentence that takes immediate effect for the term commensurate with the seriousness of the offence.
  (Sentencing Guidelines Council, 2004, p. 8)

The threshold for a community sentence can also be crossed if the offender is aged 18 or over, and on three or more occasions has only received a fine (s. 151 CJA 2003). This is so even if the individual offence was not serious enough to warrant a community sentence.

The court must then consider aggravating and/or mitigating factors. In this context, aggravating factors are those elements of an offence, which make it more serious such as committing the offence whilst on bail or being motivated by race, religion or sexual orientation. Mitigating factors are those that make an offence more understandable or less serious, including acting under duress or necessity, cooperating with the police or showing genuine remorse. The power to mitigate is contained in section 166 CJA 2003. This allows mitigating factors to change a sentence from, for example, custody to a community penalty. The court must then form a preliminary view of the sentence including taking into account any factors which might indicate a reduction in sentence due to assistance given to the prosecution (ss. 73–74 Serious Organised Crime and Police Act 2005).

The guilty plea

If applicable, the court will then consider a reduction for a guilty plea. Historically it has always been accepted that an offender should receive some kind of sentence reduction for a 'timely' guilty plea. Reasons for this include the fact that it avoids the guilty being acquitted, it spares witnesses and victims the tension of a trial, it reduces the time between charge and sentence, reduces court delay and importantly it saves public money (Sentencing Guidelines Council, 2007). The more controversial issue, however, has been how much this discount should be, with this, until 2005, set at one-third (*R v Buffrey* (1993) 14 Cr App R (S) 511). The current law, found in section 144 of the CJA 2003, states that when deciding what reduction to make, the court must take into account both the stage in the proceedings when the guilty plea is given, and the circumstances in which it is specified. Additional guidance is also provided by the guideline: *Reduction in Sentence for a Guilty Plea*, which applies to all offences sentenced on or after 10 January 2005, with the first revised version applicable to all offences sentenced on or after 23 July 2007 (Sentencing Guidelines Council, 2007) and the second revised edition applicable from 1 June 2017 (Sentencing Council, 2017e).

The Guideline refers to a sliding scale of reductions, where the timing of the guilty plea is the most important factor. Following *R v Buffrey*, the discount level starts at one third (where the guilty plea was entered at the first stage of proceedings), reducing to a recommended one quarter (after the trial date has been set) and to a recommended one tenth for a guilty plea entered at the 'door of the court'. Where the trial has actually started (defined as when cross-examination has begun), the reduction can be zero (Sentencing Council, 2017f). As well as a reduction in the length of sentence, a guilty plea can also change the type of sentence. For example, the court can, on hearing a guilty plea, decide to sentence the offender to a community penalty rather than imprisonment (*R v Okinikan*

(1993) 14 Cr App R (S) 453). Good reasons for not using the recommended approach include when there is overwhelming prosecution evidence and in these circumstances, the maximum reduction is recommended as one fifth (Sentencing Guidelines Council, 2007).

For the full one-third reduction, previous guidelines stated that the plea had to be given at the first reasonable opportunity without really clarifying what this meant. Annex 1 of the 2007 guideline suggested that it could mean at the first court hearing, although a guilty plea or at least an indication of willingness may also have been expected at the police interview stage (Sentencing Guidelines Council, 2007). The 2007 guideline therefore suggested that a person should indicate that they intended to plead guilty before they had even seen the evidence against them and in some situations before they had even had proper legal advice or been charged with an actual offence. Indicating a guilty plea at this early stage consequently meant that many of the safeguards imposed to protect defendants were not then initiated. For example, the prosecution did not need to prove its case beyond all reasonable doubt nor have its evidence tested by an independent lay tribunal. Acknowledging this problem, the Court of Appeal in *R v Caley and Others* ([2012] EWCA Crim 2821) suggested that the full one-third reduction should be given when the plea was entered at the Magistrates' Court or immediately on arrival at the Crown Court and therefore was not expected at police interview.

Despite this, data collected by the Sentencing Council in March 2015, suggested not only that the guideline was being inconsistently applied but that higher than recommended reductions in sentences were being given (Sentencing Council, 2016b). In response, the Sentencing Council published a consultation on a new guideline in February 2016 (Sentencing Council, 2016b) and issued a definitive guideline on 7 March 2017 (Sentencing Council, 2017f). Responding to criticism, the definitive guideline changes 'the first reasonable opportunity' to the first stage of proceedings, making it much clearer at what stage the full one-third reduction should now be given. For offenders aged 18 and over this is the first hearing where a plea or indication of plea is requested and recorded by the court. There are however some exceptions to this general rule:

- Where the defendant was delayed in entering their plea due to the need to seek further information, assistance or advice and without such information, it was unreasonable to expect the defendant to indicate a plea.
- If the offender is convicted of a lesser or different offence and previously indicated that they would plead guilty to this lesser offence, this should be taken into account. The stage at which this plea was indicated will determine the level of reduction.
- A guilty plea cannot reduce a sentence below its minimum threshold. (see below) (Sentencing Council, 2017f)

The fact that the Council listened and responded to this criticism is a good example of its duty to continually monitor and, if appropriate, revise guidelines.

> **Discussion Questions**
>
> 1. Should we offer a reduction in sentence to those who plead guilty?
> 2. If you think yes, what should this reduction be and at what stage in proceedings should this plea be indicated?
> 3. What effect does this have on the legal rights of the defendant?

MAXIMUM AND MINIMUM SENTENCING RESTRICTIONS

In addition to guidelines, sentencers must also be mindful of stipulations and restrictions laid out by legislation, such as maximum and minimum sentencing terms.

Maximum sentencing terms

Most statutory offences have maximum sentencing terms that are provided by government and are contained in legislation. Examples include theft where the maximum term is seven years imprisonment (s. 7 Theft Act 1968), fraud, which is 10 years (s. 1 Fraud Act 2006) and rape which is life (s. 1 Sexual Offences Act 2003). Such terms can be changed over time, for example, the maximum sentence for theft used to be ten years and was changed to seven by the CJA 1991. Even though sentencers have some discretion in their sentencing decisions, they are all restricted by maximum sentences, even if they do not think that the maximum penalty is commensurate with the seriousness of the offence. In such a case the only thing that a sentencer can do, if there is more than one offence, is to sentence consecutively (sentences are served one after the other) rather than concurrently (sentences are served at the same time). When making consecutive sentences, the judge must have regard to the principle of totality, i.e. ensure that the length of the total sentence is commensurate with the seriousness of the total offences. An example of this was seen in the case of *R v Backwell* ([2003] EWCA Crim 3213) where Justice Butterfield stated that it was lawful to impose consecutive sentences for offences of indecent assault where it was felt to be necessary to protect the public from serious harm from the offender. This was so even though the total sentence given exceeded the statutory maximum for each individual offence.

Minimum sentencing terms

Minimum sentencing terms apply to only three specific offences, two of which are contained in sections 110 and 111 of the Powers of Criminal Courts (Sentencing) Act 2000. Section 110 stipulates a minimum of seven years imprisonment for a third Class A drug trafficking offence, and section 111 imposes a minimum custodial sentence of three years for a third domestic burglary offence. Neither apply if it can be shown that such a sentence would be unjust. The third instance, under section 51A of the Firearms Act 1968, stipulates five years imprisonment where a person has been convicted of the possession, purchase, acquisition, manufacture, transfer or sale of prohibited weapons. While not plentiful, minimum sentencing provisions do, supposedly, reflect the concerns of parliament in terms of the offences that it wants to ensure are sentenced at a certain level. Such provisions therefore fetter judicial discretion, although when looking at the minimum terms it is highly unlikely that a judge would impose less than a three year custodial sentence for a third time domestic burglary or less than seven years for a third drug trafficking offence. It is therefore questionable why such provisions exist. Is it to ensure minimum sentencing, to limit judicial discretion or just to win political votes?

The life sentence

Mandatory life

Despite the fact that sentencing should be in the domain of the judiciary, a merging of executive and judicial powers can be seen in the sentencing of and review possibilities of the life sentence. When the separation of powers (executive and judiciary) is one of the fundamental principles of governance, it is therefore surprising that this blurring is found in the most severe of sentencing options. In England and Wales, there are two types of life sentence: mandatory and discretionary, with a mandatory life sentence applicable in all cases of murder. This is enshrined in statute under section 1(1) of the Murder (Abolition of Death Penalty) Act 1965 and provides no discretion, even if the offender does not pose a threat to the public. Despite the controversy which this can cause, especially in cases of mercy killings, the House of Lords (now Supreme Court) has held that the sentence is not arbitrary or disproportionate and as such does not violate either article 3 (inhuman or degrading treatment or punishment) or article 5 (right to liberty) of the European Convention on Human Rights (ECHR) (*R v Lichniak & Other* [2002] UKHL 47).

Discretionary life sentence

Discretionary life, on the other hand, is where the maximum sentence for the particular offence is life imprisonment and it is for the judge to determine whether to impose the sentence. Examples include rape, manslaughter and grievous bodily harm with intent and as these are all indictable offences such a decision would only be within the realms of the Crown Court. Such discretion however is not unfettered with guidance contained in *R v Whittaker* ([1997] 1 Cr App R (S) 261). Here, Lord Bingham set out two basic questions:

1. Has the offender been convicted of an offence of a degree of seriousness, which might properly be regarded as meriting a life sentence?
2. Are there grounds for believing that the offender might be a serious danger to the public for a period, which cannot be reliably estimated at the time of sentence?

If the answer to both of these is yes then a life sentence can be imposed. Similar advice has also been given in *R v Chapman* ([2000] 1 Cr App R 77).

Setting a life sentence term

Despite its name, only a small amount of life-sentenced prisoners will spend the remainder of their lives in custody. These are prisoners who have been given whole life tariffs and between 2003 and 2015 there were only 38 offenders who had been sentenced in this way (Ministry of Justice, 2016a). When ordering a life sentence the judge must impose a minimum term that the offender will serve in prison before they are eligible to be considered for release by the Parole Board (see Chapter 9). This minimum term is known as the first phase of the sentence and is for the length that reflects the seriousness of the offence (Lipscombe & Beard, 2015). Until 2003, the Home Secretary could amend this minimum term making the process for some offenders highly political. This political influence was seen in November 2002 when David Blunkett, the then Home Secretary, ruled that Roy Whiting who had been convicted of the abduction and murder of Sarah Payne would serve a minimum of 50 years in prison before he was eligible for parole. Whiting was not the only child killer of that year, but he was the only one who the mass media had attached itself to and arguably, this interest and public disgust was reflected in the Home Secretary's ruling. Once such a tariff had been set, prisoners were then entitled to a review of this sentence after they had served 25 years imprisonment.

The setting of minimum tariffs by the government rather than by the judiciary was challenged in the case of *Secretary of State for the Home Department ex p Anderson and Taylor* ([2002] UKHL 46). The House of Lords held that the imposition of the minimum tariff for mandatory life prisoners was a sentencing power and consequently its exercise by the Home Secretary breached article 6 of the ECHR. This requires that criminal hearings must be conducted by an independent and impartial tribunal established by law. The case therefore means that the setting of a tariff for a life sentence should always be made by the judiciary rather than by the executive. Despite this ruling, the government is still very much involved in sentencing, seen through the creation of the Sentencing Council and legislative provisions. In relation to setting minimum tariffs in life sentences, section 269 and schedule 21 of the CJA 2003 set out sentencing principles and starting points, which must be followed (see Table 4.4). It is worth noting that a whole life tariff can only be used with those offenders who were 21 years or older at the commission of the crime. The starting points of 15, 25 and 30 years can only be used where the offender was 18 or over at the time of the offence. Twelve years is the starting point for any murder where the offender was 17 or under at the time of the killing (Lipscombe & Beard, 2015).

While schedule 21 of the CJA 2003 may be viewed as useful and arguably ensures consistency in sentencing, the fact that it has been devised by parliament means that it is the executive rather than the judiciary who in effect decide on the setting of the minimum tariff. This is contrary not just to the above House of Lords

Table 4.4 Determination of minimum terms in relation to mandatory life sentence (Schedule 21 CJA 2003).

A whole life would be the starting point for adult murderers in respect of: • Multiple murders (two or more) that show a substantial degree of premeditation, involve abduction of the victim prior to the killing, or are sexual or sadistic. • Murder of a child following abduction or involving sexual or sadistic conduct. • Terrorist murder. • Murders of police and prison officers during the course of duty. • The offender has been previously convicted of murder.
The second level attracting a starting point of 30 years is appropriate for: • Murder involving the use of a firearm or explosive. • Killing done for gain (burglary, robbery etc. includes professional contract killing). • Killing intended to defeat the ends of justice for example the killing of witnesses. • Murder motivated by race/religion/sexual orientation/disability. • Simple sadistic or sexual murder of an adult. • Multiple murders (excluding those above).
The third level has a starting point of 25 years and is appropriate where the offender took a knife or any other weapon to the scene of the crime intending to use it and did use it.
The fourth level, where the starting point is 15 years, is appropriate for all other cases where the offender is at least 18 years old.
Where the offender is under 18 at the time of the murder the appropriate starting point in all circumstances is 12 years.

case but also breaches article 6 of the ECHR. This viewpoint has been shared by others including Lord Lloyd of Berwick who in 2012 argued that schedule 21 not only tied judges down so tightly that they could not realise justice but also that it turned sentencing into 'political football, with each [political] side wanting to appear tougher on sentencing than the other' (HL Deb 9 February 2012 CC426-7). The majority of the House however disagreed and a proposed amendment to the Legal Aid, Sentencing and Punishment of Offenders Bill 2010–2012 was withdrawn (Lipscombe & Beard, 2015). The problem has not gone away however and it is perhaps surprising that this issue has not been further challenged in the courts.

The lawfulness of the whole life tariff, has however been challenged. This first arose in 2012 through the case of *Vinter & Others v United Kingdom* (UK) ((2012) 55 EHRR 34) and concerned the fact that the CJA 2003 took away the automatic review of whole life sentences at the 25 year stage. The applicants, all of whom were prisoners serving whole life tariffs, argued that because their sentence did not have a review element, meant that they would be in prison for life, which they claimed breached article 3 of the ECHR. Dismissing the case, the European Court of Human Rights (ECtHR) held that the sentences were lawful: they had a penological purpose and in the circumstances were proportionate and just. The applicants appealed (*Vinter & Others v UK* (2016) 63 EHRR 1). The Grand Chamber held that the sentences in question were proportionate, but stated that in order for them to be lawful they needed to offer the possibility of review and release, as was offered in most other European countries, with review points ranging from 10 to 30 years.

Previously the UK had argued (*R v Bieber* [2008] EWCA Crim 1601) and the Court of Appeal had accepted, that the whole life tariff was reducible, i.e. there was a possibility that prisoners could be released because of a limited power under section 30 of the Crime (Sentences) Act 1997. This allows for release where 'exceptional circumstances exist which justify the prisoner's release on compassionate grounds' but the Grand Chamber did not think that this was a sufficient substitute.

The UK was given six months to respond. Seven months later, the Attorney General referred to the Court of Appeal, as unduly lenient, two life sentences where the minimum tariffs were 40 years (*AG Reference (No. 69 of 2013)* [2014] EWCA Crim 188). The Court held that some crimes were so heinous that Parliament was entitled to proscribe, compatibly with the ECHR, that the requirements of just punishment encompassed passing a sentence that included a whole life order. If however there were exceptional circumstances as designated under section 30 of the Crime (Sentences) Act 1997 then the prisoner would be released. Judges were therefore told to continue to apply the regime as set out in the CJA 2003 and to impose, where appropriate, whole life orders in accordance with schedule 21 of the Act (paras 25–36). In essence, the judgment of the Grand Chamber was ignored.

The final case in the saga, *Hutchinson v UK* ((2015) 61 EHRR 13), was decided by the ECtHR in February 2015. The case involved a prisoner who had received a whole life tariff for aggravated burglary, rape and three counts of murder. Relying on article 3, he argued that his whole life sentence was inhuman and degrading, as he had no hope of release. Arguing that the UK had confirmed that the exceptional circumstances clause provided hope and the possibility of release for whole life prisoners, the ECtHR confirmed that the whole life tariff in the UK was no longer a breach of article 3. Hutchinson appealed to the Grand Chamber (Hutchinson v UK Application no. 57592/08). Perhaps surprisingly the Grand Chamber agreed. It held there had been no violation of article 3 because of the Court of Appeals confirmation of the way in which the Secretary of State could exercise their statutory duty to release life-sentenced prisoners under section 30. The fundamental point to make here is that the UK has changed nothing. In direct contrast to many other European countries there is therefore no automatic review in England and Wales for those prisoners serving whole life tariffs. Their only hope is that they will be released one day on compassionate grounds, although as confirmed by the Ministry of Justice following a Freedom of Information request in March 2017, there have been no prisoners released under this power between 2009 (when a central electronic system came into operation) and March 2017 (Ministry of Justice, 2017c). This effectively means that there is simply no review mechanism in England and Wales.

Discussion Points

1. Who should decide on the minimum tariff of a life-sentenced prisoner, the executive or the judiciary?
2. What level of review, if any, should be given in whole life tariff cases?
3. Why do you think the Grand Chamber changed its position on whole life tariffs and the need for a review point?

CONCLUSION

Ensuring sentencing decisions are correct is fundamental; not just because of the resources required to carry out those sentences imposed but also to ensure consistency and transparency and therefore a just criminal justice system. How this is achieved, however, is the harder question. England and Wales has a sentencing system, which allows for some judicial discretion, but at the same time also imposes guidelines on its judiciary. While this is not, per se, problematic, the fact that these guidelines are influenced by the executive can mean that the lines between executive and judiciary become blurred. Who is actually making the decision is therefore unclear and if it is, the executive, then political motivations and efforts to appease a populist punitiveness public may negatively influence sentence severity. There are also serious concerns about the current makeup of the judiciary, both within the lower and senior level courts. While in the Magistrates' Court men and women are evenly represented this is not true in the higher courts, with only 25 per cent of the current Supreme Court made up of women. Statistics relating to age and BAME representation are also worrying with the need to increase the diversity of our judicial representatives vital. When there are such concerns, it is unclear which is more appropriate: an increase in judicial discretion unfettered by executive influence or, as used in the US, the introduction of stricter sentencing guidelines.

 Now read:

Hornle, T. (2013) 'Moderate and non-arbitrary sentencing without guidelines: The German experience', *Law & Contemporary Problems*, 76(1), 189–210.

Roberts, J. and Harris, L. (2017) 'Addressing the problems of the prison estate. The role of sentencing policy', *The Prison Service Journal*, 231, 8–14.

 Now watch:

Sankoff, P. (2017) 'Basic Sentencing principles', this is an account of sentencing principles in Canada, which is very similar to England and Wales, available on YouTube at: https://www.youtube.com/watch?v=6ZGR1phm8Js

Sentencing Council (2015) 'How a judge uses sentencing guidelines', available on YouTube at: https://www.youtube.com/watch?v=U_uvbthrlR4

Now consider:

Have a go at sentencing some cases yourself, using the Ministry of Justice site 'You be the Judge' website available at: ybtj.justice.gov.uk. To make this more lifelike consider the Sentencing Council Guidelines before making your sentencing decisions. These are available at: www.sentencingcouncil. org.uk with guidance available on YouTube at: https://www.youtube.com/watch?v=LP8hO29vmKM.

5 Out of Court Disposals and Fines

INTRODUCTION

As identified in the previous chapter, when making a sentencing decision the magistrate or Crown Court judge has to first identify how serious an offence is and then match it to the most proportionate response. To aid with this, England and Wales has a hierarchical system of sentences. The first option for magistrates and judges is the discharge, with the next level being the fine. Outside of this formal system, however, there are also a range of out of court disposals (OOCDs) which the police and Crown Prosecution Service (CPS) can impose. The idea of a hierarchical system is that the sentencer will start at the bottom and work their way up, each time asking whether that level of punishment is commensurate with the seriousness of the offence. Known as the lower level options, it is these three sentences which this chapter will cover. Community penalties and suspended sentence orders will be covered in Chapter 6 and custodial sentences are considered in Chapters 7–9. While these lower level options are perhaps not as exciting as studying prison or probation, they are important as they make up the vast majority of sentencing decisions in both the lower and upper courts.

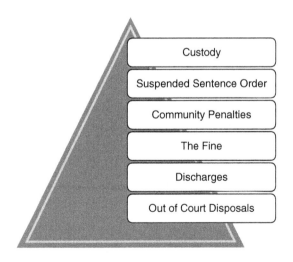

Figure 5.1 The hierarchy of sentencing in England and Wales

OUT OF COURT DISPOSALS

OOCDs are ways in which the police and in conjunction with them the CPS are able to deal with criminal behaviour without requiring a formal prosecution in court. They are often used with first time offenders who have committed low-level offences and have admitted guilt and so in accordance with sentencing principles they offer a proportionate response to this level of offending. There are a number of reasons why low-level behaviour is diverted from the criminal courts (see Figure 5.2) and especially in relation to young offenders, diversion has been used in England and Wales since the early part of the twentieth century (Smith, 2014). National guidance exists in relation to when each OOCD can be used, but in the main, it is for the police to decide whether a case is dealt with formally or is diverted away from the criminal courts. In this way, the police truly are the gate-keepers of the criminal justice system.

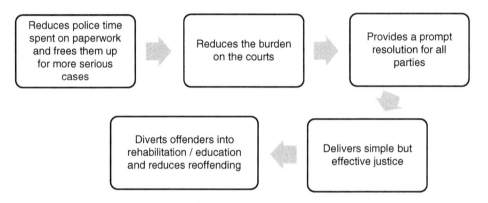

Figure 5.2   Reasons why low-level behaviour is diverted from the courts

Source: Ministry of Justice (2013d) *Quick Reference Guides to Out of Court Disposals*. London: Ministry of Justice; Ministry of Justice (2015) *Simple Cautions of Adult Offenders*. London: Ministry of Justice, p. 4.

Types of out of court disposals

There are currently a large number of OOCDs available in England and Wales, ranging from those that focus on restorative justice to those which are more punitive in nature. This section briefly considers these options, assessing how frequently they are used and whether they are a useful alternative to the more formal court sentences.

Community resolutions

Community resolutions (CRs) are available for adults and young offenders. They are non-statutory disposals that can also include elements of restorative justice (see Chapter 3). CRs are appropriate where the offender admits the offence, has shown genuine remorse and the victim has agreed that they do not want the police to take any formal action. The individual must be a first time offender, agree to accept the terms of the CR and be capable of understanding the process (Ministry of Justice, 2013d). The types of offence applicable include low-level criminal damage; minor assaults where there is no injury; anti-social behaviour and low value thefts (Ministry of Justice, 2013d). Appropriate outcomes include writing a letter of apology or repairing criminal damage. Although not a formal response, the CR will, nevertheless, be recorded on the Police National Computer (PNC) although it will not form part of an individual's criminal record.

Cannabis and khat warnings

Cannabis warnings have been available to the police since 2004 with khat warnings introduced in 2014 when khat was made an illegal Class C drug. A cannabis or khat warning can be given where a person has been found in possession of a small amount of either drug, which police believe is for personal use. The warning is the beginning of a three-stage escalation procedure for drug possession, with a second possession offence met with a penalty notice for disorder (see below) and the third with an arrest and charge (Ministry of Justice, 2013d). The drugs will be confiscated and a record of the warning made.

Fixed penalty notices

Fixed penalty notices are fines, which are fixed at a set level for a listed penalty offence. They were originally designed to deal with minor parking offences (see Part III of the Road Traffic Offenders Act 1988), but have been extended to include environmental issues such as litter (£75), nuisance parking (£100) and more recently truancy (£60). They can be administered by either local authority officers or police community support officers (PCSO) and can be given to anyone aged 10 or older. A fixed penalty notice is not a criminal conviction, but failure to pay can result in a higher fine, a community order or being sent to prison.

Penalty notices for disorder

Penalty notices for disorder (PNDs) were first announced in June 2000 as a means of reducing 'drunken, noisy, loutish and anti-social behaviour' (Roberts & Garside, 2005, p. 1) at a time when the country was in the midst of a moral panic relating to anti-social behaviour (Waiton, 2006). Contained in sections 1–11 of the Criminal Justice and Police Act 2001, a PND can be issued by either a police constable or a PCSO if they have reason to believe that an offender, aged 18 or over, has committed a 'penalty offence' (s. 2 Criminal Justice and Police Act 2001). Initially it was thought that the police would issue the on-the-spot fine and would if necessary accompany people to cash points in order to get the money. However, this was heavily criticised on the basis that it gave the police too much power and could easily lead to abuse (Roberts & Garside, 2005).

There are currently two tiers of punishment, with penalty offences divided into lower- and upper-tier offences. Examples of lower-tier offences include tres-passing on a railway, littering and consuming alcohol in a public place. Upper-tier offences encompass wasting police time, being drunk and disorderly and anti-social behaviour. In general terms the seriousness of the offence will determine whether it attracts the lower-tier fine of £60 or the upper-tier of £90 (Ministry of Justice, 2014). In response to the criticism mentioned above, the police only issue the notice and offenders are given 21 days in which to pay. The offender can pay the fine, request a court hearing if they dispute the charge or in some cases attend an educational course. This latter option was introduced by the Legal Aid, Sentencing and Punishment of Offenders Act 2012 and is available for offences committed on or after 8 April 2013. It is known as a penalty notice with an education option (PND-E) and in most police areas is used for some drug and alcohol offences (Ministry of Justice, 2014).

If the fine is paid within 21 days, all liability will be discharged (s. 2 Criminal Justice and Police Act 2001). If the fine is not paid then the Magistrates' Court will automatically register a fine one and a half times the original notice amount (s. 4 Criminal Justice and Police Act 2001). If an individual requests a court hearing and the PND is upheld then a criminal conviction will be registered by the court. If the PND-E is used then liability is discharged by paying for and completing the course (s. 2 Criminal Justice and Police Act 2001). Despite the fact that the person does not need to admit guilt and there is no actual finding of guilt a notice of the PND will be made on the PNC in addition to information relating to DNA, fingerprints and a photograph (Ministry of Justice, 2014).

Simple caution

A caution is used mainly with first time offenders, who have committed petty forms of crime. Known as the simple caution, because it has no additional add-ons or conditions, it is used with people aged 18 or over where it is not in the pub-lic's interest to prosecute, but a formal warning is nevertheless thought appropri-ate. It may be given by, or on the instructions of a senior police officer if there is evidence that:

1. the individual is guilty of an offence and guilt is admitted;
2. the offender understands the implications of accepting a simple caution; and
3. the offender agrees to be cautioned.

If the offender does not agree to receive a caution, they may be formally charged (Ministry of Justice, 2015).

The decision-making process as to whether a caution should be issued depends on the type of offence in question with guidance provided for triable either way and indictable offences. This process can be seen in Figure 5.3. Triable either way offences are those which can be tried in either the Magistrates' or Crown Court, while indictable offences can only be tried in the Crown Court (see Chapter 4).

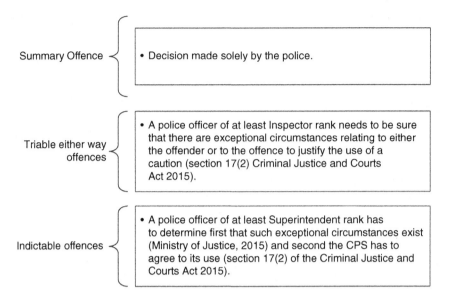

Figure 5.3 The caution decision-making process

Guidance was introduced largely in response to a number of media stories which highlighted the inappropriate use of simple cautions for quite serious offences (*The Telegraph*, 2013). As with all OOCDs, decision makers must ensure that there is sufficient evidence to prove guilt and that it is in the public's interest to proceed with the case in this way. Offences which are likely to receive a custodial sentence or a high-level community order if dealt with by the Magistrates' Court should not normally be disposed of by way of a simple caution (Ministry of Justice, 2015).

Cautions have informally existed since the advent of policing and have traditionally been used for juveniles and first time offenders; working on the principle that it is neither necessary nor desirable to prosecute every instance of offending. A simple caution is not a criminal conviction, but is an admission of guilt so will be recorded on the PNC and does form part of the offender's criminal record. This record will remain on the PNC along with photographs, fingerprints and any other evidence taken (Ministry of Justice, 2015). Accepting a simple caution for a sexual offence means that the offender will be placed on the Violent and Sex Offender Register (ViSOR) for a period of two years (Ministry of Justice, 2015). In future court proceedings, where a past caution is recent and relevant to the offence in question, a caution can be used as an aggravating factor (Sentencing Council, 2016a). If an offender has previously received a simple caution, a further caution should not normally be considered unless there has been a sufficient period of time to suggest that the previous caution had a deterrent effect, for example two years or more, and a police officer of at least inspector rank authorises it (s. 17(4) Criminal Justice and Court Act 2015). If the time period is less, the offender will be charged, even if it is for a petty offence.

Conditional caution

Conditional cautions go a step beyond the simple caution with it being conditional on the offender, who must be over 18, agreeing to abide by specified conditions. If the offender refuses, or fails to comply without reasonable excuse, they can be prosecuted in the criminal court (s. 24 Criminal Justice Act (CJA) 2003). A conditional caution can only be used where five requirements are fulfilled, as outlined in Figure 5.4. Conditions must be 'appropriate, proportionate and achievable' (Ministry of Justice, 2013a, p. 10) and be either for the purpose of 'facilitating the rehabilitation of the offender, ensuring that the offender makes reparation for the offence' or for punishment (s. 22 CJA 2003). Examples of rehabilitative conditions include attendance at drug rehabilitation or an anger management programme; reparative conditions may involve repairing the damage caused, or making an apology; and, punitive conditions could involve a financial penalty (see s. 23A CJA 2003) (Ministry of Justice, 2013a).

If the person is someone who does not have permission to be in the United Kingdom (UK), conditions may also be used to enforce departure and prevent return (s. 22(3D)–(3G) CJA 2003). Foreign offender conditions can be used even for serious offences where the public may be better served securing the offenders departure from the UK. They can be given on their own or in addition to other rehabilitative, reparative or punitive conditions. All conditions should be capable of being completed within 16–20 weeks (Ministry of Justice, 2013a). Before deciding which conditions to attach to the caution, the police officer should consult with the victim and show them the list of possible conditions outlined in the local community remedy document. Unless inappropriate, the conditions should reflect the wishes of the victim (s. 23ZA CJA 2003). Similar to simple cautions a conditional caution may be considered in court if the individual is tried for another offence. This can include using it as an aggravating factor if the conditional caution is recent and relevant to the current offence. The offender's compliance with the conditional caution may also influence the court in deciding on future interventions (Sentencing Council, 2016a).

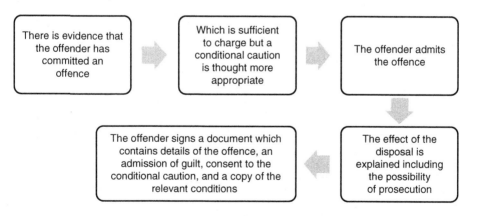

Figure 5.4 The five requirements of conditional cautions (s. 23 of the Criminal Justice Act 2003)

Youth caution

Youth Cautions are statutory disposals created by section 135 of the Legal Aid, Sentencing and Punishment of Offenders Act 2012. They are available for offenders aged 10–17 and work in a similar way to the adult version, although of importance do not require the offender's consent (Ministry of Justice, 2013d). While they are intended for low level offences, police can use them for both summary and triable either way offences and with authorisation from the CPS can also use them for indictable offences (Ministry of Justice, 2013d). The overriding criteria are that the young person admits the offence, there is sufficient evidence to charge but, it is not in the public interest to prosecute or give a youth conditional caution (s. 66ZA Crime and Disorder Act 1998). The caution must be given in the presence of an appropriate adult.

While the disposal is there to provide a proportionate and effective resolution to offending, its main aim is to prevent reoffending. Therefore, following a youth caution, the police have a statutory duty to refer the young offender to a youth offending team (YOT). If the offender has previously received either a youth caution or a youth conditional caution then the YOT must carry out an assessment and unless inappropriate arrange for participation in a rehabilitation programme. This can also be done for first time offenders, but it is not mandatory (s. 66ZB(2)–(3) Crime and Disorder Act 1998). The intervention programme cannot last for more than three months and may only be one post-assessment session. In many situations it is based on restorative justice and may involve meeting or communicating with the victim (Ministry of Justice and Youth Justice Board, 2013) (see Chapter 11 for more on YOTs and managing young people).

There is no set hierarchy between youth cautions and youth conditional cautions, but if the person has previously received two or more youth cautions and is convicted of another offence within two years, or has received a youth conditional caution followed by a youth caution and is convicted of another offence within two years, a caution would not normally be given unless there are exceptional circumstances (s. 66ZB(5)–(6) Crime and Disorder Act 1998). Any conditions or rehabilitation programmes attached are not mandatory, although if the offender fails to comply, this can be cited in future criminal proceedings (Ministry of Justice and Youth Justice Board, 2013).

Youth conditional caution

A youth conditional caution is available for offenders aged 10–17. Although introduced prior to the youth caution, it has parallel aims but is seen as more robust due to the conditions. It is available in the same circumstances as a youth caution but before it can be given, the same five requirements as necessitated for adult conditional cautions must be met (see Figure 5.4). Information concerning the effect of the caution must be given in the presence of an appropriate adult (s. 66B Crime and Disorder Act 1998).

Similar to the adult version the conditions must meet either the aims of rehabilitation, reparation or punishment and must also be appropriate, proportionate and achievable (Ministry of Justice, 2013d). The victims views should also be taken into account (s. 66BA Crime and Disorder Act 1998). Rehabilitative conditions may include a specific treatment course; reparative conditions may involve giving compensation to the victim and punitive conditions could include paying a fine or unpaid work for a maximum period of 20 hours (Ministry of Justice, 2013d). Where the offender is required to attend a specified place for a specified period of time this cannot be for longer than 20 hours (s. 66A Crime and Disorder Act 1998). Foreign offender conditions are not available (Ministry of Justice, 2013b). In addition to the conditions, the young offender will be referred to the YOT who will assess the offender and consider them for suitable intervention programmes; although these could already be part of the conditions. The conditions are mandatory and so a failure to comply will result in a prosecution for the original offence (s. 66E Crime and Disorder Act 1998). The conditional caution will be registered on the PNC and can be used in future criminal court proceedings. Also, if the young person is convicted of a criminal offence within two years of receiving the youth conditional caution, it makes them ineligible to receive a conditional discharge (see below) (s. 66F Crime and Disorder Act 1998). See Table 5.1 for a full summary of out of court disposals.

Discussion Points

1. Make a list of the advantages and disadvantages of diverting people away from the criminal courts. In your opinion how should we deal with low level offending?
2. What is your initial view of the range of OOCDs currently available in England and Wales?

Use and criticisms

Despite the benefits and long tradition of diverting people away from the criminal justice system in England and Wales, the use of OOCDs is on a downwards trend, with a steady decline seen over the last decade (Ministry of Justice and National Statistics, 2019a). For example in the year ending March 2014, OOCDs were used in 10.9 per cent of all sentencing outcomes (Home Office, 2014) with this dropping to 4.4 per cent for the year ending March 2018 (Home Office, 2018a). This is partly due to pressure from the judiciary and lawyers who argue that all cases should be dealt with by the courts to ensure that individuals understand the implications of accepting an OOCD and are not pleading guilty just because it appears to be the more convenient option. There has also arguably been a general desire to "end a 'cautions culture'", largely achieved by limiting the availability of some of the OOCDs (Allen, 2017, p. 2), coupled with other criticisms, including a lack of guidance over which OOCD should be used in which circumstance.

Perhaps one of the main criticisms concerning OOCDs focuses on the type of offences for which they are used. The Magistrates' Association, for example, has

Table 5.1 Summary of out of court disposals.

Name of disposal	Source	Available since	Age of offender	Type of offender	Type of offence	Admission of guilt	Consent needed	Victim permission	Enforceable by police or court	Criminal record	Type of disclosure	Time for conviction to be spent
Community resolution	Non-statutory	2008	10 or older	First time offender	Low level	Yes	Yes	Yes	No	No	Enhanced DBS check	N/A
Cannabis and Khat warnings	Non-statutory	2004 (cannabis) 2014 (Khat)	18 or over	First time offender	Possession for personal use	Yes	No	N/A	N/A	No	Enhanced DBS check	N/A
Fixed Penalty notices	Statutory – various pieces of legislation	1988	10 or older	All offenders	Low level	No	No	N/A	Yes, results in a higher fine, community order or prison	No	Enhanced DBS check	N/A
PND	Sections 1–11 Criminal Justice and Police Act 2001	2002	18 or over	All offenders	Penalty offences laid out in section 1 Criminal Justice and Police Act 2001	No	No	Yes – prevents compensation order	Magistrates' Court can register a fine 1.5 times original amount	No	Enhanced DBS check	N/A

(continued)

Name of disposal	Source	Available since	Age of offender	Type of offender	Type of offence	Admission of guilt	Consent needed	Victim permission	Enforceable by police or court	Criminal record	Type of disclosure	Time for conviction to be spent
Caution	Non-statutory	1984	18 or over	First time offender	Full range of offences	Yes	Yes	Views sort – prevents compensation order	N/A	Yes	DBS check, employer for certain jobs and subsequent criminal proceedings	Immediately
Conditional caution	Section 22 Criminal Justice Act 2003	2004	18 or over	All offenders	Full range of offences. Some exclusions on domestic violence and hate crime	Yes	Yes	Views sort. Can be awarded compensation or reparation	Can lead to prosecution of original offence	Yes	DBS check, employer for certain jobs and subsequent criminal proceedings	3 month if conditions complied with

(continued)

Name of disposal	Source	Available since	Age of offender	Type of offender	Type of offence	Admission of guilt	Consent needed	Victim permission	Enforceable by police or court	Criminal record	Type of disclosure	Time for conviction to be spent
Youth caution	Section 66ZA Crime and Disorder Act 1998	2013	10–17	All offenders	Full range of offences	Yes	No	Views sort. Can participate in interventions programme. Prevents compensation order	No	Yes	DBS check, employer for certain jobs and subsequent criminal proceedings. Failure to comply can be cited in future criminal proceedings	Immediately
Youth conditional caution	Section 66A Crime and Disorder Act 1998	2008 for pilot areas, 2013 nationally	10–17	All offenders	Full range of offences	Yes	Yes	Views sort. Can be awarded compensation or reparation	Can lead to prosecution of original offence	Yes	DBS check, employer for certain jobs and subsequent criminal proceedings	3 months if conditions complied with

expressed concern over the number of OOCDs which have been imposed for repeat and serious offenders, including their use for violent and sexual crimes. Even though OOCDs are designed for low level offending the police can use them for indictable offences with authorisation from the CPS and in some circumstances, this may be eminently sensible. An appropriate example could be where an under-aged sexual relationship has been reported to the police but the victim and her parents do not support a prosecution (House of Commons Home Affairs Committee, 2015). Another could be where the offender has a learning disability and there is no actual harm (Police Officer, 2017). For the year ending March 2018, only 4.5 per cent of all violent offences were dealt with by means of an OOCD, which reduced to 0.9 per cent for sexual offences. No OOCDs were issued for rape (Home Office, 2018a). While controversial, having this option for serious offences is advantageous as it allows the police to have some discretion (with CPS approval) to divert cases from the criminal justice system where to include them would not be beneficial to either offender, victim or the public at large. Bearing in mind that cautions and conditional cautions for sexual offences will include registration on ViSOR, this can mandate public protection interventions and constraints if such restrictions are thought to be necessary (see Chapter 10 for more on how sex offenders are managed in the community).

Another criticism of OOCDs relates to net widening, that is the argument that they bring more people into the criminal justice system rather than diverting them away. An example of this has been seen through the use of PNDs. Empirical research from their use in the four initial pilot areas suggested that they had been successful. In the first year of operation 6043 PNDs were issued, 49 per cent for anti-social behaviour and 42 per cent for drunk and disorderly behaviour (Spicer, 2004). However, Roberts and Garside argue that PNDs do not reduce court time because in many cases the notices are being issued against people who prior to the PND would not have been brought into the criminal justice system (Roberts & Garside, 2005). In fact, in the aforementioned evaluation it was thought that 50–75 per cent of those receiving PNDs would not have otherwise been cautioned or prosecuted (Spicer, 2004). Another concern in relation to those OOCDs which involve financial penalties is the fact that the fines are fixed and, as will be discussed in more detail below, do not therefore take income into account. This effectively allows some to 'buy themselves freedom from prosecution' (Roberts & Garside, 2005, p. 6).

There are also concerns over whether an OOCD should be issued when there is no finding or admission of guilt. This is again true for PNDs. While it is accepted that OOCDs offer swift justice, they should only do so when guilt can either be sufficiently proven or the offender admits that they were in the wrong. One of the basic principles of criminal law is that an individual is innocent until proven guilty. Furthermore, on the basis that many of the penalty offences are summary offences, approval will not even have to be sought from the CPS. While it is accepted that police decisions can be challenged in court (the very reason why OOCDs are viewed as lawful) this happens only on rare occasions; either because the individual does not think it worth the effort or because the risk of a greater sanction deters them (Padfield, et al., 2012). Without any safeguards in place, individuals can find themselves with a financial penalty to pay and a record of this 'criminal behaviour' on file, turning an administrative penalty into a 'minor court conviction' (Padfield, et al., 2012, p. 962).

The fact that OOCDs can be disclosed is also another major concern. As noted above, all OOCDs are recorded on the PNC and therefore will be on a person's police record for many years. Under sections 98–113 of the CJA 2003, these records can be relied upon in future court proceedings as evidence of a defendant's bad character and can be drawn upon to discredit prosecution witnesses and victims (see *R v Braithwaite* [2010] EWCA Crim 1082). While the Criminal Justice and Immigration Act 2003 amended the Rehabilitation of Offenders Act 1974 so that cautions are immediately spent on issue and conditional cautions spent after a period of three months, meaning that they cannot be referred to in court as convictions, this does not apply to their use as evidence of bad character (Branston, 2015). Not only is this unfair it arguably contravenes article 8 of the European Convention on Human Rights which provides respect for private and family life.

Another concern is whether it is just and fair to allow the police, public prosecutors and regulatory agencies to impose criminal sanctions, when their role is to investigate, collect evidence and prepare for trial. By giving such wide discretion to the police, which is largely exercised in an invisible way, we have a system where justice and the rule of law is replaced with the 'expression of preference' (Padfield, et al., 2012, p. 965). The existence of postcode justice is also prevalent with vast differences in use recorded between different geographical areas (Padfield, et al., 2012). Ashworth thus argues that sentences should only be imposed by fair and impartial courts and that any deviation from this gold standard 'is a matter for regret and justifiable only on pragmatic economic grounds' (Ashworth, 2010, p. 12).

Bearing in mind such criticisms, it is therefore important to consider plans and ideas for reform. In 2013–2014 the government undertook a review of and consulted on OOCDs (HM Government and College of Policing, 2013), with many of the responses reporting the criticisms mentioned above. In an attempt to simplify the system, the Government proposed a new two-tier framework where the current six disposal options would be replaced by two: suspended prosecution (akin to the conditional caution) and a new statutory community resolution. Three pilot areas, West Yorkshire, Leicestershire and Staffordshire, were announced and 12-month pilots commenced in November 2014 (HM Government and College of Policing, 2014). Through a freedom of information request, dated 27 January 2017, however, the Home Office confirmed that an evaluation would be published in due course, but declined to comment on its plans (Home Office, 2017). Despite this silence, Allen argues that if diversion is ever to fulfil its potential it is imperative that the following factors are taken into consideration:

- The police must be allowed to deal with low-level offending without the need to use formal action.
- Those cases, which are likely to result in either a discharge or a small fine in the courts, should be dealt with informally.

- The options currently available for children should also be made available for young adults.
- Treatment options, including restorative justice, should be made available. (Allen, 2017, p. 2)

Discussion Points

1. Having looked at some of the criticisms of OOCDs, has your view on them changed?
2. On the basis that a finding of guilt in not required in some of the options, should they be recordable and notifiable?
3. Should the police (even with CPS approval) have the power to sentence offenders, or is this a role which only the courts should have?
4. If you think the police are the appropriate agency, what safeguards are needed to ensure sufficient consistency and fairness?

DISCHARGES

If the prosecuting authorities feel an OOCD is inappropriate it should formally charge. Where an offender admits guilt or is found guilty, the court has a range of sentencing options, including the nominal response of a discharge. Discharges are used when the court believes that 'having regard to the circumstances including the nature of the offence and the character of the offender, it is inexpedient to inflict punishment' (s. 12 Powers of Criminal Courts (Sentencing) Act 2000). It cannot be used where the sentence is one which is fixed by law.

Absolute discharge

An absolute discharge is the most lenient of all court sentences. It imposes nothing on the offender and in most cases where an offence is dealt with by way of an absolute discharge it will not count as an actual conviction (s. 14 Powers of Criminal Courts (Sentencing Act 2000). Sexual offences are the exception, where the individual is subject to ViSOR registration. Arguably, if the court uses an absolute discharge, then the case should never have come before the court and the prosecuting authorities have erred in judgement. They can, however, be useful where the offence is excusable, i.e. where the offender has low culpability but there is no legal defence; and, where the offender has already suffered indirect loss (Ashworth, 2010).

Conditional discharge

A conditional discharge attaches the condition that the offender should not commit an offence for a set period; the maximum of which is three years. If an offence is committed within this timeframe the offender is liable to be sentenced again for the original offence (s. 13 Powers of Criminal Courts (Sentencing) Act 2000) and if this occurs the discharge becomes null and void. If the court thinks it necessary, it can appoint a person to give security for the good behaviour of the offender (s. 12 Powers of Criminal Courts (Sentencing) Act 2000). Conditional discharges work on the basis of just deserts and deterrence (see Chapter 2) and are often used as an alternative to a fine for those who cannot afford to pay. Apart for the purposes of future court proceedings, it is not seen as a criminal conviction.

FINES

The fine is one of the oldest and most commonly used punishments of the courts. For the year ending September 2018, for example, 904,306 fines were issued, equating to 76.3 per cent of all sentences imposed that year (Ministry of Justice and National Statistics, 2019a). This can be compared to 90,618 (7.6%) community sentences, 45,188 (3.8%) suspended sentences and 80,099 (6.7%) custodial sentences (Ministry of Justice and National Statistics, 2019a). The popularity of the fine is due to the fact that it is fairly easy and cheap to administer yet serves the sentencing aims of punishment, deterrence (both general and individual) and reparation (see Chapter 2). Despite these clear advantages there are generally two problems: first how should the amount of the fine be calculated and second what should be done with fine defaulters. The remainder of this chapter will consider these two fundamental questions including a consideration of how Finland administers its fine system.

Setting the level of the fine

When deciding how to set the level of any financial penalty it must first be decided whether such a system should be based on fixed penalties, as seen with OOCDs, or whether the court should take the offender's financial position into account. The advantages of having set fines are clear: they are easy to administer, sentencer discretion is reduced thus providing greater uniformity and the system is transparent in the sense that a person knows the financial cost of committing a crime. The main disadvantage, however, is that they fail to achieve equal impact and in many situations disproportionately punish those who do not have the means to pay, sometimes positively encouraging reoffending in order to do so (Ashworth, 2010). The need to achieve equal impact in sentencing decisions derives more generally from the principle of equality and the fact that 'all persons are equal before the law and are entitled to equal and effective protection against discrimination' (Art. 26 International Covenant on Civil and Political Rights). Based on these general principles all sentencing decisions should treat offenders equally and ensure that they do not discriminate on the basis of race, gender, sexual orientation, employment, social status and important here, wealth (Warner, 2012). As Warner explains, 'the principle of equality demands equality of treatment for similarly serious offences. The offender is not a variable and the impact of punishment or the punitive bite of the sanction is assumed to be the same for all offenders' (Warner, 2012, p. 226). Equality of impact can only be achieved in financial penalties therefore, if an offender's wealth is taken into account, and plays a significant part in determining the level of fine imposed.

Prior to 2005

The theoretical principle of equality of impact in relation to fines has long been accepted but how this is achieved has been more problematic. For example, under the Magistrates' Court Act 1980, the court was to 'have regard' to the offender's means, but there was no further guidance on how this would operate. Fines could be altered if the offender was poor, but there was no such alteration if the offender was wealthy. This led to a number of cases where the level of fine was reduced on appeal because while judges were trying to achieve equality of impact the legislation did not allow them to do so. In *R v Fairbairn* ((1980) 2 Cr App R (S) 315 (CA)), for example, Justice Glidewell, in reducing a fine of £7500 to £1000 stated:

> In this case the amount of the fine was over 10 times the value of the goods stolen, and in this Court's view that amount is out of scale in relation to the gravity of the offence of which he was convicted. In principle, the amount of the fine should be determined in relation to the gravity of the offence, and then, and only then, should the offender's means be considered to decide whether he has the capacity to pay such an amount. (*R v Fairbairn* (1980) 2 Cr App R (S) at 316)

In an attempt to create a fairer system, the Conservative government in October 1992 introduced a unit fine system into the Magistrates' Court. Contained within the CJA 1991, it allowed sentencers to consider an offender's disposal income in determining how much a fine should be. The system worked on a set formula of two parts. First, the offence was graded on a unit scale of 1–50 according to how serious it was. An offender's disposal income was then calculated to create a multiplier, which determined how much each unit would be worth. With units worth between £4 and £100 it allowed the situation where two people could be fined different amounts for the same criminal offence. For example, if two people committed a unit 13 offence, where one was fined £8 per unit and another £40, their respective fines would be £104 and £520. To enable the calculation of an offender's disposal income, section 20(1) of the CJA 1991 enabled the court to demand that the offender completed a means assessment form. Failure to do so was seen as a separate offence, which was punishable by a fine of up to £1200.

The system only lasted seven months with Kenneth Clarke, the then Home Secretary abolishing it in May 1993. While this was welcomed by both the Magistrates' Association and the Association of Chief Police Officers there were others who felt that by abolishing the provisions rather than amending them, such as reducing the worth of the unit range, Mr Clarke had 'thrown the baby out with the bathwater' (Independent, 1993). The sudden turnaround was in one way surprising, especially considering the evaluation of a pilot, which had looked at sentencing practice in Basingstoke, Bradford, Swansea and Teesside, six months before, and six months after a similar unit fine system had been introduced. Key findings were that means information was easy to obtain, without increasing the time taken to process the case; there was no change in the proportionate use of the penalty; the poorest offenders were fined less and the better-off paid more; disparities between courts in terms of what poor offenders were previously fined were reduced; fines were paid more quickly and there was a significant drop in the number of those who were imprisoned due to default (Moxon, et al., 1990).

The system was not abolished, therefore, due to operational reasons, with one factor being that magistrates did not like their discretion being fettered (see Chapter 4 for an explanation of how judicial discretion is currently limited). *The Guardian*, for example, reported that 30 magistrates had resigned in protest and that the Lord Chief Justice, Lord Taylor, attacked the CJA 1991 stating that it was 'an ill-fitting straitjacket' restricting sentencing powers (*The Guardian*, 1993). Moreover, it was not favoured by the middle-classes, predominantly the ones who were experiencing the higher fines. The media reported incidents where people were, they argued, being excessively fined, such as £320 for speeding and £500 for parking on double yellow lines (Sharrock, 1993). Conversely, there were also other incidents where some had not been fined enough, including the wife of a wealthy solicitor, who was fined £12 because she claimed that she had no personal income (Sharrock, 1993). There was also the infamous case of Vaughan Watkins who was initially fined £1200 for dropping litter. The media used it as another incident where the fine was not working and were slow to report that the court in question had been right to grade it as a level 12 offence and had used the £100 multiplier because Mr Watkins had not completed a means assessment form. When information became known that he was unemployed, the fine was later changed to £48 (*The Times*, 1993a). The media also focused on examples of cases where people had committed the same offence but had been fined vastly different amounts. One example was an 83-year-old woman who was fined £800 for not having a television license because she had a disposable income of more than £5000 compared to a young mother who was only fined £200 (*The Times*, 1993b). Such criticisms however were surprising, considering that this was the very point of the unit fine system. Unit fines were thus abolished by the CJA 1993. The system in part returned to that previously seen under the Magistrates' Court Act 1980, although sentencers had the power to lower and increase fines whereas before they had only had the option to decrease the amount.

Current practice

Current practice is governed by section 164 of the CJA 2003. This came into force on 4 April 2005, and outlines a four-stage process outlined in Figure 5.5. In order to gain sufficient information about an offender's financial circumstances the court can make a financial circumstances order against any convicted person prior to sentencing (s. 162 CJA 2003). This requires the offender to provide the court with

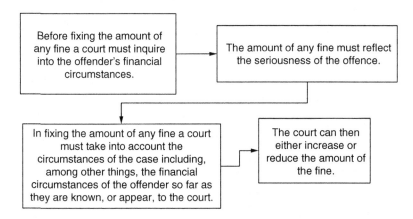

Figure 5.5 Process for setting a fine in England and Wales

a statement of their financial means within a specified period. Failure to submit a form without reasonable excuse can lead to a level 3 fine (maximum £1000). Failure to disclose information or providing false information can amount to a level 4 fine (maximum £2500). If the offender fails to provide a statement of their financial circumstances or if they have been convicted in their absence then the court can set the level of fine at the level that it 'thinks fit' (s. 164(5) CJA 2003), although there are statutory limits on this.

A unit fine system by the back door?

Despite the restoration of full sentencer discretion pleasing many magistrates, the desire to have a unit fine system has not disappeared. In 2005, there was a further attempt to introduce such a system into England and Wales but this was unsuccessful and there have been no further attempts at resuscitating a statutory scheme. A similar system was, however, introduced by the Sentencing Council (see Chapter 4) in 2008 (updated in 2015 and 2016) when it issued a Magistrates' Court Sentencing Guideline, which sets out the approach which should be taken when assessing the level of a fine. After deciding how serious the offence is, the court must then take the financial circumstances of the offender into account so that there is "an equal impact on offenders with different financial circumstances; it should be a hardship but should not force the offender below a reasonable 'subsistence' level" (Sentencing Guidelines Council, 2008, p. 148). For those offences where a fine is commensurate with seriousness, three bands (A–C) exist. Bands D–F have also been created because it may sometimes be appropriate to use a fine even where the community or custody threshold has been crossed (Sentencing Guidelines Council, 2008). Within each band there is a starting point and a range and it is the presence of aggravating and/or mitigating factors which determines where on this range the offence should lie. The bands and ranges can be seen in Table 5.2.

Table 5.2 Fine bands and ranges.

	Starting Point	Range
Fine Band A	50% of relevant weekly income	25–75% of relevant weekly income
Fine Band B	100% of relevant weekly income	75–125% of relevant weekly income
Fine Band C	150% of relevant weekly income	125–175% of relevant weekly income
Fine Band D	250% of relevant weekly income	200–300% of relevant weekly income
Fine Band E	400% of relevant weekly income	300–500% of relevant weekly income
Fine Band F	600% of relevant weekly income	500–700% of relevant weekly income

Source: Sentencing Guidelines Council (2008) *Magistrate's Court Sentencing Guidelines, Definitive Guideline*. London: Sentencing Guidelines Council, p. 148.

Once the appropriate band and position within that band has been decided, the level of the fine, based on an offender's weekly income, can then be set. This is defined in the Guideline as income 'after deduction of tax and national insurance' (Sentencing Guidelines Council, 2008, p. 148). Where this amount is more than £120 then the actual amount will be used, but where the amount is less than £120 including where the offender is on benefits (although tax credits, housing benefit and child benefit should not be included in the calculation), the relevant weekly income is set at £120. This amount should be increased to £440 where the financial circumstances of the offender cannot be reliably determined (Sentencing Guidelines Council, 2008). To aid with this calculation the Sentencing Council (2017b) has devised a fine calculator which is available on its website (see https://www.sentencingcouncil.org.uk/fine-calculator/).

Setting the minimum weekly income at £120 can be detrimental, however, with the hardship, as mentioned above, falling harder on those whose income is less than this amount or on those who have no savings, because how else are you expected to make payments of over 50 per cent of your income while also paying for your everyday subsistence costs? When the percentage can go as high as 700 per cent this, for many, is insurmountable. The system therefore favours the wealthy; especially when magistrates can lower a fine which appears to be 'disproportionately high' (Sentencing Guidelines Council, 2008, p. 150). This is despite the fact that the guideline categorically states that the seriousness of the offence and the offender's income are two separate matters and 'should be considered separately' (Sentencing Guidelines Council, 2008, p. 149).

Is this then a unit fine system by the back door? As Ashworth comments, while it is an attempt to combine flexibility with structure it is probably too woolly for real supporters of a unit fine system but too formulaic for those who believe in judicial discretion (Ashworth, 2010). There is also no evidence to suggest that the guideline is being used in any consistent way. Raine and Dunstan, for example, found that while some magistrates were using the guidelines appropriately, others 'subsequently chose to change their minds and go their own ways if and when the sentencing outcomes so derived from adherence to the guidelines failed to satisfy expectations as to their sense of justice' (Raine & Dunstan, 2009, p. 29). Some magistrates were using the guidelines, some their own version of a unit fine system and others judicial discretion alone. While Raine and Dunstan (2009) noted how magistrates were broadly in favour of having a fine-setting methodology they also spoke about not wanting their discretion fettered and their preference for flexibility in sentencing decisions. This is problematic, because, as with current OOCDs, there is a real risk that this will result in justice by geography, with some magistrate benches imposing higher fines than others. When the fine amounts to three quarters of all court disposals it is imperative that this is not the case and that there is a system in place, which is effective, transparent and fair.

An alternative to our system is the one which is found in Finland (see Spotlight Country below). There are obvious advantages to using a system such as that seen in Finland etc. Not least the fact that it enables sentencers to achieve equal impact: the wealthy are punished to the same extent as the poor and offenders are only ever sentenced to amounts, which they can truly afford to pay (see below). Taking this and the aims of fines into account, it therefore allows for a system, which is punitive, transparent and importantly fair. Due to advances in technology, there are also no problems with gaining information regarding a person's circumstances so that again, a fair result is achieved with minimum delay and expense. Also importantly, there is very little money spent on methods to ensure and enable payment, because if payment can be afforded then these are no longer necessary.

Discussion Questions

1. What do you think to the current system in England and Wales for setting the level of a fine?
2. Do you think that a unit fine system would be preferable?
3. What improvements do you think need to be made to ensure that the fine system is effective, transparent and fair?

Payment of a fine

In all cases where a fine has been imposed the court will issue a collection order (para. 13 Schedule 5 Courts Act 2003) which sets out the sum which is due. In theory, a fine should be paid on the day that it is imposed, although if this is not possible the court has the power to dispense with immediate payment allowing the offender time to pay by instalments (s. 75 Magistrates' Court Act 1980). If this option is used the payment and instalment terms will be stated in the collection order. Full payment should be achieved within 12 months, although the period can be extended to 18 months for a band D fine and to 24 months for a band E or F fine (Sentencing Guidelines Council, 2008). Payments should be set at a realistic rate and are based on weekly income, with the lowest weekly payments starting at £5 per week (Sentencing Guidelines Council, 2008). In addition to the fine there are also a number of other payments. The first of these is the victim surcharge, which for an offence committed after 8 April 2016 is 10 per cent of the fine value, with

Population	5,558,967 (Worldometers, 2019b)
Prison population (including remand prisoners)	2842 (Institute for Criminal Policy Research, 2018)
Prison population per 100,000 of national population	51 (Institute for Criminal Policy Research, 2018)
Remand prisoners	19.2% (Institute for Criminal Policy Research, 2018)
Number of establishments	26 (Institute for Criminal Policy Research, 2018)
Official capacity of prison service	2895 (Institute for Criminal Policy Research, 2018)
Occupancy level	91.3% (Institute for Criminal Policy Research, 2018)

Brief Profile

Finland is a Nordic country that neighbours Norway, Sweden and Russia. It is the eighth largest in Europe, yet the most sparsely populated (the FACTfile, 2018). Its legal system derives from Western Europe, but, unlike some other Western countries, its penal policy has been described as 'humane neo-classicism' (Lappi-Seppala, 2009, p. 334) with the central principle of sentencing focused on proportionality or just deserts (see Chapter 2).

The Day Fine System

Fines in Finland are administered through a day fines system, which takes both the seriousness of the offence and the offender's wealth into account. The number of days is determined by the severity of the offence with this ranging from a minimum of one day to a maximum of 120 (s. 1 Chapter 2(a) The Criminal Code of Finland (the Code) (550/1990)). If more than one offence is being sentenced the offender will be liable for a joint fine with a maximum of 240 days (s. 3 Chapter 7 the Code (697/1991)). The amount of each day is set according to how much the offender earns, with the aim being to set a fine that 'is reasonable in view of the solvency of the person fined' (s. 2 Chapter 2(a) the Code (808/2007)). This is calculated by taking one sixtieth of a person's average monthly net income minus a basic living allowance of €255 per month. If the offender has dependents, an extra €3 per person, per day can also be deducted (Daley, 2015). This effectively amounts to 50 per cent of an offender's daily

a £30 minimum and a £170 maximum (The CJA 2003 (Surcharge) (Amendment) Order 2016). The money does not go to the direct victim but is rather used to fund emotional and practical support services for all victims of crime. Prosecution costs will then be added on. These will vary, with a contested trial costing more than a guilty plea and will range from £85 to £965. Depending on the nature of the offence, the court may also impose a compensation order so that the disposable income. The amount of the fine is then the number of day fines multiplied by the amount (s. 3 Chapter 2(a) the Code (550/1999)). Sentencers are able to access information directly from the Finnish tax office so little time is wasted in verifying accurate details. Calculations are therefore quick, easy and importantly accurate (Lappi-Seppala, 2009).

Interestingly there are very few options for fine defaulters, with the reality being that they will be imprisoned (s. 4 Chapter 2(a) the Code (578/2008)). Unpaid fines are converted into time served with three days of fine equivalent to one day in custody. This is known as a conversion sentence and can last for between four and 60 days (s. 5 Chapter 2(a) the Code (983/2005)). A conversion sentence is given in all default situations unless the offender is under 18, the original offence is considered as petty or the sentence is unreasonable or pointless taking into account the offender's personal circumstances (s. 6 Chapter 2(a) the Code (550/1999)).

The day fines system has been used in Finland since 1921 (Zedlewski, 2010) and can be used for the majority of criminal offences, including road traffic offences. The basic structure of the system has remained relatively unchanged since its inception, with amendments largely relating to the monetary amount of the day fine, the maximum number of day fines and the rules relating to conversion into custodial time; all of which has created a credible alternative to imprisonment (Lappi-Seppala, 2009). In 2012, roughly 60 per cent of all court disposals resulted in a fine (Lappi-Seppala, 2012), although when road traffic offences are added this increases to nearly 80 per cent (Lappi-Seppala, 2009).

The system is not without its critics though, with the media again highlighting cases where large fines have been imposed due to an individual's wealth. One example is Reima Kuisla, a businessperson with an annual income of €6.5 million, who was fined €54,000 for driving at 65 mph in a 50 mph zone (Pinsker, 2015). Interestingly, however, the critics are mainly those who have to pay these large fines with most Finnish people thinking that such amounts are appropriate (Daley, 2015). Unlike England and Wales in the 1990s, the Finnish Government has not bowed to pressure from negative media publications and the system overall appears to be successful.

Discussion Points

1. What are the advantages and disadvantages of the day fines system?
2. Is this a credible alternative to the system in England and Wales?

---

victim is directly compensated. An example of these additional costs is presented in Figure 5.6. If the offender is unable to pay the total amount, payment is collected in order of priority: compensation, victim surcharge, fine and then costs (Sentencing Council, 2017d). Her Majesty's Courts and Tribunal Service (HMCTS) has the responsibility of collecting the money, which is done by a National Compliance and Enforcement Service (Ministry of Justice and National Statistics, 2016).

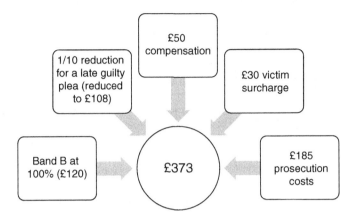

Figure 5.6 The full costs of a financial penalty

Fine defaulters

Historically the main option for fine defaulters was prison. In 1994, 22,469 people were committed to custody for the non-payment of a fine, accounting for nearly one third of all prison receptions. With the average length of time spent in custody being only seven days (Whittaker & Mackie, 1997), this was a very expensive way of enforcing a penalty which was meant to bring in revenue. In addition to the cost of imprisoning defaulters, a prison term also had a negative effect on employment, housing and the offender's family. The use of custody was also criticised because it was often being used for those who could not afford to pay their fines; rather than against those who refused to do so. This extra punishment was considered disproportionate and pressure was placed on sentencers and politicians to introduce a more equitable system. Current options for fine defaulters are outlined in legislation and involve a range of ensuring and enforcing responses (Mackie, et al., 2003).

Attachment of earnings order or application for benefit deductions

If an offender after receiving the collection order finds that they cannot pay then they can apply to a fines officer to extend the fine period, ask for instalments or an amendment to existing instalments. If payments are missed the fines officer must make either an attachment of earnings order (AEO) or an application for a benefit deduction (ABD) (para. 26 Schedule 5, Courts Act 2003). The effect of both means that a regular sum of money is deducted from the offender's wage or benefits and is paid directly to the court. Such mechanisms are useful for those who have the means to pay but perhaps due to mismanagement of money or through forgetfulness have omitted to pay. They are not useful for those who are already struggling to live on a low income, and for AEOs, rely on the cooperation of an offender's employer.

The amount that the court will order the offender to pay in relation to an AEO is based on how much the offender earns and aims to ensure that the individual is left with enough to live on. For example, where a monthly wage is between £220 and £400, the deduction rate is set at 3 per cent. This is increased to 17 per cent where monthly salary is between £1040 and £1480 (National Debtline, 2016). When it is an ABD the court can take deductions from Income Support, income-based Jobseeker's Allowance, income-related Employment and Support Allowance, Pension Credit or Universal Credit. Deductions will range from £5 to £25 per week (National Debtline, 2016). If the deduction causes the offender hardship, then they can appeal the decision to the Magistrates' Court.

Further steps

If default on payments continues the fines officer can either refer the case back to the Magistrates' Court or take a number of further steps (para. 38 schedule 5 Courts Act 2003). The first of these is a warrant of control which authorises enforcement officers, usually private firms of bailiffs, to enter a defaulter's premises and seize goods to the value of the fine. Exempted items include children's toys, a cooker or microwave, bedding and basic household and work items (National Debtline, 2016). The goods are then sold in order to pay the requisite amount. Another option is for the fines officer to include the fine on the Register of Judgments, Orders and Fines, which is likely to affect the offender's ability to get credit for the next five years. Finally under Schedule 5 of the Courts Act 2003, the fines officer can issue a clamping order. Initially the offender's car will have an immobilisation device attached, although the court can order that the car be removed and later sold if the fine is not paid within a set period of time (para. 41 Schedule 5 Courts Act 2003).

A means enquiry hearing

The fines officer can at any time remit the case back to the Magistrates' Court for enforcement. The court will then conduct a means enquiry hearing to try and ascertain why the payments have not been made. In addition to the options already discussed the court can:

- allow more time to pay.
- increase the level of the fine by 50 per cent, where it feels that the failure to pay is due to 'wilful refusal or culpable neglect' (para. 42A Schedule 5 Courts Act 2003).
- make a work order, when in view of the offender's financial circumstances all other methods of enforcing are either impractical or inappropriate. The person

must be suitable to perform unpaid work and consent to the making of the order (para 2 Schedule 6 Courts Act 2003). The specified number of hours is calculated by dividing the amount of the sum by a prescribed hourly sum (para. 3 Schedule 6 Courts Act 2003).

- make an attendance centre order where the offender is under the age of 25. This will be either at an educational or recreational centre and will be for a specified number of hours, ranging from 12 to 36 (s. 60 Powers of Criminal Courts (Sentencing) Act 2000).
- remit the whole or any part of the fine, where there has been a change in the offender's financial circumstances and the court finds that non-payment is due to an inability to pay (s. 85 Magistrates' Court Act 1980).

Committal to prison

Despite the increasing number of options for fine defaulters and the inordinate amount of money it costs to send someone to custody, committing an individual to prison for the non-payment of a fine is still possible and can arise in three circumstances:

1. where the offender is homeless and it is thought that this will affect the court's ability to enforce the fine;
2. where the offender is already serving a custodial sentence; or
3. where the original offence was imprisonable and the offender has the means to pay the fine (s. 82 Magistrate's Court Act 1980).

In the latter circumstances the court must additionally be satisfied that the default is due to the offender's 'wilful refusal or culpable neglect' and other methods of enforcing the penalty have either been unsuccessful or are inappropriate. The fact that custody should be considered as a last option has been emphasised by the courts. In *R v St Helen's Justices ex p. Jones* ([1999] 2 All ER 73), for example, the Divisional Court held that before an offender can be sent to prison for the non-payment of a fine, all other enforcement methods must either have been tried or considered first. Where other methods have been considered, but held to be inappropriate, reasons for this must be given. Furthermore and in relation to young people, Lord Justice Brown in the Queen's Bench Division held that 'Offenders generally and young offenders in particular ought not to be locked up for non-payment of fines unless no sensible alternative presents itself' (*R v Oldham Justices and Another, ex p. Crawley* [1997] Q.B. 1 at 5). If the court chooses committal to prison, it can impose either a suspended prison sentence (effectively one last chance) or sentence to immediate custody. Maximum time limits in the Magistrates' Court are detailed in Table 5.3, with additional limits appropriate for the Crown Court in Table 5.4.

Table 5.3 Maximum time limits for fine/custody conversions in the Magistrates'
Court (Magistrates' Court Act 1980, s. 76).

Amount of the original fine	Time in prison
An amount not exceeding £200	7 days
An amount exceeding £200 but not exceeding £500	14 days
An amount exceeding £500 but not exceeding £1000	28 days
An amount exceeding £1000 but not exceeding £2500	45 days
An amount exceeding £2500 but not exceeding £5000	3 months
An amount exceeding £5000 but not exceeding £10,000	6 months
An amount exceeding £10,000	12 months

Table 5.4 Maximum time limits for fine/custody conversions in the Crown Court
(Powers of Criminal Courts (Sentencing) Act 2000, s. 139(4)).

Amount of the original fine	Time in prison
An amount exceeding £10,000 but not exceeding £20,000	12 months
An amount exceeding £20,000 but not exceeding £50,000	18 months
An amount exceeding £50,000 but not exceeding £100,000	2 years
An amount exceeding £100,000 but not exceeding £250,000	3 years
An amount exceeding £250,000 but not exceeding £1 million	6 years
An amount exceeding £1 million	12 years

Discussion

One of the ways in which to assess whether the fine as a penalty is successful is to
consider how much money is collected, compared to how much is imposed. Despite
the number of different options available to the courts, the current collection rate is
only 50 per cent (Ministry of Justice and National Statistics, 2019a). This does not
mean that the other 50 per cent are outstanding, as fines can also be legally or administratively cancelled. A fine is legally cancelled when a case has been reconsidered by
the court and the sentence is altered due to new evidence, either relating to the seriousness of the offence or the offender's ability to pay. A court can also administratively
cancel a fine when HMCTS has done everything in its power to collect the money and
has been unsuccessful. This may occur when the offender has left the country; has
died; has been sent to a mental health institution for 12 months or more; where the
sum is less than £10 and enforcement would cost more; or, where the offender cannot
be traced and the fine is over 12 months old (HM Courts & Tribunals Service, 2014).
Table 5.5 contains the latest available data on the levels of fines imposed, collected and
cancelled. It is worth noting that fines often take more than 12 months to pay so collection of a fine may not take place in the year that it was imposed.

Table 5.5 Amount of financial penalties collected and administratively cancelled.

Year	Fines imposed	Value of fines collected	Total Value Legally Cancelled	Total Value Administratively Cancelled	Total Value Outstanding
2011/2012	£385,743,300	£279,248,479	£63,957,203	£63,135,442	£593,268,197
2012/2013	£404,584,213	£284,505,025	£62,594,601	£75,868,426	£575,507,170
2013/2014	£420,255,840	£290,311,831	£64,312,383	£96,801,853	£548,811,011
2014/2015	£457,415,184	£310,313,605	£61,173,156	£68,851,118	£571,061,117

Source: Data taken from Davies (2015) 'Fines'. UK Parliament: Written question, 24 June 2015, HC 4023. Available at: http://www.parliament.uk/business/publications/written-questions-answers-statements/written-question/Commons/2015-06-24/4023/ [Accessed 24 January 2017].

One way to tackle such high levels of default is to look at other ways in which fines could be enforced. One idea, which is not yet in force, is the default order under section 300 of the CJA 2003. Here, rather than committing an offender to custody, the court has the power to order the offender to comply with an unpaid work requirement, a curfew requirement with electronic monitoring, or if the offender is under 25 an attendance centre order. If the offender subsequently pays part of the fine then the number of hours of unpaid work or the days of curfew will be reduced. If all is paid then the default order will end. Likewise under section 301 CJA 2003, which is only partially in force, instead of committing to prison the court can disqualify the offender from driving for a period of up to 12 months. If part of the fine is repaid then the length is reduced pro rata and if it is paid in full then disqualification will cease to exist. Such options may be useful for both those who cannot pay as it offers them an alternative way of 'paying' (as long as there are no issues relating to childcare, disability etc.) and for those who can but will not pay as the threat of losing the ability to drive may spur many into paying. Whatever enforcement methods are employed though, they will only ever work if there is an enforcement service which is actively working to pursue those in default. This includes having a system in place, which sets the level of fines at amounts, which are equitable, affordable and consistent.

The final question is thus whether the fine is useful. The statistics in Table 5.5 do not state how much of the outstanding debt relates to those who cannot afford to pay and how much is for those who can but choose not to pay; but either way it suggests that for defaulters the fine as a penalty is ineffective in terms of punishment and reparation. It is also questionable whether the fine works as an effective deterrence especially when this high default rate is taken into consideration. Furthermore, it is unclear whether the fine reduces reoffending, because unfortunately reoffending data only differentiates between adults released from custody and those who commenced a court order, so those who were issued with a fine cannot be separately identified. Any conclusions about the worth of the fine are therefore difficult, although despite this it is always likely to remain as the most popular sentencing option because when compared to all other penalties it is, as stated at the beginning of this chapter, cheap and relatively easy to administer.

Discussion Questions

1. What can be done to improve the current enforcement rate of financial penalties? Should, for example, unpaid work be offered as an alternative to the sentence rather than as just an option when the offender defaults?
2. Should we have separate enforcement mechanisms for those who cannot afford to pay as opposed to those who will not pay?
3. Should we consider conversion sentences as used in Finland?

CONCLUSION

The sentencing options available to the police and the Magistrates' Court in relation to OOCDs and the fine are vast, cumbersome and problematic in terms of operation and enforcement. While there have been some positive ideas, such as reducing the number of OOCDs and the introduction of a unit fine system albeit by the back door, the government has been slow to implement and mandate such suggestions. This has left England and Wales in no-man's land. Change and reform are promised in respect of OOCDs but the announcement of this is vastly overdue. In relation to fines, the government appears to want some sort of a unit fine system but does not appear to have the courage to actually implement one. The answer may or may not lie with how other countries administer their fine systems. While the day fine system in Finland seems simple and effective, it is concerning that conversion sentences are the only real option for fine defaulters. For a country that has large numbers of middle class citizens, this may be appropriate, but would not work in a much more diverse country such as England and Wales. The two main questions relating to financial penalties, namely how the level of fine should be set and what should be done with fine defaulters, therefore, disappointingly remain unanswered.

 Now read:

Allen, R. (2017) *Less is More – The Case for Dealing with Offences Out of Court*. London: Transform Justice. This looks at the reduction in the use of OCCDs over the last decade and questions why this reduction has occurred.

Kantorowicz-Reznichenko, E. (2018) 'Day fines: Reviving the idea and reversing the (Costly) punitive trend', *American Criminal Law review*, 55, 333–372. This article looks at a number of European day fine systems including Sweden, Denmark, Germany, Spain, Switzerland and Romania.

Now watch:

Sentencing Council (2012) 'What types of sentence can offenders get', available on YouTube at: https://www.youtube.com/watch?v=cyZp1Hz-xaU.

Now consider:

Based on what you have read, and your own research, do you think that the fine is a useful sentence? What improvements would you make to it?

6 Community Penalties

INTRODUCTION

Staying with the hierarchy of punishment, the next option for a sentencing court, after the fine, is a community penalty. Aimed at those offenders whose offence is too serious to warrant a financial penalty, but not serious enough to justify immediate custody, community penalties make up nearly 8 per cent of all court sentences (National Statistics, 2018). Traditionally, community penalties were supervised by the Probation Service but as detailed below, the vast majority of offender management was contracted out to private operators, between 2014 and 2020, with only high-risk offenders managed by the National Probation Service (NPS). This change came about through a government initiative known as Transforming Rehabilitation (TR) and although it was originally envisaged that probation would never again be nationalised, the government announced such a reversal in May 2019. While this chapter looks at the community order with requirements and for the sake of completeness the suspended sentence order (SSO), its main function is to track the changes that have occurred in offender management due to TR and to evaluate the current state of play. As summed up in an article by Mantle the key question is whether probation is 'Dead, Dying or Poorly' (Mantle, 2006, p. 321).

THE AIMS AND ETHOS OF PROBATION

Traditionally the aims of probation have been focused on rehabilitation and treatment. As discussed in Chapter 2, rehabilitation was the primary aim of the criminal justice system for the first 60 years of the twentieth century. Under this sentencing model the seriousness of the offence was considered to be less important, with the main concern focusing on how best the offender could be treated. In this way, sentencing was offender, rather than offence driven, with sentence length determined by how long the 'cure' would take, rather than for how long the court wanted to punish the individual. This did not last however, and in the early 1970s and as a result of academics such as Martinson (1974) in the United States of America (US), and Brody (1976) in the United Kingdom (UK), it was questioned whether treatment programmes were actually working. Known as the 'Nothing Works' era, this heralded the slow demise of rehabilitation in sentencing, with our current sentencing system based on just deserts (see Chapter 2) introduced into England and Wales through the Criminal Justice Act (CJA) of 1991. As discussed in Chapter 4, this works on the basis of proportionality and tries to balance the seriousness of the offence with the gravity of the penalty. Sentencing under this system is thus offence, rather than offender driven.

Despite this change in sentencing theory, rehabilitation is still an important sentencing aim of offender management, although as Bottoms explains, there has been a conceptual shift 'from the training or expert treatment of obedient subjects to persuading rational agents to co-operate in their own longer-term interest' (Bottoms, 1995, p. 38). In this more modern day version of probation, rehabilitation is still important in sentencing policy but the offender is expected to take on a higher level of self-responsibility (Garland, 2000). As discussed below, the community order with requirements does have many rehabilitative requirements within it although, as Rex argues, in order to justify its existence, probation has had to rediscover the theory of rehabilitation, with it no longer being enough just to offer offending behaviour programmes (OBPs) as an alternative to custody (Rex, 1998). This is why there are also a number of punitive requirements in the order such as unpaid work, curfews, exclusion requirements and travel prohibitions (see below).

The ethos of probation has also changed. Starting as an agency who were there to 'advise, assist and befriend' (The Probation of Offenders Act 1907), this social work way of working lasted until the mid to late 1970s when as mentioned above the worth of rehabilitation was questioned and political parties started to include law and order promises in their election manifestos. This was therefore a time where:

> Market solutions, individual responsibility and self-help increasingly displaced welfare state collectivism and social policy came to place more emphasis on accounting and managerial expertise than upon professional social workers and clinicians. (Garland, 2000, p. 358)

In a shift from welfare principles, the public became more preoccupied with crime and the risk of crime and less tolerant of the offender. Old liberal ideas of being understanding towards an offender were in sharp decline and politicians were forced to take notice. This led to the introduction of new public management ideas into probation and saw a shift from 'Government' to 'Governance', where governance is described as:

> A shift away from government taking responsibility and authority for guaranteeing services and traditional state spheres of activity towards provision by other agencies, some private and some public, which in a sort of partnership, provide what should be full cover. (Williams, 2001, p. 541)

In this system the government maintains control over policy decisions and resources, but it is the private and public partners who actually deliver the services. By criticising the qualities of autonomy, personal discretion and self-determination, managerialism was clearly incompatible with social work values and so the traditional liberalist approach in probation went into further decline (Nellis, 1995). With the CJA 1991 and the introduction of our current just deserts sentencing system, "a focus on 'deeds' rather than 'needs' formally expunged many of the last vestiges of social democratic welfarism from the system" (McLaughlin & Muncie, 2001, p. 5). Probation became a punishment in its own right and the probation service had to change its focus from a traditional social work basis to become 'a more disciplinary correctionalist agency' (Crawford, 1997, pp. 36–37).

In addition to managerialism, probation has also seen privatisation (see below) and a focus on customer satisfaction and responsibilisation, with the latter referring to the situation where an individual is held responsible for something (such as rehabilitation) where in the past it would have been the concern of a state agency (probation) (Garland, 1996). As detailed in Chapter 2, this is arguably a shift from traditional to modern rehabilitation, where it is now considered to be the offender's responsibility to turn taught behaviour into practice and changed conduct.

These shifts in theory have meant that the probation service is now seen as a public protection agency focusing on risk rather than being predominantly concerned with helping offenders. Advise, assist and befriend has therefore been replaced with 'confront, challenge and change' (Lewis, 2014, p. 343), although as suggested by Lewis, positive changes in offenders are more likely to be achieved when the service is able to use a combination of both approaches.

COMMUNITY PENALTIES

The origins of community sentencing

On 31 March 2018, 262,758 offenders were being managed within the community, with 69,925 of these serving a community order (Ministry of Justice, 2018h). Considering this high number, it is perhaps surprising that community sentencing originates from ad hoc beginnings. The first formal use of a 'sentence' resembling probation was a power used under the Summary Jurisdiction Act of 1879. Sections 7, 10 and 16 allowed magistrates to conditionally discharge a person convicted of a trivial offence, without punishment, on the assurance that the offender would return to court for sentence if called upon and to be of good character (Bochel, 1976). Other practices in the nineteenth century included a small number of isolated experiments in England (see Table 6.1), although it is often argued, that the most direct origin of the probation order (as it was originally referred to) comes from Boston, US. In 1841, John Augustus rose in court and offered to stand bail for and supervise a man charged with drunkenness. He continued supervising offenders until 1859, overseeing nearly 2000 people, who he said, had been bailed on probation (Jones, 1981). Augustus would manage the offender between a suspension of the sentence on bail and recall for judgment, which the courts would make nominal, providing that there was evidence that the character of the offender had been reformed. Cases were chosen having regard to age, previous criminal record, home circumstances and any other information which indicated that reformation was possible (Bochel, 1976). By using a form of suspended sentence and the possibility of a custodial sentence on recall, in addition to careful selection, proper supervision and record keeping this therefore exhibits more elements of modern day probation than perhaps any of the other models used in England at the same time (Jones, 1981).

Table 6.1 Origins of offender management.

Individual and Area	Practice
County magistrates in Warwickshire	Upon finding a suitable and willing employer, the magistrates would commit a youth offender to the care of that employer so that they would avoid a lengthy prison sentence. It is thought that the magistrates would pass a one-day sentence of imprisonment, as a token punishment, but that this was the only prison time which had to be served (Mair, 1997).
Matthew Davenport Hill, Recorder of Birmingham	Hill would place young offenders with suitable guardians, even if employment could not be offered. It is thought that a nominal punishment was given and that as an addition to the sentence, there was a requirement that the guardian subjected the offender to some form of supervision (Bochel, 1976).
Edward Cox, Recorder of Portsmouth	Cox would call upon friends to act as guardians, but in addition, he would ask them to enter into recognisances agreeing to bring the offender up for judgment, if required, with sureties. Cox also appointed a 'social inquiry officer' to supervise the behaviour of the offenders sentenced in the Middlesex area (Bochel, 1976).
Police Court Missionaries employed by the Church of England Temperance Society (1875)	Magistrates who were disposing of offenders under the Summary Jurisdiction Act could ask a missionary to informally supervise the released offender. It is thought that some courts would adjourn the case, bail the offender and ask the missionary to prepare a report on the offender concerning their recent behaviour (Bochel, 1976).

After viewing the practice of Augustus in Boston, it was The Howard Association (now The Howard League for Penal Reform) that suggested that probation should be implemented into England and Wales. This took some time, with a false start seen in the Probation of First Offenders Act 1887 and a workable solution not found until 20 years later. The Probation of Offenders Act 1907 finally gave the court the power to conditionally release offenders into the community where it was 'inexpedient to inflict punishment' (s. 1 Probation of Offenders Act 1907). In such cases an offender would be released on probation, for a period not exceeding three years, on condition that they 'be of good behaviour and to appear for conviction and sentence when called on' (s. 1 Probation of Offenders Act 1907). In many cases, this would involve an additional condition of being supervised by a probation officer, a role that did not exist prior to the Act. Interestingly, when a probation order was made it was not classed as a conviction and this may be the reason why probation was viewed by many as a soft option and a let off by the courts (Mair & Rumgay, 2014).

Extensions to probation did not really occur until the CJA of 1972 and the introduction of community service. Based largely on recommendations made by the

Wootton report (Home Office, 1970) the community service order was viewed as an alternative to custody and could last for a maximum of 240 hours. The 1972 Act also contained compensation orders, restitution orders and probation orders, which required attendance at a day training centre. This expansion of probation would continue over the next few decades with other developments including curfews (with electronic monitoring), drug treatment and testing orders, exclusion orders, community rehabilitation and drug abstinence.

The community order with requirements

Historically, as outlined above, there have been a number of different community orders. Since April 2005, however, there is now only one sentence: the community order with requirements. The order has the option of 11 requirements, with these outlined in Table 6.2. Details of the order are contained in section 177 of the CJA 2003, with the court tasked with creating a package of requirements, which is best suited to individual need, with this often focused on rehabilitation. Each selected requirement must serve a specific purpose and this objective must be outlined in court and relate back to sentencing aims (s. 142 CJA 2003). In addition to what is needed, the order must also punish; so the court must either include at least one requirement imposed for the purpose of punishment (such as a curfew or unpaid work), impose a fine, or do both (s. 177 (2A) CJA 2003). This can only be ignored if there are exceptional circumstances that relate either to the offender or to the offence. The order is only available for those aged 18 or over with the available orders used for young offenders discussed in Chapter 11.

Table 6.2 Requirements available under section 177 CJA 2003.

Requirement	Brief details
Unpaid work	40–300 hours, to be completed within 12 months.
Rehabilitation activity	The court will specify the maximum number of activity days the offender must complete. The responsible officer will decide the activities to be undertaken. Where appropriate this requirement should be made in addition to, and not in place of, other requirements. Sentencers should ensure the activity length is suitable and proportionate.
Prohibited activity	Stops an offender from doing something for a period of three years, such as not attending a football match.
Curfew	To last 2–16 hours in any 24 hour period. The maximum term is 12 months. The court must consider how others may be affected and it will often be attached to electronic monitoring to ensure compliance.
Exclusion	From a specified place/places for a maximum period of two years. It may be continuous or only during specified periods; electronic monitoring is possible.

(continued)

Requirement	Brief details
Residence	To reside at a place specified or as directed by the responsible officer.
Foreign travel prohibition	Has a maximum length of 12 months.
Mental health treatment	May be residential/non-residential. Offender must be under the direction of a registered medical practitioner or chartered psychologist. The court must be satisfied: (a) that the mental condition of the offender is such that it requires and may be susceptible to treatment but is not such as to warrant the making of a hospital or guardianship order; (b) that arrangements for treatment have been made; (c) that the offender has expressed willingness to comply.
Drug rehabilitation	The court must be satisfied that the offender is dependent on or has a propensity to misuse drugs, which requires or is susceptible to treatment. The offender must consent to the order. Treatment can be residential or non-residential, and reviews must be attended by the offender at intervals of not less than a month (discretionary on requirements of up to 12 months, mandatory on requirements of over 12 months).
Alcohol treatment	Can be residential or non-residential and must have the offender's consent. The court must be satisfied that the offender is dependent on alcohol and that the dependency is susceptible to treatment.
Attendance centre	Can last between 12 and 36 hours, although it is only available for those under the age of 25.

In line with other punishments a community order can only be imposed if the offence is serious enough to warrant it (s. 148(1) CJA 2003). According to section 148(2) CJA 2003:

(a) the particular requirement or requirements forming part of the community order must be such as, in the opinion of the court, is, or taken together are, *the most suitable for the offender*, and
(b) the restrictions on liberty imposed by the order must be such as in the opinion of the court are *commensurate with the seriousness of the offence*, or the combination of the offence and one or more offences associated with it (emphasis added).

This is contradictory, however, as it creates a situation whereby the court may feel that several requirements are needed due to offending history but the seriousness of the offence in question only warrants the imposition of one or two. To help the court in deciding which and how many requirements should be imposed, the Sentencing Council (see Chapter 4) has produced a guideline (Sentencing Council, 2017c) (Table 6.3), which has been in force since 1 February 2017. Despite the

Table 6.3 Community order levels.

Low	Medium	High
Offences only just cross community order threshold, where the seriousness of the offence or the nature of the offender's record means that a discharge or fine is inappropriate	Offences that obviously fall within the community order band	Offences only just fall below the custody threshold or the custody threshold is crossed but a community order is more appropriate in the circumstances
In general, only one requirement will be appropriate and the length may be curtailed if additional requirements are necessary		More intensive sentences which combine two or more requirements may be appropriate
Suitable requirements might include:		
• Any appropriate rehabilitative requirement • 40–80 hours of unpaid work • Curfew within the lowest range (up to 16 hours per day) • Exclusion for a few months • Prohibited activity • Attendance centre where available	• Any appropriate rehabilitative requirement • Greater number of unpaid work hours (80–150) • Curfew within the middle range (up to 16 hours for 2–3 months) • Exclusion lasting for 6 months. • Prohibited activity	• Any appropriate rehabilitative requirement • 150–300 hours of unpaid work • Curfew up to 16 hours for 4–12 months • Exclusion for 12 months
If the order does not contain a punitive requirement, suggested fine levels:		
Band A fine	Band B fine	Band C Fine

Source: Sentencing Council (2017c) *Imposition of Community and Custodial Sentences Definitive Guideline*, London : Sentencing Council, p. 4.

reference to offender need in the legislation, the guidance states that the initial factor in deciding the content of the order is a determination of how serious the offence is. This therefore reiterates that just deserts and punishment is more important than rehabilitation. The court must then consider whether the offence warrants a low, medium or high response. This would therefore suggest that just deserts is being used to determine the severity and quantum of the order with offender need being used to determine exactly which requirements should be chosen.

Before a court makes its sentencing decision, it is usual that it will ask the NPS to prepare a pre-sentence report on the particular offender. This consists of an interview where the officer will enquire about the offender's background and offence. The officer's job is to assess the offender's risk of harm to the public and their risk of reoffending. Based on this, the officer will make a recommendation as to what they think should be the most suitable sentence. This does not have to be followed by the court, but in most cases, it will. When preparing the report, the offender manager will first be told within which range the judge believes the sentence to lie, i.e. low, medium or high. The officer will then select requirements, which fit within this range. They must also ensure that if more than one requirement is recommended it does not exceed what is commensurate for the offence. This is known as the principle of totality. They must also check that each requirement is compatible with each other, so for example you cannot ask the offender to participate in an activity that is within an exclusion zone or during a curfew period.

The suspended sentence order

In terms of hierarchy, the SSO sits just underneath immediate custody and above the community order. Historically, the order allowed an offender to be sentenced to a period of custody, which would be suspended due to extenuating circumstances such as ill health or childcare responsibilities. As long as the offender did not offend during this period of suspension, they would not serve any time in custody. This changed under the CJA 2003. The order is now a prison sentence (see ss. 189–194 CJA 2003) and is sometimes referred to as custody minus. It is given to an offender as a last chance to avoid imprisonment if the community requirements in the order are completed and can only be used for those prison sentences between 14 days and 2 years. The court can impose any of the requirements available for the community order with one difference being that the maximum time limit is slightly shorter for those under the SSO. For example, alcohol treatment can last up to three years for a community order, but only two for a SSO. The other difference is that on breach an offender on a SSO is more likely to be sent to custody. The order consists of two parts. First, the operational period, which is the time for which the custodial sentence is suspended, and second the supervision period, i.e. the time during which the requirements will take effect. Both periods can last between six months and two years, although the supervision period cannot be for longer than the operational period.

Enforcement

Enforcement, in probation terms, means ensuring that every element and requirement of the community order or SSO is complied with. In essence, it is ensuring that offenders turn up to their appointments, complete OBPs, carry out their allotted hours of unpaid work and follow the instructions of their responsible officers. The current enforcement procedure for NPS cases is as follows:

- On the first failure to comply, the officer should issue a warning, or if the breach is serious enough or the offender has received a previous warning in the last 12 months, breach proceedings should commence.

- The officer must make the decision whether to breach the offender by day six of the second unacceptable failure.
- Breach information must be sent to the enforcement officer (this is a person employed by the NPS who is responsible for breaches) by day eight.
- The information is checked by the enforcement officer for quality and legality.
- The enforcement officer will take the final decision whether to breach.
- The enforcement officer applies to the court for a summons and court date within 10 days of the unacceptable failure.
- Notification of the breach is sent to the offender.
- The enforcement officer presents the breach in court.
- The result is reported to the offender manager and recorded on their case management system (HM Prison and Probation Service, 2018a).

Emphasising the punitiveness of community sentences, if an offender is returned to court under breach proceedings the court must increase the severity of the original order, or revoke and re-sentence. Guidelines, issued by the Sentencing Council advise on the most appropriate penalty, with this largely dependent on the overall compliance of the order. For example, with reference to a breach of a community order, if there was wilful and persistent non-compliance then it is appropriate to 'revoke the order and re-sentence imposing a custodial sentence (even where the offence seriousness did not originally merit custody)' (Sentencing Council, 2018, p. 4). For a breach of a SSO, where the new offence is less serious than the original offence but a custodial sentence is nevertheless appropriate and there was a low level of compliance, there should be a 'full activation of the original custodial term' (Sentencing Council, 2018, p. 8).

The decline in the use of community sentences

The use of community penalties has been steadily decreasing over the last 10 years. This is perhaps surprising when evidence taken from a number of reports and studies has repeatedly shown that community sentences are more effective at reducing reoffending than short-term prison sentences (Mews, et al., 2015; Bales & Piquero, 2012). This is so even when figures are adjusted to take into account the fact that custodial sentences are often given to the more serious and risky offenders. To highlight this decrease, Table 6.4 looks at sentencing statistics for an eight year period for triable either way offences. This category of offence has been chosen as it is these which you would expect to fall within the community penalty threshold (i.e. too serious to warrant a fine but not serious enough to justify immediate custody). What is interesting here is that even though there has been a decline in the total number of people sentenced to triable either way crimes (a drop of nearly 35 per cent) the decrease in the use of custody stands at only 9.5 per cent while the decline in community sentencing stands at a staggering 58 per cent (National Statistics, 2018).

Population	5,424,800 (National Records of Scotland, 2018).
Prison population (including remand prisoners)	8213 (Institute for Criminal Policy Research, 2019c).
Prison population per 100,000 of national population	150 (Institute for Criminal Policy Research, 2019c).
Remand prisoners	20% (Institute for Criminal Policy Research, 2019c).
Number of establishments	15 (Institute for Criminal Policy Research, 2019c).
Official capacity of prison service	7918 (Institute for Criminal Policy Research, 2019c).
Occupancy level	92.9% (Institute for Criminal Policy Research, 2019c).

Brief Profile

Scotland, although a part of the United Kingdom (UK), is also a country in its own right. It is made up of the mainland, in addition to 790 islands, of which only 10 per cent are inhabited (Scottish Executive, 2003). Despite the fact that the countries of the UK share a monarch, the governance of politics is not as straightforward. Scotland has its own parliament and since 1999 has had the power to make laws on devolved matters, such as housing, health and social services.

Use of Community Penalties

In direct contrast to England and Wales, Scotland has seen an increase in its use of community sentencing over the last few years. For the period 2006–2016, Scotland saw community penalties rise by 18 per cent, while for England and Wales there was a decline of 24 per cent. (Centre for Justice Innovation, 2017). This is perhaps surprising considering that Scotland is so close to England and Wales and both share similar social and demographic features. Initially, the variance was thought to involve three factors: (1) differences in the volume of cases, (2) differences in the offence mix and (3) sentencing policy, but research carried out by the Centre for Justice Innovation (2017), found that the only significant difference between the countries was sentencing policy. In relation to England and Wales, there have been two major changes in offender management since 2011. First, the introduction of the community order with requirements and second the implementation of the TR agenda (see below). Likewise in Scotland there have also been changes, most of which were implemented by the Criminal Justice and Licensing (Scotland) Act 2010, with the most notable being the introduction of a community payback order (s. 14) and a presumption against using short-term custodial sentences of less than three months (s. 17). These have been in force since 1 February 2011, approximately

While this decrease started before the introduction of TR (see below), this has made the situation worse, especially when taking into account the more recent decline in OBPs. In the late 1990s and early 2000s the government placed great emphasis on introducing evidence-based practice into correctional services with the time when community sentencing in England and Wales saw its greatest decline in use. Scotland has also recently created one national service for offender management, merging eight previous regional authorities into the single agency of Community Justice Scotland.

The community payback order in some respects looks similar to the community order with requirements, in the sense that sentencers have the choice between nine require-ments many of which are similar to those available in England and Wales. What is differ-ent, however, is that the order sits differently in terms of a hierarchy of punishment. In England and Wales, immediate custody is at the top of the pyramid (see Chapter 5) closely followed by the SSO and then the community order with requirements. The community payback order however is to be used 'where a person is convicted of an offence punishable by imprisonment' (s. 14(1) Criminal Justice and Licensing Act), which puts it on a par with immediate custody or at least the SSO rather than the community order. This makes the order much more useable because the court does not have to concern itself with the difference between community and custody thresholds.

The presumption against short-term sentences can be found in Section 17 Criminal Justice and Licensing (Scotland) Act 2010:

> A court must not pass a sentence of imprisonment for a term of 3 months or less on a person unless the court considers that no other method of dealing with the person is appropriate. Where a court passes such a sentence the court must (a) state its reasons for the opinion that no other method of dealing with the person is appropriate, and (b) have those reasons entered in the record of the proceedings.

Since the introduction of the community payback order and the presumption against short custodial sentences, the use of community sentences in Scotland has risen by 21 per cent (Centre for Justice Innovation, 2017). At the time of writing, Scotland was also talk-ing about extending this presumption to less than 12 months (see Chapter 12 for further discussion on this).

Discussion Points

1. Why do you think that there is such a difference in the use of community penalties in Scotland when compared to England and Wales?
2. What do you think about Scotland's presumption against using custodial sentences of less than three months? Is this something which should be imple-mented into England and Wales?
3. Is the answer to increasing community penalties to get rid of a hierarchy of sentences as has arguably occurred in Scotland?

---

this referred to as the 'What Works' initiative (Home Office, 1998). While the aim was to introduce a core curriculum of accredited OBPs into prison and proba-tion, so that whatever the offending background, gender, age or ethnicity of the offender there would be a suitable programme to address that individuals need,

Table 6.4 Sentencing statistics for triable either way offences 2009–2017.

	2010	2011	2012	2013	2014	2015	2016	2017
Immediate custody	67,921	72,256	70,292	66,067	66,019	63,741	64,553	61,449
Suspended sentence	31,573	33,346	31,100	32,233	36,879	39,106	39,178	35,135
Community sentence	103,534	101,200	86,101	70,214	59,757	55,823	50,352	43,333
Fine	59,294	59,963	54,974	54,014	53,998	49,157	43,692	39,871
Total sentenced	322,494	326,852	298,197	275,985	271,406	253,733	235,228	211,279

Source: Data from National Statistics (2018) *Criminal Justice Statistics: September 2017*.
London: National Statistics.

this was never actually achieved with most programmes designed for White, male, adults. One of the consequences of TR is that while it is the Community Rehabilitation Companies (CRCs) who are involved in delivering the vast majority of the OBPs it is the NPS who present pre-sentence reports to the courts. NPS staff may not therefore have the requisite knowledge of these programmes in order to endorse them. This has resulted in the situation where programmes are no longer being recommended at the rate that they previously were (Carr, 2018). This decline in use has also occurred because there is an increasing emphasis on speed, with pre-sentence reports now often oral in nature and made without being able to assess what would be the most suitable package of requirements for the individual in question (Carr, 2018). Important work designed to address the offender's offending behaviour is therefore not being carried out, having important knock-on effects on both public protection and payment by results (PbR).

What lessons can therefore be learnt from Scotland. The obvious would appear to be that if we want to increase the use of community sentences and through this reduce reoffending, then it would appear sensible to introduce a presumption against short term custodial sentences and also to make the community order with requirements on a par with immediate custody. Arguably, we do have the SSO (see above) but community penalties have still declined despite its introduction in 2005. What is needed therefore is an abolition of the SSO and a change in the hierarchy of punishments as seen in Scotland. While such measures would be welcome, this does not detract from the fact that there needs to be good quality offender management in place. As discussed below, this is not currently the case in England and Wales, with the vast majority of CRCs underperforming. A focus on sentencing policy and the current structuring of probation services in England and Wales is therefore paramount.

Discussion Questions

1.   The fact that the court is asked to find the most suitable package for the offender makes community sentences offender driven rather than offence driven. What are the consequences of this and can this work within a sentencing system based on seriousness and just deserts?
2.   What do you think to the list of possible requirements? Are there any areas that you think are missing?
3.   Punishment is now at the core of a community order. Is this the best way for offenders to be rehabilitated?

OFFENDER MANAGEMENT

History and development

As highlighted above, the origins of community sentencing had informal beginnings, with the probation service also being created in a rather similar way. Following the introduction of the Probation of Offenders Act 1907, the vast majority of offender management was undertaken by Church of England Court Missionaries (McWilliams, 1983). Initial optimism about the system, however, soon led to disappointment, with many petty sessional divisions not appointing probation officers and probation not really used as a method of court disposal (Bochel, 1976). A change in attitude and use finally began to take place following the end of World War I. Courts began increasingly to appoint their own full time probation officers and over time called less upon the services of members from voluntary societies and the church mission. In 1934, the Home Office created a separate probation branch, appointed their first inspector and in 1936 commissioned a Probation Training Board and an Advisory Committee (Bochel, 1976). Duties of the probation officer also changed to include supervising prisoners on release and conciliation work in domestic proceedings.

Between 1909 and 1970, the government undertook several reviews in terms of evaluating how probation was working, but did not really involve itself in the day-to-day running of offender management. This meant that in 1984 there were 56 local probation services in England and Wales, all of which acted as independent and autonomous agencies. The first glimmer of a national service was seen in the *Statement of National Objectives and Priorities* (Home Office, 1984), which, against a backdrop of limited resources, set out the purpose, objectives and priorities of the probation service. This centralising of the service was emphasised through the introduction of National Standards for community service in 1989 and the 1988 Green Paper *Punishment, Custody and the Community* (Mair & Rumgay, 2014). This latter document started to change the notion of probation in the sense that the government wanted a more credible alternative to custody. To achieve this the Green Paper emphasised the punitive nature of community sentences, suggesting, for example, that day centre attendance should be raised from 60 to 90 hours, that curfews and electronic monitoring should be used to reinforce supervision and that treatment and education relating to drug and alcohol abuse would be useful. Thinking at that time, was that these options could be brought together in a new supervision and restriction order (arguably the precursor of the community order with requirements). Sanctions for breaching the order would be a fine or requirements that were more demanding. Moreover, perhaps foreseeing the resistance to such punitive responses from an agency, which had been used to social work ideals, the Green Paper also mooted the idea of using private sector agencies to deliver some or even all of these services (Home Office, 1988).

The resulting legislation was the CJA 1991, which introduced a more coherent approach to sentencing based on just deserts (see Chapter 2). Sentencing was focused on the seriousness of the offence and a graduated system of disposal was devised, with community orders being finally viewed as a sentence in their own right (Mair, 1997). As discussed above, rehabilitation and treatment had lost favour and probation officers who had trained in social work were now expected to base their working practices on just deserts and punishment. Not surprisingly, many officers found this change extremely hard. The introduction of the National Probation Service finally occurred in 2000, through the Criminal Justice and Courts Act. This resulted in 56 independent probation services being made into 42 probation areas, with each area geographically mapped to policing and the Crown Prosecution Service. All probation areas were controlled at central government level by the Home Office and the National Probation Directorate. At the local level, probation boards were created to govern local practice such as employing officers and achieving and monitoring performance standards. The Act also took away the responsibility of family court welfare from the Service by establishing a separate Children and Family Court Advisory and Support Service.

Another major structural change occurred in 2004 with the introduction of the National Offender Management Service (NOMS). This merged prison and probation together with the main purpose of this being to join up the services and provide seamless sentencing for offenders. At a basic level it allowed an offender to begin an OBP in prison and then continue it when released into the community. The decision to merge the two services was criticised however, largely due to the pace of the merger and the lack of consultation. The effect of the new service amounted to the 42 probation areas becoming 10 regions, with responsibility taken away from central government and devolved back to 10 regional offender managers (ROMs) who had the responsibility of buying in services and developing a seamless case management approach. With the vast majority of ROMs coming from the Prison Service, many in probation felt disgruntled. Despite this structural change the reality of NOMS was, however, quite different. The 42 probation areas still existed, and whilst NOMS was referred to in the literature it generally only referred to probation and not prison. HM Prison Service were not happy about merging and so, on a practical level this just did not happen.

Change again occurred in the Offender Management Act 2007. This removed the probation boards and placed overall responsibility with the Secretary of State who was assisted in their duties by the ROMs. The ROMs then commissioned services from a number of providers who may or may not have been from prison or probation. In April 2010, the 42 probation areas became 35 self-governing probation trusts, accountable to the Secretary of State for Justice through 10 regional Directors of Offender Management. Therefore over quite a short space of time responsibility for offender management was centralised, devolved, centralised and then devolved again.

Transforming rehabilitation

The greatest change in probation, however, has occurred under the auspices of the TR agenda. This first arose in 2013 when under a Conservative/Liberal Democrat Coalition Government, the Ministry of Justice published *Transforming Rehabilitation: A revolution in the way we manage offenders* (Ministry of Justice, 2013e). After only six weeks of consultation *Transforming Rehabilitation: A Strategy for Reform* (Ministry of Justice, 2013f) outlined future plans. These included:

- A new national public sector probation service, working to protect the public.
- Opening up the market to a diverse range of new rehabilitation providers.
- Statutory rehabilitation extended to all 50,000 of the most prolific offenders sentenced to less than 12 months in custody.
- A nationwide 'through the prison gate' resettlement service, giving continuous support by one provider from custody into the community.
- New payment incentives for market providers to focus on reforming offenders, but only paying them in full for real reductions in reoffending.

While some of the ideas in the report were positive, and consequently were welcomed by those working in probation, especially in relation to through the gate support for offenders; the most controversial was the opening up of probation management to the private sector.

In essence, TR has split the probation service into two sections. The first, the NPS deals with all pre-sentence reports and supervises all high and very high-risk offenders. This was originally thought to encompass 30 per cent of the pre-existing probation workload (Beard & Dent, 2018); although in practice, this has been higher. All other offenders (i.e. those classified as low and medium in risk) are supervised by Community Rehabilitation Companies (CRCs) arranged into 21 Contract Package Areas (CPAs). In September 2013, the Ministry of Justice invited competitive bids from companies to run these 21 CRCs. The contracts were for seven years and worth £3.7 billion. Over 800 organisations expressed an interest in being involved, although only 30 passed the first stage of the procurement process and only 8 new providers of probation were finally confirmed. While many existing probation areas bid for these contracts, only one of the new owners was from the public sector (Beard & Dent, 2018). The new NPS was created on 1 June 2014 and the new CRCs on 30 June 2014 (Beard & Dent, 2018). Probation staff were divided up into the two new organisations with those remaining in the NPS becoming civil servants. Staff allocation decisions were made based on which cases were held by staff on a particular day rather than on experience and skills (Burke & Collett, 2016).

Community rehabilitation companies

The eight new probation providers took ownership of the CRCs on 1 February 2015 (Beard & Dent, 2018), when the Offender Rehabilitation Act 2014 came into force. All providers were to be paid through a two-part system where the majority of the funding would come from services but also where a proportion would only be awarded for reducing reoffending, commonly known as PbR (Strickland, 2016). This was one of the main reforms identified under TR with the government's plan being to incentivise companies to drive down offending (Ministry of Justice, 2013f). It was initially thought that about 10 per cent of the contract price would be paid on a PbR basis (Beard & Dent, 2018). During the planning for TR, PbR pilots were taking place at HMP Doncaster and HMP Peterborough, but decisions relating to its use within probation were made before evaluation data on these studies were released (Beard & Dent, 2018).

The contracts with the CRCs allow for three tiers of probation providers. The first tier is the owner of the CRC. This is a prime provider or lead organisation made up of a number of other smaller organisations and charities. An example can be seen with Purple Futures, the lead provider in the Humberside, Lincolnshire, and North Yorkshire CPA, which is made up of five different organisations. The second and third tiers are made up of charities and the voluntary sector who are commissioned and paid to provide those services, which are required for offender management but are not able to be supplied by the lead organisation. These could include services for housing, health, drugs and alcohol, relationships, mentoring and employment. As noted below there have been, however, real concerns about the level at which second and especially third tier organisations are now actually involved in probation services.

Discussed in more detail in Chapter 9, one of the main tasks of the CRCs in addition to supervising those sentenced to a community penalty, is the provision of through the prison gate services. This is provided to all short-term prisoners (sentences of under 12 months), who previously had not received any support when released into the community. The idea is that by offering pre-release supervision and a through the gate service this will help to reduce reoffending rates and bring to an end the revolving prison door of crime. To help with this the government has established a network of resettlement prisons (see Chapter 8) in which offenders spend the last three months of their sentence and in which resettlement services are provided.

The National Probation Service

The changes to probation meant that 35 self-governing probation trusts had to merge into one NPS, further divided into seven areas (London, Midlands, North East, North West, South East, South West and South Central and Wales). Change did not take place overnight, however, with significant differences found between each probation area. National policies and processes have therefore been devised and implemented on issues such as job roles, approved premises and what risk assessment tools should be used, with this being the first phase of the E3 agenda (effectiveness, efficiency and excellence). This focused on offender management and victims, and took nearly three years to implement. The NPS has also introduced a national workload management tool, which has indicated that the vast majority of offender managers are massively overloaded due to the intense and serious nature of the offenders that they now manage. Common offences for NPS staff are thus murder, rape, manslaughter, GBH, wounding and sexual offences. Phase two of the agenda related to multi-agency working (see Chapter 10), with phase three concentrating on offender management in prisons, with probation officers now supervising all high-risk offenders in prison. This represents quite a significant change for the NPS in terms of its previous job role. This allows the resettlement process to start while the offender is still in prison and provides for better resources to allow probation officers to be involved at the prison stage. The NPS is now a part of HM Prison and Probation Service (HMPPS) which, similar to its predecessor NOMS, creates a whole system approach which aims to create a stronger and more united approach between prison and probation.

The main tasks of probation officers are therefore to assist the courts with pre-sentence reports and then to effectively supervise high-risk offenders while in prison and in the community. Probation officers offer a range of services including one-to-one counselling, group work programmes including sex offender treatment programmes (see Chapter 10) and will also tap into other resources and services where needed. This may include advice focused on healthcare, housing, employment and training, mentoring and services for those who suffer from personality disorders. One of the most limiting factors of the new model, however, is that the NPS cannot commission services itself and so can only use those, which are provided by the CRC. This has meant that in some cases they have been prevented from being innovative.

Discussion Points

1. What do you think to the changes introduced into probation by the TR agenda? What are the advantages and disadvantages of these changes?
2. Should the funding of probation services be dependent on reducing reoffending?
3. What is your view of privatising probation?

Has rehabilitation been transformed?

The overarching objective of TR is to reduce reoffending with many of the reforms designed to offer better support to offenders both in prison and in the community. Views on the restructuring and how successful the programme has been have been mixed, although in the main largely negative. Anecdotal evidence from probation staff in the early days of TR was largely adverse with many of these views not changing over time. As highlighted throughout this section, there have been numerous problems including the pace and lack of consultation on the changes, incompatible IT systems, staff morale and CRCs making less investment than promised in their bids and ultimately being less successful than anticipated. In a reflection piece in 2016, Burke and Collett referred to the 'Transforming Rehabilitation juggernaut' (Burke & Collett, 2016, p. 129) remarking how most of the reforms were introduced without the need for legislation. They further noted how early research carried out on CRC staff highlighted how they were struggling to cope with the changes that TR had brought about, with this extending to feelings of a loss of status as they were no longer probation officers. Significant concerns, as highlighted below, have also been raised about the operational relationship and communication practices between the NPS and the CRCs (Burke & Collett, 2016).

The early implementation of TR was the subject of five HM Inspectorate of Probation reports (2014–2016), all of which focused primarily on the systems and processes needed to create effective offender management. Although some progress was noted in the final report (HM Inspectorate of Probation, 2016d), on the whole they have described delays, low staff morale (HM Inspectorate of Probation, 2014), insufficient risk assessment information, incorrect allocation decisions, ineffective IT systems (HM Inspectorate of Probation, 2015b), variable enforcement procedures (HM Inspectorate of Probation, 2015c), insufficient progress in terms of reducing reoffending (HM Inspectorate of Probation, 2016c), and even in the last report, insufficient pre-release support, little progress in training and employment prospects and inconsistent quality of pre-sentence reports (HM Inspectorate of Probation, 2016d). The fact that HM Inspectorate of Probation felt the need to inspect 5 times in a 15 month period, is in itself of concern.

There have also been a number of inspections in individual areas, although these are carried out in geographical police service areas rather than CPAs (see https://www.justiceinspectorates.gov.uk/hmiprobation/inspections?probation-inspection-type=inspection-of-probation-services). Rather than focusing on systems and processes these inspections have looked at the effectiveness of the organisations in reducing reoffending, protecting the public and enforcement. Bearing in mind the thematic inspection reports noted above, it is not surprising that the reports on individual CRCs and local delivery units for the NPS were similarly critical, although in most cases the inspectors have been more positive about the NPS than they have the CRCs. In London, for example Chief Probation Inspector Dame Glenys Stacey stated:

> We found the quality of work by the CRC poor. There was some welcome good practice by individual officers and first-line managers but generally, practice

was well below standard, with the public exposed unduly to the risk of harm. (HM Inspectorate of Probation, 2016a, p. 4)

And in Gloucestershire:

When we looked at the quality of work undertaken, we found that the NPS in Gloucestershire was performing reasonably well in many respects .... We did not find such a coherent picture at the CRC. At the time of the inspection, Working Links had not been able to implement its plan that a single responsible officer would support the offender throughout. Instead, offenders were being transferred between workers for operational reasons, and also as a result of painful staff reductions. (HM Inspectorate of Probation, 2017b, p. 4)

TR has therefore effectively created a two-tier service where most CRCs are underperforming and an appropriate level of service is only being provided by the NPS (Carr, 2018).

The effectiveness of probation work in Gwent (South Wales)

Main CRC findings

- Work to protect the public was not of sufficient quality.
- Assessments and planning were good, but quality of subsequent work was not good enough.
- The CRC was not sufficiently effective in delivering interventions to reduce reoffending.
- Specific services were not available when needed, or at all in some cases.
- The needs of female service users were given specific consideration, with women-specific interventions available.
- Enforcement processes were followed, but there were too many cases, where the CRC judged the service user's non-attendance as acceptable.
- Managers and responsible officers spent too long on administrative tasks at a cost to the quality of work.
- More effective management oversight was required.
- Overall the work of the CRC in Gwent was troubling.

Main NPS findings

- The quality of work to protect the public was acceptable.
- Assessments and planning were good, but the quality of subsequent work varied. In a small number of cases the work delivered was poor.
- Positive progress had been made towards reoffending outcomes.
- Sufficient progress had been made in delivering the requirements of the sentence in four out of every five cases.
- Appropriate breach action had been taken in every case where it was necessary to do so (HM Inspectorate of Probation, 2017c).

There have also been significant concerns over the financial viability of some of the CRC owners. In July 2016, the House of Commons Committee of Public Accounts reported that nearly two years into the reform programme the aims of it had not been achieved. One of the problems it cited was the fact that the predicted caseloads for the CRCs were wrong, with more cases allocated to the NPS than originally thought, meaning that CRCs were receiving less offenders than predicted and consequently less income. This meant that the CRCs did not have the money to create the new IT systems and the examples of innovative practice which they had promised in their bids (House of Commons Committee of Public Accounts, 2016). In July 2017 the Ministry of Justice announced a further £342 million to enable CRCs to provide 'critical frontline services' (House of Commons Committee of Public Accounts, 2018, p. 4), but despite this injection of cash, in March 2018, 14 of the 21 CRCs were still forecasting losses on the contract. Furthermore in February 2019, three CRCs (Wales; Bristol, Gloucestershire, Somerset and Wiltshire; and, Dorset, Devon and Cornwall) run by the company Working Links went into administration (Cockburn, 2019). This was expected to worsen when PbR was fully introduced, with 19 out of the 21 CRCs in March 2018 not meeting their reduction in reoffending targets (House of Commons Committee of Public Accounts, 2018).

This has arguably created a vicious circle for the CRCs: low caseloads, means less money, which results in reduced investment and innovation, resulting in lower than predicted reoffending reductions. This has meant that CRCs have made a number of staff redundant, which again affects reoffending reductions. One point to make here though is that the number of offenders that need to be managed has not changed, it is just that they are being managed by the NPS rather than by CRCs. This system of allocation between the NPS and the CRCs, which depends solely on risk is therefore inflexible and illogical (Carr, 2018). It does not take account of trends in sentencing and has meant that the CRCs have been forced to lose highly skilled employees who could be helping with the high and demanding caseloads in the NPS.

Another criticism is the fact the CRCs are not in general collaborating with enough third sector organisations, so are not offering probation services from a diverse enough range of rehabilitation providers, with this again potentially linked to affordability. In August 2015 Clinks, an organisation which supports voluntary organisations that work with offenders and their families, published a report on the voluntary sector's collective experience of the changes which had been undertaken in probation following the TR agenda (Clinks, 2015). Reporting the views of practitioners, during May 2015, Clinks found:

- There is very little clarity about what services the voluntary sector will deliver and how it will be funded.
- The pace of change has been slower than anticipated, leaving organisations in a state of limbo, waiting to see how or if they will be involved in service delivery, making strategic planning and staff retention difficult.
- A small number of larger voluntary sector organisations secured contracts with CRCs to deliver services.

- The level of NPS engagement with the voluntary sector is largely unknown and needs to be investigated further.
- The voluntary sector is reporting a sense of confusion amongst funders and commissioners around what CRCs and the NPS will resource.

A follow up survey published by Clinks in 2016 was as negative, with concerns focused on the still slow progress, which had been made in terms of involving third sector organisations in probation services. Prior to TR, 70 per cent of the survey's respondents had been funded by probation but this had since dropped to 25 per cent, with the CRCs preferring to use large voluntary sector organisations rather than the small or medium sized ones (Clinks, 2016). The third and final report (*Under represented, under pressure, under resourced*) was published in April 2018 with the name of the report typifying the unchanged state for the voluntary sector (TrackTR partnership, 2018).

Despite this high level of negativity, the NPS manager interviewed for this book, expressed more positive views about TR. In terms of organisational structure, she felt that it was a progressive change for probation to be part of a national organisation as this gave them a greater voice. The changes had also resulted in better national policies and processes and communication had become more effective. Managing offenders in prison was also seen as a constructive change as probation officers were thought to be in a much better position to offer the rehabilitative support that was needed and had previously been lacking for many high-risk offenders. She also reported positive working relationships with her staff and that many were pleased and proud to be working in the NPS. Nevertheless, she still felt that privatising the majority of probation was a significant waste of money and that probation trusts could have achieved a lot more if they had been allowed to. The split, in her opinion, had created dysfunction and a huge amount of bureaucracy, which got in the way of staff being able to do their jobs. Staff, for instance, felt that they had not been consulted enough about the changes and there were additional concerns over pay and benefits, especially as their caseloads were now entirely high-risk in nature. The manager also reported that while in her area there was a good relationship between the NPS and the CRC, she knew that this was not the case across the board, which was particularly important when an offender was showing signs of risk escalation. She also thought that both the local NPS division and CRC lacked the staff capacity to properly manage its offenders, which was of concern. As highlighted by Clinks (2015; 2016), she confirmed how splitting the service had had a negative impact on the partners which they had previously worked with. Her final thought was that change would have to happen because the current structure was just not working, although she noted how this could not happen until at least 2021 because of the penalties, which would need to be paid if contracts were ended early. If alteration did occur, she thought it probable that rather than accept that it had it wrong, the government was likely to present such change as another transformation programme. While this would be frustrating for practitioners, if it resulted in the joining up again of all probation services, this level of repeated disruption was viewed as worthwhile.

Some positive views have also been recorded from those offenders supervised since the introduction of the reforms. While many did not know whether they were being supervised by a CRC or the NPS, many service users were happy with the way that probation was running. Very few had noticed any real changes since TR had been implemented although where change had been noticed this was largely positive with some offenders noting that provision relating to education, offender behaviour programmes and substance misuse was good. Some however thought that probation did not meet their needs and more work was needed to help with housing and employment. In relation to those offenders who were supervised by the CRCs, many noted that their relationships with practitioners had suffered, with many reporting that they had experienced multiple changes in responsible officers (National Audit Office, 2016).

GOVERNMENTAL RESPONSE

The government finally responded to this high level of criticism in July 2018, when it announced a consultation on probation providers, which ran from July to September 2018. It promised an extra £22 million to improve through the gate services and to the surprise of many announced that CRC contracts would be ended in 2020, 14 months earlier than expected (Ministry of Justice, 2018k). This was again confirmed in May 2019, when the Justice Secretary published a blueprint for the future of probation. This promises up to £280 million for voluntary and private sector organisations, to allow them to deliver innovative rehabilitation services and importantly brings the management of all offenders back under the auspices of the NPS. Each NPS region, of which there will be 11, will have an 'Innovation Partner', who will be responsible for delivering unpaid work and OBPs and could be from the private or voluntary sector. Such changes were expected to take place by the end of 2019 for Wales and from December 2020 for England (Ministry of Justice, 2019b). The detail on what this will actually look like is, at the time of writing, unknown, although as stated by Garside, due to the continued involvement of private companies, 'this is not the wholesale renationalisation of the probation service' (Garside, 2019) that many working in probation want.

Discussion Points

1. What is your view of probation and offender management? Is it dead, dying or poorly?
2. What changes need to be made to offender management to secure its future?

CONCLUSION

Community penalties and the management of offenders in the community have probably experienced the most change of any other subject in this book. From ad hoc beginnings, we have seen the expansion of community orders to the curtailing of this through the two current options of the community order with requirements and the SSO. While the community order with requirements appears to focus on offender need, which has to be paramount in reducing reoffending rates, it is questionable how this can work in a sentencing system that is based on just deserts rather than on rehabilitation. It is also disappointing that despite community penalties being more effective at reducing recidivism than short-term custodial sentences and significantly cheaper for the taxpayer; the number of community sanctions ordered by the courts has significantly decreased since 2011. Ideas from Scotland may help to improve this use, but as noted, we still have the problem of good quality offender management and it is this factor that is causing the most concern. In her annual inspection report in 2017 the Chief Inspector of Probation stated that 'regrettably, none of the government's stated aspiration for Transforming Rehabilitation have been met in any meaningful way' (HM Inspectorate of Probation, 2017a, p. 12). Furthermore, she questioned whether the current model of probation (the split between the NPS and CRCs) could ever 'deliver sufficiently well' (HM Inspectorate of Probation, 2017a, p. 6). Change must occur and it must occur quickly, not just to protect the public but also to secure the survival of the probation service. It is currently poorly and may even be dying so the government need to step in fast before it is dead (Mantle, 2006).

 Now read:

Probation Journal (2019) 'Special edition: Five Years of Transforming rehabilitation: Markets, management and vales', *Probation Journal*, 66(1).

 Now watch:

File on 4 (2016) 'Transforming rehabilitation: At what cost?', BBC Radio 4, available at: https://learningonscreen.ac.uk/ondemand/index.php/prog/0D79D8A3?bcast=122662676

Liverpool John Moores University (2019) Transforming rehabilitation. Privatising probation and the failure of marketization by Lol Burke and Steve Collett, available on YouTube at: https://www.youtube.com/watch?v=7TTGEDovJjU

National Audit Office (2019) 'Transforming Rehabilitation: progress review', available on YouTube at: https://www.youtube.com/watch?v=XSvKWVe9tPg

Now consider:

If you were creating an agency whose task it was to manage offenders, what would the key aims and ethos of this organisation be? How would you effectively manage offenders in the community and who would provide the rehabilitative services?

7 Prisons and the Use of Imprisonment

INTRODUCTION

Since the Murder (Abolition of Death Penalty) Act 1965, imprisonment is the most serious sentence that a court in England and Wales can impose. Despite the fact that it is only used in approximately 7 per cent of all criminal offences, there are almost 83,000 men, women and children, deprived of their liberty and held securely in penal establishments. Prisons and the use of them are never out of the headlines with the media focusing on issues such as drugs, violence, low staffing levels, overcrowding and when prisoners should be released. These and other pertinent areas of discussion are dealt with in Chapters 8 and 9. This chapter however acts as an introduction to this discussion including a brief history of how prison establishments came about. It explains how male prisoners are categorised, the many functions which prisons are expected to perform and discusses whether holding people in custody should be done for a profit. Reference is made throughout to current penological research and to the prisons which were visited for this book, with five of these establishments included below.

A BRIEF HISTORY

Originating from the Latin word, carpare, meaning to seize (Coyle, 2005), prisons in one form or another have always existed; although the prison as an institution was not formally recognised in England and Wales until after the Norman Conquest in 1066, when William I ordered the building of the Tower of London as the first royal prison. Imprisonment is the most obvious way in which we incapacitate people (see Chapter 2), although prisons were not originally used to detain people as a form of punishment, with this meted out through branding, mutilation, the stocks, burning, hanging, decapitation and then later transportation (Peters, 1998). Prison as a sentence was therefore largely insignificant, with no more than 10 per cent of people receiving custodial sentences in the third quarter of the eighteenth century (Spierenburg, 1998). Jails were used to hold those awaiting trial or sentence and Houses of Correction held petty offenders sentenced to short periods of custody, with large amounts of these inhabitants being debtors (McGowen, 1998). Both types of establishment were governed by local authorities and magistrates (Johnston, 2016).

The first national prison in England was Millbank, London, which opened in 1816 and although thought was put into its design, the network of corridors was later found to be unsatisfactory, leading to Pentonville being opened in 1842

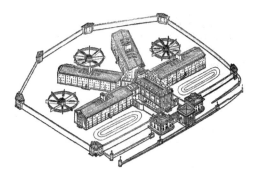

Figure 7.1 Pentonville Prison in 1844

(McGowen, 1998) (Figure 7.1). The architecture of Pentonville was to keep prisoners isolated and was the introduction of the separate system into England and
Wales as previously used in Philadelphia in the United States of America (US) (see
Henriques, 1972). In Pentonville, this was achieved through one central hub with
four radiating wings all of which were visible to staff in the centre. Prisoners could
not see or communicate with each other with there being separate exercise yards
and separate stalls in church (McGowen, 1998). Religious instruction was the only
time that silence would be interrupted, with a separate system church still available to see today at Lincoln Castle. Life in the separate system was focused on thinking about past behaviour and indeed prisons were originally called penitentiaries
because they were places where offenders were sent to give penance and repent.
The separate system represented the first stage of a prison sentence and was
originally for 18 months; although this was later reduced to 12 months and then
to 9 due to its effects on physical and mental health (Johnston, 2016). The second
stage of the sentence then focused on either transportation (which ceased in 1869)
and/or work and for this purpose working prisons were built between 1847 and
1856 at Portland, Dartmoor, Portsmouth and Chatham (McGowen, 1998).

In 1865, the Prison Act amalgamated the local jails and Houses of Correction
into local prisons. The national prisons were referred to as convict prisons
(McConville, 1998). As the popularity for transportation diminished and then
ceased, long term imprisonment (penal servitude) with hard labour became the
preferred option also replacing the corporal punish-
ments noted above (Johnston, 2016). Hard labour was
achieved through the treadmill (similar to modern day
step machines), the crank and the capstan wheel; all
of which involved non-productive labour. Sentences
of two years or less were served in the local prisons,
while convict prisons held those sentenced to penal
servitude where the minimum period was for three
years (McConville, 1998). This distinction and separate
administration of the two types of prison lasted until
the national prison system was created by the Prison
Act of 1877 (Coyle, 2005).

> Crank wheels could be tightened to make the task more arduous and the nick-name of 'screws' for contemporary prison officers comes from this time when crank wheel screws were tightened by them.

Historically the period of greatest prison building was during Victorian times (1837–1901), with most of these designed to accommodate the separate system. With funds needed for two subsequent World Wars and the resulting clean-up operations there was little money available for prison repair or redesign even when the separate system was finally abandoned by the Prison Rules of 1930 (Coyle, 2005). At the end of the 1970s there were 46 prisons: 42 of which had been built before 1900 and four built between 1900 and 1939 (McConville, 1998). Many of these Victorian prisons are still functional today, despite the fact that their design is no longer conducive to contemporary aims of imprisonment (see below). The architecture of a prison is however important. Historically, as mentioned above, the design of a prison was set at what would aid security and control, but there is now an emerging focus on how design can help with rehabilitation and reform. One of the leading researchers in this field is Yvonne Jewkes, whose work on carceral spaces has highlighted how prison design can have a 'profound psychological and physiological influence on those who live and work within them' (Jewkes, 2018, p. 319). Best practice in this area is often attributed to Scandinavian countries with Storstrom Prison in Denmark and Halden Prison in Norway designed to resemble small urban communities 'with streets, squares and centrally located community buildings' (Jewkes & Gooch, 2019). Other differences to prisons found in England and Wales include the fact that there are no bars on the windows, furniture and rooms are curved (so as to minimise self-harm), and all cells have views of landscaped gardens or open countryside. While some of this good practice is evident in HMP Berwyn, a purpose-built prison in Wales, where the prisoners are referred to as men and there is evidence of soft furnishings and inspirational quotes on the walls (Jewkes & Gooch, 2019), this does not represent the vast majority of the current prison estate in England and Wales.

THE AIMS AND PAINS OF IMPRISONMENT

The aims of imprisonment have arguably changed over time, although traditionally these have focused on incapacitation (now referred to as public protection), deterrence, retribution and reformation. Today, these four aims are still evident, although a prison's core endeavour is the deprivation of liberty and the exclusion of an individual from society. Contrary to traditional imprisonment where penal servitude and forced labour were common, offenders today are not sent to prison to be punished. This is neatly summed up in a famous quote from Alexander Paterson, an English Prison Commissioner in the early part of the twentieth century:

> It is the sentence of imprisonment, and not the treatment accorded in prison, that constitutes the punishment. Men come to prison as a punishment, not *for* punishment. (Coyle, 2005, p. 13)

Punishment is therefore delivered through curtailing an individual's freedom and their ability to make autonomous decisions, a fact which has been confirmed by the House of Lords (now Supreme Court) in *Raymond v Honey* ((1983) 1 AC 1). Four statutory aims of imprisonment, specifically omitting punishment, were proposed in Clause 1 of the Prisons and Court Bill, but after the dissolution of Parliament in May 2017 this was not included in the subsequent Queen's speech and there are no plans to resurrect this element of the Bill. Prison Rule 3, which talks about training prisoners to lead good and useful lives, therefore remains the most up-to-date provision on what contemporary imprisonment is for.

> **Prisons and Courts Bill**
>
> Clause 1: 'prisons must aim to protect the public, reform and rehabilitate offenders, prepare prisoners for life outside prison, and maintain an environment that is safe and secure' (Strickland, 2017, p. 17).

While, in theory, there are positive purposes to imprisonment, the practice of being detained has been documented as being far different. Perhaps one of the most well-known studies by Gresham Sykes (1958), identified five 'pains of imprisonment'. Writing at a time when imprisonment was not meant to inflict punishment on prisoners, he nevertheless argued that inmates suffered deprivation of liberty, deprivation of goods and services, deprivation of heterosexual relationships, deprivation of autonomy, and deprivation of security. These psychological pains of imprisonment, were, Sykes argued, just as damaging as the physical pains that prisoners had previously endured (Sykes, 1958). Nearly 20 years later, Foucault (1977) made similar comments in his classic text *Discipline and Punish*, where he questioned whether new psychological ways of controlling prisoners were worse than the physical punishments of the past. Further work (King & McDermott, 1990; 1995) has focused on prison life and the dehumanising conditions in which prisoners are kept (see Chapter 8), in addition to the misuse of prison officer authority (Jameson & Allison, 1995). More recently, Crewe (2011) has added pains associated with tightness, where

> The term 'tightness' captures the feelings of tension and anxiety generated by uncertainty and the sense of not knowing which way to move, for fear of getting things wrong. It conveys the way that power operates both closely and anonymously, working like an invisible harness on the self. It is all-encompassing and invasive, in that it promotes the self-regulation of all aspects of conduct, addressing both the psyche and the body. (Crewe, 2011, p. 522)

In all of these accounts prison is viewed as damaging rather than purposeful and while such effects are not always intended they are nevertheless ever present. These pains of imprisonment are discussed in more detail in Chapter 8.

Discussion Questions

1. What do you think the aims of imprisonment should be?
2. Is it possible to avoid the pains mentioned above?
3. If you were asked to design a new prison what architectural elements would you include and what sort of regime would you run? Would your focus be on security and control or rehabilitation and reform?

THE PRISON ESTATE

Structure

The prison estate is currently made up of 116 prisons and young offender institutions, 1 immigration removal centre (IRC) and 3 secure training centres. Of these 116 establishments, 13 are contracted out and managed by the private companies of Serco, G4S and Sodexo Justice Services on behalf of HMPPS (HM Prison and Probation Service, 2018b). The remaining 103 are public sector prisons. All institutions are governed on a national basis by the Ministry of Justice, which is a ministerial department of the government. Prison establishments are geographically dispersed throughout England and Wales, from Northumberland in the North to the Isle of Wight and Dartmoor in the South and for male adult prisons are divided into two geographical regions: North and South. There are also separate directorates for Wales, young people, high security, contracted out prisons and women (Ministry of Justice, 2019f).

Prison capacity and populations

In April 2019, the useable operational capacity in prison establishments in England and Wales was 84,756 (Ministry of Justice, 2019d). The operational capacity of a prison or IRC is the total number of people that an establishment can hold, taking into account its needs for control, security and other operational factors. The useable operational capacity for HMPPS is the sum of all prison places minus 2,000 which gives the service an operating margin. This margin is needed to reflect constraints imposed by the requirement to provide separate accommodation for different classes of prisoner for example based on sex, age and conviction status. Each prison will have a designated operational capacity but also a certified normal accommodation (CNA) figure with the CNA representing 'the good, decent standard of accommodation that the Service aspires to provide all prisoners' (Ministry of Justice, 2012a, p. 11). Any cell or prison establishment which is operating above the CNA is referred to as crowded. In May 2019, the prison population in England and Wales was 82,599 (Ministry of Justice, 2019d). This would suggest that there is no crowding, but as highlighted in the case studies below and discussed in more detail in Chapter 8 this is not true. In terms of comparisons, England and Wales (excepting Turkey and the Russian Federation) holds more people in prison than any other European country and on a World basis is ranked 21/225 (World Prison Brief, 2019b).

Categorisation

In addition to separating prisoners in terms of age (see Chapter 11) and gender (see Chapter 12), the male prison estate is also classified in terms of security risk. Once an adult male has received a custodial sentence he will be risk assessed, first on the likelihood that he will escape and second, what level of risk he would pose to the public if he did. This is known as categorisation. The categorisation system dates back to 1966 following the recommendations of the Mountbatten Inquiry

(Mountbatten Report, 1966) which looked at a number of high profile escapes (McEwan, 1986). To allow categorisation to work, different prisons are allocated a particular categorisation with their security conditions reflecting this. Due to prison crowding and geographical location many prison establishments will be multi-functional so they may have a high security wing, but will also cater for Category B and C prisoners. The categorisation system is detailed in Figure 7.2

In 1987, two Category A prisoners escaped from HMP Gartree, prompting a further review of security and categorisation (Coyle, 2005). Consequently, Category A is now divided into three additional classifications: standard, high-risk and exceptional risk. Standard prisoners make up the bulk of the high security estate and include those who have no history of escape planning; are not considered to have the skill or determination to escape and/or do not have access to outside resources to assist with such an escape. High-risk prisoners do, however, have such a history and are perceived to have both the skill and determination to overcome the security measures applied to them to affect an escape. Exceptional-risk prisoners have the same characteristics as high-risk but are thought to be even more risky in terms of escape.

Prison function

In addition to security category, each prison has a specific task or function which it is expected to perform. Prisons are therefore designated both as to categorisation and function.

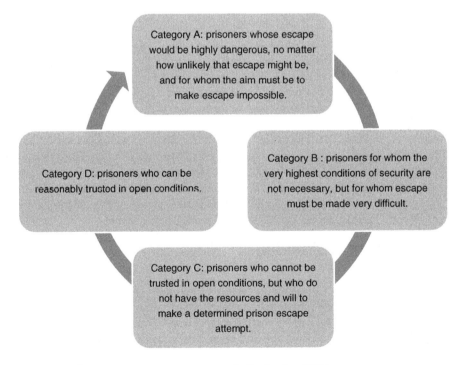

Category A: prisoners whose escape would be highly dangerous, no matter how unlikely that escape might be, and for whom the aim must be to make escape impossible.

Category B : prisoners for whom the very highest conditions of security are not necessary, but for whom escape must be made very difficult.

Category C: prisoners who cannot be trusted in open conditions, but who do not have the resources and will to make a determined prison escape attempt.

Category D: prisoners who can be reasonably trusted in open conditions.

Figure 7.2 The prison categorisation system in England and Wales

High security

The high security directorate is made up of 13 prison establishments: 4 dispersal prisons, 3 local prisons with separate Category A units, 5 Category B training prisons, which specialise in managing life sentenced prisoners and 1 designated for young adults (HM Prison and Probation Service, 2018b). These are illustrated in Figure 7.3. HMP Frankland also has a separation centre which houses dangerous and radicalised extremists. This was opened in July 2017 and is part of the government's wider strategy to tackle extremism in prisons. The operational capacity for dispersal prisons in 2017 was 3283 (Ministry of Justice, 2017j), despite the fact that in July 2017 the high security estate held only 946 Category A prisoners, of which 811 were held in dispersal prisons and 27 in close supervision centres (CSCs) (Ministry of Justice, 2017d). While this means that many Category B prisoners are being held under more secure conditions than necessary this is the aim of the dispersal system.

Dispersal prisons have existed since the Radzinowicz Report of 1968, which argued that it was safer to disperse dangerous Category A offenders across a number of different prisons rather than having them all in one establishment (McEwan, 1986). Due to the function of containing the most dangerous, the regime in a high security prison is the most severe in terms of security measures. This can include frequent cell and personal searches, control of movement, restrictions on communications, limitations on visits, closer observations and special measures for outside transfers. More stringent measures are used for those who pose a high risk, as opposed to just a standard risk and all exceptional-risk inmates are kept within CSCs. In July 2017 there were CSCs at HMP Full Sutton, HMP Wakefield and HMP Whitemoor (Ministry of Justice, 2017d). As seen in HMP Full Sutton below, despite the regime being more severe in terms of security, living conditions are often better in dispersal prisons, especially regarding crowding, staff/prisoner ratios and time out of cell.

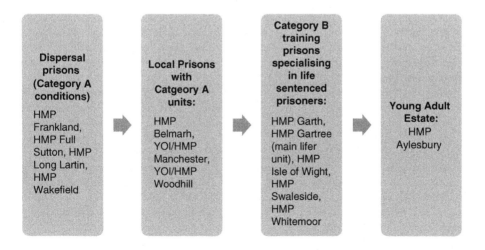

Figure 7.3 The high security estate in England and Wales

PRISON

Category and function	Adult male Category A and B Dispersal prison
Prison status	Public
Location	Full Sutton, 11 miles east of York
Building	Purpose built in 1987
Operational capacity	626
CNA	606
Population	566
Reception criteria	Sentenced to 4 years or more and have at least 12 months left to serve.
Residential units	Nine residential units plus healthcare: three general wings, three for vulnerable prisoners, one induction unit, one segregation wing and one reintegration unit following time spent in segregation.
Inspection details	Safe prison (HM Chief Inspector of Prisons, 2016a).
IMB report	Well managed and succeeding in creating a stable environment that is as safe as possible (Independent Monitoring Board, 2017c).
Prison performance rating	Where 1 is serious concern and 4 is exceptional 4
Date of visit	17 May 2017

Regime

The prison had two standard regimes: the first ran Monday–Thursday and the second Friday–Sunday, with the four-day week imposed to save money. In the first, cell doors were opened at 8.15 am. Men would already have had their breakfast, which was provided, in weekly breakfast packs. Those going off the wing, for gym, healthcare, treatment programmes, work or education would then leave. Those remaining were locked up, with only cleaners, laundry orderlies and pensioners allowed out. Lunch was provided through the form of a packed lunch (sandwich, crisps and a drink) which was collected by those in education and work before they left. The men returned to the wing at approximately 3.20 pm and would be locked up until dinner at 5.00 pm. Hot food was collected from the servery on the wing with the men returning to their cells to eat. Provision existed to eat in the servery but this was rarely used with the men preferring to eat either alone or with friends in cells, although no more than three were allowed in a cell at any one time. Cells were locked up at 6.40 pm for the night. In the second regime, the men would stay on the wing but would have most of this time as free association. Many of the men filled their time with hobbies such as painting and model making. Individual hobby boxes were kept in the office with many men collecting these just before lock up.

The wing visited had the capacity for 108 prisoners. All had single cells with a toilet and sink. Enhanced prisoners (see Chapter 8) had the choice to cook their own food and, if appropriate, were given an opt-out food allowance, with the men commonly ordering and cooking together. Most prisoners were allowed to wear their own clothes. All standard prisoners (see Chapter 8) were allowed a TV and enhanced prisoners a play station. From walking around, at least two of the men had canary birds. One officer noted: 'They do have a lot here but they live here, forever, they aren't going anywhere'. To reflect the high security status of the prison, three cells were searched each day. Category A prisoners were targeted more and had a full cell search at least once a month. They also moved cells every six months.

Education and Work

The prison offered a number of work opportunities including textile workshops, desktop publishing, Braille transcription, assembly and packaging lines, bicycle refurbishment and waste management. Employed prisoners received between £13 and £18 per week. Educational courses ranged from functional skills to basic Maths and English, GSCEs and degrees.

Prison Officer/Prisoner Relationships

Prison officer/prisoner ratios were quite high: for 108 prisoners there were 30 officers, although not all would be working at the same time. When all prisoners were on the wing there were 12 officers, with this reduced to seven when many were in education or work. All officers were allocated four personal prisoners with whom they were expected to help with sentence planning and show an interest in their well-being. Because many of the men had been there for a long time, staff knew the prisoners well and were able to create meaningful relationships. Consequently, officers commonly knew what an individual's risk factors and danger signs were and could use this knowledge to reduce the risk of an incident. The prison was not crowded and gave many men a stable life. When compared to other prisons, there was thought to be no real drug problem.

Visits and Family

Visits were available Thursday–Sunday with each session being approximately two–three hours. Prisoners had two statutory visits per month, which could be put together so many would only see family on a monthly basis. Despite this allowance, the visits hall was rarely full, partly because of the distances that family had to travel but also due to the nature of some of the prisoners' offences.

Current Challenges

The main challenge reported at the time of the visit was how to work with some very entrenched men in terms of helping them to progress. Due to the nature of the offences and the prevalence of mental health issues, the officers were working with some very complex individuals. One explained: 'some days it's mentally draining because of the prisoners cutting up and not being able to cope and offloading onto the officers'. Another felt that better mental health training and provision of programmes was needed for both staff and prisoners so that officers in particular were better equipped to deal with such multifaceted individuals.

Two concerns in relation to high security prisons focus on the management of risky individuals and the life experience of those prisoners serving very long sentences. In terms of risk management, this can be made more difficult when prisoners are mentally ill (see HMP Full Sutton and Adams & Ferrandino, 2008), but can also be heavily influenced by the relationships which exists between prison officers and prisoners, with trust playing a key role in this. Work by King and McDermott (1990) and more recently by Liebling and colleagues (2015), for instance, has suggested that trust between prison officers and prisoners can be negatively affected by an officers prejudicial bias. One example, given by Liebling and Williams (2018) is when security information reports are based on a prisoner's membership of a 'security threat group', rather than anything more concrete. This they say is borne out of officers fears of radicalisation, gang culture and violence in prison and while White long-term prisoners are also subject to security reporting, being Black (dangerous) and Muslim (terrorist) is viewed, by many officers, as 'added risk' (Liebling & Williams, 2018, p. 1196). This misjudgement consequently affects trust and contributes to problems of religious and racial injustice. Trust between prisoners and officers can also be influenced by a prisons approach to risk management, with Liebling and colleagues noting that while staff at HMP Full Sutton were 'professionally outstanding ... there was a general tendency on some of the wings for staff to take only a superficial interest in prisoner circumstances and dynamics' (Liebling, et al., 2015, p. 5). Conversely, staff at HMP Frankland were described as 'competent, professional and relationally-based ... [where] first names were routinely used'. Despite this, prisoners still commented that relationships with officers were 'superficial' (Liebling, et al., 2015, p. 5).

As highlighted by an officer at HMP Full Sutton, many men held within high security prisons live there for long periods of time. While some will stay in prison for the remainder of their lives, the vast majority will one day be released, although when that end-date is, is often unknown. Long-term prisoners inevitably suffer from the pains of imprisonment as described above, but perhaps what sets these prisoners apart is the length of time that they are subjected to such conditions. One study, which specifically looked at the problems of long-term imprisonment for men (see Crewe, et al., (2017b), which compares problems experienced by men and women who received sentences at a young age, noted how the most severe problems, as reported by prisoners, were missing somebody, missing social life, worry relating to release, concern about wasting life and being sexually frustrated (Hulley, et al., 2016). These findings closely mirror similar research carried out in the late 1970s (Richards, 1978; Flanagan, 1980), although this more recent study did note how 'different types of problems emerge as more or less severe at different stages of the life sentence' (Hulley, et al., 2016, p. 779). For example, missing luxuries, social life and being sexually frustrated was recorded as being more severe for those in the early days of their sentence, with this group also more likely to raise issues relating to unfairness of the sentence and thinking about the time they had left to serve (Hulley, et al., 2016). This might simplistically suggest that the pains of imprisonment for long-term male prisoners lessen as sentence length increases, but this is not how Hulley and colleagues view it. Rather they argue that it shows how long-term prisoners are altered by their environment, learning to swim with the tide rather than against it (Crewe, et al., 2017a) and warn how resulting coping mechanisms, such as distrusting others may inhibit future release and reintegration plans (Hulley, et al., 2016). Another study goes further arguing that long-term imprisonment can result in post-incarceration syndrome, a condition similar to post-traumatic stress disorder (PTSD) (Liem & Kunst, 2013).

Discussion Questions

1. What do you think of the 'comforts' allowed to high security prisoners such as single cells, cooking their own food, having canaries and access to hobby boxes? Should such privileges be given to those who have committed the worst crimes?
2. How important do you think trust is in behaviour management? If you think it is important, how can prison officer/prisoner relationships be improved?
3. What do you think to the view that long-term imprisonment can change a person so fundamentally so as to cause a psychological disorder?

Local

The traditional function of the local prison was to hold unconvicted and unsentenced prisoners, but now, most will hold a large number of sentenced prisoners, either because they are serving short terms of imprisonment or because there is no space within training prisons. All local prisons are closed and commensurate with Category B status, although they will often contain Category C and sometimes even Category D prisoners. In December 2018, there were 30 male local prisons (HM Prison and Probation Service, 2018b), many of which date back to the Victorian era, meaning they are often the least fit for purpose. Examples include HMP Bedford built in 1801, HMP Birmingham built in 1849 and HMP Hull which opened in 1870. Many local prisons are therefore 'old and shabby, chronically over-crowded, poorly resourced and with higher suicide rates than any other prison' (Jewkes, 2008, p. 156). As seen in the case study of HMP Wandsworth, other common issues include high levels of violence, increased drug use and problems with recruiting and keeping staff. All of these issues will be discussed in more detail in Chapter 8.

Discussion Questions

1. Local prisons are often the most overcrowded and least fit for purpose, but hold the majority of unsentenced and in some cases unconvicted prisoners. Should the factually innocent be held in such conditions?
2. In the design of your new prison what would the prison officer/prisoner ratio be?
3. Why do you think that HMPPS has experienced such difficulties in recruiting prison staff? Would it be a job that you would currently consider?

Category and function	Adult male Category B with a Category C resettlement unit Local prison
Prison status	Public
Location	Wandsworth, South London
Building	Built in 1851 although extensive refurbishment in 1989
Operational capacity	1628
CNA	963
Population	1570 – 163 per cent crowded
Reception criteria	See below
Residential units	The Heathfield Centre: A and B wings housed general population and workers; C half smoke free and half vulnerable prisoners; D drug maintenance and general population; E first night and segregation units. Trinity: resettlement unit
Inspection details	Six self-inflicted deaths since 2015, not all staff carrying anti-ligature knives and cell bells often not answered. Living conditions inadequate (HM Chief Inspector of Prisons, 2018c).
IMB report	The continuing staff shortfall affected every aspect of prison life … the prison did not consistently manage to provide a safe, decent and humane environment (Independent Monitoring Board, 2017b).
Prison performance rating	Where 1 is serious concern and 4 is exceptional 1
Date of visit	11 May 2017

Although designated as a local Category B prison, at the time of the visit, Wandsworth was holding virtually every kind of male prisoner including Category Bs and Cs, Category Ds waiting to go into the open estate, remand prisoners, those who had served their sentence but were subject to an immigration hold and a number of foreign national prisoners. In May 2017, Wandsworth was a reform prison and the only prison in the estate which dealt with extradition prisoners. This has now changed with its new function being a reception prison, although it still holds a number of Category C prisoners, largely to create a workforce so that the prison can run. The rest of the prison houses remand (unsentenced) prisoners with Wandsworth being the main reception/remand prison for the London area. To accommodate this, the reception area has been increased in size, the video conferencing suite extended from 5 to 22 rooms and the visits hall made larger. This latter requirement is because those on remand have the right to receive more visits than sentenced prisoners.

Regime

Due to staff shortages, in May 2017, the prison was running an emergency regime, which was first implemented in the summer of 2016. The prison was not fully staffed with there being a high level of sickness and many staff working under restricted duties that are office based rather than on the wings because of advice from occupational health. Initially, free flow, moving prisoners around the prison for activities, was only taking place on Trinity unit, although at the time of the visit this had been extended to B and C wings in Heathfield. Prisoners on A and D wings had very few employment or educational opportunities.

Education and Work

As a reform prison, Wandsworth had several work, educational and partnership opportunities. These included a business hub where men learnt how to make posters and menus, barbering on Trinity, barista skills and NVQs in the kitchen. Other courses focused on responsible pet ownership, money management, victim awareness (Sycamore Tree Project), music production, reading and a choir. Plans for the future included creating centres of excellence in catering and barbering with the hope that the public would come into the prison to have their hair cut. While such opportunities were plentiful, they were not open to many of the men due to the emergency regime imposed. As a reception prison, much of this intervention work will disappear although drug intervention and maintenance work will still be needed and programmes such as Cell Workout (see www.cell-workout.com), mindfulness, mentoring skills, learning how to read and yoga will still be useful.

Prison Officer/Prisoner Relationships

Staffing levels were identified as needing to change, to allow for improved officer/prisoner relationships. Staff could then identify issues much earlier, be able to watch, observe and build relationships with prisoners and potentially reduce incidences of violence and other frustrations. One of the wing officers spoke about the demise of 'prison craft', that is, the lack of experience on the wing in terms of dealing with and working with prisoners. In May 2017, wings of up to 300 men, which used to have 12 officers, had only 6. When HMP Full Sutton had a 1:9 officer/prisoner ratio, the ratio here of 1:50 is starkly different.

Visits and Family

The visits centre was run by Spurgeons, a children's charity, with social visits available every day. There were also monthly family days for specific groups including events for pre-school children, Halloween and Christmas. These were designed to allow men to interact with their families. Officers tried to create as 'normal' an environment for the children as possible and while family days were well received, they were only held for a small number of the men, again due to staffing constraints. The prison also had a family support worker, was involved in Storybook Dads (see www.storybookdads.org.uk) and had a number of short programmes that helped to build family relationships. The visits room had a 'tuck shop', soft play and a children's area with toys, books and a Wendy house.

Current Challenges

Staffing was identified as the main challenge at the time of the visit. Shortages meant that officers could not give prisoners the amount of attention that they would have liked meaning that prisoner issues were sometimes left unresolved. High levels of violence partly caused by the rise in new psychoactive substances, contraband, the use of drones and gang culture were also identified.

Category and function	Adult male Category C Training prison
Prison status	Public sector
Location	Doncaster
Building	Former RAF base, opened as a prison in 1985.
Operational capacity	1017
CNA	924
Population	1015 – 110 per cent crowded.
Reception criteria	Category C convicted males over 21 serving sentences of over 4 years.
Residential units	Ten residential units: six dormitory design, with prisoners having keys to their own cell; three modern wings and a purpose built segregation unit. Mainly single cells.
Inspection details	October 2017 – some improvement in safety, but levels of violence still high, with a quarter of prisoners feeling unsafe (HM Chief Inspector of Prisons, 2017b).
IMB report	Some progress made in setting up work contracts, although the availability of new psychoactive substances was a major concern (Independent Monitoring Board, 2016b).
Prison performance rating	Where 1 is serious concern and 4 is exceptional 1
Date of visit	21 July 2017

Regime

A typical day at Lindholme began at 7.45 am when a bell rang to tell the men that they would soon be unlocked for work. Work began at 8.30 am; with this time needed to move the men, as Lindholme, with a three-mile perimeter fence, is the largest prison site in Europe. The men returned to their units at 11.45 am for lunch and were locked up at 12.30 pm for one hour. Lunch consisted of, a roll, crisps/chocolate bar and a piece of fruit. Hot soup was often served in winter. At 1.30 pm, the cycle would start again. Dinner, a hot meal, was served at 5.15–5.30 pm. Prisoners were then unlocked until 7.00 pm for association, games, sports, gymnasium etc.

Education and Work

Lindholme is a working prison. To facilitate this it had a number of inter-governmental contracts with the Ministry of Defence including refurbishing flat racks (used to carry cargo in planes) and the making of camouflage nets. Other contracts existed with DHL to refurbish white goods and Doncaster Council to recycle old streetlights. The prison also had a bakery,

Training

Training prisons house medium to long-sentenced prisoners who on reception have at least four years left to serve. Their main function is to provide men with full employment and training so that they can progress through the estate, and were which provided bread for Lindholme and two other neighbouring prisons and was sold to staff and the local community. Profits from these initiatives were invested back into the fabric of the jail. There were employment opportunities on the wings including cleaners, peer mentors and servery workers and the prison also had a day centre for pensioners.

Training and qualification opportunities included an autotechnic course, plastering, welding, tiling, a waste management unit and barbering. The old RAF hangers were industrial units with one of them used for building; a true to scale house had been built and when completed would be taken down for construction to begin again. The prison also had a number of catering and hospitality courses, the head chef used to work at Buckingham Palace and the hospitality manager used to be a butler at the House of Lords. For men who gained NVQ qualifications in hospitality, the prison had a partnership with Q Hotels, which guaranteed a job interview on release. Through this, two men had earnt jobs. The prison also offered educational courses, including basic literacy and numeracy, GCSEs and degrees. At the time of the visit, Lindholme had the second largest education and training budget in the prison estate worth £2.6 million.

Prison Officer/Prisoner Relationships

Prisoner/staff relationships were described by the governor as good. At the time of the interview the prison had 164 'white shirt' officers, although they had been promised another 40. The governor felt this would help to further improve relationships.

Visits and Family

Visits were daily, except on Tuesday and Thursday. Prisoners used to be able to block book visits, so that their family could choose on which day to come, although this had recently stopped. This was to ensure that there were enough visits but mainly to try and stop the influx of drugs, as some would come to the prison, see a drug dog and decide to try again the next day. If a prisoner had a visit, they would have the morning or afternoon off work. The visits hall had a servery that sold food, with profits from this used to upgrade the crèche and visiting facilities. The aspiration was that prisoners would soon be able to buy bread made at the prison and give it to their families. The prison also worked with Storybook Dads and had family days.

Current Challenges

One of the main challenges in the prison at the time of the interview was Spice. Due to the large perimeter fence it was difficult for the prison to stop illegal drugs getting in. All work areas were searched at the beginning of the day but over 700 men were being moved twice a day with only four–five prison officers monitoring this. With Lindholme being such a huge site, it was impossible to cover all areas; prisoners could cause a fight at one end to distract officers while packages were coming over the perimeter fence at the other end. There had also been problems with drones. Violence was on a downward trend and due to their relationships with the prisoners, prison officers were in full control of the prison; although it was acknowledged that this could change at any point. This fear was partly related to the fact that the prison had approximately 160 organised criminal gang members. Another challenge, similar to HMP Wandsworth was the retention of staff.

described by one prison worker as holding grounds to provide men skills, training and qualifications for their back pocket when they move on. Ordinarily training prisons do not release prisoners, so the men will be moved either to a resettlement or an open establishment. Some training prisons have special facilities, for example HMP Gartree is the main lifer unit, HMP Grendon has a therapeutic unit, HMP

Whatton specialises in sex offenders and HMP Coldingley and HMP Lindholme are working prisons. Training prisons are often less overcrowded than local prisons, but are usually in more remote locations and thus further away from the offender's family. In December 2018, there were 8 Category B training prisons and 43 Category C training prisons, with two of the Category Cs only holding Foreign National Offenders (FNOs) (HM Prison and Probation Service, 2018b). In December 2018, there were 9090 FNOs in England and Wales. Of these 6745 had been sentenced to a criminal offence, 1587 were being held on remand and 758 were held for non-criminal reasons (National Statistics and Ministry of Justice, 2019b). As evidenced above, and discussed in more detail in Chapter 8, training prisons share similar challenges to local prisons. While the buildings tend to be newer, there are still problems with drugs, violence and perhaps due to this, staff retention.

Resettlement

The main difference between a training and a resettlement prison is that while the former focuses on equipping the men with employment skills it is the latter, which actually prepares them for release. Because there is this distinct difference, a number of Category C training prisons have been identified as resettlement prisons. These hold Category C prisoners serving sentences of between 12 months and under 4 years and will help them work towards release in the last 3 months of their sentence. Prisoners serving 12 months or less serve the entirety of their sentence in a resettlement prison (Taylor, et al., 2017). Resettlement prisons include HMP Humber, HMP Onley and HMP Parc (see below). The resettlement regime concentrates on release and resettlement by increasing an individual's level of personal responsibility, thereby reducing institutionalisation and ensuring that they can manage in the community independently. This is achieved by focusing on the three key areas of accommodation, employment and finances.

Resettlement prisons came about under the Transforming Rehabilitation agenda, which saw the introduction of competition into the field of rehabilitation and through this the creation of community rehabilitation companies (see Chapter 6) and the extension of mandatory community supervision to all offenders who had spent more than one day in custody. The aim behind the policy was to ensure that all offenders in custody would have effective resettlement support

---

Discussion Questions

1. Training prisons arguably offer the best opportunities for prisoners in terms of education and training, but are generally only available to those serving sentences of four years or more. Should this stipulation be changed so that all prisoners have access to these opportunities?
2. For those prisons able to, such as HMP Lindholme, should they be more self-sufficient in terms of growing their own food, selling the products of their work and carrying out their own maintenance work?
3. Prisoner wages (on average £10 per week) are considerably lower when compared to the minimum wage. What do you think to this?

in place prior to and following on from their release; with the hope being that this would make a step change in rehabilitation and would help to reduce reoffending rates (Taylor, et al., 2017) (for a critical discussion on this see Chapter 9).

Open

Open prisons operate on the belief that by allowing prisoners more interaction with the community, they provide the opportunity for offenders to make links and resettle back into the community. As stated by Sir Alexander Paterson 'you cannot train a man for freedom under conditions of captivity' (Morris & Rotham, 1998, p. 332). Most open prisons do not have a perimeter fence and so due to this minimal security, they are only suitable for those who present a minimum security risk and are unlikely to escape or misbehave. Open prisons detain approximately 5 per cent of the total prison population (HL Deb, 18 February 2016, cW), which is low when compared to Norway where approximately one third of all prisoners are held in open conditions (Shammas, 2015) (for more on the differences between England and Wales, and Norway see Prisons Research Centre, 2019). Open prisons house a mixture of people, from white-collar criminals who have gone straight to open conditions to long-term prisoners who have spent several years in the prison estate. Prisoners will often leave the prison, on temporary license, either to spend time with their family or to work. As long as they return by a given time this is viewed as working towards full resettlement back into the community. If the offender has spent a significant period of time in prison and has become institutionalised in the sense that they become used to the prison environment, this progressive re-entry is often necessary with evidence suggesting that a life sentenced prisoner is three times less likely to reoffend if released from an open rather than a closed prison (Crewe, 2015). Reductions in reoffending rates for all prisoners has also been noted by Hillier and Mews (2018) who found that for each additional resettlement day that a prisoner was given prior to release, this equated to a 0.5 per cent reduction in reoffending. This increased to a 5 per cent reduction when the temporary release included an overnight stay (Hillier & Mews, 2018). In December 2018, there were 12 open prisons in England and Wales (HM Prison and Probation Service, 2018b).

Open prisons and release on temporary license (ROTL) hit the headlines in 2013 when three serious offences (murder, robbery and rape) were committed by Ian McLoughlin (HMP Springhill), Al-Foday Fofnah (HMP Ford) and Alan Wilmot (HMP North Sea Camp) (HM Inspectorate of Prisons, 2014). This sparked a number of investigations and reviews and consequentially a tightening up of the ROTL process. Two ROTL schemes now exist: a standard regime and a restricted regime for serious offenders. Offenders who have a history of escape or abscond are no longer allowed to live under open conditions. The main difference for offenders is that ROTL is now seen as a privilege rather than as a right and there is a greater emphasis on assessing the risk of the individual (Crewe, 2015). While this is necessary, it is important that the Ministry of Justice does not restrict ROTL too much, especially as research has shown that ROTL reduces reoffending and is key in helping offenders obtain employment (Pedder, 2017). Based on a two-year action-learning project at HMP Brixton, Pedder recommends not only that ROTL

PRISON

Category and function	Adult male Category D Open prison
Prison status	Public
Location	Grendon Underwood, Buckinghamshire
Building	House built in 1872, became the first male open prison in 1953.
Operational capacity	335
CNA	335
Population	Near to operational capacity – not crowded
Reception criteria	Those suitable for open conditions although no sex offenders, foreign national prisoners, those presenting a risk to children, those convicted of arson or those with outstanding court appearances.
Residential units	Prisoners housed in huts: 9 held 22 prisoners in shared accommodation; 3 have 40 single rooms; and 1 a 16-bed substance misuse unit. All had communal lounges, showers, kitchens and toilets, with one having en-suite facilities.
Inspection details	Communal and external areas clean, some of the residential units were dilapidated, the heating system was inadequate and the hot water supply was unreliable. Prisoners continued to be less positive about staff–prisoner relationships than in other open prisons (HM Chief Inspector of Prisons, 2018b).
IMB report	Men are treated humanely although the deteriorating condition and fabric of the prison remains a constant negative to the positive efforts to foster a more rehabilitative culture (Independent Monitoring Board, 2017e).
Prison performance rating	Where 1 is serious concern and 4 is exceptional 4
Date of visit	7 March 2017

Regime

As an open prison, Springhill had no fence or wall and when compared to other prisons had a relaxed regime. Cells were referred to as rooms with the men having their own keys. This allowed them to come and go as they pleased, although they were expected to be inside their huts between the hours of 10 pm and 6 am, unless they were off site working. The day began for most at 7.45 am when roll check (register) took place in the communal dining room, where the men collected their breakfast. Most would then either leave the site for work or go to their work placement on site. Roll check occurred again at lunchtime. Dinner was at 5.00 pm when a hot meal was served. The first evening roll check took place at 8.30 pm in the huts with the final roll call at midnight.

Education and Work

The prison's main function was resettlement with the ultimate goal being to release offenders with employment. At the time of the visit approximately 70 per cent left with a job, either set up by themselves or the prison. To enable this, the prison ran a range of educational opportunities including literacy and numeracy courses, IT and employment skills. The men also had the opportunity to gain experience and/or qualifications in catering, horticulture, basic plumbing, carpentry, forklift truck driving and call centre work. There were also apprenticeship schemes, for example, Rail Track, taught men the skills to lay tracks and cabling. They were paid by Rail Track and would have fulltime employment on release. At any one time, approximately one third of the population would be working off site, which could include night and shift work. To facilitate this some of the prisoners had their own cars. Jobs included building, carpentry, painting, film set building, IT support and window fitting. Placements were set up either by individual prisoners or by the prison itself. Full risk assessments and disclosures were carried out and random on site checks were made. The rest of the men were employed to help run the prison or were involved in other training or educational activities.

Prison Officer/Prisoner Relationships

Due to the open nature of the prison, there was a lot of freedom and the men wanted to engage and talk to officers as they walked around the site. Staff numbers had recently increased to further improve resettlement and educational opportunities and working at Springhill was described as enjoyable. Officers were not just 'turn keys, [however] but Mum, Dad, Postman, Nanny, Nurse, [and] First Aider'. On an ordinary day, there would be five officers to operate the site, reduced to three at night. At night, the vast majority of the men were on the site and while the risk of a serious incident was low, if one did occur it would be difficult for staff to manage.

Visits and Family

Prisoners were able to spend periods at home in addition to having visits at the site. This was facilitated through Resettlement Day Release or 'townies'. These were licences lasting four–six hours, which allowed them to leave the site and spend time in the local town or at home. This could also be extended to an overnight licence (Resettlement Overnight Release) which could last for a few days. Perhaps due to this, there was no separate visits hall in Springhill with the dining room doubling up for this purpose. Unlike closed prisons, prisoners and their visitors could leave the dining room and move around the gardens. Visits took place Friday–Sunday. Facilities for visits included a play area for children and the availability of refreshments. There was no visitor centre.

Current Challenges

Motivation of prison officers was cited by one officer as one of the biggest challenges for the prison, partly due to the number of changes which had occurred in the last few years. Wages were described as poor as there had been no pay rise in the last seven years and the pension age had been increased to 68. This was viewed as problematic when over that same time period, the job has become more pressurised and in some prisons, dangerous.

should be used more but also that it should be routinely used in both open and resettlement prisons. Interestingly the research found that "it was not primarily employers' attitudes but the policies and practices of prisons, and the lack of priority given to finding prisoners employment on release, which were the main barriers to getting more prisoners into work" (Pedder, 2017, p. 28). Discussed in more detail in Chapter 9, employment is fundamental in resettlement and so practices which help to reduce crime and prevent reoffending must be increased rather than diminished.

Discussion Questions

1.   What do you think about the mechanism of temporary license? Should it be used across the prison estate to help with resettlement or are the government right in restricting it to those in open prisons?
2.   The regime in open prisons could be described as part time prison. Could this be extended across the prison estate to allow people to maintain employment and other community links?

Immigration removal centres

IRCs, previously known as detention centres, are holding establishments for foreign nationals who are awaiting asylum claim decisions or awaiting deportation following a failed application. There are currently ten IRCs in England and Wales, nine of which are run by private providers and one, IRC Morton Hall, operated by HMPPS (HM Prison and Probation Service, 2018b). The regulation of IRCs and their conditions are met through the Detention Centre Rules 2001 with their purpose set out in section 3:

> To provide for the secure but humane accommodation of detained persons in a relaxed regime with as much freedom of movement and association as possible, consistent with maintaining a safe and secure environment, and to encourage and assist detained persons to make the most productive use of their time, whilst respecting in particular their dignity and the right to individual expression.

The use of IRCs has been controversial, not only because detainees are not offenders, but also because of the overcrowded and unacceptable conditions in which many are kept (politics.co.uk, 2017). While it is the policy of HMPPS to treat all immigration detainees as unconvicted prisoners, this in practice has not always been the case (HM Inspectorate of Prisons, 2015). Perhaps due to such conditions, there have been 29 deaths in IRCs between 1989 and 2017 (Institute of Race Relations, 2017). There is no statutory upper limit for how long someone can be held and while many will only be held for short periods of time, others will remain for much longer (Bosworth & Vannier, 2016). General uncertainties relating to a release date can therefore lead to high levels of anxiety and depression (Bosworth & Kellezi, 2015), with research suggesting that detained asylum seekers are significantly more likely to suffer from depression, anxiety and PTSD symptoms when compared to community based asylum seekers (Robjant, et al., 2009).

Discussion Questions

1. What do you think to the use of IRCs?
2. Should HMPPS be involved in detaining non-criminals?
3. In what conditions should foreign nationals be kept and what regime should the establishments operate under?

PRISON PRIVATISATION

Prison privatisation in England and Wales can be traced back to 1986 when the parliamentary Select Committee on Home Affairs reflecting on a prison estate which was at record levels (51,000) and following practice in the US, thought that by contracting out the building and running of penal establishments it would: (1) save the taxpayer money; (2) ensure buildings were built quicker and (3) achieve greater architectural efficiency and excellence when compared to old Victorian prisons (Nathan, 2003). Section 84 of the Criminal Justice Act (CJA) 1991 thereby allowed for the contracting out of prisons and in 1992 HMP Wolds became the first privately run prison (Panchamia, 2012). Amendments to the CJA in 1993 further extended this to existing establishments rather than to just new buildings (Panchamia, 2012).

> **Privatisation** refers to a process whereby the state hands over, under contract, the delivery of new or existing services to private operators.

This was then followed by the Private Finance Initiative (PFI) which was first introduced in 1992 by a Conservative government but not fully implemented until Labour came into power in 1997; despite the fact that in opposition Labour had opposed the idea (Nathan, 2003). The PFI scheme covers new prisons and involves the financing, design, construction and operation of prison establishments. The first PFI prison in England and Wales was HMP Altcourse in Liverpool, closely followed by HMP Parc in Bridgend, which were both built and opened in 1997. Contracts under the PFI scheme last for a period of 25 years, with many of them still in existence. In 1996, the aspiration was that at least 25 per cent of the prison estate would be managed by the private sector (Nathan, 2003). In 2019, this stood at just over 11 per cent. A full list of contracted out prisons can be seen in Table 7.1. At the end of 2012 the government stated that it had abolished whole prison contracting out (Tanner, 2013), this was seen with HMP Berwyn which was designed and built by the private sector but then given to the public sector to run.

Table 7.1 Prisons which have been or are currently privatised.

Prison/YOIv	Opened	Contractor	Contract	Current situation	Performance rating
Wolds	1992	G4S	Operational	Returned to the public sector in 2013	3
Blakenhurst	1992	UK Detention Services Ltd	Operational	Returned to the public sector in 2001	N/A
Doncaster	1994	Serco	Operational	Extended in 1999 and remains under Serco	2
Buckley Hall	1994	Group 4 (now G4S)	Operational	Returned to the public sector in 2000	3
Parc	1997	G4S	PFI	Contract ends in 2022	3
Altcourse	1997	G4S	PFI	Contract ends in 2022	3
Lowdham Grange	1998	Serco	PFI	Contract ends in 2023	3
Ashfield	1999	Serco	PFI	Contract ends 2024	3
Forest Bank	2000	Sodexo Justice Services	PFI	Contract ends 2025	3
Rye Hill	2001	G4S	PFI	Contract ends 2026	3
Dovegate	2001	Serco	PFI	Contract ends 2026	3
Bronzefield	2004	Sodexo Justice Services	PFI	Contract ends 2029	3
Peterborough	2005	Sodexo Justice Services	PFI	Contract ends 2030	3

Prison/YOIv	Opened	Contractor	Contract	Current situation	Performance rating
Birmingham	Transferred in 2011	G4S	Operational	Contract set to end in 2026. First public sector prison to be transferred, but was transferred back in 2018.	
Birmingham	Transferred in 2011	G4S	Operational	Contract set to end in 2026. First public sector prison to be transferred, but was transferred back in 2018.	1
Thameside	2012	Serco	PFI	Contract ends 2037	3
Oakwood	2012	G4S	Operational	Contract ends 2027	3
Northumberland	Transferred to in 2013	Sodexo Justice Services	Operational	Contract ends 2028	2

One of the main differences between private and public sector prisons relates to accountability in terms of what they are expected to deliver. The Ministry of Justice will set a number of targets, which become the baseline figures for delivery. This might include a minimum number of hours of constructive activity or, one taken from HMP Parc, providing prisoners with seven sets of underwear per week. In the tendering process providers are given the opportunity to bid against this baseline with the provider offering the best value for money (i.e. the cheapest) awarded the contract. If it is awarded to the private sector and the operator doesn't deliver to this baseline then penalty or performance points will be attached. Performance points can be linked to failures to comply with procedures (e.g. £9000 for leaving a gate unlocked), incidents and also failures to comply with prison regime, with there being no comparison in the public sector. Baseline targets derive from the decency agenda which was initiated by Martin Narey in 1999 in his role as HM Prison Service Director General and which tried to ensure that every prisoner was treated with decency and respect. Due to the threat of financial penalties, levels of decency are therefore more likely to be achieved in private sector rather than public sector prisons. Another distinction is that private sector prisons only work to their contract in terms of prisoner numbers. Once the number of prisoners agreed to in the contract has been reached then the prison is full. If the Ministry of Justice wants to send more prisoners, then in theory, the contract should be altered, with more accommodation and ancillary facilities built to accommodate this. Despite this, however, many private prisons are crowded with HMP Doncaster in 2019 being the most overcrowded by 146 per cent (Howard League for Penal Reform, 2019).

While prison privatisation may be sound in theory, there have been countless problems. Incidents at HMP Birmingham, HMP Northumberland and Medway Secure Training Centre (once run by G4S) have all painted private sector prisons in a bad light. Problems in some of these establishments were arguably linked to inexperienced staff who were paid less and received insufficient training when compared to their public sector counterparts. In 2005, basic salaries for staff not transferred over from the public sector were nearly one third less; private sector officers also had a longer working week, fewer holidays and less generous pensions (Prison Reform Trust, 2005). Other issues relate to personal relationships. One public sector prison governor stated how their relationship with the director of the local private prison was not as good as it was with other local prisons. The private prison was not willing to share best practice or help the public sector prison out. Those in private prisons were not happy either, feeling that sometimes they were at a disadvantage and that their staff were often treated like second class citizens even when, as in the case of HMP Birmingham, the staff had not chosen to work for the private sector. Tanner, who is more positive about prison privatisation, argues, as detailed in Figure 7.4 that as the private sector performs at a far greater level than the public sector, its stake in the market should be increased.

One of the main questions regarding private prisons is therefore whether they do perform better than their public sector counterparts, because if Tanner is right,

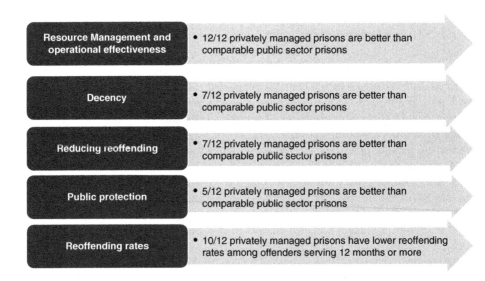

Figure 7.4 The case for private prisons

Source: Tanner, W. (2013) *The Case for Private Prisons*. London: Reform.

then privatisation should be increasing rather than being on the current decline that it is. The evaluation of differences between private and public sector prisons is under researched, although a few studies do exist. One of the first, which looked at HMP Wolds and compared it with HMP Woodhill, a public sector prison, found that in terms of relationships with and treatment by prison officers, prisoners far preferred the private prison (James, et al., 1997). Research by Liebling and Arnold further supported this thesis with them stating that private prisons were rated better in areas such as wellbeing, prisoner autonomy and relationships between prisoners and officers, although there were concerns with safety, structure and security (Liebling & Arnold, 2002). More recently, Crewe and Liebling (2018) have carried out a larger study looking at the differences between public sector and private sector prisons, and, in contrast to Tanner (2013), found that private sector prisons 'appeared at both the top and bottom end of the quality spectrum' (Crewe & Liebling, 2018, p. 171). Scoring institutions on aspects such as prisoner safety, drugs and exploitation, policing and security, decency, and staff–prisoner relationships, three private prisons were rated as either poor or average, two public sector prisons rated as good and two private establishments rated as very good (Crewe & Liebling, 2018, p. 172). It is therefore far too simplistic to demarcate the quality of prison down a public sector/private sector divide.

In addition to effectiveness, there is also the question of whether companies should profit from imprisoning people, in short is this ethically defensible? On the basis that it is the state that imposes the sentence of imprisonment should it not also be the state that oversees and manages those establishments which carry out this sentence? When many charities and non-governmental organisations are working to reduce prison populations, it is arguably unhelpful 'to create an interest in their growth among companies and their shareholders' (Prison Reform Trust, 2005, p. 1). Shichor (1998) therefore warns how large companies can sway governmental policy which could result in corporate influence working 'in favour of more and longer prison sentences' (Shichor, 1998, p. 85). Similar concerns are also cited by others (see Geis, et al., 1999; Schwartz & Nurge, 2004).

Of the public sector staff interviewed, most were opposed to private prisons. One stated, 'making money out of putting people in custody only benefits the person who is getting that money, as a public servant we are there to serve the public, the public don't gain it's not any cheaper, no-one should be locked up for someone else to gain pocket'. Another said 'personally I think that it is absolutely disgusting that people make money from people and that's what they are doing', while another 'I am absolutely against the private sector'. This view was put to a senior staff member at HMP Parc who argued:

In terms of the company [G4S] their reward is only for delivering against a contract and they should only win that contract if they have gone through a full procurement process and they are the cheaper provider than the alternative. If you can demonstrate in a fair and open competition that you can provide the baseline (with an aspiration to achieve more) that you will deliver that for the best value for money that looks after tax payers money then the profit becomes irrelevant.

Category and function	Adult male and young people Category B Local, training and resettlement
Prison status	Private – G4S
Location	Bridgend, South Wales
Building	Purpose built in 1997
Operational capacity	1723 but can hold up to 2058
CNA	1559
Population	Slightly under the operational capacity – crowded.
Reception criteria	Remand and sentenced (young people, young adults and sex offenders); sentenced (adult men).
Residential units	A and B held sentenced young adults and adults; C was a resettlement unit; D offered substance misuse support; X held convicted and remand prisoners including an assisted living unit and an older prisoners unit; T housed enhanced prisoners including units for ex-service personnel, a family unit and cells with wheelchair access. The prison also had a safer custody unit and a segregation unit.
Inspection details	'Despite the issues around safety and violence, outcomes for prisoners in terms of both purposeful activity and resettlement were found to be good' (HM Chief Inspector of Prisons, 2016b, p. 5).
IMB report	'well managed, the safety of the prisoners is of paramount importance and the purposeful activity provision is generally very good' (Independent Monitoring Board, 2016a, p. 4).
Prison performance rating	Where 1 is serious concern and 4 is exceptional 2
Date of visit	19 May 2017

At the time of the visit, HMP Parc was the only PFI prison in Wales. The contracted consortium was made up of a construction company, an operational company (G4S) and a conglomerate of bankers, who financed the initial venture. When opened in November 1997 the prison had 838 beds with a capacity of up to 1200, as some of the cells were big enough to be doubled up. An extension was opened in 2010 for an extra 326 men allowing the prison to look after longer-term prisoners. In 2015, a second house block was built for 387 prisoners, which gave Parc a self-contained sex offender prison; this has its own visits area, sports facilities and multi-faith area, making healthcare the only shared function. The prison was designed and built to a Category B standard even though 60 per cent of the prisoners were of Category C status. The PFI contract is due for completion in 2022, when the original consortium will be dissolved and the property will be handed back and owned by the Ministry of Justice. A decision will then be made whether to continue to outsource it, put it out for competition or take it back in-house.

Regime

Cells were unlocked at 7.30 am to enable the men to go to work. Breakfast was provided in a bag the night before, although on weekends they would have brunch cooked on the wing. The men would return to the wing for lunch at 12.15 pm and would dine out. They would be locked up after lunch and would later return to work or other purposeful activity. Dinner was served on the wing at 5.15–5.30 pm, followed by free association. Final lock up was at 8.00 pm. A more restricted regime ran from Friday afternoon to Sunday night. Many of the cells had telephones and each wing had its own computers (for making applications), showers and a laundry.

Education and Work

As part of its hybrid function, Parc was a resettlement prison and as such offered a wide range of educational and work opportunities. These included 'Welsh in the Workplace', ICT, numeracy, literacy, music and art. Programmes aimed at substance misuse, anger management and debt were also available. Parc offered a number of vocational courses including electrical installation, woodwork, graphic design, painting and decorating, industrial cleaning, carpentry, catering and horticulture. The catering department prepared meals for the local community 'Meals on Wheels' and operated the staff canteen. The men also had access to a wide range of sporting facilities, with accredited educational courses involving the Princes' Trust, the Welsh Rugby Union, Welsh Rowing and the British Weightlifting Association.

Prison Officer/Prisoner Relationships

Prison officer/prisoner ratios were reasonably good; although this was largely because Parc only took the number of prisoners stipulated in the contract. Good relationships were evident, especially on the family unit.

Visits and Family

Parc had a visitor centre, run by Barnardo's and a functional visits room. The prison held family days and also ran a homework club. In terms of supporting families, Parc was distinctive in that it had a Family Interventions Unit (FIU) for 62 men. The unit focused on 'repairing, enhancing and taking responsibility for relationships, parenting and family' (G4S, 2016, p. 6), achieved through a range of parenting interventions. Men who lived on the wing, had to be drug free and of model behaviour. As residents of the FIU, the men had access to the Family Interventions lounge, which was a separate room in the visits hall. This provided a nicer space in which to have visits and was seen as a privilege. Residents also received an extra one-hour visit per month.

Current Challenges

Parc had seen an increase in violence, partly due to the use of Spice. While there was no pressure on the regime in terms of being able to provide programmes and purposeful activities, when violence increased, some staff would leave. Parc was one of the first prisons to go non-smoking and even though most of the prisoners were embracing it, some thought this had contributed to the increase in Spice.

Benchmarking

In 2012 the Secretary of State for Justice announced that the prison privatisation programme would be replaced with public sector benchmarking (HC [Session 2012–13] 741-i). Public sector staffing levels were therefore benchmarked or matched against those in the private sector. There are two main reasons, however, why private sector prisons can operate with fewer staff than public sector prisons, neither of which were taken into account by the Minister. First, all PFI prisons are purpose built, and second they have up-to-date IT facilities which streamline back-office procedures. This difference can be seen in the cost per place comparison between HMP Oakwood a purpose built new prison (£12,133 per place excluding education and healthcare) and HMP Brixton a Victorian prison (£33,649 per place) (Warrell & Plimmer, 2015). The consequence was the loss of many prison officer jobs; largely achieved through voluntary severance and retirement which resulted in the loss of experienced staff. The supervision rank of senior officer, was also removed, so new staff coming into the service no longer have the experienced supervision, which their predecessors did. Between 2010–11 and 2014–15 HMPPS made savings of £900 million, which was largely achieved through staff cuts: in the Summer of 2017, there were 6428 fewer staff looking after more prisoners when compared to the Summer of 2010 (Prison Reform Trust, 2017). The knock on effect for prisoners was that they received less support and as stated by one senior staff member were basically left to fend for themselves. As discussed in Chapter 8, benchmarking has significantly contributed to a rise in violence, assaults against prison staff and the use of Spice, and while the government is currently trying to increase staff numbers, the effects of benchmarking will take years to eradicate.

Discussion Questions

1. What do you think about private prisons? It is ethically acceptable for the state to hand over offender management to the cheapest provider?
2. When designing your prison would you want the operator to guarantee certain baseline targets so that prisoner decency was maintained? If so, how would you enforce this?
3. Prisons under PFI contracts arguably have the best facilities, architecture and are liked by prisoners. Bearing this in mind, why do you think whole prison contracting out has been abolished?

CONCLUSION

The prison estate in England and Wales is a multi-faceted entity, serving a number of different types of prisoners and geographically spread across England and Wales. While largely descriptive, this chapter has tried to show the breadth of these prisons and allow you to start to think about some of the current issues relating to prisons, including privatisation and benchmarking. It has also tried to get you to think about your own prison: what architecture and design would you have, what would be your aims and regime, what prison officer/prisoner ratios would you have and how would you ensure your operator was accountable? It is only by ensuring that these elements of a custodial sentence are correct that we can hope to achieve positive aims of imprisonment rather than just pains (Sykes, 1958; Crewe, 2011). These pains are explored in much more detail in the next two chapters.

Now read:

Morris, N. and Rotham, D. (1998). *The Oxford History of the Prison*. Oxford: Oxford University Press.

Jewkes, Y., Crewe, B. and Bennett, J. (2016). *Handbook on Prisons*. 2nd edition. London: Routledge.

Jewkes, Y. and Johnston, H. (2006) *Prison Readings*. Cullompton: Willan Publishing.

Crewe, B. and Bennett, J. (2011) *The Prisoner*. London: Routledge

A prison map of establishments can be found at:

https://www.justice.gov.uk/downloads/contacts/hmps/prison-finder/prison-map.pdf

Now watch:

Life inside Wandsworth Prison. Available at: https://learningonscreen.ac.uk/ondemand/index.php/prog/0D24852C?bcast=122319058

Do the Dutch have the answer to the UK's prison crisis? Available at: https://www.youtube.com/watch?v=Fw_E2t2Wl-Q

Norwegian Prison – Michael Moore (Bastoy Prison and Halden Maximum Security Prison, Norway). Available at: https://www.youtube.com/watch?v=0IepJqxRCZY

Now consider:

What does an ideal prison look like? Take some time to consider this and compare your thoughts and design plans with others.

8 The Prison Experience

INTRODUCTION

In January 2016, Lord Fowler stated, 'In 1970, we faced a prisons crisis; today we face a prisons scandal' (HC Deb 27 January 2016 Col. 334). This view has been additionally expressed by HM Inspectorate for Prisons (HMIP), The Howard League for Penal Reform, the Prison Reform Trust and, importantly, prisoners themselves. Notwithstanding these shared views, the government refuses to accept that the prison estate is currently in crisis. In a House of Commons debate, Michael Gove stated, 'I agree that we face a problem ... but I do not wish to use the word crisis' (HC Deb 27 January 2016 Col. 339). This is despite the fact that in the nine months between December 2016 and August 2017 prison riots occurred at HMP Birmingham (Evans & Willgress, 2016), HMP Swaleside (Weaver, 2016), HMP Hewell (*The Guardian*, 2017) and HMP The Mount (Farmer, 2017). Furthermore, between April and September 2018, there were further riots at HMP/YOI Aylesbury, HMP Lowdham Grange, HMP Bedford and HMP Long Lartin. In August 2018, following a HMIP inspection, HMP Birmingham was taken off G4S and brought back under the control of Her Majesty's Prison and Probation Service (HMPPS) (Ministry of Justice, 2018l) and, in April 2019, 13 prison officers were hospitalised after a riot at HMP/YOI Feltham (Shaw, 2019).

The treatment of prisoners and subsequently an offender's experience of being imprisoned is regulated by a number of national and international rules. These include The Prison Rules 1999, The European Prison Rules 1987 and the United Nations Standard Minimum Rules for the Treatment of Prisoners (the Nelson Mandela Rules). The basic principles in all are that imprisonment should be carried out in material and moral conditions, which ensure respect for human dignity. Despite the government's reassurances, this chapter argues that the operation of imprisonment in England and Wales is currently in breach of many of these minimum standards.

INSPECTION

Role and expectations

One of the main ways in which the prison experience is assessed is through inspection. HMIP is an independent agency, which has a statutory duty to 'inspect or arrange for the inspection of prisons in England and Wales and to report ... on the treatment of prisoners and conditions in prisons' (section 5A Prison Act 1952 (as amended)). This applies to all establishments and institutions where people are detained. All inspections are conducted against a list of expectations. Examples include having enough clean clothing of the right kind, size, quality and design and having a palatable, varied, healthy and balanced diet (HM Inspectorate of Prisons, 2017b). In male prisons, for example, the expectations cover the four broad areas of safety, respect, purposeful activity and rehabilitation and release planning; with these collectively known as the healthy prison test (HM Inspectorate of Prisons, 2017b). This is designed to promote treatment and conditions in detention that meet international human rights standards with HMIP also providing indicators that show how these expectations can be met.

When an establishment is assessed against the healthy prison test, outcomes are rated between good and poor.

- Good: there is no evidence that outcomes for prisoners are being adversely affected in any significant areas.
- Reasonably good: there is evidence of adverse outcomes for prisoners in only a small number of areas. For the majority, there are no significant concerns. Procedures to safeguard outcomes are in place.
- Not sufficiently good: there is evidence that outcomes for prisoners are being adversely affected in many areas or particularly in these areas of greatest importance to their well-being. Problems/concerns, if left unattended, are likely to become areas of serious concern.
- Poor: there is evidence that the outcomes for prisoners are seriously affected by current practice. There is a failure to ensure even adequate treatment of and/ or conditions for prisoners. Immediate remedial action is required (HM Chief Inspector of Prisons, 2017a).

All inspections of adult prisons and immigration detention centres (IRC) are unannounced; the governor will receive a phone call to let them know that the inspection team are in the car park waiting to come in. All prisons are inspected at least once every five years, although those that display poor outcomes will be inspected more frequently. Follow-up inspections can also occur, which in the main will be announced. Establishments holding children under 18 are inspected annually and IRCs every four years (or every two if they also hold children) (HM Chief Inspector of Prisons, 2017a).

Until recently, the powers of HMIP had no legal basis. While an internal agreement existed between HMIP and HMPPS for prisons to respond to and act on stated recommendations, there was no actual legal requirement to do so. This changed in November 2017, when the Ministry of Justice announced the urgent notification process. This allows HM Chief Inspector of Prisons to alert the Justice Secretary in a published letter, where they have urgent and significant concerns about the performance of a prison. The process, illustrated in Figure 8.1, outlines what must happen within a 28-day period, with this culminating in an action plan and a written response from the Justice Secretary.

Findings

In 2015–16, the headline from HMIP, relating to prison establishments in England and Wales was 'unacceptably violent and dangerous places'. In 2016–17 the Chief Inspector stated, 'the situation has not improved – in fact, it has become worse'

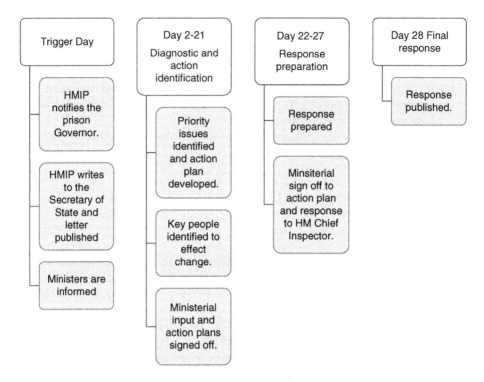

Figure 8.1 The urgent notification process

Source: Ministry of Justice (2017m). *The Urgent Notification process: Overview.* London: Ministry of Justice.

(HM Chief Inspector of Prisons, 2017a, p. 7). In 2017–18, we 'documented some of the most disturbing prison conditions we have ever seen – conditions which have no place in an advanced nation in the 21st Century' (HM Chief Inspector of Prisons, 2018a, p. 7). Of the 31 local and training prisons inspected in 2017–18, 22 (67%) were either 'poor' or 'not sufficiently good' in their safety outcomes (HM Chief Inspector of Prisons, 2018a). Other issues of concern related to the prevalence of drugs inside prisons, insufficient staffing levels, good order and discipline, out of cell time and general overcrowding, which was found to exacerbate everything else. Due to the importance of these issues, it will be these which will be assessed in more detail.

In terms of the urgent notification process, in the first nine months of 2018, there were urgent notifications issued for HMP Nottingham, HMP Exeter, HMP Birmingham and HMP Bedford. If the process had been in place, they would also have been made in respect of HMP Wormwood Scrubs and HMP Liverpool (HM Chief Inspector of Prisons, 2018a). Copies of the notification letters, replies from the Secretary of State and subsequent action plans can be found on the HMIP website (see https://www.justiceinspectorates.gov.uk/hmiprisons/about-hmi-prisons/urgent-notifications/).

Discussion Questions

1. If you were tasked with the job of inspecting prisons, what criteria would you use to do this?
2. Are you surprised by these initial findings of imprisonment in England and Wales?
3. What is your view of the urgent notification process? What needs to be put in place to ensure that positive results are achieved?

CROWDING AND ACCOMMODATION

Crowding in prison has become a fact, and has been present in the prison system since 1994 (Prison Reform Trust, 2018c). A crowded prison is one, which contains more prisoners than the establishment's Certified Normal Accommodation (CNA), defined as the good, decent standard of accommodation that the service aspires to provide all prisoners. In 2017–18, of the 120 prisons in England and Wales, 81 (68%) were overcrowded, with nearly 20,700 people held in crowded conditions (Prison Reform Trust, 2018c). In 2016–17 nearly one quarter of prisoners were held in crowded conditions, with this figure being fairly static since 2009 (Ministry of Justice, 2018e). As highlighted in Chapter 7 and in Table 8.1 prison populations are not distributed evenly across the prison estate, with male local prisons being the most crowded. Crowded prisons are also amongst the oldest establishments in the estate and consequentially the least fit for purpose.

Table 8.1 The most overcrowded prisons in England and Wales.

Prison establishment	Certified Normal Accommodation	Population	Crowding (%)	Prison function	Prison design
Lincoln	318	538	169	Local male	Opened 1872
Preston	433	701	162	Local male	Built 1790
Winchester	334	540	162	Local male	Built 1846
Exeter	302	486	161	Local male	Built 1853
Durham	595	948	159	Local male	Built 1819
Wandsworth	929	1468	158	Local male	Built 1851
Leeds	669	1055	158	Local male	Built 1847
Pentonville	694	1082	156	Local male	Opened 1842
Doncaster	738	1107	150	Local male (private)	Built 1994
Brixton	520	751	144	Resettlement male	Opened 1819

Source: Data from Howard League for Penal Reform (2019) *Most overcrowded prisons in England and Wales*. [Online] Available at: http://howardleague.org/prisons-information/ [Accessed 2 May 2019].

While this situation is unacceptable, it is important to add some context in terms of how England and Wales compares to other countries around the world. Table 8.2 therefore illustrates global occupancy/crowding levels, showing not only the top 10 countries but also the other countries featured in this book. Of interest, while England and Wales are ranked 104/205 in the World they are 9/57 when judged on a European basis (World Prison Brief, 2019a).

Table 8.2 Prison occupancy levels based on official capacity.

Ranking	Country	Occupancy level (%)
1	Philippines	463.6
2	Haiti	454.4
3	El Salvador	333.3
4	Guatemala	333.2
5	Comoros	318.3
6	Uganda	312.3
7	Zambia	303.0
8	Burundi	262.0
9	Sudan	255.3
10	Bolivia	253.9
11	Bangladesh	241.5
25	Kenya	201.7
49	Venezuela	153.9
104	UK: England and Wales	109.4
110	New Zealand	106.1
112	United States of America	103.9
134	UK: Scotland	92.9
141	Finland	91.3
179	Spain	71.8
205 (last on the list)	Nauru	14.0

Source: Data from World Prison Brief (2019a) 'Highest to lowest – occupancy level (based on official capacity)'. [Online] Available at: http://www.prisonstudies.org/highest-to-lowest/occupancy-level?field_region_taxonomy_tid=All [Accessed 2 May 2019].

Being detained in a crowded prison has a number of consequences for a prisoner, not least the fact that they have to share; cells originally designed to hold one person now contain bunk beds to allow for a larger capacity of offenders. Most crowded conditions are where two are sharing a cell designed for one, but three sharing a cell built for one also exists in some prisons (Prison Reform Trust, 2018c). Prisoners will not usually get to choose with whom they share and so mixing a range of personalities, mental health needs, category offences and regional/gang affiliations can create problems. The biggest problem however is space, or more to the point the lack of it. In relation to space, Prison Service Instruction 17/2012 sets out accommodation standards for both uncrowded and crowded conditions as seen in Table 8.3.

Table 8.3 Prisoner accommodation standards.

Requirements for uncrowded conditions	Requirements for crowded conditions
In cell activities: • Sleep • Dress and undress • Storage • Personal pursuits (reading, writing, TV/Music) • Take meals • Use WC (in private) and wash basin • Circulation, movement and seating	In cell activities: • Sleep • Dress and undress • Storage (subject to space) • Personal pursuits (subject to space) • Take meals • Use WC (with some privacy) and wash basin • Circulation, movement and seating

Source: Silvestri, A. (2013) *Prison Conditions in the United Kingdom*. Rome: European Prison Observatory.

The most striking difference between the two standards is the difference in privacy when using the toilet. In uncrowded conditions private is defined as 'full body visual screening from all points in the cell or room, as would be provided at a minimum by a cubicle'. Furthermore, 'in double cells or rooms containing a WC cubicle the WC area must be ventilated separately to the living area.' (Ministry

---

European Prison Rule 14

1. Prisoners shall normally be lodged during the night in individual cells except in cases where it is considered that there are advantages in sharing accommodation with other prisoners.

2. Where accommodation is shared it shall be occupied by prisoners suitable to associate with others in those conditions.

---

of Justice, 2012a, pp. 13–14). When the cell is crowded, the stipulation is 'with some privacy', defined as 'body screening, when using the WC, from the fixed points of the cell that is the table and beds'. Furthermore, 'the WC area need not be ventilated' (Ministry of Justice, 2012a, p. 14). The need to have in-cell sanitation or at least access to sanitation was included as one of the recommendations in the Woolf report (Prison Reform Trust, 1991), which looked into prison conditions in England and Wales following a number of prison disturbances in 1990. Prior to Woolf, the practice of slopping out (the emptying of buckets used as in-cell toilets) was rife and while the eradication of this is welcome, the current situation of men having to share cells with minimum privacy is not acceptable. Of note, however, in October 2016 there were still 1287 cells, located at HMP Isle of Wight, HMP Bristol, HMP Coldingley, HMP Grendon, and HMP Long Lartin, which did not have in-cell sanitation (Ministry of Justice, 2017b). In Grendon, for example, men at night have to press a button in their cell, which, as long as there is no other prisoner out, will unlock their cell for a few minutes. While this is not ideal in the sense that the men have to wait to use the facilities, arguably this is much better than having to use them in front of up to two strangers with minimal visual screening and no ventilation. When most prisoners now have to eat in their cells, lack of space may mean that one will sit at a small table and the other sits on the bed or even the toilet balancing the tray on their knee.

The Nelson Mandela Rules – Rule 12

It is not desirable to have two prisoners in a cell or room.

The Nelson Mandela Rules – Rule 1

All prisoners shall be treated with the respect due to their inherent dignity and value as human beings. No prisoner shall be subjected to, and all prisoners shall be protected from, torture and other cruel, inhuman or degrading treatment or punishment.

The basic rights of privacy and respect are therefore not being adhered to in crowded cells and arguably, such conditions breach Article 3 of the European Convention on Human Rights (ECHR), which protects against torture, inhuman and degrading treatment or punishment. The Council of Europe for some time has recognised that crowding is a problem across Europe and in 1999 Committee Members adopted Recommendation No. R (99) 22, which contained advice and practical steps to reduce prison crowding. Nearly 20 years on, however, very little has changed (Council of Europe, 2016). The European Court of Human Rights (ECtHR) has consequentially had to consider whether crowding and prison conditions in general can amount to a breach of Article 3. In *Peers v Greece* (2001) 33 E.H.R.R. 51, for example, the ECtHR held that inadequate prison conditions could breach Article 3. The applicant had to spend a considerable part of each day practically confined to his bed in a cell with no ventilation and no window, and had to use the toilet in the presence of another inmate (and be present while the toilet was being used by his cellmate). Furthermore, in *Ananyev and Others v Russia* (nos. 42525/07 and 60800/08, 10 January 2012) the ECtHR set out a test for crowding in cells stating that 'each detainee must have at least 3 metres square of living space and the overall surface area of the cell must be such as to allow detainees to move freely between items of furniture' (Council of Europe, 2016, p. 9). In the particular case the ECtHR held Russia in breach of Article 3 because the applicants remained inside the cell for 23 hours a day, they had their meals and used sanitary facilities inside the cell in cramped conditions and one of them had been living in such conditions for over three years (Council of Europe, 2016). Other important factors to take into consideration are access to natural light, ventilation, air and privacy when using sanitary facilities. On the latter aspect in *Szafranski v Poland* (no. 17249/12, 15 December 2015) the ECtHR held that Poland had breached the applicants Article 8 right of privacy because of in-cell sanitation: 'a sanitary annex which is only partially separated off is not acceptable in a cell occupied by more than one detainee. The in-cell toilets should be provided with a full partition i.e. up to the ceiling' (para. 38). The applicant was awarded €1800. Using these cases to assess prison conditions in England and Wales would suggest that the UK Government are currently breaching both Articles 3 and 8 of the ECHR.

The government's answer to crowding is to build its way out of the problem. In March 2017 it announced plans to build four new large prisons to be sited in Port Talbot, South Wales; adjacent to HMP Full Sutton in Yorkshire; and redevelopment plans at HMP/YOI Rochester, Kent and HMP/YOI Hindley, Wigan, which would have added up to 10,000 modern prison places (Ministry of Justice, 2017b). The Prison Estate Transformation Programme has been beset by problems however; not least because local residents and businesses in many of these proposed sites objected to planning applications. In 2019, focus was taken away from these locations with the construction of a new prison on the site of HMP Wellingborough (which closed in 2012). The proposed prison will be a category C resettlement prison (see Chapter 7) with the capacity for 1680 people. Another new prison is planned for the place where HMP/YOI Glen Parva used to be and a new house block is to be built at HMP Stocken (Ministry of Justice, 2019a).

A building programme is not the only answer, however, with alternatives including letting out non-dangerous prisoners and/or reducing the number that are sent to prison in the first place:

> The easy answer to overcrowding is to build more prisons, but we cannot afford that. The other answer is to send fewer people to prison. Drug addicts should be rehabilitated outside prison; the mentally ill should be treated and helped within the health system. Prisons should be reserved for the dangerous, the violent and the depraved. The government has more to do than just dealing with Brexit and it should deal with our prisons urgently. (Garnier, 2017)

In Romania, for example, the government are currently considering the use of electronic monitoring in an attempt to overcome its prison crowding problem (Romania-insider.com, 2017) and Turkey has reportedly let out 38,000 ordinary criminals to free up prison space, albeit to refill it with coup plotters (France 24 International News, 2016). Northern Ireland are concentrating on using alternatives to custody and has been piloting an enhanced combination probation order of unpaid work and strict supervision which has shown a 40 per cent reduction in reoffending rates and is one tenth the cost of imprisonment (Fitzpatrick, 2017). Furthermore, in Rwanda, a more robust form of alternative sentencing has been seen which offers all offenders who have committed an offence punishable by imprisonment by up to five years, the alternative of spending time working six days a week in a work camp. Not only has this enabled a number of infrastructure projects to be completed at a fraction of the cost, it has enhanced skills and employment opportunities and has enabled the prisoners to pay back to society. Conditions in the camps have, however, been criticised but the payoff for the prisoners is that they spend far less time in detention and because of this many prefer this option (Allen, 2016).

Discussion Questions

1. How should the problem of crowding be solved?
2. Imagine sharing a small room (even with your closest family or friends) for up to 23 hours a day with non-private in-cell sanitation. Would you regard this as degrading?
3. Should the Ministry of Justice build its way out of the problem or should the money instead be used to provide more credible alternatives to custody?
4. What is your view of the work camps in Rwanda? Are these a credible alternative?

CONSTRUCTIVE ACTIVITIES AND TIME OUT OF CELL

Crowding on its own is not necessarily an issue. As identified by several of the prison staff spoken to for this book, many prisoners actually enjoy double bunking. Problems occur, however, when the level of crowding affects how prisoners are treated within the prison environment. Privacy as discussed above is one consequence with another being the availability of constructive activities and out of cell time. HMIP expectations are that prisoners should be unlocked for at least 10 hours a day. In 2017–18, however, HMIP reported that this was only being achieved on average with 16 per cent of adult male prisoners. In local prisons, the average dropped to 8 per cent and for young adults was as low as 4 per cent (HM Chief Inspector of Prisons, 2018a). In HMP Lewes (a local male prison) for example:

> [It is] currently a 21-hour-per-day bang-up. Cells open 1415–1730ish to include lunch in cell, association, phone calls, shower, and exercise. Not my turn for the gym today. All other classes – education, library, etc. – cancelled. (Smith, P., 2016)

One of the main ways in which prisoners escape the confines of their cells is through work or education, with examples of the different opportunities available in prison considered in the case studies in Chapter 7. The importance of prisoners engaging in purposeful activities is well known with benefits including preserving prisoner wellbeing (Leese, et al., 2006), aiding reform and rehabilitation and providing skills and experience to aid reintegration and reset-tlement on release (Scottish Parliament, 2013). In many prisons, however, and especially in local prisons, there are not enough placements. Moreover, even where opportunities do exist there are not always the requisite staff to escort the prisoners between the landings and workshops/classrooms. On the day of the visit to HMP/YOI Feltham, for example, the education block was closed because there was not enough staff to transport the young people around the prison. In 2016–17, there were on average 11,200 prisoners and detainees working in custody delivering approximately 16 million hours of work (Ministry of Justice, 2017a). In 2017–18, this had increased to 12,330 prisoners and 17 million hours of work (Ministry of Justice, 2018d). While, other prisoners will attend education and/or accredited treatment programmes and there is an increasing number of retired prisoners in prison, this still shows a vastly unemployed prison popula-tion. In 2017/18, for example, of the 39 adult male prisons inspected that year by HMIP, 18 (46%) did not have enough education, skills or work placements (HM Chief Inspector of Prisons, 2018a). In 2016, the European Committee for the Prevention of Torture and Inhuman or Degrading Treatment or Punishment visited the United Kingdom and noted:

> regimes in all prison establishments visited were inadequate, with a consider-able number of prisoners spending up to 22 hours per day locked up in their cells. Many inmates stated that the long lock-up times contributed to a sense of frustration. The [committee] recommends that steps be taken to ensure that inmates attend education and purposeful activities on a daily basis, with the aim that all inmates on a normal regime spend at least eight hours out-of-cell. (Council of Europe, 2017, p. 9)

Discussion Questions

1. Is it sufficient that HMPPS hold people securely or should they also have a duty to provide constructive activities and sufficient out of cell time?
2. Returning to the idea of designing your own prison, what would the prison regime be like? Would you have any minimum criteria in terms of respecting dignity and human rights?

DRUGS AND CONTRABAND

Arguably, due to boredom and long periods spent locked up, there has been a sharp increase in the use of drugs, particularly new psychoactive substances. The drug economy in prisons has therefore changed, moving from 'hard' drugs to psychoactive substances. The use of Spice, for example, has been on the increase since 2014 with it becoming illegal in 2016 (Psychoactive Substances Act 2016). Spice, a synthetic form of marijuana, is more dangerous and addictive than its natural form, causing seizures and psychotic symptoms such as hallucinations, panic attacks, aggression and paranoia. Longer-term effects include damage to the heart and kidneys (Ayer, 2017). The increase in the use of Spice can be correlated to a rise in violence but it has also been linked to organised crime, debt (which can lead to further rises in violence) and an increase in medical emergencies.

One of the issues for HMPPS, therefore, is to stop the flow of drugs into prisons, although this is problematic when it is not always clear how they are getting in. Common methods include packages dropped over prison walls, drones delivering to cell windows, and smuggling by visitors, inmates and prison staff. Recognising that prison staff do contribute to the problem, one initiative has been the introduction of the Counter Corruption Unit, which is working to reduce the amount of drugs and contraband brought into prison by prison staff (Ministry of Justice, 2019c). Another mechanism is the use of drug dogs, which predominantly targets drugs being brought in on social visits. Dogs used to be allocated to individual prisons although now are provided on a regional basis. In August 2017, there were 300 trained drug dogs across the prison estate (Liddington, 2017a). This change of organisation may be viewed positively as sickness can be managed better but it does mean that dogs are not always available at every prison. One governor for example stated how he thought that some of the social visitors to the prison would check to see whether the drug dogs were there before deciding whether to come in. Some prisons also have expensive technology, with HMP Wandsworth, for example having a £1 million body scanner, which is used to check all prisoners on reception for drugs and other forms of contraband. Other methods of disruption can be more subtle. One senior staff member explained how they had improved the food in the staff canteen in an attempt to keep officers on site all day so as to reduce the flow of officers coming in and out of the jail, while another had spent some of their budget on a quad bike which was used to patrol the perimeter fence. Even with such measures in place drugs are still getting in, with it generally accepted that it is impossible to completely stop the flow. When drugs in prison are worth up to ten times more than on the outside, gangs will risk losing eight out of ten packages knowing that if they manage to get two inside undetected, they are still making a profit.

Other detection methods include random mandatory drug testing (RMDT), with the aim being to test between 5 and 10 per cent of prisoners in each prison, each month. Failure of the test can lead to time added on to the prisoner's custodial term (Ministry of Justice, 2017a). Considering the widespread problem of drugs, it is perhaps surprising that in 2017–18 only 10.6 per cent of RMDTs were positive. However, when new psychoactive substances are also included, the rate increases to 20.4 per cent (Ministry of Justice, 2018d). Furthermore, in May 2017, Les Nicolles prison on Guernsey became the first prison in the world to install an anti-drone device (Sky Fence), which effectively puts a 600 metre shield around the prison to deflect and detect drones and this maybe something which we should consider (*The Telegraph*, 2017).

In addition to drugs, prisons also have to deal with the influx of other forms of contraband such as mobile phones and SIM cards. The fact that phones are now Internet enabled creates a whole new set of problems, because prisoners can now use them to make and demand financial transactions. Other uses include social media, the 'dark' web and crypto-currencies (Gooch & Treadwell, 2019). In 2015, nearly 17,000 mobile phones and SIM cards were found in prisons across England and Wales, a 243 per cent increase from 2013. All prisons have hand-held mobile detectors (Liddington, 2017a), but even these are not solving the problem. Having telephones in each cell may go some way to reduce illegal phones, although even if this did occur some prisoners would still want to have unmonitored conversations.

Discussion Questions

1. Why do you think that there has been such a sharp increase in drug use in prisons over the last few years?
2. What does HMPPS need to do in order to reduce the use and impact of Spice?

SAFETY

Self-inflicted deaths and self-harm

The rise in drug use, frustrations caused by inadequate living conditions and the unavailability of constructive activities in some prisons, has contributed to a sharp deterioration in prison safety. The Prison Reform Trust argues, 'people in prison, prisoners and staff, are less safe than they have been at any other point, with more self-inflicted deaths, self-harm and assaults than ever before' (Prison Reform Trust, 2018c, p. 4). In the year to March 2019, there were 317 deaths in prison: 87 self-inflicted and 3 homicides (National Statistics and Ministry of Justice, 2019a). Levels of self-harm in prison are also unacceptably high as evidenced in Figure 8.2 and have particularly increased over the last few years. For example, for the year ending December 2018, there were 55,598 self-harm incidents involving 12,570 prisoners (National Statistics and Ministry of Justice, 2019a). Self-harm has always been a problem in women's prisons (see Chapter 12), but what is striking in recent years is the change in self-harm rates in men.

Due to these concerning statistics it is imperative that we discover why these increases are taking place and whether any correlations can be found with things such as prison function, security level, drug use or any of the other issues mentioned here. One evaluation, which tried to do this was the Harris Review, which in 2015 focused on the high rates of suicide in relation to 18–24 year olds held in custody (Harris, 2015). While the Review acknowledged there were no easy answers, it felt that significant factors which contributed to the risk of young adults committing suicide included the harsh environment of the prison, too few constructive activities, unsafe cell conditions, bullying and being locked in their cells for too long periods of time (Harris, 2015). Another study has looked at whether there is a link between prison crowding and suicide rates, with the premise for the research being that crowded prisons tend to have higher suicide rates than those operating at, or

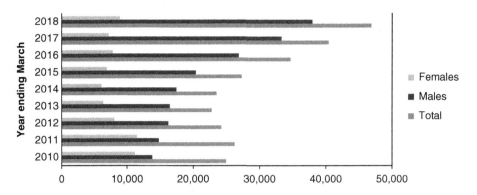

Figure 8.2 Incidents of self-harm in prison

Source: National Statistics and Ministry of Justice (2019a). *Safety in Custody Statistics Bulletin, England and Wales, Deaths in prison custody to March 2019, Assualts and Self-Harm to December 2019.* London: Ministry of Justice.

below, their CNA (van Ginneken, et al., 2017). The research, which looked at suicide rates in prisons between 2000 and 2014 in England and Wales, found that crowding on its own could not be correlated to higher suicide rates. Prison characteristics which could be however included 'a larger population size, public management of a prison, higher security category, a male population and high [prisoner] turnover' (van Ginneken, et al., 2017, p. 80). A wider study looked at prison suicide rates between 2011 and 2014 in 24 countries, including Europe, Australasia and North America, but came to no real conclusion as to what was causing such high rates:

> Most of the examined prison-level factors were not associated with prison sui-
> cide rates, suggesting that prison suicides are likely to be the result of a complex
> interaction of different factors, and not merely due to the prison environment.
> Nevertheless ... there are replicable associations with ethnicity, sentence length,
> self-harm, and a number of clinical factors. (Fazel, et al., 2017, p. 951)

Further suicide risk factors found in custodial settings include prison officer short-ages, which have contributed to a deterioration in the support that prisoner offic-ers are now able to provide (IIoward League for Penal Reform, 2016b). This isn't to say that prison staff don't work effectively with vulnerable prisoners, but just that they do not have the time and in some cases the necessary training to work with all of those in need. Other aspects of prison life that can impact on vulnerability to suicide and self-harm additionally include isolation, boredom, initial entry into prison (and release), loss of liberty and control and feeling unsafe (Howard League for Penal Reform, 2016b). HMIP also add mental health problems, bullying, debt and the rise of Spice (HM Chief Inspector of Prisons, 2017a). When staffing is at appropriate levels, both in terms of numbers and experience, such vulnerabilities can be managed but, prison officers no longer have the freedom to spend time talking to prisoners getting to know them and understanding their vulnerabilities

(Howard League for Penal Reform, 2016b). Officers are rather rushing from one crisis to another meaning that they can no longer prevent situations but only deal with them when they occur.

Perhaps due to this lack of clarity behind what the risk factors are for suicides and self-harm in custodial institutions, one recent study has looked at the experiences of male prisoners who had ceased from self-harming, hoping that this can provide clearer answers (Fitzalan Howard & Pope, 2019). Although small in scale, the research suggests that key points of consideration include the men 'feeling as though they matter and are cared for', 'developing trusting relationships' and 'having an accurate understanding of the complex reasons for their harming' and importantly 'prison staff having a good understanding of these reasons' (Fitzalan Howard & Pope, 2019, p. 1). All factors which require appropriate staffing levels.

Levels of violence

In addition to high levels of self-harm, incidences of violence perpetrated against others is also on the rise. For the year ending December 2018 there were 34,223 assault incidents, an increase of 16 per cent from the previous year, of which 3918 (11%) were considered serious (i.e. was sexual, required hospital detention, required medical treatment for internal injuries or concussion, or caused: fracture, scald/burn, stabbing, crushing, extensive bruising, broken nose, black eye, broken tooth, deep cuts, bites or temporary/permanent blinding) (National Statistics and Ministry of Justice, 2019a, p. 8). Since March 2013, serious assaults have almost trebled (National Statistics and Ministry of Justice, 2019a) with assaults on staff increasing by 88 per cent (Prison Reform Trust, 2018c). In the year ending December 2018 30 per cent of all assaults were against staff with the percentage being higher in female establishments (38 per cent) than in male (29 per cent) (National Statistics and Ministry of Justice, 2019a).

HMIP attribute much of this increase in violence to drugs and associated debt but prisoners also reported that it was due to frustration caused by unpredictable and restricted regimes (HM Chief Inspector of Prisons, 2017a). Having a predictable regime was the reason why HMP Wandsworth stopped free flow on some of its wings, although this has exacerbated rather than prevented prisoner frustrations. Also of concern to HMIP is the fact that in 2016–17, they found very few positive interventions with violent prisoners: 'prisons relied heavily on punitive measures through the incentives and earned privileges scheme and adjudication process' (HM Chief Inspector of Prisons, 2017a, p. 24), further exacerbating tensions and prison officer/prisoner relationships.

It is well known that prisons are emotionally charged and volatile places (James, 2003) and that especially in male establishments, some prisoners will construct themselves as hyper masculine so as to blend in. Moreover, in order to negotiate an acceptable position in the prison hierarchy, some prisoners will put "on excessive displays of manliness, constructing a public identity that allows them to 'fit in' with the dominant culture" (Jewkes, 2005, p. 46). As the dominant culture over recent years has seen a rise in violence, arguably some prisoners are acting more violently so as to conform and make surviving their sentence easier. Linked to this is Goffman's idea of prison life being a performance, with 'frontstage' and 'backstage' behaviour. Acting on the frontstage requires behaviour which conforms to, as mentioned above, the dominant culture. It is only in private (backstage behaviour), where an individual's guard can be dropped (Goffman, 1959). Crewe and colleagues take this further, arguing that while some prisoners will put on 'masks ... of masculine bravado' (Crewe, et al., 2014, p. 56) these are removable, with many prisoners behaving differently depending on which 'emotion zone' (Crewe, et al., 2014, p. 57) they are within. In a study carried out in HMP Wellingborough, it was found that masks of masculinity were more likely to be used in the residential wings and prison workshops, with some prisoners stating that they 'were only able to relax and release their feelings when in their cells, listening to music or watching television' (Crewe, et al., 2014, p. 65). While this accords with Goffman (1959), the study also found that masks could additionally be dropped in visits rooms, educational activities and the prison chapel. Such environments were seen as 'less prison like' where prisoners were treated as students or worshippers and where 'personnel created places where the fundamentals of power, liberty and authority could, for brief periods, be put aside' (Crewe, et al., 2014, p. 69).

The emotions of prisoners, and more importantly the way in which prisoners control these emotions, is potentially fundamental if we want to address and consequentially reduce current levels of violence in the custodial estate. Laws (2014), for examples talks about how prisoners simultaneously use masks to hide or supress their emotions while also seeking out other avenues of 'emotional ventilation' (Laws, 2014, p. 26). In terms of suppressing feelings, prisoners at HMP Moorland reported how they were able to either consciously stop thinking about something or could rationalise or work through an event so as to reduce potential anger and conflict. In many situations, seeking out distractions through activities or routines was how this masking was achieved (Laws, 2014). Others used activities, such as physical activity, creative writing or music to release pent up frustrations, which otherwise may have manifested themselves in violent behaviour. Of concern, two participants explained how they used self-harm to release tension (Laws, 2014) (see also Laws & Crewe, 2016). Notable in all of this research is the need for constructive activities and the ability to have reasonable out of cell time. Coupled with the presence of supportive prison staff, it is perhaps these three factors which have the biggest influence on rates of violence in penal institutions.

Discipline and control

Due to such high levels of violence within the prison estate and without the available resources to reduce it (such as ensuring reasonable out of cell time, purposeful activities and proper pastoral care), prison officers are having to resort to a number of measures in order to maintain discipline and control, with this often involving force and/or segregation. The use of force is regulated by Prison Rules 6 and 47, with Prison Rule 45 concerned with segregation. This states that a person can be removed from association (the main prison landings) 'for the maintenance of good order or discipline', but this needs to be approved by an Independent Monitoring Board (IMB) member. Each prison will have its own IMB made up of independent, unpaid, members of the public, who work to ensure that proper standards of care and decency are maintained (Independent Monitoring Board, 2017a). They will visit the prison regularly to ensure that day-to-day life is as positive as it can be and are on call in situations of emergency (such as a riot or a death in custody) so that they can witness how the prison deals with it. Segregation can only last for one month, although can be renewed on a month-by-month basis. Under Prison Rule 48, violent prisoners can be temporarily confined in special cells for an initial period of 24 hours, although again this can be extended. Three types of special cell exist:

- Stripped cells: unfurnished with only a mattress.
- Special cells: sound proofing, a double door and furniture which cannot cause injury.
- Protected cells: soundproofing, a double door, no furniture and padded walls (Loucks, 2000).

Prison Rule 49 also allows for the restraint of prisoners where this is deemed 'necessary to prevent the prisoner from injuring himself or others, damaging property or creating a disturbance'.

Force, as a measure of discipline and control is available to all prison personnel with officers receiving training in control and restraint methods on employment. In response to the almost regular occurrence of prison riots, HMPPS also have specialist Tornado units, made up of prison officers who receive an additional five days of advanced control and restraint training. Each prison governor must ensure that they have sufficient numbers of Tornado trained staff, although in major incidents prisons will deploy staff from neighbouring establishments. Equipment issued to a Tornado trained officer will include: riot helmet, flame retardant overalls, side arm baton and holder, shin guards, elbow protectors, flame retardant balaclava and shield (HM Prison Service, 2005).

In 2017, HMIP found high levels of force in two thirds of the prisons it inspected, coupled with significant gaps in its governance (HM Chief Inspector of Prisons, 2017a). Concerns were also expressed about the overuse of segregation, with HMP Full Sutton picked out as one example:

> For many segregated prisoners, care planning was inadequate and too many remained segregated for long periods. The regime was impoverished for long-stay prisoners, with little in place to help prevent psychological deterioration caused by prolonged segregation. (HM Chief Inspector of Prisons, 2017a, p. 26)

Concerns about the overuse of segregation/solitary confinement are not new. In Chapter 7, it was noted how the separate system was abolished partly due to deteriorations in offender's mental health with this concern still apparent today. The Istanbul Statement on the use and effects of solitary confinement defines solitary confinement as the physical isolation of individuals who are confined to their cells for 22–24 hours a day and on this basis many prisoners held in single cells across local prisons in England and Wales are currently held in solitary conditions. Conditions associated with solitary confinement include paranoia, visual and auditory hallucinations, self-mutilation, suicidal thoughts, debilitating depression, anger, bitterness, boredom, stress, loss of a sense of reality, impaired concentration and fantasy of revenge (Harrison & Tamony, 2010). O'Donnell (2014) explains how solitary conditions often results in lethargy, injustice, passivity and disintegration. Haney additionally describes how some prisoners actually become uncomfortable with small periods of liberty, being too accustomed to an environment where everything is organised for them. In other cases, prisoners act out in order to feel alive, filling their idleness with plans of attack against prison officers and officials (Haney, 2009) (For a personal account of incarceration in solitary conditions see Ambort, 2018).

Another way in which prisoners can be 'punished' is through the incentive and earned privilege (IEP) scheme. Introduced in 1995, the aim is that prisoners can earn and lose privileges depending on their general behaviour and participation in work and/or constructive activity. The scheme operates on four levels: basic, entry, standard and enhanced. When an individual comes into the prison, they will be placed on the entry privilege level, with a review of behaviour taken after 14 days. This will determine which level they are then assigned. Key earnable privileges include:

- extra and improved visits (better surroundings for enhanced prisoners);
- access to in-cell television (entry and above);
- access to games consoles (enhanced);
- opportunity to wear own clothes (standard and enhanced);
- time out of cell for association;
- eligibility to earn higher rates of pay (standard and enhanced); and,
- access to private cash.

Establishments can also provide other privileges depending on the local circumstances and facilities. For example, one of the prisons visited used to incentivise good behaviour by allowing prisoners' access to Sky Sports at the weekend, although the practice was stopped when the media published negative reports about it.

Due to the restrictive nature of the basic regime, all prisons have to keep a record of how many basic prisoners it has, with the number of prisoners on basic continuing to rise. When visited, 12 per cent of the prison population at HMP Lindholme were on basic, largely due to the use of illicit drugs. At HMP Wandsworth, this was lower at only 5 per cent. While it is unclear why this rise has occurred it does mirror the rise in Spice use and violence recently seen in the majority of prisons. HMIP further argue that too often prisons view the IEP scheme as a way to punish rather than to reward prisoners, with the numbers of basic prisoners at HMP Risely trebling since its last inspection. Also of concern was that at HMP Swinfen Hall, prisoners on basic were not allowed out of their cell often enough to allow them to demonstrate that their behaviour levels had actually improved (HM Chief Inspector of Prisons, 2017a).

A study conducted by Scott (2011) also identified how the IEP scheme was a way in which prisoner deference could be established:

Prisoners had to deserve, or earn the right, to be treated humanely. As one officer put it, additional 'rights' could be given to those prisoners who demonstrate that they accept their subjugated position or occasionally for those prisoners who were in trouble, such as 'giving an extra phone call for a prisoner experiencing a family crisis'. Those prisoners who resist or 'try to abuse the system' should have only the most limited of entitlements. (Scott, 2011, p. 9)

Officers commonly referred to the IEP scheme as a game of snakes and ladders, with it thought to work best 'when considered as a means of disciplining prisoners' (Scott, 2011, p. 9). In the first national evaluation of the IEP scheme in 1999, vast differences were found between the ways in which different prison establishments and different prison wings within the same establishments were implementing it. Where good prison officer/prisoner relationships existed, there was minimal use of the scheme as a punitive measure. However, where the opposite was true in terms of relationships, several prisoners had been downgraded to the basic regime, often without sufficient warning (Liebling, 1999). Unsurprisingly, 'On the wing with poor staff–prisoner relationships and a high resort to formal sanctions, a major disturbance followed' (Liebling, 2000, p. 337). Positive and supportive prisoner officer/prisoner relationships, are once again cited as being key.

Discussion Questions

1. What needs to change so that prisons are safer for both staff and inmates? In October 2017, the use of body-worn cameras, police style handcuffs and incapacitant (pepper) spray was announced. Will this make a difference?
2. Should prisons use the IEP scheme to reward good behaviour or to maintain good order and discipline? Can it be used for both?
3. In the design of your prison, how would you ensure that it was a safe and decent institution?

STAFFING

Many of the problems cited above are caused by inadequate staffing levels, with this making 'it impossible to provide a decent, rehabilitative environment' (HM Chief Inspector of Prisons, 2017a, p. 8). The government's response has been to increase staffing, i.e. to effectively undo the benchmarking process detailed in Chapter 7, although this will not reverse the loss of experience that HMPPS has also suffered. In 2016, using a new offender management model, the government promised 2500 extra band 3–5 prison officer jobs. It stated that each prison would have 'new dedicated officers, each responsible for supervising and supporting around six offenders, [who] will make sure prisoners get the help they need to quit drugs and get the skills they need to turn their lives around' (Ministry of Justice, 2016c, p. 7). This was to happen on a national basis with full implementation expected by 2018. In HMP Lindholme, for example, the number of 'white shirt' officers was set to increase from 164 to 204, which the governor stated would allow significant improvements in safety and prisoner/staff relationships. Ten pathfinder prisons were given extra staffing first, with HMP Leeds and HMP Moorland receiving nearly 60 and 40 more staff respectively. Such recruitment however, must be considered in light of the numbers leaving HMPPS and in the early days of officer recruitment this was negligible (see Figure 8.3). In the year

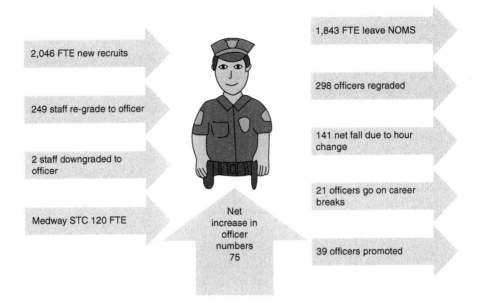

Figure 8.3 Movements into and out of band 3–5 prison officer jobs March 2016–March 2017
Source: Ministry of Justice (2017i) *NOMS Annual Workforce Statistics Bulletin 31 March 2017*. London: Ministry of Justice

ending June 2018, however, there was a net gain of 2,853 band 3–5 officers, with this being the highest number of officers in post since January 2013. Emphasising the point about experience however, 37.8 per cent of all band 3–5 officers had less than three years' experience (Ministry of Justice, 2018f).

While this increase in officer numbers is encouraging, one problem identified during the prison visits was the reduced pool of people who want to work in prisons. One senior officer in particular, commented on how he was unable to fill vacant posts and had been at the job centre the previous morning promoting the benefits of working for HMPPS. The main problem was that there were competing employers nearby who were offering similar amounts of money but opportunities in a less stressful and safer working environment. This was seen as less of a problem in the North of England, but with a starting salary of between £22,751 and £23,052, this was not competitive in the South.

Discussion Questions

1. Do you think that increasing staff numbers will solve the issues that many prisons currently face or are things much more complicated than that?
2. In the design of your prison what prison officer/prisoner ratios do you intend to have and how will you ensure positive relationships between prisoners and staff?

THE PRISON OFFICER EXPERIENCE

In a chapter concentrating on the prison experience, it is also important to include the experiences of prison staff. While it is accepted that all operational staff (including governors and managers) experience prison life, band 3–5 officers are focused on here, as they are the ones who operate the landings and are, as one officer remarked 'banged up in the same way as the men'. During the course of the prison visits, a number of wing officers were spoken to, both formally and informally. Most lamented about deteriorating conditions, the rise in violence and the fear that loved ones had that they may go to work one day and not return. One officer in particular spoke about the loss of 'prison craft' a term that was used to describe the experience, which had previously existed on the wing and the way in which colleagues, would interact with the prisoners. As discussed in Chapter 7, because of benchmarking, this prison craft had been lost. When this officer joined the service they were able to learn from the wealth of experience around them but now the wings were manned by less than half the number of officers with very few having more than two or three years' experience. Another officer stated that they often tried to get to the gym at lunchtime to get out of the prison environment, while another went further and explained how they had created an all-weather patio in their garden, as they needed to spend time outside when they were at home, due to the enclosed environment in which they worked. One described the situation as 'my own life sentence'.

All of these accounts describe the impact of prison life on officers with this often described as emotional labour (Crawley, 2004). In the same way that prisoners put on masks (Crewe, et al., 2014) (see above), prison officers must also 'play parts and stage manage their actions' (Crawley, 2004, p. 414) so as to control the impression of themselves that they are portraying both to prisoners and other officers. As detailed above, prisons are emotionally charged places and for officers working on landings they are working in highly pressurised environments, often spending significant periods of time with the same inmates 'many of whom will have suffered a variety of personal traumas, difficulties and disappointments during their sentence' (Crawley, 2004, p. 414). Such tensions can be further exacerbated when mental health problems and long-term imprisonment are added into the mix. Crawley also notes how officers,

> were fearful of certain prisoners, that they were jealous of colleagues who were able to do 'quality work' while they pounded the landings, that they were disappointed that their prison had 'gone downhill', that they were frustrated by their managers ... that they were bewildered (and disgusted) that some of their fellow officers actually wanted to work with sex offenders (some of whom had committed the most heinous offences against children) and that they were bored working on a wing that was 'more like an old folks' home than a prison' because it was inhabited by elderly prisoners. (Crawley, 2004, p. 414)

Due to this highly charged environment, it is therefore imperative that prison officers (like prisoners) are able to control their emotions, with going to the gym at lunchtime and spending time outdoors examples of this management. Other

Population	32,714,752 (Worldometers, 2019g)
Prison population (including remand prisoners)	57,096 plus another 32,000 in police jails (Institute for Criminal Policy Research, 2019e)
Prison population per 100,000 of national population	178 (Institute for Criminal Policy Research, 2019e)
Remand prisoners	35,970 (63%) (Institute for Criminal Policy Research, 2019e)
Number of establishments	58 (Institute for Criminal Policy Research, 2019e)
Official capacity of prison service	35,562 (Institute for Criminal Policy Research, 2019e)
Occupancy level	153.9% (Institute for Criminal Policy Research, 2019e)

Brief Profile

Venezuela is a Spanish-speaking South American country bordering Colombia, Brazil, and Guyana. It is the thirty-third largest country in the world and is home to the highest uninterrupted waterfall – Angel Falls. Governed by a President and consisting of 23 states, it is one of the most urbanized countries in Latin America with the vast majority of the population either living in its capital, Caracas, or in the North. The country has the world's largest oil reserves but has been in economic crisis since the 1980s.

Prison Conditions

In 2016, prison conditions in Venezuela were described as 'life threatening' (United States Department of State, 2016, p. 5) and 'seriously overcrowded' (Amnesty International, 2017, p. 395). Prison capacity was thought to be as high as 190 per cent in the first six months of the year, with pre-trial detention facilities depicted as 'critical' (Amnesty International, 2017, p. 395). Such problems were thought to be due to insufficient numbers of staff, many of whom were inexperienced and undertrained. The Venezuelan Observatory for Prison (OVP), a non-governmental agency that monitors compliance and respect for human rights, estimated a 90 per cent staffing gap in prison personnel, with one guard for every 100 inmates. Other issues related to weak security, inadequate medical care, corrupt staff, shortages of food and water and armed gangs within the prison (United States Department of State, 2016).

Inmate Governance

Due to staff shortages and material deprivations, some Venezuelan prisons are being controlled by armed inmates. Known as inmate governance, this is the substitute of 'prison administrators in the task of maintaining order and regulating life [with] the replacement of informal, inmate-controlled structures and practices' (Antillano, 2017). The practice is relatively prevalent across Latin America (see Darke & Garces, 2017), with it being distinguishable from prison gangs. While the presence of prison gangs may, precede inmate governance, the latter offers a complete and often exclusive level of control over the prison. While control is initially secured through violence and disorder, a set of rules 'la rutina' (Antillano, 2017, p. 27) will subsequently govern every aspect of prison life, with infractions punished severely. Cooperation with the State is also punished (Antillano, 2017).

The 'El Carro' (Antillano, 2017, p. 28), armed prisoners, will decide on issues such as resource management, food distribution, cell and bed allocation, the imposition of penalties, the regulation of visits and will conduct negotiations with the State. In this way, it serves the same function as the State in the sense that it maintains internal order. The 'poblacion' (Antillano, 2017, p. 28), the remaining prisoners, must abide by the rules of the Carro or face punishment, although prisoners tend to comply not just out of fear but also because the Carro offer a better form of governance (Antillano, 2017). This is funded through the *causa* (Antillano, 2017, p. 28) a tax that must be paid weekly by the prisoners. The Carro also secure money from providing goods and services, which the State was previously unable to supply (Antillano, 2017) and in this way is able to fund automatic rifles, pistols and high-calibre revolvers.

In 2013, Time Magazine claimed that Wilmer Brizuela, a convicted murderer and kidnapper was the leader of Vista Hermosa, one of Venezuela's most dangerous prisons. He and his gang took control of the prison in 2005, when governmental authorities were unable to control overcrowding and rising violence. While drug use and violence is problematic, Brizuela claimed that conditions were better than under state control as drugs were more tightly controlled. He argued that his Carro had 'achieved peace and a minimum of decent human living standards' (Benezra, 2013). Experiences are not always positive however. In October 2016, four mass graves were found at the Venezuelan General Prison holding the bodies of inmates who had not paid the leader of the prison their causa. (Prison Insider, 2015).

In response to inmate governance, the Ministry of Popular Power for Correctional Services announced a new prison regime in 2013 in an attempt to regain control of the country's prisons. In prisons where the new regime has been implemented, prisoners are subject to corporal punishment and prolonged solitary confinement. Women at Uribana prison, for example, have experienced tear gas and had their heads shaved when in solitary confinement (Prison Insider, 2015). Where the new regime is in force, inmates are assigned different coloured uniforms based on prisoner status. Untried wear blue, sentenced yellow and women fuchsia. The regime has not however been implemented across all prisons and carceral self-rule still largely exists (Prison Insider, 2015).

Discussion Questions

1. Are there any similarities in prison conditions in Venezuela and England and Wales?
2. What do you think to the idea of inmate governance in Venezuela?
3. In a different and more accountable form, would this be something you might consider in the design of your prison?

officers spoke about the importance of prison humour which was said to help the day along, a coping strategy mentioned by Crawley (2004) in addition to becoming emotionally detached from situations, which was also seen as a mechanism to avoid prisoner manipulation. If an officer cannot find a way in which their emotions can be released and managed it is likely that they will leave the service, with one governor in the study noting a high correlation between violent incidents and staff resignations in their prison. Other factors which relate to 'burn-out' include overload, low social status of occupation, poor social relationships at work and role characteristics (Cieslak, et al., 2008).

Discussion Questions

1.   The benchmarking process is attributed with causing many of the problems covered in this chapter. Are there any other issues, which have contributed to overcrowding, lack of safety and an increase in the use of contraband?
2.   What qualities do you think are needed in a good prison officer?
3.   What training would you want to provide the officers in your prison?

THE VISITOR EXPERIENCE

The final category of people commented on here are visitors. The very essence of imprisonment means that prisoners are restricted in their contact with family and friends. In recognition of this, and to preserve a prisoners' right to family life under Article 8 of the ECHR, Prison Rules 'require prisons to actively encourage prisoners to maintain outside contacts and meaningful family ties' (National Offender Management Service, 2016, p. 2). The benefits of family contact are thought to include an incentive not to reoffend, help with employment and accommodation on release, and, on the proviso that the visit is a positive experience, it can assist in maintaining good order. Convicted prisoners are allowed at least two one-hour visits every four weeks (National Offender Management Service, 2016), with prisoners often putting these together to save on family travel. Enhanced prisoners normally receive more visits than those on basic and standard. Unconvicted or remand prisoners are given at least three one-hour visits each week. Each prisoner is allowed a maximum of three adults and their accompanying children (National Offender Management Service, 2016). If a prisoner wants visitors then they have to request and then send out visiting orders to those whom they want to see. If the prisoner does not have anyone to visit, they can apply for a visit from an Official Prison Visitor (see www.naopv.com). These are independent volunteers who are appointed by prison governors to visit and offer friendship.

The experience of a prison visit will often begin with trying to book it. All prisons should have booking lines although in the past these have received a fair amount of criticism in terms of not being adequately staffed and visitors being unable to get through (Light & Campbell, 2007). Part of the reason for the installation of in-cell technology is therefore so that these booking lines can be eradicated and that prisoners can book visits online while speaking to their family/ friends. Sufficient visit space and when sessions are available can also be problematic, especially if visitors work and/or live vast distances from the prison establishment. While some prisons offer visits every days others limit the amount of days on which visits can occur; with weekend sessions often booked weeks in advance (HM Inspectorate of Prisons, 2016a).

On arrival at the prison, most prisons will have a visitors' centre, many of which are manned by charities. Of the centres visited for this book, most were airy, bright, operated by friendly and efficient staff, with play and care facilities for children and lockers for visitors to leave their personal possessions. Most were situated outside of the main prison gate. It is generally accepted that prison visitors' centres play a valuable role in supporting the families of prisoners and can also improve the experience of social visits. They tend to offer several types of support, including bureaucratic support (facilitating the necessary paperwork), functional support (providing shelter, food and drink) and stress-reducing support (Woodall, et al., 2009). Visitors' Centres have also been seen as integral in supporting children who make prison visits (Barnardo's, 2014).

Once booked in, visitors are escorted into the prison and will have to undergo a number of security checks, with the intensity of these depending on the security category of the prison. In HMP Full Sutton, for example, X-ray machines as seen in airports were used, while at HMP Parc it was a bag search and external pat down. Drugs dogs are also sometimes used. Each prison has a designated visits area with examples of the facilities outlined in the case studies in Chapter 7. The decor and general environment, including the furniture should be in a good and decent condition (National Offender Management Service, 2016) and certainly, this was what was witnessed at those prisons visited. Even where other parts of the prison were deteriorating and unfit for purpose, the visits area appeared to be functional, clean and in most cases attractive.

Aside from facilities, information and friendly staff, prison visits can however be problematic and bittersweet experiences (Codd, 2008), with 'some prisons more survivable than others' (Liebling, 2011, p. 550). This diversity in prison experience is also reported by Hutton (2016) who looked at the visiting experience of two prisons, one of which was HMP Doncaster. Problems witnessed in both prisons related to the three key areas of security and surveillance, restrictions on movement and restrictions on physical contact. In terms of security, while visitors understood the need for searches prior to entering the visits hall, many were then resentful at being watched and sometimes listened to during the actual visit. They felt that they were all being treated as potential drug smugglers and that this feeling of distrust affected the visit experience (Hutton, 2016). Comfort describes this as secondary prisonisation, where family members are made to feel like prisoners rather than as free citizens (Comfort, 2007).

Perhaps more damaging, however, is that prisoners must sit in their chair at all times. So while the visits area may have a plethora of play facilities, the prisoner is not actually allowed to accompany their child when they are using them, a situation which can be upsetting and frustrating for all (Hutton, 2016). This may explain why, in many of the visit halls visited, there were good play facilities, but very few were being used. Relationships with adults were also affected with spouses stating that they did not see why they were not allowed to sit next to their partners, especially when everyone had gone through prior searches and security checks. This also extended to restrictions placed on physical contact. While this was not problematic for parents or siblings, romantic partners were more concerned: when a partner was having a bad day, they could not even comfort them with a hug (Hutton, 2016). Some of these problems can be overcome through family days where there is more free flow of movement and children are given more opportunities to engage with their parents. HMP Doncaster, for example, additionally had weekly toddler days, homework clubs, daddy newborn visits, play projects and a social kitchen when children could cook and eat with their father (Hutton, 2016). HMP Parc, as evidenced in Chapter 7, also run a number of positive family interventions and despite the criticism levied at private prisons, it is acknowledged that HMP Parc and HMP Doncaster are run by G4S and Serco respectively. In the other prison assessed by Hutton (2016), she saw evidence of disrespect and mistrust between prison officers and social visitors. Legal visitors were often ushered to the front of queues and social visitors made to wait while prison staff finished their cigarette break (Hutton, 2016).

Discussion Questions

1. What provision should be made for prisoners' families and how should prisons ensure that family contact is maintained?
2. How do you balance the needs of security and respect for social visitors?
3. In your prison, how would you improve the current experience of social visits?

CONCLUSION

The lived experience of being in prison in England and Wales at this current time is, as described by one prisoner, no trip to a holiday park (Smith, P., 2016). With increases in violence, self-harm, suicide, drug usage and time spent in crowded cells, it is unsurprising that prison disturbances are so common. Staffing numbers are slowly improving, but it will take many more years before the prison craft that benchmarking helped to deteriorate is replaced and prison officer/prisoner relationships see a marked improvement. In my view, the government has two choices. Either it can continue to receive more and more urgent notification letters or it can make a concerted effort to change the prison experience. To do this, it has to release those prisoners who do not need to be imprisoned. Detaining low-level, low-risk offenders in this type of environment only has the potential to make them worse. If this does occur then not only is the state prioritising the punishment of offenders above all other sentencing principles but, it is doing so to the detriment of society and at great risk to the safety of many prison officers. Emphasising the points made throughout this chapter three key areas of focus are more supportive prison officer/prisoner relationships, more time out of cell and allowing inmates to engage in positive and constructive activities.

Now read:

Crewe, B. and Bennett, J. (2011) *The Prisoner*. London: Routledge. This provides first-hand accounts of the prison experience.

Scott, D. (2017) *Against Imprisonment. An Anthology of Abolitionist Essays*. Hook: Waterside Press.

The Butler Trust (2019) *The Good Book of Prisons*, available at: http://www.goodbookofprisons.com/. It is easy to be negative about the prison estate so this is worth a look as it focuses on the positive aspects of prisons.

Prison Bag: this is a blog written by the wife of a prisoner, available at: http://prisonbag.com/?p=684

Now watch:

Everyday, 21:00 15/11/2012, Channel 4, 110 mins. https://learning onscreen.ac.uk/ondemand/index.php/prog/02DBEA84?bcast=91722796 (Accessed 04 May 2019). This is a drama about a man in prison separated from his four children and wife.

Prison, My Parents and Me (2016) available at: https://realstories.pixel.video/watch/30523121

Van Buren, D. (2017) What a World without prisons could look like. TED Talk available at: https://www.ted.com/talks/deanna_van_buren_what_a_world_without_prisons_could_look_like?language=en

Now consider:

Read a HMIP inspection report. You may choose your local prison or one whose function you are particularly interested in (recent reports can be accessed at: http://www.justiceinspectorates.gov.uk/hmiprisons/inspections/). Consider what improvements could be made, and how you would go about making such changes if this was your prison. You may want to do this exercise in groups so that you can compare your thoughts with each other.

9 Release, Recall and Reintegration

INTRODUCTION

At any one time, there are more than 80,000 men, women and children held within custodial institutions in England and Wales. Except for a small minority, that is those serving whole life tariffs (see Chapter 4), these individuals will one day be released into the community. For the majority, freedom will be automatic, but for others and particularly in relation to dangerous offenders (see Chapter 10), it is for the Parole Board to decide when an individual is safe to be released. Whichever process is followed, for there to be successful reintegration, it is important that offenders are prepared for release. As highlighted in Chapters 6 and 7, this is achieved with resettlement prisons, open prisons and through the gate support offered by community rehabilitation companies (CRCs) and the National Probation Service (NPS). For those who have served short sentences, release into the community may not be too much of a shock, but for some who have spent a considerable period in custody, this can be a daunting prospect. Even for those who are caught within the revolving door of prison, constantly spending short periods in custodial institutions, imprisonment can cause them to lose accommodation, employment and social support. When it is these, that influence whether a person returns to crime, it is crucial that there is the necessary provision in place to try to prevent this. This chapter therefore looks at these factors in more detail, with separate sections on release, recall and reintegration.

RELEASE

The release of prisoners into the community is often referred to as parole, with the original sense of parole meaning 'word of honour' (Justice, 2017c). In most cases prisoners will be eligible for release before the end of their sentence (sentence expiry date (SED)) and so will be released into the community to be supervised, either by CRCs or the NPS. The statutory provisions relating to parole are contained in the Criminal Justice Act (CJA) 2003, but this has been updated on many occasions meaning that the process of parole can be quite complicated. Eligibility for parole will therefore depend first, on whether the individual is serving a determinate or indeterminate sentence and second when that sentence was imposed. All determinate or fixed-term prisoners, regardless of sentence length, are eligible for release at the halfway stage, but what happens after this point can be complex. Any time which has been spent in custody either on remand (s. 240ZA CJA 2003) or bail (s. 240A CJA 2003) will be taken into account and will count towards this marker. A prisoner's release date can however be delayed if they have incurred additional days added on for disciplinary reasons. For example, in 2015, more than 215,000 additional days (590 years) were imposed on prisoners for disciplinary reasons. Since 2010, there have been more than one million (3000 years) additional days imposed (Howard League for Penal Reform, 2016a). This can mean that a prisoner, whose behaviour is exceptionally poor, could spend their entire sentence in prison, although this cannot extend beyond the SED.

Home detention curfew

All prisoners aged 18 or over who have been sentenced to at least 12 weeks but under four years are eligible to be considered for the Home Detention Curfew (HDC) scheme, unless statutorily exempt. These exemptions are listed in section 246 CJA 2003 and include those who have previously breached a HDC, those who are serving an extended sentence for a sexual or violent offence and those who are liable to be removed from the UK. The essence of the scheme is to allow prisoners to be released before they have served their requisite custodial term and allows release to occur up to 135 days early (s. 246(1) CJA 2003), as long as they have served at least one quarter of their sentence or a minimum of 28 days. Early release is not an entitlement, however, and so prisoners must not only meet the eligibility criteria but also pass a risk assessment and a home circumstances check (Ministry of Justice, 2017g). If released, prisoners are required to wear an electronic tag, which monitors whether they are abiding by their curfew requirements. These requirements may differ depending on the circumstances of the individual prisoner but will normally be from 7 pm–7 am and must not be for less than nine hours per day. If the curfew is broken, the prisoner may be recalled to prison and will serve time in custody until their automatic or conditional release date is reached (see below). Breach of the curfew will also prevent further release under the HDC scheme, which will also apply to all future periods in custody (Ministry of Justice, 2017g). The HDC scheme has been operative in England and Wales since January 1999 and was introduced partly in an attempt to reduce crowding in prisons.

The first national evaluation of the HDC scheme was carried out in 2001. Of those prisoners released within the first 16 months, only 5 per cent were recalled to prison, with only 1 per cent of these recalled because the individual was perceived to be a serious risk of harm to the public (Dodgson, et al., 2001). Interestingly, the evaluation found that HDC was more likely to be granted to women than men, with age and race also a factor. Older prisoners were more likely to be granted HDC than younger ones and Black, South Asian and Chinese prisoners were more likely to be released when compared to their White counterparts. The higher the reconviction rate for the prisoner's index offence (i.e. the offence for which they were imprisoned) the less likely they were released under the HDC scheme. The vast majority of curfewees spoken to were positive about the scheme, with only 2 per cent saying that they would have preferred to have stayed in prison. Family members were also happy, not just because their loved one was home but also because it eradicated the need for prison visits (see Chapter 8). In the first 12 months of the scheme, an estimated saving of £36.7 million was made (Dodgson, et al., 2001). Further research on the reconviction rates of those released on HDC looked at those released

Table 9.1 Rates of reoffending while on HDC April 2003–March 2008.

Year	Number of offenders on HDC	Number of offenders who reoffended while on HDC	Reoffending rate (%)
2003–2004	20,802	1244	6.0
2004–2005	18,587	839	4.5
2005–2006	15,443	688	4.5
2006–2007	12,626	484	3.8
2007–2008	11,316	486	4.3

Source: HC Deb, 14 September 2009, c142WS.

between April 2003 and March 2008, with the results in Table 9.1. This can be compared to a current proven reoffending rate of 64.4 per cent for all adults released from custodial sentences of less than 12 months (Ministry of Justice and National Statistics, 2019c), which when taking into account the sentence length would appear to be a fair comparator. This therefore suggests that HDC is a far more positive way of releasing prisoners into the community.

Standard determinate sentences less than 12 months

All offenders serving standard determinate sentences (SDS) of at least two days but less than 12 months are released by the Secretary of State at the halfway point. Where the offence was committed before 1 February 2015, release into the community is unconditional (s. 243A CJA 2003). There used to be an 'at risk' period until the SED, where if a further offence was committed the prisoner would be recalled to prison, but this was abolished by the Legal Aid, Sentencing and Punishment of Offenders Act (LASPOA) 2012. If a person commits an offence before the SED, this can now be used as an aggravating factor in the sentencing of the new offence.

Where the offence was committed after 1 February 2015, release is conditional with the offender released subject to restrictions, often referred to as license conditions:

- To be well behaved, not to commit any offence nor do anything which undermines the purpose of supervision.
- To keep in touch with the supervising officer.
- To receive visits from this officer at the offender's place of residence.
- To reside at the address previously approved and notify the officer of any changes.
- To only undertake previously approved work and notify the officer of any changes.
- To not travel outside the UK without prior permission (HM Prison Service, 2012).

License conditions are imposed to protect the public, prevent reoffending, and to secure the successful reintegration of the prisoner into the community (s. 250 CJA 2003). Any breach of them will justify recall to prison and subsequently further periods of imprisonment. For those serving a SDS of less than 12 months, supervision will last until the end of the sentence (the sentence and license expiry date (SLED)) plus a further period of post sentence supervision to ensure that the time spent under supervision lasts for 12 months. This then creates a top up supervision end date (TUSED) (National Offender Management Service, 2015c). The process and options are illustrated in Figure 9.1.

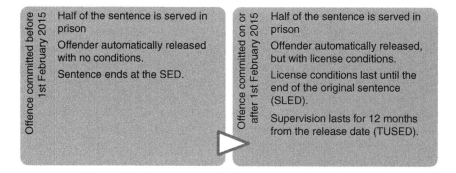

Figure 9.1 Release options for those serving less than 12 months

Standard determinate sentences 12 months but less than two years

The next category is offenders serving sentences of 12 months but less than 2 years. In all circumstances, the offender is again released at the halfway stage but regardless of when the offence was committed, release is conditional and as above, license conditions will be imposed. While there are a number of standard conditions it is also possible for the sentencing court to recommend particular license conditions where the sentence is 12 months or more (s. 238 CJA 2003). All license conditions will last until the SLED (s. 249 CJA 2003). If the offence was committed on or after 1 February 2015, post sentence supervision will be imposed, which again will expire 12 months after the halfway point (National Offender Management Service, 2015c). This is illustrated in Figure 9.2.

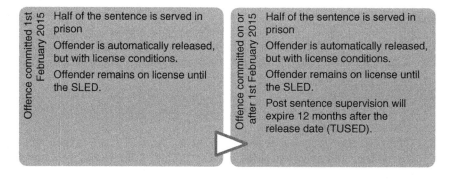

Figure 9.2 Release options for those serving 12 months but less than 2 years

Standard determinate sentences over two years

While 1 February 2015 is an important date for short-term sentences, it is 4 April 2005 when the sentence is over two years. Where an offender has committed an offence on or after 4 April 2005, conditional release will come at the halfway stage. License conditions will be put in place, which will last until the end of the sentence (SLED). Post sentence supervision is not required as there will be at least 12 months of supervision before the SLED (National Offender Management Service, 2015c). This also applies to prisoners sentenced on or after 3 December 2012, even where they committed their offences before 4 April 2005 (Ministry of Justice, 2012b). Where the offence was committed prior to 4 April 2005, sentencing took place before 3 December 2012 and the sentence was over 12 months but less than 4 years, the offender was automatically released at the halfway stage but was only on license until the three-quarter point. This is now obsolete due to the passing of time, but included here for completeness. Where the sentence is four years or more and sentencing took place before 3 December 2012 the process is the same as it currently stands for two years or more. Conditional release is granted at the halfway stage with license conditions in force until the SLED (National Offender Management Service, 2015c). Amalgamating these complex processes means, put simply that there is one procedure for sentences of two years and over as summarised in Figure 9.3.

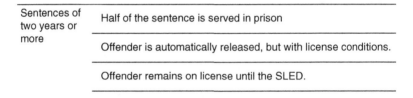

Sentences of two years or more	Half of the sentence is served in prison
	Offender is automatically released, but with license conditions.
	Offender remains on license until the SLED.

Figure 9.3 Release for standard determinate sentences over two years

---

Discussion Questions

1. Should prison governors have the power to add on additional days for misbehaviour in prison? Should these be treated as separate incidents or is it right that they can delay the release of a prisoner?
2. What do you think to the HDC scheme? Should the punishment of the original offence be cut by up to 135 days? How do you think you would feel if you were the victim?
3. Most offenders are eligible for release at the halfway stage of their custodial term. What do you think to this? Should a sentence of four years mean four years in custody?

The Parole Board

Automatic release does not however apply to three categories of prisoner:

1. Some serving determinate sentences including:
   a) Discretionary conditional release prisoners serving more than four years whose offence was committed before 4 April 2005. Offenders can apply for parole at the halfway stage but are released in any event at the two-thirds point. Supervision in the community is provided up until the three-quarter stage with a 'at risk' period existing until the SED.
   b) Extended sentences for public protection prisoners sentenced before 14 July 2008.
   c) Prisoners given an extended determinate sentence after 3 December 2012.
   d) Prisoners given a sentence for offenders of particular concern on or after 13 April 2015, who have committed a qualifying offence.
2. Those serving life or indeterminate sentences.
3. Those who have been recalled who had previously been serving life or an indeterminate sentence.

In these circumstances, decisions regarding release are made by the Parole Board for England and Wales. The Parole Board is an independent agency that has existed since 1967. Initially set up to advise the Home Secretary on release decisions, it is now an executive non-departmental public body, which determines the length of time that certain prisoners will serve in custody (Justice, 2017c). The test for this is contained in the LASPO Act 2012, with the Board being required to determine whether it is 'satisfied that it is no longer necessary for the protection of the public' that the prisoner be detained. To carry out these assessments, the Board has a broad membership of up to 240 members (Parole Board for England and Wales, 2018). Most of these work part-time for the Parole Board and part-time in other professions, including the judiciary, psychiatry, psychology and offender management.

Paper hearings

The Parole Board first becomes involved in a case when it receives a referral letter from the Secretary of State concerning a particular prisoner. This will initiate the appointment of a single Board member who will look at the papers (rule 5 The Parole Board Rules 2016). The papers contain information about the prisoner including:

- pre-trial and pre-sentence reports;
- current reports on risk factors, reduction in risk and behaviour in prison;
- compliance with the sentence plan and courses completed;
- views on suitability for release; and
- risk management reports prepared by the NPS detailing plans for managing risk in the community.

Where the prisoner is serving an indeterminate sentence (other than an IPP (imprisonment for public protection) sentence) this single member can decide either that the prisoner is unsuitable for release or that the case should be directed to an oral panel (rule 14). For those serving IPP sentences the single member can additionally decide that the prisoner is suitable for release as long as they have completed their minimum tariff (rule 14(4)), or they can recommend transfer to open conditions (The Parole Board, 2017a).

If the single member decides that the prisoner is not eligible for release, the prisoner has the right to ask an oral panel to determine their case (rule 15). Rule 15 is the product of *Osborn and Booth v Parole Board* ([2013] UKSC 61), where the Supreme Court held that in order to comply with the common law duty of fairness and Article 5(4) of the European Convention on Human Rights (ECHR), the Board had to hold an open hearing where fairness to the prisoner required it. Such a request needs to be made within 28 days, although it is for the Board to decide whether it will grant it. This is known as the request hearing. Life sentenced prisoners also have the right to an oral hearing where they have been classed as 'not suitable' on the papers. In 2017/18, there were 16,436 paper hearings conducted, resulting in 293 release decisions and 629 requests for an oral hearing (Parole Board for England and Wales, 2018). The estimated unit cost for a paper hearing is £320, compared to £1406 for an oral hearing (Parole Board for England and Wales, 2018).

Oral hearings

If used, an oral panel must take place within 26 weeks of the original referral from the Secretary of State (rule 16). Although panels used to take place with every party in the same room, it is now common for them to occur using video link, telephone conferencing or other forms of technology. As previously mentioned, it is for to the prisoner to decide whether they want their case to be heard by an oral panel and whether they want to be present. Prisoners can call witnesses and have an observer accompany them if they do intend to be present. The panel will consist of one to three members of the Board, depending on the complexity of the case and if appropriate will include either a psychologist or psychiatrist member. The prisoner's victim may also be present. The decision of the oral panel must be communicated to the prisoner not more than 14 days after the end of the hearing (rule 24). The oral hearing panel can:

- direct release;
- direct release at a future date (for determinate recalled prisoners);
- recommend a transfer to open conditions (for indeterminate prisoners);
- make no direction to release;
- adjourn the case for further information; or
- defer the case for a set period of time (The Parole Board, 2017a, p. 44).

Discussion

Over the last few years, there have been a number of issues, which have negatively affected the efficiency of the Parole Board, of which the first is delay. The effect of the Osbourne case was that the Parole Board was expected to carry out significantly more oral hearings than it had previously and in the years following the judgment it simply did not have the resources to do this. Delay in processing cases, therefore reached its peak in January 2015 when the parole case backlog stood at 3163. This has been reduced over time, but is still significant. In April 2016, there were 2422 outstanding cases, 2033 at the end of March 2017 (The Parole Board, 2017b) and 1296 on 18 October 2017 (Hardwick & Jones, 2017). In April 2018, the number of outstanding cases stood at 1247 (Parole Board for England and Wales, 2018). Furthermore, in March 2016, there were 563 prisoners whose orals hearings were 90 days or more overdue (The Parole Board, 2017a). Such delays in 2016/17 resulted in £938,000 being paid to prisoners in compensation (The Parole Board, 2017a), with a further £455,000 paid in 2017/18 (Parole Board for England and Wales, 2018). This is a massive increase from the £144,000 paid in 2014/15 and the £154,000 paid in 2015/16; although bizarrely the increase shows that the Board is reducing its backlog as compensation claims cannot be processed until the prisoner's case has been concluded. Recognising such problems the Ministry of Justice allowed the Board to increase its membership adding a further 50 Board members in June 2017 (The Parole Board, 2017b), but such a crisis should not have been allowed to happen in the first place. Between 2010 and 2016, the number of Board members reduced from 284 to 171 and during this time, the Board was not allowed to recruit (Hardwick & Jones, 2017). This was inevitably due to austerity measures, but these cost savings have been counterproductive when you take into account the almost £1 million paid in compensation in 2016/17 alone.

Another issue resulting in delay is caused, not by the Parole Board, but by the failure of HM Prison and Probation Staff (HMPPS) to deliver reports on time. When this occurs, hearings are either cancelled or decisions are made based on incomplete paperwork. Decisions made under these circumstances often result in the prisoner not progressing. In 2016/17, it was thought that approximately 50 per cent of all deferred hearings were because the necessary reports were not ready on time, with the overall deferment rate standing at 39 per cent (Hardwick & Jones, 2017). Allowing staff to work remotely and to 'attend' hearings through live links has helped to ease the time pressure for some staff, but this relies on technology working within all prison establishments. Resources in the community are also needed so that the Board can be reassured that the correct supervision and support in the community is in place if a release decision is made.

Linked with delay is also how the Parole Board, in conjunction with HMPPS has contributed to the high number of IPP prisoners still in custody. Sentences of IPP lasted for seven years (2005–2012) and were part of the government's agenda to increase custodial terms for those classified as dangerous (see Chapter 10). When offenders were sentenced to an IPP, the sentencing judge would impose a minimum term of custody. This was set to be commensurate with the seriousness of the offence and was designed for reasons of punishment and just deserts. Release only occurs when the offender has demonstrated to the Parole Board that it is no longer necessary, on the grounds of public protection, for them to be detained in custody. The most common way in which this is proven is through the completion of accredited offending behaviour programmes, but as we have seen in Chapter 8, these are severely lacking in number and often prisoners will have to join long waiting lists and in some cases apply to transfer to alternative prisons where suitable programmes are running. Due to this insufficient provision, many prisoners were unable to evidence within their minimum terms that they had shown the required reduction in their risk. This has resulted in a large amount of offenders detained in custody past their minimum tariff. Admittedly, the government did not expect the sentence to be used as widely as it was, but in 2012, when the sentence was finally abolished, of the 8711 people who had been issued with an IPP sentence (HM Inspectorate of Prisons, 2016b) 6080 who had served their minimum tariffs were still in custody (The Parole Board, 2017a). While it is accepted that some IPP prisoners should be in prison beyond their minimum tariff, David Blunkett MP, who is attributed with having introduced the sentence stated in 2014 'we certainly got the implementation wrong. The consequences of bringing that Act [CJA 2003] in had led, in some cases, to an injustice and I regret that' (Conway, 2014). This has been exacerbated further by the fact that when the sentence was abolished this was not applied retrospectively and no provision was made for those IPP prisoners still in custody. There are therefore three categories of IPP prisoners:

1. Those who remain dangerous, and should not be released.
2. Those who could show a reduction in risk if given access to the necessary support and programmes.
3. Those who are ready for release, but are waiting to be seen by the Parole Board.

The number of IPP sentenced prisoners in prison, waiting to be released has significantly contributed to the delays discussed above. One of the most publicised cases was James Ward, who in September 2017 was finally released having served 11 years in prison for an IPP sentence that had a minimum tariff of less than 1 year (Allison, 2017). While the Parole Board has made steady progress in dealing with these cases, in 2018, six years after the sentence was abolished, there were still 2884 offenders waiting to be seen. Some changes have been made. For example, in 2016, the Parole Board Rules were changed so that decisions relating to IPP prisoners could be made on the paperwork and this has helped to process IPP prisoners much quicker. However, if an IPP prisoner is recalled (see below), the Parole Board has to be involved before release can be granted. One proposal, which would significantly reduce the IPP backlog, is to reverse the burden of proof in these cases. Nick Hardwick (Chair of the Parole Board March 2016–March 2018) argues that in the case of those serving minimum tariffs of less than two years, rather than asking a prisoner to prove that they have reduced in risk, it should be for the state to prove that they are likely to commit a further offence (*Insidetime*, 2017). For some, however, this does not go far enough. Allison for example argues that on the basis the government has accepted that the IPP sentence was wrong and that it has led to injustice in many cases, the state should have to prove the need to detain IPP prisoners beyond their minimum tariff in *all* cases (Allison, 2017). Another suggestion is to resentence IPP prisoners, giving them the sentence they would have received if the IPP option had not existed. This would inevitably mean that many would be immediately released from prison. Such a task would inevitably take a long time, however, especially if it required court hearings for all those effected, meaning that this too may not be workable until, at least, the backlog is at a more manageable level.

It is clear that something must be done and while an increase in staff at the Parole Board is welcome, it is unlikely to make the significant changes, which are urgently required. This is partly due to the high number of IPP prisoners who are being recalled following release:

> The most significant issue with the IPP problem now is that more than 50% are being recalled, not necessarily because they've committed another offence, but because they've broken their licence conditions – and that's a real problem. So, we're letting them out, but they're getting recalled. (Hardwick & Jones, 2017)

For the period April 2016–March 2017, 581 IPP prisoners were processed and released by the Parole Board, but also within that same period 472 of them (not necessarily the same prisoners) were recalled to prison (Ministry of Justice and National Statistics, 2017). This therefore only gave a net release of 109. Even if the IPP backlog is reduced to levels that are more manageable it is predicted that by 2020, the number of recalled IPP prisoners in prison will exceed the number of IPP prisoners waiting to be released for the first time (Hardwick & Jones, 2017). If such practice continues, it is difficult to see how the IPP problem will ever be solved unless IPP prisoners are resentenced and the sentence retrospectively eradicated.

Another pertinent issue is whether the Parole Board is sufficiently independent from the executive (the Ministry of Justice). In R. *(on the application of Brooke) v Parole Board for England and Wales* ([2008] EWCA Civ 29), the Court of Appeal held that it was not, meaning that there had been a breach of Article 5(4) of the ECHR:

> Everyone who is deprived of his liberty by arrest or detention shall be entitled to take proceedings by which the lawfulness of his detention shall be decided speedily by a court and his release ordered if the detention is not lawful.

This is because the Secretary of State has influence over appointing Board members, implements rules of procedure, allocates funding and has the power to give the Board directions. Bearing in mind the judicial role that the Board undertakes in deciding whether the continued deprivation of a prisoner's liberty is justified, the Board was seen not to meet the requirements of a 'court'. Furthermore, and again, due to the influence of the Ministry of Justice, under Article 6 of the ECHR, the Board was held not be 'an independent and impartial tribunal'. The decision initiated a government consultation in 2009 (Ministry of Justice, 2009) although very little change has occurred because of it.

Perhaps the most obvious solution would be to transfer the sponsorship of the Parole Board from the Ministry of Justice to HM Courts and Tribunal Service (HMCTS); allowing the Board to be within the remit of the judiciary rather than the executive and indeed following on from the government's consultation this was what the Parole Board wanted. This would have the added advantage of placing the Board with other similar tribunals, such as those dealing with mental health, immigration and asylum. JUSTICE, argues that such a move could save resources in the sense that HMCTS already has the administration and infrastructure which could serve the Parole Board and which could be used to quicken up the current parole process (Epstein, 2010). The Parole Board could also then use the Upper Tier of the HMCTS as an appeal court rather than having to look at appeal cases itself, again quickening up the parole process and making in fairer. Board members would be appointed by the Judicial Appointments Commission, rather than by the Secretary of State and independence from the executive would be achieved.

While the issue of independence continues, this was overshadowed in 2018 when a parole release decision in the case of John Radford (previously known as John Worboys) was overturned by the High Court, following a judicial review case brought by two of Radford's victims. Focusing on inadequate risk information, the Court felt that the Board had not enquired enough into evidence of the offender's wider offending. As noted above this could have been due to a lack of resources experienced by both the Parole Board and HMPPS. In addition to reversing the decision, the court stated that rule 25, which had previously prohibited information about proceedings being made public, was unlawful. This brought into issue whether policies and procedures previously followed by the Parole Board were correct and whether its decision making process was transparent enough. The case also raised concerns over whether the Board were sufficiently communicating with victims. The initial reaction from government was to amend rule 25. This now provides that the Board must provide a summary of its reasons in release cases to the victim, unless there are exceptional circumstances why it should not be produced, and if the interests of open justice demand it, this can also be given to other interested parties (The Parole Board (Amendment) Rules 2018). The Secretary of State for Justice commissioned a comprehensive review of all Parole Board Rules (Ministry of Justice, 2018m) and in an attempt to deflect responsibility away from the Ministry of Justice and onto the Parole Board, he forced Nick Hardwick, the Chair of the Parole Board to resign. This was met with widespread condemnation from academics, policymakers and practitioners. In his resignation letter, Nick Hardwick expressed his concern about the

Discussion Questions

1. Should release decisions be made just on the papers? Does there need to be a balance between fairness and cost or is one fundamentally more important than the other?
2. Is the current level of delay acceptable? What more do you think needs to be done?
3. What do you think about the amount of money, which the Board is paying out in compensation? Is this justified?
4. What changes should be made to ease the situation for IPP prisoners?
5. What changes need to take place to ensure that the Board is 'an independent and impartial tribunal'?

independence of the Board and how the Radford case raised, 'very troubling questions about how the Board's independence can be safeguarded' (Hardwick, 2018).

RECALL

Released offenders may be recalled if they:

- commit another crime or are charged with another crime; or
- are behaving in a way that leads the offender manager to think they might be about to commit another crime; or
- break the conditions of their licence.

Decisions relating to recall will be made either by the individual's offender manager or by a separate HDC recall team. If a recall is initiated, the offender will be notified in writing and if necessary, the police will be involved in ensuring that the offender is returned to custody. Those recalled offenders who are serving a sentence of 12 months or longer and who are assessed as not presenting a high risk of serious harm will be subject to a fixed term recall period of 28 days, after which time they will be automatically released, as long as there has not been any escalation in risk. For those serving sentences of less than 12 months this fixed recall period is 14 days (Offender Rehabilitation Act (ORA) 2014). If the offender is high risk or is serving an indeterminate sentence, they will be subject to a standard recall, which could mean serving the remainder of the sentence in custody, although this is rare. If the offender is subject to a standard recall, their case must be referred to the Parole Board after 28 days. This allows the Board to review whether continued detention is necessary. If the Board authorises continued detention then the case is referred back to the Board on an annual basis (National Offender Management Service, 2017).

In all cases, the offender has the right to challenge their recall, which is known as making representations against recall. If they decide to do this, the case will go before the Parole Board. The recalled prisoner can make representations to the Board against their recall, although in practice, even where such an application has been made the Board will sometimes confirm the recall decision without hearing from the prisoner (Padfield, 2016). In all hearings, the Board can make one of four decisions:

- order immediate release back onto licence;
- refuse immediate release but order release at a future date;
- make no recommendation at all; or
- send the case to an oral hearing.

If the offender is not happy with the Parole Board decision this can be appealed by way of an oral hearing, but this is an oral hearing before the Parole Board, where once again it will make one of the above four decisions. Moving the Parole Board to the remit of the HMCTS would therefore be beneficial for recall prisoners as there would then be the option of an independent appeal court with the upper tier tribunal.

Population	46,434,265 (Worldometers, 2019e)
Prison population (including remand prisoners)	59,218 (Institute of Criminal Policy Research, 2019d)
Prison population per 100,000 of national population	127 (Institute of Criminal Policy Research, 2019d)
Remand prisoners	9238 (15.6%) (Institute of Criminal Policy Research, 2019d)
Number of establishments	82 (Institute of Criminal Policy Research, 2019d)
Official capacity of prison service	84,478 (Institute of Criminal Policy Research, 2019d)
Occupancy level	71.8% (Institute of Criminal Policy Research, 2019d)

Brief Profile

Spain, located in Southern Europe, is the fourth largest country in Europe in terms of size, and the sixth largest in terms of population. As a developed country, it enjoys a good standard of living, although in 2015 it had the second highest unemployment rate in all of Europe.

Release Mechanisms

Open Regime

The release of prisoners in Spain can be achieved either through transfer to an open regime or through the process of parole. As part of the open regime and similar to release on temporary license (Chapter 7) in England and Wales, offenders will often work in the community during the day only returning to prison at night. This applies from Monday–Thursday with Friday–Sunday often spent at home on weekend leave. For monitoring purposes, open regimes often work in conjunction with HDCs which can be used instead of returning to prison. This may mean that an offender only comes to the establishment for meetings with their offender manager. The curfew element of the scheme will normally run from 11 pm to 7 am with the electronic monitoring aspect supervised by the police (Cid & Tebar, 2012). Any breach of the electronic monitoring requirements will result in a recall to prison (Cid & Tebar, 2010). The open regime is the third category of regimes in Spanish prisons as seen in Table 9.2.

Table 9.2 The Spanish prison system.

The Spanish Prison System	
Prison Treatment Categories	**Prison Regime**
First category	Closed or maximum security
Second category	Ordinary regime
Third category	Open regime or HDC
Fourth category	Parole

Source: Cid, J. & Tebar, B. (2012) 'Revoking early conditional release measures in Spain', *European Journal of Probation*, 4(1), pp. 112–124.

For an offender to be considered suitable for an open regime they must either have an initial 'good risk prognosis', for example, first time offenders sentenced to short custodial terms; or have progressed from the ordinary regime (Cid & Tebar, 2012). Under the 1996 Prison Rules, progression can be achieved when the prisoner has served one quarter of their sentence and they are assessed as being ready for resettlement. However, where the sentence exceeds five years and the offence is listed as a felony offence the offender must serve one half (Article 36 Spanish Criminal Code). A minimum term can also be ordered by the sentencing judge where the custodial term exceeds five years (Article 36 Spanish Criminal Code). Decisions relating to parole are made by a prison judge, a member of the judiciary who has experience in dealing with prison related court applications. Emphasising the judicial nature of the role, decisions of the prison judge can be appealed to the Spanish High Court (Bachmaier & Garcia, 2010).

Parole

In addition to the open regime, early release in Spain can also be granted through parole. There are currently four ways in which this can be achieved:

1. Ordinary parole: release at the three-quarter point.
2. Earlier parole: release at the two-thirds or half-way point where the prisoner has engaged in treatment and continuous labour requirements (Cid & Tebar, 2012).
3. Humanitarian parole: reserved for all prisoners, aged 70 or over who are suffering from an incurable illness and can occur at any stage (Cid & Tebar, 2010).
4. Convictions for terrorism and organised crime: release delayed until between three quarters and seven eighths of the sentence.

The common element is that the offender must meet the requirements of being transferred to the open regime i.e. they must have been of good behaviour and show a good prognosis of risk. This normally requires them to have already spent some time out of the prison on home leave and/or to have been in an open regime (Cid & Tebar, 2010). Prisoners may also be obliged to comply with any civil liabilities arising from their offence such as compensating the victim for their losses.

Prisoners released on parole are required to observe certain rules and conditions, the main being not to reoffend. Others may tell them what not to do (restrictive) or be more positive, for example, participating in a treatment programme (Cid & Tebar, 2010). Parole will remain in force until the SED with revocation occurring when either a license condition is breached or reoffending occurs. Revocation decisions and the setting of license conditions will be made by the prison judge. Prisoners have the right to present written statements at parole hearings but there is no option of an oral hearing (Cid & Tebar, 2010). Interestingly, and in direct contrast to England and Wales, any license conditions set by the prison judge must have the consent of the prisoner.

Discussion Questions

1. Are there any similarities in the release mechanisms in Spain and England and Wales? Which system do you prefer?
2. What do you think is the most appropriate minimum term, which should be served in closed conditions before release or pre-release, should begin?
3. What do you think to the idea of a prison judge? Would this solve many of the problems which the Parole Board in England and Wales are currently facing?

Discussion

The number of prisoners subject to recall is staggering, with numbers increasing on an annual basis. This increase is shown in Figure 9.4.

Looking at the year April 2016 to March 2017 in more detail, 21,721 prisoners were recalled, 20,982 of whom were returned to custody (Ministry of Justice and National Statistics, 2017). How this is broken down by sentence can be seen in Table 9.3

In June 1995, the average number of recalled prisoners in custody was approximately 150. In June 2016, this had increased by 4300 per cent to 6600 (Howard League for Penal Reform, 2017b). Part of this increase is due to the implementation of the ORA 2014, which introduced conditional release with a period of at least 12 months supervision for all prisoners serving more than one day in custody. This has increased the number of recalls to prison by approximately 7500 each year (Howard League for Penal Reform, 2017b).

Interestingly, however, most recalls are not because the individual has committed a further offence: for example, for the 12 months ending September 2016, 7798 people were recalled to prison for failing to keep in touch and a further 5228 were recalled due to failing to reside at a particular address (Howard League for Penal Reform, 2017b). Figures for April 2016–March 2017 are illustrated in figure 9.5 (Webster, 2017). While issues such as drugs, alcohol and place of residence need to be addressed, they should be dealt with in the community through effective supervision and support rather than through recall to prison. It is also essential that offender managers consider whether, for example, drinking actually increases the risk levels of an offender and actually makes it more likely that they will reoffend. If this is not the case then a recall should not be initiated (Hardwick & Jones, 2017). The reason for conditional release was to provide extra support and through the gate services for those offenders

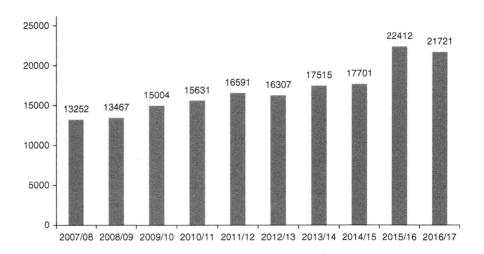

Figure 9.4 Number of offenders recalled to prison in each year since 2007

Source: Gyimah, S. (2017) 'Reoffenders'. Written question 107703. [Online] Available at: http://www.parliament.uk/business/publications/written-questions-answers-statements/written-question/Commons/2017-10-13/107703/ [Accessed 20 October 2017].

Table 9.3 Offenders returned to custody after license recall April 2016–March 2017.

	April–June 2016	July–September 2016	October–December 2016	January–March 2017	April–March 2017
Total recall admissions	5317	5410	5097	5158	20,982
Total determinate sentences	5142	5228	4930	5012	20,312
Less than 12 months	1972	1927	1977	2037	7913
12 months or more	3170	3301	2953	2975	12,399
Total indeterminate Sentences	175	182	167	146	670
Life sentence	55	58	46	40	199
IPP	120	124	121	106	471

Source: Ministry of Justice and National Statistics (2017) *Offender Management Statistics Quarterly, England and Wales.* London: Ministry of Justice and National Statistics.

who were constantly in and out of custody; but by making such offenders subject to recall as well, the legislation has arguably increased rather than decreased their likelihood of being returned to prison. This is especially disruptive if some inroads have been made in terms of reintegration and desistance. In this sense, the extension of conditional release to all prisoners has been arguably counterproductive.

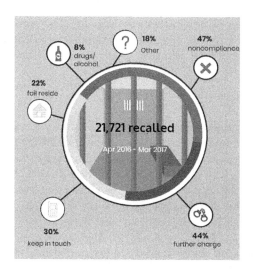

Figure 9.5 Why are people recalled to prison?
Source: Webster, 2017,

It is therefore imperative that the frequency of recalled prisoners is reduced. Some suggestions come from Padfield (2012) who spoke to 46 recalled prisoners. Of the prisoners interviewed (10 women and 36 men), 13 had been recalled for breaching their license conditions while the remainder (33) had been accused of committing a further offence. Interestingly, several of those in the latter group, were either not charged, had their charges subsequently dropped or were found not guilty by a court; but remained in custody. Many across the board felt that their license conditions were 'unreasonable' and that their conditions had been 'inadequately discussed with them' (Padfield, 2012, p. 20), especially in terms of how they would practically work. Furthermore, while they had been given a recall pack or dossier when they were first returned to the prison, for many this was too complicated to understand and created too negative an image of themselves. Echoing similar research carried out by Bottomley and Bilton (Bilton & Bottomley, 2012) in 1969, in Hull prison, Padfield found that most 'had little knowledge or understanding of what was being done to progress their case' (Padfield, 2012, p. 20). Padfield therefore makes four suggestions: 'more information, more advice, more certainty and much less delay' (Padfield, 2012, p. 21).

The addition of recall cases in the Parole Board's remit is therefore another reason why there is a parole case backlog, with the Board receiving on average 1000 recall cases a month, many of which go to a full oral hearing (Jones, 2017b). On 18 October 2017 there were approximately 500 recall cases waiting to be heard with approximately 100 who had been waiting over 90 days (Hardwick & Jones, 2017). Martin Jones, the Chief Executive of the Parole Board argues that 'Whilst it is quite right that prisoners have the right to challenge the lawfulness of their recall, I believe that more could be done to encourage probation officers to exercise their professional judgement to keep people in the community' (Jones, 2017b). Alternatively, he wonders whether the Parole Board should have the final say on recalling offenders in a similar way to how the Scottish Parole Board currently works (Jones, 2017a). Although this may initially cause a further increase in the Board's work, it could eventually reduce the number of prisoners, especially those serving sentences of IPP, from being returned to custody.

Recall of women to prison

Since the implementation of the ORA 2014, the number of women who have been recalled to custody or committed to prison following a breach of a community order has tripled (Beard, et al., 2019). For the year ending September 2018, male offenders were recalled at a rate of 34 recalls for every 100, with women recalled at 29 per 100. While the rate for men is higher, the recall rate for women has risen much more steeply since the changes brought in by the ORA 2014. For example, for the year ending September 2015 the recall rate was 29 recalls per 100 for men but only 16 per 100 for women (Beard, et al., 2019). Also worth noting is that while there was an increase in recalls for both men and women initially, this rise plateaued for men during 2016/17 but did not for women (Prison Reform Trust, 2018a).

Some work has been undertaken to try and discover why women are being disproportionality affected by the ORA 2014 with the Prison Reform Trust (2018a) being one charity to report on this. Interestingly, the Trust is not surprised with this additional impact on women, with this being predicted before the ORA 2014 came into force, despite the fact that the arrangements in the ORA were supposed to reflect the differences which women face (see Chapter 12). This has been further emphasised by the government's Female Offender Strategy:

> We know that many offenders are amongst the most vulnerable people in society .... Female offenders can be amongst the most vulnerable of all, in both the prevalence and complexity of their needs. Many experience chaotic life-styles involving substance misuse, mental health problems, homelessness, and offending behaviour – these are often the product of a life of abuse and trauma. (Ministry of Justice, 2018c, p. 5)

In their report, the Prison Reform Trust cite housing, drugs, benefits, employment, mental health, counselling and banking as the main areas which women needed support with on release from prison. Help was also needed for debt, accessing a GP, domestic violence and children (Prison Reform Trust, 2018a). Women also spoke about frequently finding themselves in dangerous situations, such as unstable housing, drug misuse and abusive relationships, with some saying that they felt safer in prison. As with men, CRCs were failing to provide women with sufficient support, but in addition to this it was found that both the CRCS and the NPS lacked access to women-only provision, which was again impacting on the women. Due to this 83 per cent of the women thought that they 'had been set up to fail' (Prison Reform Trust, 2018a, p. 31). Recommendations include:

- Repealing the relevant provisions in the ORA 2014.
- Providing more women-only services.
- Legislating for a presumption that custody should only be used for sentences of 12 months or over (Prison Reform Trust, 2018a).

Discussion Questions

1. The extension of post sentence supervision to offenders serving custodial sentences of less than 12 months has dramatically increased the number of recalls. Is this a correct use of limited resources?
2. Should offenders only be recalled if they have committed a further criminal offence or are other circumstances also justifiable?
3. What changes need to be made to reduce recall numbers to more manageable levels? Are additional measures needed for women?

REINTEGRATION

The reintegration of a prisoner back into their community is key, especially if there is to be any hope that that individual will desist from future offending. This involves ensuring that on release they have somewhere to live and for the first few months have adequate support in terms of finances, employment and, depending on how long they have been in prison, the practicalities of everyday living. While the terms reintegration and resettlement are used here, it is worth noting that these assume that the offender was once settled and/or integrated into the community, which may not have been the case. Work towards integrating or settling the offender may therefore be needed, rather than work to reintegrate/resettle them.

Through the Gate

One of the main governmental ways in which short-term prisoners are helped to resettle into the community is known as 'Through the Gate' (TTG). This is a flagship policy, which intends a step change in rehabilitation and through this a reduction in reoffending rates (HM Inspectorate of Probation/Criminal Justice Joint Inspection, 2016). It was launched on 1 May 2015 with the aim being that CRCs (see Chapter 6) and resettlement prisons (see Chapter 7) would work far more closely to bridge the gap that was previously thought to exist between prison and the community. The main tasks are to ensure that on release, individuals have somewhere to live, can find employment or be registered for training and that any financial issues are resolved. TTG is part of the Transforming Rehabilitation agenda (see Chapter 6) which opened up the market of rehabilitation to competition through the creation of the CRCs and, as outlined above, enacted at least 12 months of community supervision for all offenders released from custody. It was therefore designed to ensure that the extra 45,000 prisoners released on license into the community would be effectively supervised and that through this effective support the 64 per cent reoffending rate of these prisoners (who had previously not been supervised following release) would be reduced (Taylor, et al., 2017).

The main responsibilities of TTG lie with the CRCs who are paid by the Ministry of Justice on a fee-for-service basis to provide resettlement services in all resettlement prisons. The eventual aim is that the CRCs will eventually be paid on a payment by results basis but in May 2019 (four years on from the policy's introduction) this had still not been brought into operation. Under the contract, the CRCs must:

- Prepare a resettlement plan.
- Help prisoners find accommodation.
- Help prisoners retain employment held pre-custody and gain employment or training opportunities post-release.
- Provide help with finance, benefits and debt.
- Provide support for victims of domestic abuse and sex workers.
- Undertake pre-release coordination (HM Inspectorate of Probation/Criminal Justice Joint Inspection, 2016).

The resettlement process begins once an offender enters custody: within 72 hours, the offender must be screened using a Basic Custody Screening Tool (BCST), which aims to identify resettlement needs. Part two of this screening is then carried out by the CRC within 5 days of the initial screening, with the aim here being for the CRC to outline how they intend to meet these needs. This then forms the basis of the individual resettlement plan. The full resettlement process can be seen in Figure 9.6.

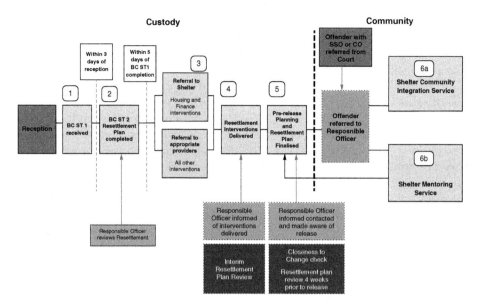

Figure 9.6 CRC resettlement process

Source: Burke, L. (2017) 'Transforming Rehabilitation and Through the Gate: Research from a Resettlement prison'. Cardiff: Paper given at the European Society of Criminology 13th–16th September 2017.

While TTG sounds laudable, the practice has been somewhat different. Between October 2015 and September 2016, 31,715 prisoners had been released on licence following determinate sentences of 12 months or more, but very few had received the help which they required in order to resettle into the community and desist from offending. HM Inspectorate for Probation, for example, stated that only 44 per cent received accommodation support; 53 per cent received support related to employment/training and 41 per cent received financial advice (HM Inspectorate of Probation, 2017d). Of their 98 offender sample, none had found employment through using TTG services and 10 were homeless on release. Within 12 weeks of release, 10 per cent had been charged with new offences and 11 per cent had breached their license conditions (HM Inspectorate of Probation, 2017d). Disappointment about TTG has also been expressed by Dame Glenys Stacey (the Chief Inspector of Probation from 2016 to 2019):

> None of the early hopes for Through the Gate have been realised. The gap between aspiration and reality is so great, that we wonder whether there is any prospect that these services will deliver the desired impact on rates of reoffending. To succeed, the government and HM Prison and Probation Service must review and develop the contractual arrangements with CRCs, improve IT systems materially and align systems, processes and resettlement targets for prisons, CRCs and the National Probation Service to both incentivise and enable effective work. (HM Inspectorate of Probation, 2017d, p. 3)

Such pessimism has also been shared by Lloyd et al. who in 2017 evaluated 10 pilot drug recovery wings in 8 men's and 2 women's prisons in England and Wales.

Despite some progress being made while the individuals were in prison, 'a central theme of this study [was] the lack of support for prisoners on release' (Lloyd, et al., 2017, p. 6). Of the 109 interviewed, only 6 (5.5%) reported receiving support from professionals and the vast majority were not met by anyone at the prison gate. Housing was identified as the most important issue on release with hostels described as 'deeply unpleasant' (Lloyd, et al., 2017, p. 6).

A further study by Taylor et al. (2017) shows equal pessimism, with them arguing that 'instead of enhancing resettlement, Through the Gate is actually enhancing resentment' (Taylor, et al., 2017, p. 115). Part of the noted failures were due to a lack of prison resources in the resettlement prison, which the project was focused on. Prisoners were often confined in their cells due to staff shortages and so the provision of 'sustained, ordered and seamless resettlement provision' (Taylor, et al., 2017, p. 119) was incredibly difficult. While the researchers observed a clear will from both prison and CRC staff to help prisoners, the lack of resources meant that resentment was felt by both prisoners and professionals. Other disabling factors included a lack of clear leadership on prioritising resettlement over other demands and the 'inadequacy and integrity of current service provision' (Taylor, et al., 2017, p. 120). This latter point included the fact that the CRCs had been unable to deliver on the diverse supply chain of services, which were required, and a feeling by all professional staff that communication channels needed to be much clearer and more effective (Taylor, et al., 2017). Rather than prisons being places of rehabilitation, the study concludes by stating that they are places of 'dehabilitation' (Taylor, et al., 2017, p. 127). Early research would therefore suggest the TTG is not working. Whether this will change in time, when CRCs have been able to put in place the full range of third sector agencies, which are desperately needed to provide the necessary support, is unclear, although as with many other aspects of offender management the main issue here appears to be, once again, a lack of resources.

Discussion Questions

1. What are the three keys factors, which would help an offender to stay crime free? Why do you think these particular factors are so important?
2. Should post sentence supervision have been extended in the way that it has?
3. What are your thoughts on the 'Through the Gate' policy? Early research would suggest that it is not achieving what it set out to accomplish, why do you think this is the case? What more needs to be done to effectively support released offenders?

CONCLUSION

Grouped with Chapters 7 and 8, this is the last prisons chapter. In common with the other prison chapters (7 & 8), this chapter also paints a bleak picture of offender management, and highlights a number of problems. These include the fact that several prisoners are being held in custody for too long, not because they are deemed to be risky but because of administrative delay. Furthermore, release decisions should be undertaken by an impartial court or tribunal, but rather they are being administered by a body that is effectively being sponsored by the Ministry of Justice. The future of the Parole Board and the policies and processes which it must follow is now under review, with plans from the government currently awaited. While many believe that the only correct option is to transfer prison release decisions to a body under HMCTS, another choice could be to introduce a system of prison judges as evidenced in Spain. Whatever the decision, the government needs to act fast so that compensation claims do not continue to mount up and millions of pounds are not spent because of organisational deferments.

The government also needs to act fast to remedy the current recall situation. Far too many prisoners are being returned to prison, often not because of reoffending. This has been exacerbated by the ORA 2014, which adds license conditions to all those offenders serving custodial sentences of more than one day. While such a policy had laudable aims, until proper resources are put into a TTG system that supports rather than hinders offenders, recall rates are going to continue to rise, exacerbating crowding and the other issues identified in Chapter 8. The scandal as referred to at the beginning of Chapter 7 thus permeates throughout the entirety of the prison estate in England and Wales, and without much needed change it is envisaged that this will only get worse, rather than better over the next few years.

Now read:

Fitzalan Howard, et al. (2018) *Understanding the Process and Experience of Recall to Prison*. Analytical Summary 2018. London: HMPPS.

Prison Reform Trust (2018d) *More Carrot, Less Stick. Proposals for a Radical Reassessment of the use of Release on Temporary Licence in Prisons to Support Work, Training and Resettlement*. London: Prison Reform Trust.

Prison Service Journal (2018) *Special Edition 50 Years of the Parole System for England and Wales*. May, No. 237.

Now watch:

The Parole Board for England and Wales has a YouTube channel available at: https://www.youtube.com/channel/UCMFx5D7PNeVfP680-no-GSw/featured.

A Westminster Hall debate on Recall of Women to Prisons available at: https://parliamentlive.tv/event/index/3ad01d8a-abad-4576–8251–dfeca23e10d4?in=14:29:34

Now consider:

In the design of your prison think about how the prisoners would be released. Issues which you might want to consider include: What would the process be? Who would make the decisions? What support would be in place to help with a transition into the community? How long would this support last? On what basis would you recall prisoners? Would you have special support in place if you housed women prisoners?

10 Dangerous Offenders

INTRODUCTION

So far, the main focus of this book has been on 'normal' offenders, that is, those offenders who are sentenced using a proportional just deserts approach (see Chapter 4). This chapter however looks at those who are classified as 'dangerous', and in particular considers how we should sentence, manage and reduce the levels of risk which such offenders pose. The first task, in such a chapter, is to identify what is meant when using the term 'dangerous', with this concept changing over time. In fact dangerous offenders in the past have ranged from beggars and street children to political activists, counter revolutionists and habitual, but generally petty offenders. More recent notions include sexual and violent offenders, terrorists, the mentally disordered, habitually drunken drivers, keepers of unsafe factories, white collar criminals, health and safety violators and also environmental polluters (Harrison, 2011). As Floud and Young argue 'harmful behaviour and unacceptable risks are socially constructed and people are socially defined as dangerous accordingly' (Floud & Young, 1981, p. 20). People are therefore dangerous if they are dangerous to us, that is, they threaten our security, our property or those we care about. This is also emphasised by Brown and Pratt who argue that the way in which we classify offenders as dangerous, tells us more about ourselves than about the particular offender; because it shows what types of offending we fear the most and on what we place the most value (Brown & Pratt, 2000). Moreover, when we talk about sentencing dangerous offenders it shows the lengths that we are prepared to go to reduce our risk of having to encounter them. Despite the potential breadth of the term, priority in this chapter is given to those whom the government considers to be dangerous, both in terms of sentencing and public protection policies. This chapter therefore focuses on serious violent and sexual offenders, with a particular emphasis on high-risk sex offenders.

Discussion Questions

1. How would you define the term 'dangerous offender'? Can you think of anymore potential categories that have not been included here?
2. Should the categorisation of those considered to be dangerous include those we fear, or just those who have been proven to have caused harm?

SENTENCING POLICY

While normal offenders are sentenced using an approach based on commensurability and just deserts, a separate sentencing policy exists for those who are classified
as dangerous. The rationale for this is based on public protection, with sentencers
able to impose longer than commensurate sentences on such individuals. This
is directed at what the offender may do in the future rather than on what they
have done in the past and is therefore based on the theory of incapacitation (see
Chapter 2). The rise of modern day dangerousness legislation is in direct correlation with the rise of the new penology. This is the identification and management
of high-risk categories and sub-populations, which are sorted according to their
levels of dangerousness, with such strategies and techniques existing since the
early 1990s (Feeley & Simon, 1992). Instead of focusing on the individual and trying to rehabilitate them, the new penology is focused on notions of risk and how
groups of individuals can be managed according to these risk classifications. In
particular 'it seeks to regulate levels of deviance, not intervene or respond to individual deviants or social malformations' (Feeley & Simon, 1992, p. 452). Under this
model, risk management is much more important than rehabilitation, with a focus
placed on surveillance, confinement and control. In addition to the new penology, dangerousness legislation has also been influenced by populist punitiveness
(Bottoms, 1995), the notion that the public are in favour of harsh punishments,
especially in relation to dangerous offenders. Thinking that this is true and that
the introduction of punitive penalties will win votes, policy makers have increasingly introduced more severe measures for those classified as high-risk (however,
see Hutton, 2005, who offers a more nuanced account of this view).

Previous dangerousness legislation

Prior to considering current dangerousness legislation, it may be useful to briefly
look at previous policy and in particular the sentence of imprisonment for public
protection (IPP). This is important for two reasons: first because it allows for a comparison between the two, but also because there are still offenders who are currently
being held in custody under the IPP sentence (see Chapter 9 for a discussion on this).
IPPs were first introduced into England and Wales on 4 April 2005, through the
Criminal Justice Act (CJA) 2003. Its introduction into sentencing policy for dangerous offenders was radical in the sense that it extended the use of dangerousness legislation to those people who, on the face of things, had not committed serious offences.
Prior to the CJA 2003, life sentences were mandatory for murder and then discretionary for other serious offences. The CJA 2003, however, extended public protection
sentences to include criminal damage; offences involving threats; keeping a brothel;
exposure and voyeurism. While these latter offences are criminal and deserve censure, few would classify them as dangerous. The relevant offences were contained in
Schedule 15 of the Act and included 65 violent offences and 88 sex offences.

   The test for an IPP was that the offender was over 18, had committed a sexual
or violent offence where the maximum penalty was at least ten years and had been
assessed as dangerous. The assessment of this was notoriously difficult, made worse

by the fact that when the Act was first enacted section 229(3) contained a presumption of dangerousness where the offender was 18 or over, had been convicted of one of the aforementioned relevant offences and the court felt that it was reasonable to conclude that the offender was dangerous. Bearing this in mind, and the fact that the relevant offences involved a number of minor offences, it is not surprising that Judges were forced to impose life sentences in wholly unsuitable cases. Judges were able to impose low minimum tariffs, but nevertheless these were still indeterminate sentences. The government thus made changes in 2008 (s. 13 Criminal Justice and Immigration Act (CJIA) 2008). These included a new Schedule 15A CJA 2003 which meant that the sentence was now only relevant to 23 rather than 153 offences and a restriction that the sentence could only be used if under normal sentencing policy the appropriate custodial term would have been at least four years. Despite such amendments, the consequence of introducing IPPs into dangerousness laws was a rapid expansion of the lifer population as evidenced in Table 10.1.

While the amendments made by the CJIA 2008 did result in a reduction in use, in an 8 year period over 8500 people were given the sentence with only 11 per cent released. When offenders were sentenced to an IPP, the sentencing judge would impose a minimum term of custody. This was set to be commensurate with the seriousness of the offence and was designed for reasons of punishment and just deserts (see Chapter 2 for explanations of these sentencing aims). Release however would only occur when the offender had demonstrated to the Parole Board that it was no longer necessary, on the grounds of public protection, for them to be detained in custody. The most common way in which an offender could prove this was through the completion of accredited offending behaviour programmes (OBPs). Due to the insufficient provision of these however (see Chapter 8), many prisoners were unable to evidence within their minimum terms that they had shown a reduction in their risk. This resulted in a large amount of offenders detained in custody who were past their minimum tariff (see Chapter 9 for further discussion on this). In September 2012, two months before the sentence was abolished, this was 3538 or 60 per cent of the IPP population (Ministry of

Table 10.1 Growth of IPP prisoners 2005–2012.

Year	No. sentenced to IPP	No. of IPP prisoners released
2005	147	0
2006	1283	3
2007	1687	13
2008	1691	36
2009	1132	53
2010	959	97
2011	867	300
2012	792	444
Total	8558	946 (11%)

Source: Ministry of Justice (2013c) *Criminal Justice Statistics September 2012.*
London: Ministry of Justice.

Justice, 2013c). The situation was therefore challenged in a series of cases as seen in Figure 10.1. In response, the UK government did very little. As discussed in Chapters 7–9 increased resources have not been given to HM Prison and Probation Service (HMPPS) and so the situation regarding insufficient programme provision remains. Significant delays in parole decisions (see Chapter 9) have also played a significant part in the IPP problem although the Parole Board is now making some advances in reducing this backlog. On 3 March 2019, however, there were still 2403 people serving IPP sentences, 91 per cent of whom were over their minimum tariff (Ministry of Justice and National Statistics, 2019b).

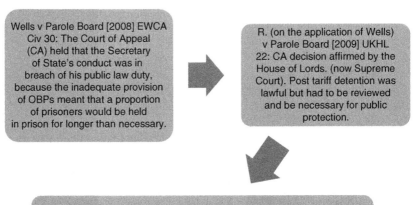

Figure 10.1 Challenges against the sentence of IPP

Current dangerousness legislation

Current sentences for public protection are found within the Legal Aid, Sentencing and Punishment of Offenders Act (LASPOA) 2012, which abolishes and updates previous sections of the CJA 2003. There are two main sentences with the first being a mandatory life sentence (s. 224A CJA 2003). This is different, however, to the life sentence discussed in Chapter 4. Here, the sentence is available where a number of criteria have been met, with the predominant factor being that the offender has committed a second listed offence. The listed offences are contained in Schedule 15B of the Act and comprise of 43 offences with attempting, conspiring, inciting, aiding, abetting, counselling or procuring any of the listed offences also included. In short there are 8 violent offences, 10 security/terrorist offences and 25 sexual offences. If the necessary criteria are met, the court must impose a life sentence, unless there are particular circumstances which would make it unjust to do so (s. 224A(2) CJA 2003). The criteria for the sentence are illustrated in Figure 10.2.

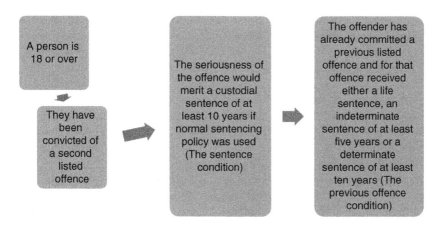

Figure 10.2 The life sentence for a second listed offence

The second available sentence is the extended sentence, which provides for a determinate custodial sentence but an indeterminate supervision period following release. The sentence originally came into force at the same time as the IPP sentence, although has been updated by the LASPOA 2012. It is only available for sexual and violent offenders, because even though in theory it could be used with terrorist offenders, since the listed offences in Schedule 15B are also relevant here, there are only extended supervision periods mentioned for sexual and violent offenders. Again the offender must meet a number of criteria which are outlined in Figure 10.3. The sentence is effectively divided into two parts. The first, the custodial stage, is set at whatever length is deemed to be appropriate based on proportionality and just deserts. At first glance this appears to be very similar to sentencing under 'normal' principles, although release arrangements are slightly different. Covered in Chapter 9, where an offender is serving a determinate

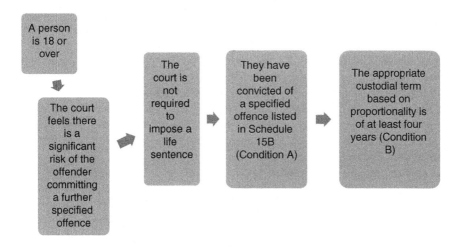

Figure 10.3 The extended sentence

sentence they can expect to be released at the halfway stage. Under an extended sentence however, release will not occur until the offender has served two thirds of their sentence in custody (s. 246A CJA 2003), although it is worth noting that originally release arrangements were the same as for 'normal' offenders. This time in custody can also be extended if the individual has received a custodial term of 10 years or more *and* the offence in question is listed in parts 1–3 of Schedule 15B CJA 2003 (this includes the 43 offences mentioned above, murder and any other offences which existed prior to the Act). In these circumstances the release of the offender is decided by the Parole Board and in such conditions the determinate custodial term effectively becomes an indeterminate one.

Once the custodial term has been served the offender then has an additional supervision period. Under normal sentencing rules an offender would serve the remainder of their prison sentence in the community under the supervision of either the National Probation Service (NPS) or the relevant Community Rehabilitation Companies (CRC) (see Chapters 6 and 9). So if for example the custodial term is for 24 months then they would spend 12 months in prison and 12 months being supervised within the community. Under an extended sentence however, the supervision period is extended by up to five years for violent offenders and by up to eight years for sex offenders. The length chosen will be what the court considers to be necessary in order to protect the public and is not intended to be proportionate with the seriousness of the original offence.

The key question is whether current sentencing options are an improvement on previous provisions. Taking the extended sentence first, the main change is that the offender will serve longer in custody than a normal offender and additionally if the appropriate custodial term is 10 years or more then the Parole Board are involved in the release decision. On the basis that we are talking about dangerous offenders, this change is appropriate. Due to the requirements of the new life sentence, it is unlikely that as many offenders will be caught within its net, when compared to the IPP. One consequence of this, in public protection terms however, is that those offenders who previously would have been assessed as dangerous and would previously have qualified for an indeterminate sentence will now receive a determinate sentence. This will have a determined release date; including a definite end date for license conditions. In that sense, it could be argued that the new life sentence will provide less public protection as fewer offenders will be held on life license. If sentencing judges agree then there may be an explosion in the use of the extended sentence and in order to ensure that the offender is kept in a custodial setting until they are considered safe for release, we could therefore see an increase in the appropriate custodial term to at least 10 years. While the court will need to justify this on the basis of commensurability, if the offender has already been assessed as dangerous and if there are also associated offences to take into consideration this shouldn't be too hard to do. This will result in a number of offenders again being held at the mercy of the Parole Board (see Chapter 9). There is therefore the risk that in the future while we may not have as many IPP prisoners being held in post-tariff detention, there may well be significant others held post-tariff serving extended sentences. Time will tell, but it may be that the extended sentence becomes the new IPP!

Discussion Questions

1. What do you think to the idea that dangerous offenders are kept in custody for what they may do in the future, rather than for what they have done in the past?
2. While the government openly acknowledges that it got it wrong with the IPP, are the current sentencing options for dangerous offenders any better? What further changes would you like to see?

PRISON CLIMATES FOR DANGEROUS OFFENDERS

The most obvious way in which to manage the risk of dangerous offenders is to lock them up. On the basis, however, that there are very few offenders serving whole life tariffs, the key question is how such offenders can be progressed through the prison system. This section builds on Chapter 7 by looking at two more prisons and discusses the different types of prison climates which have been shown to be useful with dangerous offenders.

The sex offender prison

Whether a custodial sentence is given for any particular offence will depend on how serious that offence is and also whether previous similar offences have been committed. Following such principles means that it is not uncommon for serious sex offenders to spend some time in custody. It used to be the case that sex offenders, along with other vulnerable prisoners (such as those in debt, or those who had informed on others), would be kept on vulnerable prisoner wings under Prison Rule 43. This segregation was to protect them from other prisoners; with sex offenders and in particular child sex offenders at risk of serious assults from mainstream prisoners. While such wings still exist, for example HMP Hull, in more recent years there has been a move towards sex offender only prisons, with these currently existing at HMP Whatton, HMP Stafford, HMP Isle of Wight, HMP Bure and HMP Littlehey. Apart from HMP Isle of Wight (Category B) all of the current sex offender only prisons are Category C training prisons, with an obvious omission being that there are no Category D prisons. Currently there are only two Category D prisons which will accept sex offenders: HMP Leyhill in the West and HMP North Camp in the East. The increase of sex offender prisons was partly due to the influx of historical sex offenders which were dealt with by the courts in light of the Jimmy Saville scandal in 2012, but also because it is easier to coordinate sex offender treatment programmes when they are being delivered in a smaller number of sites. While such prisons solve the problem of having to segregate offenders away from the general population and also allow for programmes of work to focus exclusively on sex offences, housing so many sex offenders under one roof may encourage the building up of sex offender networks and may also be counterproductive in terms of normalising deviant sexual attitudes and beliefs.

Category and function	Category C Adult male sex offender training prison
Prison status	Public
Location	Whatton, Nottingham
Building	Opened as a detention centre in 1966, but previously a RAF base. Has held sex offenders since 1990 and was the first sex offender only prison in England and Wales.
Operational capacity	841
CNA	775
Population	841
Reception criteria	All applicants must be (1) Cat. C; (2) have at least six months left to serve; (3) have a sexual conviction.
Residential units	11 wings: 8 new which house the majority in mostly single en-suite cells and 3 old style dorms (4 beds to a room). A separate unit for over 55s and an end of life suite.
Inspection details	15–26 August 2016: 'Whatton remained an overwhelmingly safe prison. There was comparatively little violence or anti-social behaviour' (HM Chief Inspector of Prisons, 2017d, p. 5).
IMB report	'a safe environment where prisoners are treated with fairness and decency' (Independent Monitoring Board, 2017d, p. 4).
Prison performance rating	Where 1 is serious concern and 4 is exceptional 3
Date of visit	3 March 2017

The main function of Whatton is treatment, with it achieving approximately one third of the national completion targets for living skills and sex offender treatment programmes (SOTPs). Whatton holds a very diverse population of sex offenders including deaf prisoners, transgender women, disabled offenders and the elderly. This is largely because the prison makes provision for such inmates, with it, for example, being the only institution to offer a deaf SOTP. Whatton also holds indeterminate prisoners, on the day of the visit, for example, there were over 150 IPP prisoners who had been through at least 2 parole reviews and were still in custody. The prison has a settled environment, it was one of the quietest prisons visited and incidences of violence or disorder are rare. This is partly because it houses longer-term prisoners but also because many are specialist sex offenders and therefore not on the anti-social criminality pathway, which you would encounter in other mainstream prisons.

Treatment Programmes

At the time of the visit, Whatton was still running the Core and Extended SOTPs. The Core was for everyone, except those who were classified as intellectually disabled (ID), and the extended, an additional programme, was being used for those who presented as very high-risk. For those who completed both this meant undertaking up to 77 sessions, at a rate of 4 or 5 sessions a week with each session lasting up to 2½ hours. The transition to Horizon (medium-risk) and Kaizen (high-risk) (new treatment programmes) had however begun with the notable difference being the fact that high-risk men no longer have to complete two programmes (they can go straight onto Kaizen) and both programmes are suitable for deniers, which the previous SOTPs were not. The prison also ran a SOTP designed for ID offenders (Becoming New Me) and a maintenance programme (Living as new me). In addition, there were healthy sex programmes and a number of living skills programmes such as healthy relationships, thinking skills and resolve. Different to the new penology (see introduction) the aim at Whatton is to treat the men as individuals.

Employment and Other Opportunities

In addition to treatment, there are also a number of work and training opportunities ranging from NVQs in building, plastering and decorating, to catering qualifications in the kitchens and horticultural opportunities in the gardens. There were textile workshops where the men made slippers and clothes, a woodwork craft shop and the laundry. Furthermore, DHL, who has the prison contract to provide canteen items for prisoners, ran their warehouse from the prison. Prisoners also take part in a wide variety of educational programmes ranging from entry-level basic skills to Open University degree programmes. This wide variety of constructive activities is partly because the prison is categorised as a training prison (see Chapter 7).

Medication

An innovative aspect of Whatton is its use of medication with sex offenders in order to reduce sexual drive and deviant fantasies. Medication is offered to those men who are sexually preoccupied and it helps them to be able to concentrate more on treatment and ultimately progress through the system. Referrals are accepted by psychiatrists who are involved in the process throughout, with referrals being made by any member of prison staff. At any one time approximately 5 per cent of the population will be on medication, with the majority taking SSRIs (see below for more detail). The national service runs out of six prisons (HMP Hull, HMP Whatton, HMP North Sea Camp, HMP Leyhill, HMP Frankland and HMP Isle of Wight) and is funded under the offender personality disorder pathway.

Current Challenges

One of the problems cited at the time of the visit was the fact that offenders were often reluctant to leave Whatton. This bed blocking was causing problems in terms of being able to accept other men. While men should be moved to resettlement prisons once treatment has ended, the resettlement system (see Chapter 9) is not working for sex offenders. This is because there are no sex offender only sites and mixed sites present several safety issues, which can undo much of the positive work, which has previously been achieved. At the time of the visit, Whatton was funding its own resettlement initiatives and was also discussing creating its own safe community accommodation for prisoners to move to.

The climate which a prison like HMP Whatton can provide is a fairly stable one, especially when compared to the prisons considered in Chapter 7. Illegal drug use is low, violence and diosorder is rare and there are sufficient resources and staffing available to ensure that the prison can focus on its treatment aims. Having this type of prison climate is important to the success of treatment, with research establishing that the context in which treatment takes place can be more influential than the actual treatment procedure. In one study, for example, it was found that while treatment gains could be made in community and forensic settings, the same gains were not replicated in prisons (Schmucker & Losel, 2015). Until recently the academic literature on prison climates and treatment gains has largely focused on therapeutic communities (see below), although now some evidence is emerging that treatment success can also take place within sex offender only prisons. As highlighted in Chapter 8, key factors in providing a good prison experience are supportive prison officer/prisoner relationships, sufficient out of cell time and sufficient constructive activities, but additional benefits of being in a sex offender only prison included having 'greater headspace and [a] reduction in anxiety and fear' (Blagden & Wilson, 2019, p. 7) with both facilitating personal development and change. As discussed in Chapter 8, orthodox prison environments often require men to wear 'masks' so that they blend into the dominant culture, but at a sex offender only prison, particpants of the research felt that they had the space to be themselves, reflect on their past and their behaviour and importantly start on a journey of change (Blagden & Wilson, 2019).

The therapeutic community

Rather than separate sex offenders from the general prison population, some prisons integrate them and treat them as any other prisoner. Two prisons which do this include HMP Full Sutton (see Chapter 6) which is a Category A, maximum security prison and HMP Grendon which runs a democratic therapeutic community (TC). TCs have been found to be useful not only with sex offenders but also with those who have committed serious violent offences and with those who have personality disorders. A TC has been defined as a 'structured psychologically informed environment ... where the social relationships, structure of the day and different activities together are all deliberately designed to help people's health and well-being' (The Consortium of Therapeutic Communities, 2013). TCs designed for the treatment of offenders have existed in England and Wales since 1962 when HMP Grendon, in Buckinghamshire, opened. Although Grendon was originally set up as a psychiatric experiment under the control of a medical superintendent, it came under the control of the main prison estate in 1985 and is now run by a prison governor, assisted by a director of therapy. TCs exist at HMP Grendon, a 200 bed unit at HMP Dovegate, one wing at HMP Wymott, two wings at HMP Gartree (one for those with learning disabilities), one 65 bed unit at HMP Holme House (used for treating severe drug misusing prisoners), a 40 bed unit at HMP Warren Hill and one wing at HMP Send (a women's prison) (Ministry of Justice, 2017j).

While TCs sound expensive, they only cost an extra £5000 per year per resident than a standard Category B prison. Such investment has been found to be beneficial, not just for the health and wellbeing of residents but also because prisoners in TCs cause significantly less damage and destruction than in other Category B prisons. For example, for every £1 invested into Grendon there is £2.33 worth of benefits (Bennett & Shuker, 2017). Two reconviction studies on Grendon (Marshall, 1997; Taylor, 2000), show that residents who stay for 18 months or more experience a significant reduction in their future reoffending by up to 25 per cent. When Grendon and other TCs house some of the most dangerous offenders in the country, this is significant.

Psychologically Informed Planned Environment (PIPE) units

PIPE units are a relatively new creation, having only existed within HMPPS since 2012. They arose out of a recognition that there were some offenders who had completed treatment in specialist prisons but on their return to mainstream prison, many were not psychologically equipped to deal with this change and therefore any progress which had previously been made was lost (Turley, et al., 2013). The aim of the unit is therefore to provide a progressive environment for prisoners to come to after they have completed therapy in either a TC, a high security prison or a sex offender only prison. They are not treatment, as such, rather they work to provide prisoners with opportunities to show that they have learnt from previous treatment with the intention being that the individual will be able to progress to a lower security classification or release. Staff on the units receive additional training so that they are able to develop an increased psychological understanding of the experiences and behaviours of the prisoners and help towards a more positive resettlement experience. There are currently PIPE units at HMP Gartree, HMP Send, HMP Frankland, HMP Hull and HMP Warren Hill.

Research on PIPE units is currently limited although one study has focused on the hopes and expectations of offenders on the high-secure unit in HMP Frankland, which, similar to HMP Grendon, houses sex offenders and mainstream prisoners together. Having congruence with the aims of a PIPE unit, the men interviewed said they hoped the unit would allow them to feel part of a community and that the environment would also help in their progression through the prison system (Bennett, 2014). Whether this has actually happened is currently unknown, with there being a need for more research in this area.

Discussion Questions

1. Should dangerous offenders be allowed back into the community or should more whole life tariffs be used (you may want to refer to the discussion in Chapter 4 to help answer this)?
2. What should be done with dangerous offenders when they are in custody?
3. Would you consider any of the prison environments discussed above in your prison?

Category and function	Category B Training prison
Prison status	Public
Location	Grendon Underwood, Buckinghamshire
Building	Originally a psychiatric hospital; it has been a prison since 1962.
Operational capacity	233
CAN	235
Population	220
Reception criteria	Cat. B or C; more than 18 months to serve; meets 'drug-free' criteria; no current diagnosis of major mental illness; accepts responsibility for offence and no self-harm within 2 months of referral (Ministry of Justice, 2017f).
Residential units	Six wings (A–G). A wing is for sex offenders, F for men with mild learning disabilities and G wing an assessment and induction unit.
Inspection details	'The physical fabric of the prison was shabby, and the automated night sanitation system outdated …. Relationships between staff and the men, and between prisoners and their peers, were outstanding' (HM Chief Inspector of Prisons, 2017c).
IMB report	'The Board wishes to commend the impressive work carried out by both the residents and the staff' (Independent Monitoring Board, 2018b, p. 4).
Prison performance rating	Where 1 is serious concern and 4 is exceptional 4
Date of visit	7 March 2017

The vast majority of men at Grendon are serving indeterminate sentences and have committed serious sexual and/or violent offences. They generally have a longer history in the criminal justice system, so offending behaviour is more entrenched in their lives. They tend to have been more disruptive in prison and two thirds have been child victims of sexual or violent abuse, often finding dysfunctional ways of coping with this distress, either through substance misuse or self-harm. Over 50 per cent have considered suicide. Grendon residents are often described as the most difficult, damaged and dangerous people in the prison system, but despite this Grendon is the only prison at this category level without a segregation unit.

Therapeutic Community

Grendon takes a psychotherapeutic approach to treatment, which acknowledges that a person's personality and behaviours are often shaped by childhood experiences and that this is often the root of their offending. It has a number of wings, or communities, with each housing approximately 40 residents (not prisoners). On Monday and

Friday mornings the whole community (residents and staff) meet, with this chaired by an elected resident. They will discuss issues of interest to the community including matters of conflict or needed change. They will also make decisions regarding people's lives, so if someone wants to apply for a job or they want to go off the community to participate in an activity, the meeting will discuss and vote on this. If there has been rule breaking the community will decide on the appropriate sanction and if there has been a breach of the fundamental rules (no sex, no drugs, no violence) they will vote on whether they still want to work with that person or whether they should be asked to leave the prison. The community meetings teach about decision-making and account-ability but in a living and learning way, so residents are making decisions and thinking through actions and holding each other to account.

On Tuesday, Wednesday and Thursday morning the community breaks down into smaller groups of 8–10 residents, facilitated by trained members of staff. The residents will go through their background, history and offences and explore how that links to their behaviour and thinking today. This helps them to make sense of their experiences and allows them to learn how they can manage it more effectively. Creative therapies such as psychodrama and art therapy may also be used. Residents at Grendon have to be mentally ready to engage with the therapeutic experience, because unless they do success will not be achieved. For some this may not happen until they come to Grendon for a second time. Others may not be able to cope with the intrusive nature of the environment so will actually ask to be transferred elsewhere.

'Grendon hasn't changed me, I've changed me, but Grendon has given me the opportunity to change' (Prisoner at Grendon).

In the afternoons, every resident has a job or goes to education. Residents are also encouraged to take part in community life, so all residents have a voluntary job ranging from being the chair of the community to feeding the fish and watering the plants. Each community also has a nominated charity, which they will raise money for and twice a year the wing will host a social day where they invite in interested professionals. There are also a number of clubs and societies including an artist in residence, the learning together pro-gramme (residents learn with students from Cambridge University), debating clubs and music opportunities. This enables residents to further develop their talents and interests. Every year the prison hosts 'visits with a difference' where residents can invite family members in to go through their therapeutic journey with them. Family members are also invited in for significant events, such as award ceremonies.

Resettlement and Progression

Due to the risk levels of those found at Grendon very few are released directly into the community, with most progressing to other Category C or D institutions. Grendon will work with these individuals to identify which is the best prison climate for them, whether this is a sex offender only prison, or a prison with a PIPE unit (see above). Prisoners will also be moved into open prisons so that they can work towards an eventual release.

RISK MANAGEMENT IN COMMUNITY SETTINGS

Multi-Agency Public Protection Arrangements (MAPPA)

Despite the fact that many dangerous offenders will spend some time in custody, the vast majority will one day be released into the community (see Chapter 9). One of the main ways in which sexual and violent offenders are managed within the community is through MAPPA. Under sections 325–327 of the CJA 2003, the Police, the NPS and the Prison Service (the responsible authorities) are under a statutory duty to establish arrangements for assessing and managing the risks posed by both sexual and violent offenders. There is also a duty on what are known as 'duty to co-operate agencies', which includes housing, social services, health and education, to co-operate with the responsible authorities. Panels are therefore often made up of police, probation, social services, health and housing. It is also good practice to involve, when appropriate, the expertise of forensic psychiatrists and psychologists (Maguire, et al., 2001). The main purpose of MAPPA is to help reduce the reoffending behaviour of sexual and violent offenders in order to protect the public, including previous victims, from serious harm. This is achieved by ensuring that all of the relevant authorities work effectively together so that relevant offenders are identified, appropriate risk assessments are completed and, leading on from this, suitable risk management plans are formulated. The key to this is the sharing of information between MAPPA agencies. In all decisions, resources follow risk, so MAPPA needs to ensure that it focuses its available resources in a way which best protects the public from serious harm. The responsible authorities are also under a duty to decide whether they should disclose information regarding the previous convictions of those whom it supervises, with this duty operational irrespective of whether information is actually requested (see below for more on this).

To qualify for MAPPA, offenders must fall into one of three categories:

1. Registered sex offenders: these will be managed by the police and, if under a court order or on license from prison, by the NPS as well.
2. Violent offenders, registered terrorist offenders and other sex offenders: includes offenders who have been sentenced to 12 months or more in custody or to detention in hospital with restrictions, now living in the community and subject to NPS supervision and management.
3. Other dangerous offenders: includes people who have committed an offence in the past, indicating a capacity to cause a serious risk of harm to the public and who because of their assessed risk it is thought needs multi-agency management.

Once it has been identified that an individual is MAPPA eligible it will then be decided at what level that individual needs monitoring. There are three levels of MAPPA supervision with this illustrated in Figure 10.4.

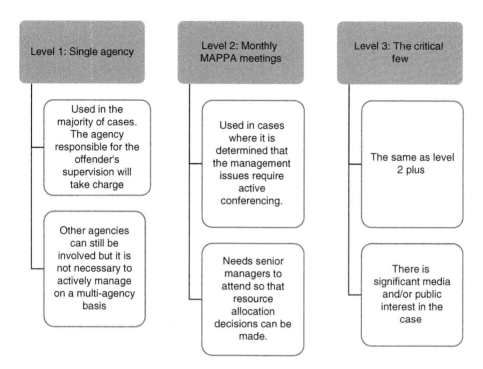

Figure 10.4 The three levels of MAPPA involvement

On 31 March 2018 there were 80,983 MAPPA-eligible offenders. Of these, 72.4 per cent were Category 1 offenders, 27.2 per cent Category 2 and less than 0.4 per cent Category 3. The large majority of cases (98.2 per cent) were managed at Level 1 (Ministry of Justice, 2018g). Data is also available for each MAPPA area with some examples seen in Table 10.2.

Looking at Table 10.2 in more detail, the last column is probably the most interesting, because it is the only one which offers a direct comparison between MAPPA areas. This is because areas are of unequal geographical size, with some being more urban or rural than others, so it is misleading to look at numbers apart from when comparing how many sex offenders a MAPPA area has per 100,000 of population. The top three MAPPA areas for this statistic are consistently Teeside, Humberside and Lancashire, although not always in that order. Preliminary research in Humberside has tried to identify why it is always in the top three, but no firm conclusions have yet been reached. Anecdotal evidence from practitioners suggests it is because it has two approved premises (places where some sex offenders will live after release), it has a sex offender unit at one of its prisons, it has a preponderance of seaside resorts which are thought to attract child sex offenders and it is a relatively cheap area in which to live. While some of these factors may also apply to Lancashire and Teeside there are also other issues which separate these areas (such as Humberside having two ports) and additionally there are other MAPPA areas which share these factors with Humberside but which do not

Table 10.2 MAPPA area data 2017–18.

Area	Cat. 1	Cat. 2	Cat. 3	Level 1	Level 2	Level 3	Total MAPPA offenders	Cat. 1 per 100,000 of population
Avon and Somerset	1592	989	15	2524	64	8	2596	106
Dorset	779	173	2	935	18	1	954	113
Essex	1427	343	6	1731	42	3	1776	89
Gwent	760	438	5	1136	62	5	1203	147
Hertfordshire	759	281	0	1036	4	0	1040	74
Humberside	1303	280	3	1570	15	1	1586	159
Lancashire	2088	899	5	2971	19	2	2992	159
London	6317	3833	24	10,068	84	22	10,174	83
Surrey	765	211	3	965	12	2	979	74
Teesside	814	338	5	1142	15	0	1157	164
Thames Valley	1417	554	8	1923	54	2	1979	68

Source: Ministry of Justice (2018g) *Multi-Agency Public Protection Arrangements Annual Report 2017/18.* London: Ministry of Justice.

have large amounts of sex offenders. Looking at the data there also appears to be a clear North–South divide, with the areas housing less offenders per 100,000 of the population (Thames Valley, Surrey, Hertfordshire, London and Essex) based in the South, but again there is currently no research to explain why this is so.

Over the years there have been a number of studies which have considered how effective MAPPA is, with the first looking at the predecessor to MAPPA, namely public protection panels (Maguire, et al., 2001). This has been updated by further studies (Kemshall, et al., 2005; Kemshall & Wood, 2007; Wood & Kemshall, 2010; HM Inspectorate of Probation, 2011; HM Inspectorate of Probation, 2015a) all of which have been largely favourable and which have produced advice on process and procedure. There is less research, however, on whether MAPPA works as a risk management method, that is, whether it reduces reoffending and adequately protects the public. This can be measured in two ways: first by the rate of breach and second by looking at the number of serious further offences (SFOs) committed by MAPPA eligible offenders. In 2017/18, 587 level 2 and 3 MAPPA offenders were returned to custody for breaching their licence conditions. This was a reduction of 16 per cent from 2016/17 and continues a steady decrease in recalls since 2006 (Ministry of Justice, 2018g). During the same time period, however, 242 MAPPA offenders were charged with a SFO, a 12 per cent increase from the previous year and the highest number for 10 years (Ministry of Justice, 2018g). While 242 may sound high when put into the context of the total number of MAPPA eligible offenders (80,983) this only represents 0.3 per cent of all cases (Ministry of Justice, 2018g). As noted by Wood and Kemshall, therefore, the real threat to the effectiveness of MAPPA is often not the offenders themselves but the impossible expectations placed on it by politicians and the public and the lack of adequate resources to facilitate it (Wood & Kemshall, 2010).

Although SFOs are rare they are nevertheless a serious breach of public protection and therefore must be seen as a failure of MAPPA. A further offence qualifies as a SFO where it is one of either 45 violent or 31 sexual offences which are listed in operational instructions (National Offender Management Service, 2015b). When this occurs a SFO review is undertaken to ascertain the circumstances which led to the commission of the offence and whether there are any lessons which need to be learnt. This will normally be undertaken by the relevant NPS or CRC, although in serious circumstances will be delegated to HM Inspectorate of Probation. An example of an independent SFO review can be seen in Figure 10.5. The findings and recommendations from such reviews can be useful, but often point to inadequate resources and overburdened staff – a common theme running throughout much of this book.

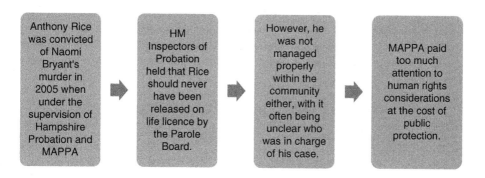

Figure 10.5 SFO review: Anthony Rice

Source: HM Inspectorate of Probation (2006) *An Independent Review of a Serious Further Offence Case: Anthony Rice*. London: HMIP.

Violent and sex offender register

Another way in which the public is protected from dangerous offenders is through a notification system. The registration of sex offenders was first introduced into England and Wales by the Sex Offenders Act (SOA) 1997. All offenders who had been convicted or cautioned for a listed sexual offence or found not guilty by reason of insanity had to submit their details to the police. The relevant sexual offences were listed in Schedule 1 of the Act and included offences such as rape, sexual intercourse with a child, causing or encouraging prostitution, incest and taking or possessing indecent photographs of children. This is why, even today, many refer to sex offenders as Schedule 1 offenders. Registration is now governed by the SOA 2003 and is known as the violent and sex offenders register (ViSOR). Within three days of release from custody or from receiving a community order, an offender must inform the police of their name, address, date of birth, banking details and national insurance number. There is also an ongoing duty to notify the police of any changes, with a failure to provide either the initial information or updates punishable by up to five years in custody. ViSOR went live on 19 August 2005 and works through a national database which is linked to every police force in England and Wales. HMPPS also have access to the data. Length of registration will depend on the original offence, with periods halved if the offender is under 18. This is known as the notification period as identified in Table 10.3.

For sentences over 30 months, registration used to be for life without any possibility for review. This, however, was held to contravene Article 8 of the European Convention on Human Rights (ECHR) (see *R (on the application of F) and Thompson v Secretary of State for the Home Department* [2010] UKSC 17), and so on 1 September 2012, the law was changed to allow those offenders subject to lifetime registration to apply to have this revoked. The earliest point at which an application can be made is 15 years from the date on which the offender made their first notification to the police (or 8 years if the offender was aged under 18 on that date). The application will be determined by reference to specified considerations, including information secured from HMPPS, the seriousness of the applicant's offending and their risk of sexual harm, and any submissions from the offender's victims. If an applicant is unsuccessful, they may not reapply for a further 8 years, though in exceptional cases the police may extend this minimum to up to 15 years (see ss. 91A–F SOA 2003).

Table 10.3 ViSOR registration terms (s. 82 SOA 2003).

Description of relevant offender	Notification period
A person who, in respect of the offence, is or has been sentenced to imprisonment for life or to imprisonment for a term of 30 months or more	An indefinite period beginning with the relevant date
A person who, in respect of the offence or finding, is or has been admitted to a hospital subject to a restriction order	An indefinite period beginning with that date
A person who, in respect of the offence, is or has been sentenced to imprisonment for a term of more than 6 months but less than 30 months	10 years beginning with that date
A person who, in respect of the offence, is or has been sentenced to imprisonment for a term of 6 months or less	7 years beginning with that date
A person who, in respect of the offence or finding, is or has been admitted to a hospital without being subject to a restriction order	7 years beginning with that date
A person within section 80(1)(d)	2 years beginning with that date
A person of any other description	5 years beginning with the relevant date

Community notification

While most people accept that registration is a good idea, the more controversial question is whether the public should be made aware of who is on the register. The United States of America (US) is one of the leading nations in terms of sex offender community notification. This is collectively known as Megan's Law, named after Megan Kanka who was raped and murdered by a known sex offender. In all 50 states, the public have a right to access their own state's sex offender register with this often provided through websites (see for example https://meganslaw.ca.gov). Despite several calls for a Sarah's Law in England and Wales (named after Sarah Payne who was also killed by a known sex offender), ViSOR is not open to the general public. Until fairly recently information contained on the register could only be passed in a controlled fashion to agencies who needed to know, such as housing, social services and schools, but this has now been extended.

This first extension was through a common law duty where the court had upheld a number of police decisions where women had been informed about the previous convictions of men who were close to their children (see for example *R v Chief Constable of North Wales Police and Others ex p. Thorpe and Another*, The Times Law Report 23 March 1998 and *R v Devon CC ex p. L* [1991] 2 FLR). Guidance from the Home Office did advise however that although such disclosures could be made, the police should be mindful about the 'potentially serious effect on the ability of an offender to live a normal life, the risk of violence to offenders and the risk that disclosure might drive them underground' (Home Office, 1999). On the basis that it was for the responsible authorities to decide whether to disclose, this was known as discretionary disclosure. Furthermore, in November 2006, the Child Exploitation and Online Protection Centre created a 'Most Wanted' website. This was used to display images and details of convicted sex offenders who had gone missing and failed to comply with notification requirements. When the website was first set up, five offenders were placed on it. One of these contacted the police within days scared for his own safety. Another, who had been on the run since 2000, having failed to register with the police when released from prison, was found in October 2007 due to information from the site. In the first year of the website, nine offenders were traced (Harrison, 2011). The website is now run by the National Crime Agency and contains all dangerous offenders, including sex offenders, violent offenders, white-collar criminals and drug related offenders (see https://nationalcrimeagency.gov.uk/most-wanted).

Despite the fact that the 1999 Home Office guidance stated that 'the general presumption is that information should not be disclosed' (Home Office, 1999) this changed in 2008 when new disclosure duties were enacted. Section 327A CJA 2003 creates a legal duty whereby responsible authorities (such as the police) have to consider whether information concerning an offender's previous convictions should be disclosed. Instead of this being discretionary however, the Act states that there is a presumption that information will be disclosed if:

(a)   a child sex offender managed by it poses a risk in that or any other area of causing serious harm to any particular child or children or to children of any particular description, and

(b)   the disclosure of information about the relevant previous convictions of the offender to the particular member of the public is necessary for the purpose of protecting the particular child or children, or the children of that description, from serious harm caused by the offender.

The scheme therefore gives parents, carers and guardians a statutory right to register an interest in a person whom they have suspicions or concerns about, if they have access to their children. Disclosure pilots began in September 2008 and due to their success were extended in March 2009 to 18 police areas. It is now available across all 43 police forces and known as the Child Sexual Offender Disclosure Scheme (CSODS).

During the first 12 months of the pilots, the police received 585 enquiries under the scheme, of which 315 were proceeded with as applications and 21 sexual offending disclosures were made. A further 11 general disclosures (including violence) were also given, while another 43 cases led to a range of other child safeguarding actions, including referral to Children's Social Care. The Home Office claimed that this had protected approximately 60 children (Home Office, 2010). Subsequent research on the CSODS has, however, shown relatively low take up rates. In 2015/16 for example, there were only 1252 applications in 21 police forces, resulting in 192 disclosures (McCartan, et al., 2018). This has brought into question whether (a) the scheme is really needed and (b) whether it is working in the way that it was hoped it would be (Kemshall & Weaver, 2012).

Presumptive disclosure has also been extended to violence between intimate partners. The domestic violence disclosure scheme or Clare's Law (named after Clare Wood who was killed by her violent ex-partner) was piloted in four police areas between July 2012 and September 2013 and became nationwide on 8 March 2014. It works in a comparable way to the CSODS, so there is a right to ask and a right to know, with the latter being where the police will proactively trigger an application in order to protect a potential victim from their partner (Fitz-Gibbon & Walklate, 2017). Information will be disclosed where a Multi-Agency Risk Assessment Conference establishes that there is a pressing need. Similar to the CSODS, there is limited evidence of its benefits (Fitz-Gibbon & Walklate, 2017).

Discussion Questions

1.   What is you view on community notification? In the US, community notification practices include providing informational leaflets, community notification meetings, marking car licenses, requiring the offender to approach neighbours and publishing information in local newspapers. Would you like to see any of these used in England and Wales?

2.   Do current notification practices in England and Wales offer the right balance between public protection and offender privacy? If not, what changes are required?

Other risk management strategies

Another available option, this time just for sex offenders, is the polygraph, which is said to measure physiological activity associated with the autonomic nervous system. During the test, responses to a carefully structured set of questions are measured and recorded, with the thought being that such measures can determine whether the subject is telling the truth. This is quite controversial, especially as there are disputes over the accuracy of the tests. Despite such concerns its use with sex offenders in England and Wales, dates back to 1999 when it was first piloted in the West Midlands (Wilcox, et al., 1999). Positive results, from this study, led to further research, where sex offenders had volunteered to undertake sexual history tests (Madsen, et al., 2004; Wilcox & Sosnowski, 2005). In the latter study, researchers found that the testing uncovered much more information, from the offender, about their number of victims, paraphilic interests and age at first offence. In short it allowed the NPS to appreciate that they were dealing with much riskier men then they had previously thought; essential knowledge when formulating effective risk management plans.

Despite the pilots only covering voluntary testing, the ability to include mandatory polygraph conditions in a sex offender's parole license has been available since April 2009. Initially this was restricted to nine police areas in the East and West Midlands, but has been force-wide since January 2014. The condition is available where the offender has served a custodial sentence of 12 months or more, the offence was sexual and the offender is 18 or over (see ss. 28–30 Offender Management Act 2007). One of the first evaluations into the condition stated:

> Polygraph testing has increased the chances that a sexual offender under supervision in the community will reveal information relevant to their management, supervision, treatment, or risk assessment. It has also increased the likelihood of preventative actions being taken by offender managers to protect the public from harm (Gannon, et al., 2012, p. iii).

Despite the fact that sexual history disclosure has increased and arguably offender managers are better informed about the risk factors of individuals, there is no evidence that the use of polygraphy effects reconviction rates or has an impact on the offender's behaviour (Grubin, et al., 2019).

Finally, responsible authorities can make use of civil orders. There are currently three, as outlined in Figure 10.6. The orders can be made by a Magistrates' Court acting in a civil capacity and on the application of a Chief of Police or the Director General of the National Crime Agency. Although the orders are civil in nature, it is a separate criminal offence if any of the prohibitions are breached, with this punishable by up to five years in custody.

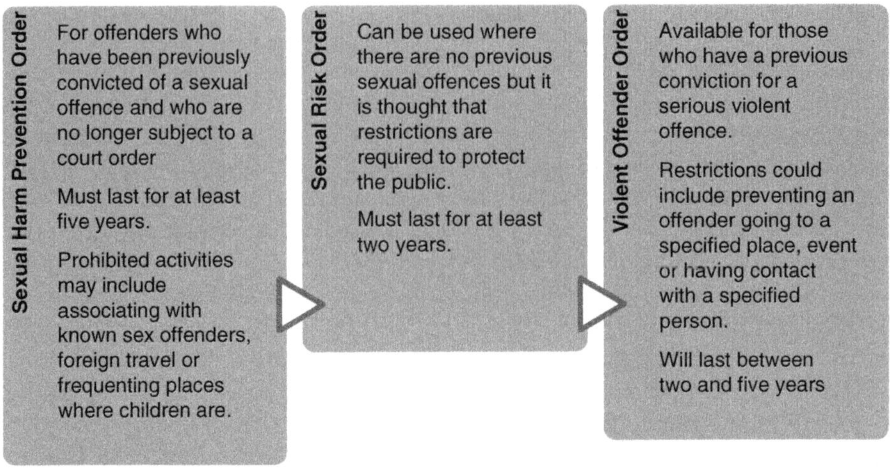

Figure 10.6   Civil orders available for dangerous offenders

Discussion Points

1. What is your view on the range of risk management strategies outlined above? Do they offer sufficient public protection or is more required?
2. How can human rights considerations be reconciled with community notification and/or polygraph testing, especially when there are validity concerns over the latter?
3. Should civil orders be used against those who have not been convicted of an actual offence, especially when these orders have criminal consequences? Why do you think that this option exists for sex offenders but not for violent offenders?

RISK REDUCTION STRATEGIES

However effective risk management strategies are, they are not designed to lower risk and so in addition to managing dangerous offenders, responsible authorities are also committed to interventions which focus on risk reduction. While there are a number of strategies used to achieve this goal, the methods considered here are psychotherapy, pharmacotherapy and Circles of Support and Accountablity (CoSA).

Psychotherapy

The main use of psychotherapy in England and Wales is through OBPs. In line with the purposes of psychotherapy, these educate and teach self-control mechanisms and the re-evaluation of attitudes. This is achieved by focusing on a number of key areas which have been shown to help in the reduction of risk, including enhancing self-esteem; challenging cognitive distortions and minimisation; stress management and relapse prevention (Harrison, 2011). HMPPS have an array of general OBPs including Thinking Skills, Think First, Reasoning and Rehabilitation and the Priestley 1:1 programme, although this section will focus on programmes for sex offenders and those specifically designed for anger management and domestic violence perpetrators.

Since March 2017, there are two treatment programmes used for sex offenders in prisons in England and Wales. The first, Kaizen, is for high-risk, high-need, high-priority offenders and the second, Horizon, is for medium-risk offenders, with there nothing currently available for low-risk offenders. Both programmes are based on the Good Lives Model (Ward & Brown, 2004), which works with offenders to build better lives for themselves and are available to deniers and those who maintain their innocence. Previously deniers were not allowed to participate on the SOTPs, which not only hindered their progression and release, if they were serving an indeterminate sentence (see Chapter 9) but also because they were not participating in treatment it meant that they would be placed on the basic level of the incentive and earned privilege scheme (see Chapter 8). In addition to the prison programmes, there are also a number of community SOTPs, with the duration and intensity of these dependent on what treatment if any the offender has previously received. Typical modules focus on relapse prevention, victim empathy, lifestyle change, self-management and interpersonal skills with completion sometimes taking up to two years to achieve (Harrison, 2011).

Historically, research has suggested that some success can be achieved with sex offenders (see Hedderman & Sugg, 1996; Hanson, et al., 2002; Losel & Schmucker, 2005; Schmucker & Losel, 2015). Other research has shown that while treatment programmes can have an effect on the reoffending rates of low deviancy and low denial offenders, they do not have the same effect for those who are high in deviancy and/or high denial. Indeed one study found that 'more than half [of the high deviance group] showed no treatment change at all' (Beech, et al., 1998, p. 4). Perhaps due to this uncertainty the Ministry of Justice undertook an evaluation of prison-based SOTPs in 2017 (Mews, et al., 2017). As part of the study, 2562 convicted sex offenders undertaking a programme were compared to 13,219 other untreated sex offenders using 87 matching factors. Although the reoffending rates were fairly similar for both groups:

- More treated sex offenders committed at least one sexual reoffence (excluding breach) during the follow-up period when compared with the matched comparison offenders (10% compared with 8%).
- More treated sex offenders committed at least one child image reoffence during the follow-up period when compared with the matched comparison offenders (4.4% compared with 2.9%).

The results suggested that the prison-based programme was generally associated with little or no change in sexual and non-sexual reoffending, and that in fact the 'treatment' may actually have been making the offenders worse. This may have been caused by the programmes emphasis on group work, with this having the potential to normalise deviant behaviour, or even lead to the sharing of contacts or sources. The results were fairly controversial and led to the Ministry of Justice introducing Horizon and Kaizen as outlined above. Whether or not these are any better in terms of effectiveness is currently unknown.

There are also a number of treatment programmes designed specifically for violent offenders, with one example being CALM (Controlling Anger and Learning to Manage it), which is an emotional management programme designed for those whose offending behaviour is precipitated by intense emotions. The goals of the programme are to help offenders to understand the factors that trigger their anger and to support them in learning skills to manage these emotions (Ministry of Justice, 2010). Another example is IDAP (Integrated Domestic Abuse Programme) which is a community-based programme specifically designed for domestic violence perpetrators. It is suitable for heterosexual male offenders, aged over 17 who have committed at least one violent act against an intimate partner and helps offenders to change their attitudes and behaviours towards women (Harrison, 2011). A final example is the Self Change Programme which aims to reduce violence in high-risk repetitively violent offenders. It is based predominantly in prison settings, although it's final learning block does extend to practice in the community and consolidation of the offender's relapse prevention plan.

Despite the plethora of studies concerning sex offender programmes, research concerning the efficacy of violent offending has been minimal, with Polasckek claiming that 'the most optimistic conclusion that can be reached is that the best programmes may help a little' (Polasckek, 2006, p. 127). Research in England and Wales has been negligible, with most research taking place either in North America, Canada, or Northern Ireland (for example, see Henning & Frueh, (1996) for an evaluation on the Self Change Programme in Vermont, Canada). Much more research on efficiacy in England and Wales is therefore required.

Pharmacotherapy

In addition to psychotherapy, another option for high-risk sex offenders is the use of pharmacotherapy (see HMP Whatton). Usually, and wrongly, referred to under its more emotive title of chemical castration, pharmacotherapy is the use of anti-libidinal and/or psychotropic medications to reduce sexual desires. Anti-libidinal medication works by reducing testosterone levels in adult males to those found in pre-pubescent boys, thereby decreasing sexual interest and arousal. Although offenders can still be sexually aroused by relevant stimuli, they are generally less interested in sex, and there is a great reduction in spontaneous sexual behaviour. SSRIs (selective serotonin reuptake inhibitors) a psychotropic medication, are commonly prescribed for depression, anxiety and compulsive disorders. They work by increasing the concentration of serotonin, a chemical messenger found in the brain which relates to mood, impulsivity, appetitive behaviours and sexual activity. They are less potent than anti-libidinals and aim to reduce the intensity of sexual fantasies and sexual urges. Due to the fact that both drugs reduce or in some cases eradicate sexual desire and fantasies, they are only likely to work on those who offend due to uncontrollable urges. Limited success will be found with those who offend for reasons of power (rapists) or under the influence of drink or drugs (for more details see Harrison, 2007).

A number of research studies suggest that medication can be effective in reducing deviant sexual fantasies, sexual ability, erectile function and consequently recidivism rates of sexual offending (see Khan, et al., 2015; Winder, et al., 2017). It is important to note, however, that the use of both anti-libidinal and SSRIs can result in a myriad of negative side effects with some academics arguing that the true extent of these is simply unknown. Reported effects include fatigue, hypersomnia, lethargy, depression, a decrease in body hair, an increase in scalp hair, weight gain, gynaecomastia (the growth of breasts), liver damage, bone mineral loss, nausea, indigestion, skin rashes, galactorrhoea (abnormal production of breast milk), shortness of breath and decreased production of oil from sebaceous glands in the skin (Harrison, 2007). Due to the severity of some of these conditions it is questionable whether the use of anti-libidinals, in particular, contravene Article 3 of the ECHR which protects against torture, inhuman or degrading treatment. Whilst the pain and suffering involved with such conditions may not pass the threshold for torture, the effects could be described as inhuman and/or degrading. With regard to gynaecomastia this can easily be seen as degrading and humiliating for the offender involved, especially considering the fact that any growth is irreversible even when treatment is withdrawn (for more discussion on this and also how Articles 8 and 12 ECHR may be engaged see Harrison & Rainey, 2009). It is therefore imperative that the offender's suitability for such medication is assessed and that practitioners involved have knowledge of the offender's full medical history. If pharmacotherapy is given to an offender whose pre-existing medical condition is worsened or whose quality of life is seriously curtailed by taking part in such a programme, Article 3 may be engaged. As with other practices discussed throughout this chapter the balance between public protection and the rights of the offender need to be considered.

Circles of Support and Accountability

The final strategy is CoSA, which could be viewed as both a risk management and a risk reduction tool. The development of CoSA can be traced back to the restorative work carried out by the Canadian Mennonite Church in 1994 and in particular to Charlie Taylor a prolific and high-risk sex offender who, in addition to the responsible authorities, was released from prison into the care of a small group of church volunteers. Through their support and accountability, Charlie remained crime free, with this quickly spreading to other Mennonite fellowships across Canada (Hanvey & Hoing, 2013). England and Wales have been piloting Circles since 2002. They consist of four to six people who surround the offender, known as the core member, with support and accountability. In terms of support this could be in relation to finding accommodation and/or employment but could also involve encouraging the core member to get involved with suitable clubs and socities. Coupled with this though is an appropriate amount of disapproval and challenge concerning inappropriate behaviour, thoughts and feelings. It is thought that support at this level can help the Core Member grow in self esteem, develop healthy adult relationships and maximise their chances of successful reintegration. The core member and the volunteers are known as the inner circle with the outer circle made up of MAPPA professionals and the CoSA coordinator. Members will initially meet weekly, with mid-week telephone support, dropping to fortnightly contact as the core member becomes more integrated into the community. Each circle will last approximately 12 months, although will usually continue until it is thought that the offender no longer requires the support.

Different to their Canadian forefathers, CoSA in England and Wales has developed in a systemic way, being professionally driven but community supported. Most initiatives since 2008 are managed by Circles UK; who work in partnership with police, probation and local MAPPA professionals and who are funded by the Ministry of Justice, statutory agencies and a number of charitable trusts and foundations. Research conducted on circles both in Canada and England and Wales has been positive. In one study, those involved in CoSA reoffended 70 per cent less for sexual reoffending; 35 per cent less for general reoffending and 57 per cent less for violent reoffending, when compared to the matched control. This was also confirmed in a second study where recidivism rates were 2 per cent versus 13 per cent for sexual reoffending, 9 per cent versus 32 per cent for violent reoffending and 11 per cent versus 38 per cent for general recidivisim (Wilson, et al., 2008). Research has also shown that participation in circles can reduce the isolation and loneliness of sex offenders (Wilson, et al., 2009; Fox, 2015) and increase an offender's emotional wellbeing (Bates, et al., 2012).

A recent development to CoSA has been initiated by the Safer Living Foundation which is a joint venture between HMP Whatton and Nottingham Trent University (see http://saferlivingfoundation.org). Rather than waiting until the offender has been released into the community, sex offenders at HMP Whatton get the opportunity to engage with a prison-based circle approximately 3 months prior to their relase and then this circle (with the same volunteers) will continue in the community for around 18 months after release (Kitson-Boyce, et al., 2019). The main benefits of starting the circles early include the fact that the offenders are not as fearful about being released into a community. This was classified as 'no longer being alone' (Kitson-Boyce, et al., 2018, p. 19) and provided the offenders with a greater sense of support during this incredibly stressful time.

Discussion Questions

1. What do you think to the risk reduction options discussed above? Do they raise any significant human rights or other ethical issues? If they do, can you still justify their use?

2. Pharmacotherapy in some US States is used on a mandatory basis and precedes release from prison. In England and Wales it is only available if the offender consents to its use. In your opinion which is the preferential practice?

3.   CoSA is said to work because it attempts to reintegrate offenders rather than trying to stigmatise and isolate them. Is this way of working with offenders better than disintegrative policies such as community notification and bars on obtaining employment?

CONCLUSION

When compared to 'normal' offenders there are relatively few dangerous offenders held in custodial institutions and/or supervised within our communities. Despite this, the potential harm and the long-term damage which these offenders can cause means that it is appropriate that special attention is paid to those who represent a high-risk in terms of public protection. As illustrated throughout this chapter this is why such offenders are dealt with under separate sentencing principles and why a number of risk management strategies exist so that as far as possible public protection is maintained. While this is important, there is a real tension between the need to protect the public on the one hand and the desire to honour the rights of the offender on the other. This is especially the case when sentencing policies are based on what the offender *might* do in the future rather than what they have done in the past, and the questionable efficacy of some of the strategies covered here. Respecting the rights, of especially child sex offenders, is not a popular notion however, with many preferring to lock such offenders up forever rather than trying to work with them in a more reintegrative way. Despite this populist view, it is only through initiatives such as OBPs and CoSA that real change can occur and for this reason more resources to fund such programmes are desperately needed. If an offender is treated like an offender throughout their life it makes it very difficult for them to change; but with help, time and compassion even someone as high-risk as Charlie Taylor can turn their life around.

 Now read:

Thomas, T. (2003) 'Sex offender community notification: Experiences from America', *Howard Journal*, 42(3), 217–228.
Harrison, K. and Rainey, B. (2009) 'Suppressing human rights? A rights-based approach to the use of pharmacotherapy with sex offenders', *Legal Studies*, 29(1), 47–74.
Thompson, D. and Thomas, T. (2017) *The Resettlement of Sex Offenders after Custody: Circles of Support and Accountability*. Abingdon: Routledge.

Now watch:

CNN News (2009) Castration as a cure to sex offenders, available on You-Tube at: https://www.youtube.com/watch?v=Esntuis_3so

Sky News (2019) Special report: Inside the 'Circle', available on YouTube at: https://www.youtube.com/watch?v=r8Hdcz_fXQk

 Now consider:

Assess reasons for and against making the sex offender register in England and Wales open? Are current disclosure mechanisms sufficient or would you like full community notification as seen in the US?

11 Children and Young People

INTRODUCTION

The commission of crime and the need to sentence those who commit it, is not limited to adults. In recognition of this and in order to adhere to international and national laws there is a separate system designed to deal with children and young people. In theory, the primary consideration of the youth justice system (YJS) is 'the best interests of the child', with this outlined in Article 3 of the United Nations (UN) Convention on the Rights of the Child. Furthermore, the Convention advances that states must develop measures for dealing with young people through non-judicial measures (Art. 40), custody should 'only be used as a measure of last resort and for the shortest appropriate period of time' and that while in custody every child 'shall be treated with humanity and respect' (Art. 37). National law also recognises this welfare principle, although only states that the court should 'have regard to the welfare of the child' (s. 44(1) Children and Young Person Act 1933). The welfare principle works on the basis that all decisions concerning a child should be made in the best interests of that child. It is more sympathetic than punishment and accepts that there could be reasons behind the offending behaviour and that these should be solved before the child develops into an adult. In addition to welfare, the prevention of offending is also seen as a recognised aim. While there was an attempt to put this on a statutory footing in 2008, the relevant legislative section (s. 9 Criminal Justice and Immigration Act 2008) still has no commencement date. Historically, there have therefore been opposing approaches when it comes to sentencing young people, with particular tension between welfare and justice. In more recent times we have also seen the introduction of restorative justice (see Chapter 3).

For the purposes of this chapter a young person is anyone under the age of 18, although in England and Wales you need to be at least 10 years old to be held criminally responsible for your behaviour. This is known as the age of criminal responsibility, with England and Wales setting this at quite a low age when compared to some other countries around the world. Some examples can be seen in Table 11.1. It used to be the case, in England and Wales, that it was presumed that those aged 10–13 were not capable of committing criminal offences, although this presumption could be disproved. Known as the rebuttable presumption of doli incapax this was abolished in 1998 by the Crime and Disorder Act, making it far easier to prosecute and convict young children of criminal activity. It is also worth noting, that children under the age of 10 can still be subject to civil care and supervision orders, including placement in secure accommodation. The use of civil proceedings to deal with criminal and anti-social behaviour has also been prevalent in England and Wales since 1998. This saw the introduction and rapid use of the anti-social behaviour order. While this has now been abolished, other similar civil orders remain, with the main aim behind their use being to divert young people from the YJS.

Table 11.1 Examples of the age of criminal responsibility around the World.

Europe		Americas		Africa		Asia	
Andorra	12	Argentina	16	Angola	14	Bangladesh	9
Austria	14	Barbados	11	Cameroon	10	India	7
Finland	15	Peru	18	Egypt	12	Indonesia	8
Scotland	12	USA	7–10	Kenya	8	Iran	9–15
Spain	14	Cuba	16	Liberia	7	Iraq	9
Ukraine	16	Panama	12	S. Africa	10	Japan	14

Source: Child Rights International Network (2018) *Minimum Ages of Criminal Responsibility Around the World*. [Online] Available at: https://www.crin.org/en/home/ages.

In order to provide an overview of the YJS this chapter will reflect on the range of criminal orders available to the courts when sentencing young people and also which courts young people are dealt in. When considering these criminal options attention will primarily be paid to the referral order, the youth rehabilitation order and the young people's estate including a focus on HMYOI Feltham and New Zealand as the spotlight country. Finally a brief consideration of civil options is included.

FACTS AND FIGURES

To add some context it may be useful to begin with some facts relating to young people and their involvement in the YJS. Between April 2017 and March 2018:

- There were 4,877,000 crimes recorded by the police (age not recorded at this point).
- 65,833 children and young people were arrested, of which approximately 31 per cent were from Black, Asian and Minority Ethnic (BAME) groups (BAME young people make up 18 per cent of the population).
- Approximately 10,999 cautions were given.
- 31,509 were proceeded against in the criminal courts.
- 22,996 were convicted and sentenced:
  - 1585 were sent to immediate custody, with the average custodial term being 16.7 months, an increase of 5 months in the last 10 years. The average monthly population in the youth secure estate was 894. BAME young people made up 45 per cent of the custodial population.
  - 15,635 were given a community sentence, with the most common sentence being the Referral Order.
  - 5776 were given other court sentences.
- 40.9 per cent reoffended (Youth Justice Board and Ministry of Justice, 2019).

THE YOUTH COURT

In recognition of the differences between adults and young people, all those aged between 10 and 17 will normally be tried in a Youth Court, rather than an adult Magistrates' Court. In essence the two are very similar, although Youth Court magistrates are drawn from a special panel who have experience or a special interest in young people and it is not held in public. Youth Court magistrates have similar powers to those serving in the adult court, although they have a different range of options to choose from and can sentence offenders to longer periods in custody (see Chapter 4). As with the adult system, all cases will start in the Youth Court with serious offences such as murder and rape usually committed to the Crown Court. Different from the adult system, however, is the fact that indictable offences do not have to be sent to the Crown Court. In the year ending March 2018, for example, 55 per cent of the proceedings in the Youth Court were for indictable offences (Youth Justice Board and Ministry of Justice, 2019). An offender can also be sent to the Crown Court for sentencing if it is thought that the powers of the Youth Court are insufficient. However, in the year ending March 2018, only 4 per cent of those young people sentenced, were sentenced by the Crown Court (Youth Justice Board and Ministry of Justice, 2019).

There is currently no separate Crown Court for young offenders, despite the fact that in 2000, using such a court for two 11-year-old boys was heavily criticised by the European Court of Human Rights (ECtHR). A summary of the case and the findings of the ECtHR can be seen below. Despite the fact that in the instance case using an adult Crown Court was held to violate Article 6 of the European Convention on Human Rights (ECHR) very little has since changed. The only current modifications are that the lawyers 'may take off their wigs and robes during proceedings to put the defendants at ease' (Crown Prosecution Service, 2018b) and consideration should be given to the physical layout of the court, the court's timetable, splitting the defendant away from adult defendants (if applicable) and ensuring that the child is not exposed to humiliation or distress (Practice Direction: (Crown Court: Trial of Children and Young Persons) (2000) (Archbold 4-96a)). How the latter can be guaranteed, however, especially considering there are no limits identified in relation to public attendance, is difficult to fathom.

Discussion Questions

1. What do you think the age of criminal responsibility should be in England and Wales? Scotland recently increased theirs from 8 to 12 and the average age in Europe is 14. Should the age of 10 therefore be increased?
2. What do you think of the ruling in V v UK and T v UK? Do you think that the ECtHR, in relation to Article 6 was right?
3. If such a case was to happen again are the adjustments mentioned in the Practice Direction sufficient or alternatively should a Youth Crown Court be introduced?

V v United Kingdom (UK) (2000) 30 E.H.R.R. 121; T v UK (Application No. 24724/94)

The two appellants, Jon Venables and Robert Thompson were tried and convicted in an adult Crown Court for the abduction and murder of two-year-old James Bulger. They argued that their trial, in a public adult Crown Court, plus the punitive nature of their sentence was in breach of Article 3 of the ECHR, protecting against the use of inhuman or degrading treatment or punishment and/or a breach of Article 6 which guarantees a fair trial. By 12 votes to 5 the ECtHR held that there had not been a violation of Article 3, but unanimously held that there had been a breach of Article 6. While the court said that trying a child of 11 was not automatically a violation of Article 6, 'it is essential that a child charged with an offence is dealt with in a manner which takes full account of his age, level of maturity and intellectual and emotional capacities, and that steps are taken to promote his ability to understand and participate in the proceedings' (p. 126). Despite the court in question making some effort (the procedure was explained to them, hearing times were shortened and they visited the court prior to the trial starting), the boys were on public display and exposed to the scrutiny of the public and press. This was made worse by the high profile nature of the case. In such cases the ECtHR thought that better protection could have been offered to the boys by limiting the public's access to the court. It was also noted how the trial followed all of the formality and ritual of an adult case including the Judge and barristers wearing wigs and gowns.

The court also found it unlikely that either boy was able to properly participate in the trial. With reference to V he stated that he was 'terrified of being looked at in court and had frequently found himself worrying what people were thinking about him. He had not been able to pay attention to the proceedings and had spent time counting in his head or making shapes with his shoes'. Expert witnesses argued that it was 'very doubtful that he understood the situation and was able to give informed instructions to his lawyers' (p. 126–127). Evidence relating to T stated that 'due to the conditions in which he was put on trial, he was unable to follow the trial or take decisions in his own best interests' (p. 127).

SENTENCING APPROACHES

When penalising adults, the sentencing court will generally think about what it is that it is trying to achieve with that individual (see Chapter 4). While the intention may be for the sentence to act as both a general and an individual deterrent and that it also has some rehabilitative content, sentencing policy in England and Wales is largely based on just deserts (see Chapter 2 for an explanation of these sentencing aims). Under the justice model it is therefore the seriousness of the offence that is used to decide what the most appropriate disposal will be in any particular case. The situation for young people is, however, slightly different with sentencers having to often choose between the opposing models of welfare and justice, with restorative justice also being a further consideration. Just deserts is covered in detail in Chapter 2 and restorative justice in Chapter 3 so it is only the welfare model which is considered here.

The welfare approach

The welfare model takes as its premise the belief that a young person is a product of both environmental and social factors and that it is this which is the cause of their offending behaviour. Under this model, the aim of the YJS is to correct these factors and to provide help and treatment (rehabilitation), with the best interests of the child given primary consideration over punishment. In England and Wales, this welfare approach can be seen through the existence of a separate youth court and also through the fact that when in custody children and young people are separated from adults. It also explains why there are a number of low level and diversionary options available to the police (see Chapter 5) and the sentencing courts with custody only used as the last resort. Furthermore the Sentencing Council (see Chapter 4) states that when sentencing children and young people, wherever possible, the focus should always be on rehabilitation (Sentencing Council, 2017g). While this is positive it is worth reminding ourselves that this doesn't make welfare the paramount consideration. The YJS in England and Wales is therefore welfare orientated but cannot be called a true welfare model. Countries, which do have their youth justice systems based on a welfare model, include Japan, Sweden, Norway, Denmark and Finland (see Cavadino & Dignan, 2006; Lappi-Seppala, 2011).

Discussion Points

1. Thinking about the different sentencing approaches that can be used with young people, which do you think is the most appropriate?
2. Is the approach that you've chosen suitable for all types of offence or is it necessary to use different approaches for different types of criminal behaviour?

COMMUNITY SENTENCING

On the basis that nominal and financial penalties for young people are considered in Chapter 5 the next option in terms of hierarchy for the court to consider is a community penalty. In the year ending March 2018, 68 per cent of all young people who were sentenced by the criminal courts were given a community sentence. Of this number 64 per cent received a referral order and 35 per cent a youth rehabilitation order (Youth Justice Board and Ministry of Justice, 2019). It will be these two options that will be discussed further.

Referral order

The referral order is available to all those aged 10 to 17 who have pleaded guilty to their offence and is only available in the Youth Courts. Where compulsory referral conditions are met (i.e. the offender pleads guilty to an imprisonable offence, it is their first offence and the court does not think that custody is appropriate) the court 'shall' make the order. Where discretionary referral conditions exist (i.e. the compulsory conditions are not met but the offender pleads guilty) the court 'may' make the order (ss. 16–17 Powers of Criminal Courts (Sentencing) Act 2000). If a young person has pleaded guilty, is a first time offender but is on the custody threshold (i.e. the court is unsure whether they should go to custody or not) the Youth Offending Team (YOT) can convene a youth offending panel (YOP) (see below) prior to sentence, where an intensive contract will be agreed upon. The youth court can then decide whether this is sufficient to save the young person from custody (Sentencing Council, 2017g).

Once made, the Order is implemented by the local YOT, which is a multi-agency team made up of representatives from police, probation, local authorities, social services, health, education and housing. There is a YOT in every local authority with it being their statutory duty to coordinate youth justice services for all those who need them (s. 39 Crime and Disorder Act 1998). The order can last between 3 and 12 months, with length dependent on the seriousness of the offence/s (a just deserts approach).

As the name suggests, the order involves the referral of the young person, with this referral being made to a YOP. The YOP is made up of at least three people, one of whom will be a member of the local YOT and the other two trained volunteers from the local community. If the young person is under 16, the court will make a supplementary order requiring that at least one appropriate adult attends the meetings. In addition, the young person can ask another adult to accompany them and, if relevant, the victim of the offence will be asked whether they wish to attend. If the victim does attend they can also bring someone with them. The YOP will work with the young person to agree a youth offending contract which in essence sets out a programme of behaviour. The contract will usually focus on two points: interventions that reduce the likelihood of the young person reoffending (for example, being at home during specified times and/or participating in specified activities) and activities which will repair the harm which the original offence caused (mediation sessions, unpaid community work, and/or financial compensation to the victim).

Three-monthly review meetings and a final panel meeting will monitor the offender's compliance and progression. If a contract cannot be agreed on or is later breached, the young offender risks being sent back to court and re-sentenced for the original offence. If the contract has been successfully completed when the order comes to an end then the conviction will be 'spent'. The order could originally only be used once, but changes made in the Legal Aid, Sentencing and Punishment of Offender Act 2012, allow the court to use a referral order even if it had been used before. In the past if a referral order was breached or there was further offending the court would have had no choice but to revoke it, which arguably had the effect of undermining any restorative work which had been completed. This was also changed by sections 43–45 of the Criminal Justice and Courts Act 2015, which now allows the original referral order to remain and the offender to be fined or the referral order amended. The maximum fine is £2500 and the order can be extended by up to 12 months.

The referral order, while not a diversionary mechanism (see Chapter 5) is a low level response from the court. Its emphasis is on reparation and the reduction of reoffending, with it also being an opportunity for parents to become involved in helping their child to engage in the programme of behaviour. The central principles behind the order are therefore restoration, reintegration and responsibility, with the guidance for the order stating that YOPs 'should operate on restorative justice principles, enabling the young offender, by taking responsibility and making reparation, to achieve reintegration into the law-abiding community' (Edwards, 2011, p. 45). As discussed in more detail in Chapter 3, the YOPs allow the opportunity for all those affected by the crime to come together and implement a plan of action, which will help to repair the harm caused. The fact that the conviction is spent at the end of the order also ties in with restorative values and especially Braithwaite's theory of reintegrative, rather than disintegrative shaming (Braithwaite, 1989). This way of working with young people has been shown to be effective (Earle, et al., 2002) and is a positive way of dealing with young people, especially when it is their first encounter with the YJS (Edwards, 2011). Offenders have also stated that they found the YOPs positive and that they were treated fairly throughout:

> Panels made me feel better about myself because everything they said was positive … I ended up feeling good about myself because of the way they treated me. (HM Inspectorate of Probation, 2016b, p. 30)

One criticism of the order, however, is its use with serious offences. Referring back to the compulsory referral conditions above, in such situations, the court has no choice but to make a referral order, even if they think that a financial penalty or a youth rehabilitation order would be more appropriate. This has led to some situations where the YOP is faced with dealing with quite serious offences. Edwards, for example recounts a situation where a YOP he was involved in was faced with a young person who had pleaded guilty to making and distributing images of child sexual abuse. He states:

> As well as being beyond the type of offence for which CPMs [community panel members] receive training, we were surprised that the youth court had opted for a RO [referral order] and not a custodial sentence, and puzzled as to how to apply restorative principles. (Edwards, 2011, p. 61)

Concern has also been expressed about the suitability of the referral order for young people who have mental health issues (Youth Justice Board, n/d). Furthermore, The Magistrates' Association has expressed its frustration at its lack of discretion in this regard, but the government have remained firm. This is somewhat surprising when the youth rehabilitation order (see below) has so many other options than the referral order and may be more effective for those on the borderline of the custody threshold. Indeed it would be a travesty of justice if a first time offender was sent to custody because a referral order was not suitable, but a youth rehabilitation order would have been.

A review on how effective referral orders are was carried out by HM Inspectorate of Probation in 2016 (HM Inspectorate of Probation, 2016b). Overall it was found that the order was more successful in terms of preventing reoffending and reintegrating the offender back into the community than any other option, although it was accepted that this could have also been because the order was generally used with first time and low level offenders. Some areas for improvement were found however, including giving the young person a greater voice in the programme of work and ensuring that they understood everything that was happening. The key to the order's success was found to be the fact that it was grounded in restorative justice and adhered to the three primary aims of restoration, reparation and reintegration (HM Inspectorate of Probation, 2016b).

Discussion Questions

1. What do you think to the referral order? Is it appropriate that the most popular sentence for young people is based on reparation and the prevention of reoffending?
2. Should it be extended to those young people who haven't pleaded guilty but have been found guilty?
3. Should it be used for serious offences or should more discretion and the option of the youth rehabilitation order also be available?

Youth Rehabilitation Order (YRO)

If the criteria for a referral order are not met and the custody threshold has not been reached, the court will look to impose a YRO. This option has been available since 2009 and in many respects is very similar to the adult community order with requirements (see Chapter 6), except the YRO has the option of 18 requirements (see Figure 11.1) rather than just 11. The last two options (intensive supervision and surveillance and fostering) are only available for those aged 15–17, unless the offender is

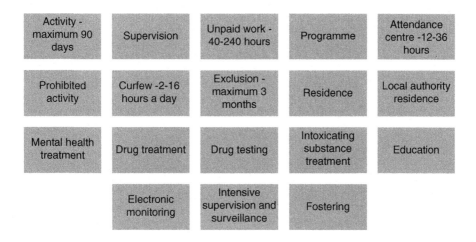

Figure 11.1 The requirements of the YRO (s. 1 Criminal Justice and Immigration Act 2008)

classed as persistent and then it can be used with 12–14 year olds. Unpaid work and the residence requirement are also only available for 16 and 17 year olds. All of the other 14 requirements are available across the age range of 10–17. In order to promote the use of community sentencing, sentencers must provide a reason if they do not use an alternative to custody for those young people who are on the custody threshold. Depending on which requirements are chosen, the court is able to focus on punishment, public protection, reparation, reducing reoffending and/or rehabilitation (see Chapters 2 and 3 for more details on these sentencing aims). While the order will be made for a set length of time, with the maximum period being three years, it will end once all of the requirements have been completed. Conversely, it can be extended by up to six months if the requirements have not been achieved, although this can only be done once.

To help sentencers determine which and how many requirements should be given, after the individual has either pleaded or been found guilty, the court must retire until a pre-sentence report (PSR) has been prepared by the local YOT. In recommending requirements, they will be endeavouring to find a balance between (1) the seriousness of the offence and the risk which the young person poses, with (2) their needs (Crown Prosecution Service, 2017). As illustrated in Table 11.2 further guidance on which requirement to opt for is provided by the Sentencing Council (see Chapter 4).

A breach of any of the requirements will result in the young person being returned to the youth court. If this happens, the court has the option to do nothing and allow the order to continue, impose a fine of up to £2500 (and allow the order to continue), amend the terms of the order or revoke the order and resentence for the original offence. Where the offence was originally on the custody threshold, a breach is likely to result in a custodial sentence.

Table 11.2 Intervention levels and suggested requirements for young people.

Intervention level	Child or young person profile	Requirements of order
Standard	Low likelihood of reoffending **and** a low risk of serious harm	Primarily seek to repair harm caused through, for example: • reparation; • unpaid work; • supervision; and/or • attendance centre.
Enhanced	Medium likelihood of re-offending **or** a medium risk of serious harm	Seek to repair harm caused and to enable help or change through, for example: • supervision; • reparation; • requirement to address behaviour e.g. drug treatment, offending behaviour programme, education programme; and/or • a combination of the above.
Intensive	High likelihood of re-offending **or** a very high risk of serious harm	Seek to ensure the control of and enable help or change for the child or young person through, for example: • supervision; • reparation; • requirement to address behaviour; • requirement to monitor or restrict movement, e.g. prohibited activity, curfew, exclusion or electronic monitoring; and/or • a combination of the above.

Source: Sentencing Council (2017g) *Sentencing Children and Young People. Overarching Principles and Offence Specific Guidelines for Sexual Offences and Robbery – Definitive Guideline.* London: Sentencing Council, p. 27.

Discussion Questions

1. What comparisons can you make between the YRO and the adult version? Does the YRO offer anything better?
2. If you were a sentencer and deciding which combination of requirements to impose on a young person what considerations would be important to you?

THE YOUNG PEOPLE'S ESTATE

When discussing the young people's estate the first question that must be asked is whether young people should be locked up. Referring back to international treaties, the UN Convention on the Rights of the Child states that while non-judicial measures should be used first, custody can be used as an option of last resort. Just because something can be used, however, doesn't necessarily mean, that it should be. While there will be some young people who need to be detained in order to protect others and/or themselves, this does not make up the majority of the young people's estate. In fact, for the year ending March 2018 the median time spent in youth custody was only 87 nights and 24 per cent of those held were only there for remand purposes (Youth Justice Board and Ministry of Justice, 2018). As outlined below there are serious concerns with how some of the current custodial units for young people are run, coupled with staffing issues which prevent education provision and leave many boys locked in their cells for hours at a time. In Chapter 8, it was argued that the adult secure estate is failing, with the picture for young people being no better.

The young people's estate is the collective name for all youth custodial and secure facilities for those under 18. It is managed by the Youth Custody Service (YCS), part of HM Prison and Probation Service (HMPPS), which has a commitment to safeguard and promote the welfare of children who are in contact with the YJS. The YCS has been operational since September 2017, with the Youth Justice Board (YJB) in charge before this. The YJB now functions as a monitoring board and provides government with advice on the YJS including custodial institutions (HM Chief Inspector of Prisons, 2018a). Young people can be contained in secure units from the age of 10. If the person is under 15, rather than being sent to a young offender institution (YOI), they will be contained in either a secure training centre (STC) (12–17) or a secure children's home (SCH) (10–17). Opposite to dangerous offenders (see Chapter 10), however, resources do not follow risk in the young people's estate. SCHs, for example, receive £210,000 per year per child, STCs receive £160,000 and YOIs only £76,000 (HC Deb, 23 May 2018, cW). Generally, a child with the lowest possible risk level will therefore be placed in a SCH, which has the highest staffing levels and the most opportunities for therapeutic input. If they become more difficult they will go to a STC and if they become too complex for a STC they will be moved to a YOI. Interestingly and by way of comparison, in 2019 it was cheaper (£42,501) to send a child to Eton College, one of the most prestigious public schools in England, than to lock them up in a YOI.

In February 2019 the population of the secure estate for children and young people under 18 was 834, of whom 37 were 14 or younger (HM Prison and Probation Service, 2019). Over the last decade the number of young people who have been detained by the courts has fallen by 71 per cent (Prison Reform Trust, 2018b). While this reduction is positive, the downside is that it has concentrated the amount of violent and serious offenders and those with the most complex needs into a small estate. Before the reduction in youth custody there would be perhaps one or two complex cases on each custodial housing unit but now it is the majority of offenders. This has also made it more difficult to separate and manage disruptions and problems associated with gang affiliation. Another consequence is that a number of YOIs have been closed which has meant that many more children are being accommodated further away from home, with often long and difficult journeys for families if they wish to visit (Taylor, 2016). Another statistic worthy of note is the increase of BAME children in the young people's estate. In February 2019, of the 834 children detained, 391 (46.8 per cent) were from BAME backgrounds (HM Prison and Probation Service, 2019). Ten years ago, BAME young people only accounted for 26 per cent (Prison Reform Trust, 2018b). While this percentage is still too high, when we take into account the percentage of BAME young people in the general population (18 per cent), the fact that it is further increasing is of real concern.

Custodial sentences

Detention and Training Order (DTO)

The detention and training order (DTO) is by far the most common custodial sentence used with young people, with it imposed in 80 per cent of custodial cases in the year ending March 2018 (Youth Justice Board and Ministry of Justice, 2019). It is available to all 15–17 year olds and for those aged 12–14 if they are regarded as being persistent offenders. The offender must have committed an offence which, in the case of an adult, would be punishable by imprisonment. The order can last between 4 and 24 months but cannot exceed the maximum term of imprisonment that the Crown Court could impose on an adult offender for the same offence. For summary offences, where the maximum term is 51 weeks for an adult, the maximum term for a DTO is 6 months. As its name suggests it is made up of two parts:

1. Detention: this will make up one half of the whole order.
2. Training: this takes the form of supervision within the community, carried out by the local YOTs. The needs of the young person will determine what this will involve but it will often include aspects of surveillance, unpaid work, training and education.

In combining elements of custody and supervision, the order is designed to be used with persistent and/or serious offending.

Other custodial sentences

Even though the DTO is the most common custodial sentence, there are two others available under the Powers of Criminal Courts (Sentencing) Act 2000:

- Where someone aged under 18 commits murder, they can be held at Her Majesty's pleasure (section 90).

- Long-term detention of under 18s is available where the offence is punishable (in the case of an adult) with 14 years or more and it is either a relevant sexual or firearms offence (section 91).

In the case of Her Majesty's pleasure this is an indeterminate sentence. As with adults the young person will have a minimum custodial term set, but will not be released from prison until such time that the Parole Board think that it is safe to do so. The individual, depending on age may therefore find themselves detained in a SCH, moved to a STC and then a YOI before being transferred to the adult secure estate. The maximum length of detention under a section 91 sentence is the same as that which can be imposed on an adult offender. If the maximum is life, then this can be ordered under section 91, although the standard length is usually no more than two years.

Custodial institutions for young people

Secure Children's Home

There are currently eight SCHs in England and Wales, housing young people generally between the ages of 10 and 14, although in theory young people up to the age of 17 can be placed there. On 31 March 2018, there were 255 places (Department for Education/National Statistics, 2018). They are small residential units with high staff/resident ratios, housing both boys and girls and are run by local authorities. While some of the young people will be serving criminal court orders, others will have been placed there for welfare reasons (see s. 25 Children Act 1989). For example, on the 31 March 2018, 47 per cent of children held in SCHs were placed there by the local authority on welfare grounds, 48 per cent were placed by the YCS either due to a court remand or sentence and 5 per cent had been placed by the local authority but this time in a criminal justice context (Department for Education/National Statistics, 2018). Of the 204 children who were detained on 31 March 2018, 33 per cent were female and 66 per cent were male. Although this gender split has been pretty static over the last few years it is in direct contrast to the gender split in the adult secure estate where women only make up approximately 5 per cent of the prison population (see Chapter 12 for more on women offenders). At the homes, individual teaching programmes will be formulated and the children will follow a school day timetable, with outside agencies also able to provide counselling, anger management, drug and alcohol treatment and other therapeutic interventions.

Secure Training Centres

STCs are predominantly for 12–14 year olds, although again anyone up to the age of 17 can be accommodated there. Usually, girls aged 12 and over and boys aged 12–14 will be placed in a STC. There are currently three centres in England and Wales, namely Medway, Oakhill and Rainsbrook. Originally all three were run by private providers but Medway was taken over by HMPPS from G4S in 2017 following a BBC Panorama programme which highlighted allegations of abuse and mistreatment. Rainsbrook was also taken away from G4S and given to another private provider (MTCnovo) in 2016, again following complaints. They are slightly larger than SCHs, housing between 50 and 80 young people per site and similar to SCHs focus on education, rehabilitation and the prevention of reoffending.

Young Offender Institutions

The final option is the YOI which is used predominantly for 15–17-year-olds. There are currently four YOIs in England (Cookham Wood, Feltham, Werrington and Wetherby) run by HMPPS and one in Wales (Parc) which is contracted out to G4S. As highlighted above, despite the fact that these will house the most disruptive and complex individuals they receive the least amount of money, have the smallest staff to resident ratio and are the largest in size.

For the purposes of this book, HMYOI Feltham was visited in an attempt to get a flavour of what a YOI is like. While Feltham was chosen due to ease of access (the author knowing one of the deputy governors) it is important to acknowledge that it is probably one of the most notorious YOIs in the current estate. For reasons of context, it might be useful to initially consider previous inspection reports before looking at it today. HM Inspectorate of Prisons (HMIP) first inspected Feltham in 1989 and at that point noted a lack of staff; not enough constructive activities; the fact that the boys had to eat in their cells and too little education and exercise (Crook, 2018). Since that first report similar concerns have been raised, made worse by additional issues relating to the use of unnecessary control and restraint and in later years problems associated with crowding. In 1998, for example,

> the Chief Inspector said his inspection of Feltham was the most disturbing he had done in his three years as HM Chief Inspector. He said treatment and conditions were totally unacceptable, even worse than two years previously with a marked deterioration in the treatment of boys. (Crook, 2018)

In 2010 the prison was described as 'a volatile and difficult environment in which to ensure safety ... [where] staff placed heavy reliance on the use of force, segregation and special accommodation' (HM Chief Inspector of Prisons, 2010, p. 5). Some improvements were noted in 2012, but deterioration had again occurred in 2013:

> We had serious concerns about the safety of young people held at Feltham A. Many told us they were frightened at the time of the inspection, and that they had little confidence in staff to keep them safe. Gang-related graffiti was endemic. There was an average of almost two fights or assaults every day. Some of these were very serious and involved groups of young people in very violent, pre-meditated attacks on a single individual with a risk of very serious injury resulting. (HM Chief Inspector of Prisons, 2013, p. 5)

Some improvements were then seen (see inspection details below), partly because the number of young people kept at Feltham had decreased, but in July 2019 the urgent notification process (see Chapter 8) was invoked in relation to Feltham A. This was due to 'very high levels of violence, between boys and against staff, high use of staff force, poor care, long periods of lock-up in cells and escalating self-harm' (HM Inspectorate of Prisons, 2019).

Restraint and control

One of the most controversial issues relating to youth custody is the use of force through techniques designed to restrain and control. One way in which this is achieved is through restrictive physical interventions (RPIs), that is, when 'force is used to overpower or with the intention of overpowering a child or young person' (Youth Justice Board and Ministry of Justice, 2019). In the year ending March 2018, there were approximately 5400 RPIs, in the youth secure estate, which was a 20 per cent increase from the previous year. Worryingly, this is the largest year on year increase in the last five years (Youth Justice Board and Ministry of Justice, 2019). In the same time period there were also 3800 single separation incidents (where children in SCHs or STCs are forcibly separated from others) and nearly 6600 use of force incidents across STCs and YOIs. This represents on average 52.4 use of force incidents per 100 children per month (Youth Justice Board and Ministry of Justice, 2019).

The use of force in the young people's estate came to the forefront of public attention in 2004 after the death of Gareth Myatt, a 15-year-old who died after being restrained by three adults at Rainsbrook STC, for refusing to clean a sandwich toaster. He was held in the seated double embrace and died, choking on his own vomit. Four months later Adam Rickwood, at 14, was found hanged in his cell following a restraint incident at another STC. Techniques used at this time included pain complaint and pain-inflicting distraction methods, including bending the upper joint of the thumb forwards and down towards the palm of the hand and exerting pressure with knuckles on a child's lower ribs (Howard League for Penal Reform, 2011). An independent inquiry into the deaths found not only that the methods of restraint were unsafe, but that there were systemic failures across the whole youth secure estate (Carlile, 2006).

A fundamental question which must be asked is whether force should be used against children, especially considering that custodial institutions hold some of the most vulnerable children in society. This is despite the fact that some children and young people can be severely disruptive, some though because of mental health issues. One interesting study carried out by Gooch (2015), looks at the experiences of 21 young people held in a YOI, in relation to physical restraint and force. While the study acknowledges that violence was an everyday occurrence, including in some instances serious violence, it was nevertheless felt that force was too routinely used against the young people (Gooch, 2015). Guidance stated that force could only be used as a last resort, but the study unearthed that officers were sometimes using it in order to get the young people to comply with their

PRISON

Function	A closed YOI
Prison status	Public
Location	Feltham, Middlesex
Building	Originally built in 1854 as an Industrial School, used as a Borstal in 1910 and a remand centre in 1988.
Operational capacity	180
CNA	240
Population	140
Residential units	Feltham A: nine units including an induction and enhanced support unit for the most difficult offenders.
Inspection details	'There had been some very good initiatives and some significant investment in Feltham. However, the progress could easily prove to be fragile if investment falls away or leadership loses its focus' (HM Chief Inspector of Prisons, 2018d, p. 5).
IMB report	'All prisoners endured frequent and unpredictable daily regime changes, often caused by a shortage of uniformed staff ... it is an unusual week that passes without several violent incidents' (Independent Monitoring Board, 2018a, p. 5).
Prison performance rating	Where 1 is serious concern and 4 is exceptional 2
Date of visit	8 March 2017

HMYOI Feltham is a young person and young adult establishment split into Feltham A (predominantly 15–17 year olds) and Feltham B (for those aged 18–21). Feltham A has up to 180 young people, housing a mixture of children on remand and those who have been sentenced. Sentences range from three month DTOs to indeterminate life. Accommodation consists of small units, each housing approximately 30 young people. The majority of the cells are single, except one corner double cell. Feltham is on a large site encompassing 93 acres with a lot of green space and a number of sports fields. The young people come from a large geographical area including London, the South East, the South West and the Midlands.

Regime

A typical day at Feltham begins at 7.30 am when cells are unlocked. Inmates get a chance to have some breakfast and make applications before being moved to education, programmes or workshops, which begin at 8.30 am. At 11.30 am they return for lunch which they will eat locked in their cell. Three hours of activities will also take place in the afternoon with these ending at 4.30 pm when they will be locked up again.

From Monday to Thursday, evening association is held between 6.00 and 8.00 pm. On Friday, activities only take place in the morning which is followed by Muslim service and some association. Weekends are used for visits, association and other religious services.

Constructive Activities

The main focus for Feltham A is on education with the aim being to achieve 30 hours of education per week. There is a very extensive education block and many opportunities available for the offenders, including regular parent's evenings. On the day of the visit, however, education was closed, as there weren't enough staff to escort the young people to and from the wings. Offenders can also access psychological programmes focusing on anger management, control and violence, and there are workshops split evenly between Feltham A and B, including a laundry and an area to teach cleaning. A wish for the future was to have some more practical opportunities for the young people; with maths, for example, being taught through bricklaying rather than in a classroom. This acknowledged the fact that not all of the young people would be able to attain academic qualifications and that these were often children who out in the community would not have been attending school.

The prison worked with a number of charities including Barnardo's to provide an advocacy service and Kinetic Youth which ran a Youth Council. It was noted that some of the young people had brain injuries and mental health issues and a lot of children had experienced significant trauma in their upbringing, including physical, sexual and emotional abuse. For many of these young people this was why they behaved in the way that they did, so there was a desire to have more trauma counselling available. This, it was felt, had the potential to be more worthwhile than education, in terms of reducing reoffending and improving social relationships with family and friends.

Current Challenges

One of the major challenges at the time of the visit was staffing, both in terms of retention and recruitment. Like other prisons Feltham had lost a lot of experienced staff over the last few years and these were being replaced with less experienced younger staff who weren't always as resilient to the pressures of working in a YOI. They were also losing staff to other professions, largely because the pay which used to be fairly good was now decidedly average. Staff, for example, could earn just as much, if not more, working next door at Heathrow Airport.

The other challenge was violence, with a lot of sporadic, spontaneous, quite intense and often gang-related incidents. Some of this was about survival (bravado and swagger), with some of the young people thinking that they needed to hit out first in order to get respect. Prison officers noted however that these were still young children and while many appeared brave on the unit they would often cry behind a locked door. The prison also had to be careful to separate rival gangs although could not always prevent rival members seeing each other in the corridors. It was noted that while adults tend to have one-on-one fights this was unusual with young people, with five or six attacking one person being more the norm.

instructions. Furthermore, 'notions of care were largely missing, as was any recognition that officers were dealing with children' (Gooch, 2015, p. 9).

In response to such criticisms, the government introduced a Minimising and Managing Physical Restraint (MMPR) system. This is currently in place in all STCs and YOIs and all frontline staff at these institutions must undergo MMPR training, with understanding assessed through a written test and scenario-based exercises. Top-up training is also required every six months (National Offender Management Service, 2015a). The system is designed to reduce the use of physical restraint on young people and make restraints safer, although according to Allison & Hattenstone, 28 of the 66 restraint scenarios have at least a 40 per cent chance of causing harm with some having the potential to result in 'catastrophic injury'. For example:

> Moving a child through a door way with a waist restraint belt on has a three out of five chance of causing breathing difficulties resulting in death or permanent severe disability affecting everyday life. (Allison & Hattenstone, 2016)

Data on injuries caused through the use of restraint techniques is available in Table 11.3. While the incidence of injury has decreased over the last few years this must be read in the context of a decreasing youth custody population, although as noted above the most complex children are still being managed within these custodial units.

Table 11.3 Injuries sustained as a result of a restrictive physical intervention 2012–2017.

	2012/13	*2013/14*	*2014/15*	*2015/16*	*2016/17*
SCHs	169	158	156	123	123
STCs	336	243	247	136	148
YOIs	685	590	309	170	106

Source: HL Deb, 1 November 2017 cW.

Inspection reports

As with the adult estate all STCs and YOTs are inspected by HMIP. In 2017/18 six inspections took place in YOIs (The Keppel Unit in Wetherby was inspected separately) and three in STCs meaning that every custodial unit was inspected. Units are inspected on four areas (safety, respect, purposeful activity and resettlement) with there being four possible outcomes (good, reasonably good, not sufficiently good and poor). A summary of these results can be seen in Table 11.4. HM Chief Inspector of Prisons noted that:

> children continued to feel unsafe in YOIs and bullying was still a problem ... rates of violence against staff and boys were higher than in previous years ... [and] time out of cell was very poor, education provision was not always good, and too few boys attended activities. (HM Chief Inspector of Prisons, 2018a, p. 63)

Table 11.4 Outcomes in YOI inspection reports published in 2017–18.

	Safety	*Respect*	*Purposeful activity*	*Resettlement*
Cookham Wood	Not sufficiently good	Reasonably good	Not sufficiently good	Not sufficiently good
Feltham A	Poor	Reasonably good	Poor	Reasonably good
Keppel Unit	Reasonably good	Reasonably good	Not sufficiently good	Reasonably good
Parc	Reasonably good	Reasonably good	Reasonably good	Reasonably good
Werrington	Reasonably good	Reasonably good	Reasonably good	Good
Wetherby	Not sufficiently good	Not sufficiently good	Not sufficiently good	Reasonably good

Source: HM Chief Inspector of Prisons (2018a) *Annual Report 2017–18*. London: HMIP, p. 63.

Ofsted inspections of YOIs in England rated one YOI as inadequate, three as requiring improvement and only one as good in terms of education provision. Even if the provision had have been up to scratch, the average out of cell time on weekdays at Cookham Wood and Feltham was only 4.5 hours, with some only having as little as 30 minutes out of cell time per day (HM Chief Inspector of Prisons, 2018a).

The picture was no better for STCs. In 2017–18, outcomes across the three sites were either inadequate or required improvement. The Chief Inspector of Prisons noted that:

> levels of violence in STCs were the highest per head of those held in any type of institution ... violent incidents had increased from the already high levels at Rainsbrook and Oakhill, ... [and] at Oakhill, use of force had increased to 100 incidents a month in a centre holding 75 children. (HM Chief Inspector of Prisons, 2018a, p. 70)

Secure schools

In response to these issues the government has talked about abolishing STCs and YOIs and replacing them with secure schools. This came from a recommendation from a review of the YJS carried out by Charlie Taylor (Taylor, 2016). Recognising the strong link between education and offending and the fact that many young people in custodial units were either behind in their education or had stopped going to school, the recommendation was to place education at 'the heart of youth custody' (Taylor, 2016, p. 40) by reconceiving youth prisons as schools. Taylor visioned that secure schools would be small custodial units located on a more regional basis than existing YOIs. Headteachers would have autonomy to recruit and train staff and also commission other services such as mental health and

Population	4,786,213 (Worldometers, 2019d)
Prison population (including remand prisoners)	10,053 (Department of Corrections, 2019)
Prison population per 100,000 of national population	214 (Institute for Criminal Policy Research, 2019b)
Remand prisoners	31.15% (Department of Corrections, 2019)
Number of establishments	15 male and 2 women prisons and 4 youth justice residences (Department of Corrections, 2019)
Official capacity of prison service	8393 (Institute for Criminal Policy Research, 2019b)
Occupancy level	106.1% (Institute for Criminal Policy Research, 2019b)

Brief Profile

New Zealand is a country in the south-western Pacific Ocean, next to Australia, consisting of North Island and South Island. It is made up of two dominant cultural groups namely the Māori, the descendants of the original Polynesian settlers and New Zealanders of European descent. It is a relatively small country, roughly the size of Great Britain, but with under five million people is relatively unpopulated.

Youth Justice in New Zealand

Similar to England and Wales, the age of criminal responsibility in New Zealand is 10. However, in contrast those aged 10–13 can only be held liable for a criminal offence if it can be shown that they understood that either the act or omission was wrong, or they knew that it was against the law. Historically New Zealand followed a welfare model of practice, although this still saw large numbers of children being locked up, with a disproportionate number of Māori children being affected (Cavadino & Dignan, 2006).

Family Group Conferencing

Partly in recognition of this disparity and in an attempt to bring restorative justice more to the forefront of youth justice, family group conferencing (FGC) has replaced the traditional criminal justice system for most young people under the age of 17. Decisions regarding restitution and other outcomes are made by FGC participants, rather than by a court, and in this way it acts as 'the hub of an entire youth justice system' (MacRae & Zehr, 2004, p. 13). In contrast to England and Wales, the conferences are used for all types of offences and not just for first time offenders. Save for murder and manslaughter, all cases will endeavour to be resolved in this way, although even in homicide cases a FGC can be used to address some issues, such as visits in custody or to discuss alternatives to custody (MacRae & Zehr, 2004). Acknowledging age and mental capacity there are two forms of FGC: one based on welfare and the interests of the child for 10–13-year-olds and the other for 14–17-year-olds, which focuses more on criminal accountability (MacRae & Zehr, 2004). To ensure that the conferences suit each circumstance there are four types, as outlined in Figure 11.2.

For most conferences, the process is the same. A Youth Justice Coordinator is passed a case from the police and will then prepare the parties by consulting with the offender (and the offender's family), the victim and all other relevant parties. The coordinator will facilitate the meeting and will communicate decisions and proposals to the appropriate people (MacRae & Zehr, 2004). Meetings do not have to be face-to-face with contact sometimes occurring through telephone calls and written correspondence, although the victim cannot be compelled to take part. In cases of drink driving or drug offences there

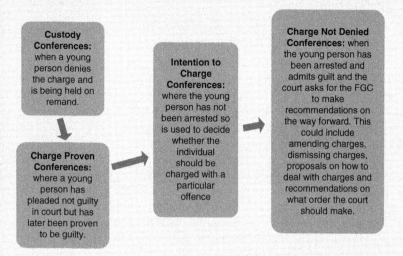

Figure 11.2 The four types of FGC in New Zealand's youth justice system

may not be a readily identifiable victim, so the community (police representatives) or surrogate victims are used (MacRae & Zehr, 2004).

The content of the meeting will differ depending on who the parties are and what they are seeking to achieve, for example some may start with a prayer if this is culturally appropriate. The main aim is that the offender understands the consequences and impact of their behaviour. The victim is given the opportunity to ask questions and in the majority of cases, there will be a 'family caucus' (MacRae & Zehr, 2004, p. 13) where the offender and their family will discuss what has happened and come up with a proposal to present to the victim. A consensus is then reached and a plan outlined. Consensus and agreement is achieved in 95 per cent of all FGCs held in New Zealand with the best results attained when members of the extended family are involved (MacRae & Zehr, 2004).

Youth Justice Residences

As mentioned, FGC cannot be used for murder or manslaughter and may not be suitable in other serious offences. If custody is found to be unavoidable there are currently four youth justice residences (three in North Island and one in South Island) which keep 14–17-year-olds. The units have higher staffing levels than the adult estate and focus on rehabilitation, education, employment skills and psychological services (Department of Corrections, 2018). They are relatively small units housing between 30 and 40 young people and house girls and boys together. The young person will have a single room and shared access to a living/dining room, a gym and an activities area (Ministry for Children, 2018). Support is also offered post-release including residential home placements if it is not appropriate for the young person to return home (*Young People Tell Their Stories – Inside a Youth Justice Residence*, 2018).

Discussion Questions

1. What is your view of FGC? Is it something which you think could be implemented into England and Wales?
2. Compare youth justice residences with the custodial units in England and Wales. Can we learn anything from New Zealand?

speech therapy. At the core would be education, offender desistance programmes and health (Taylor, 2016).

In June 2018 the Ministry of Justice published its vision on what it thought the secure schools would look like (Ministry of Justice, 2018j). The intention is that each school will have a head teacher who will have the autonomy to decide on curriculum and timetable – as long as the subjects of English, maths, science, IT, PE and vocational training are included. Importantly they can also decide the best way in which the children will be taught, with the ambition being that children in secure schools will make the same educational progress as their peers in the community:

> On entry, each young person will have a full assessment of needs to establish a baseline against which progress can be measured and identify unmet health and special educational needs. They will have personalised programmes that build on their strengths and develop their potential, with the use of evidence-based interventions that help them build resilience and develop life and social skills. Curriculum delivery will take place in appropriate-sized groups, including one-to-one intervention where needed. (Ministry of Justice, 2018j)

The vision explicitly states that 'they will be akin to a special residential school or secure children's home and not simply prisons with education' (Ministry of Justice, 2018j). The Schools will accommodate both boys and girls aged 12–17 and will have up to 70 places in each unit. Moving away from the model of STCs they will not be run for profit. The vision is laudable, but in some respects is reminiscent of what the government wanted to achieve with STCs, so whether such ambitions will in reality be achieved in unknown.

Discussion Questions

1.   Should we lock up young people?
2.   Are our current custodial institutions for young people fit for purpose?
3.   What do you think to the idea of secure schools? If you were the head teacher of a secure school what would your curriculum and timetable look like and what additional services would you provide?

STANDARDS FOR CHILDREN IN THE YJS

In response to some of the criticisms levied above, the Ministry of Justice in 2019, issued minimum standards for those children involved in the YJS (Ministry of Justice and Youth Justice Board, 2019). While these do not raise the age of criminal responsibility or abolish our juvenile justice system as New Zealand and the Nordic countries of Norway, Finland, Sweden and Denmark (see Lappi-Seppala, 2011), have effectively done, it does perhaps for the first time confirm that practitioners should see 'the child first [and] the offender second' (Ministry of Justice and Youth Justice Board, 2019, p. 2). This means that the best interests of the child should now be the priority and that agencies working with young people must ensure this. The standards are divided into five areas and cover proceedings 'out of court, at court, in the community, in secure settings and on transition and resettlement' (Ministry of Justice and Youth Justice Board, 2019). Looking at the standards for secure settings in more detail, it does contain some nice ideals: 'the environment that children live in is rehabilitative and safe and one where there is a culture that enables children to develop, grow and learn' and 'children are motivated by staff to have an opportunity to engage in appropriate, high-quality education and training that helps them to make good progress' (Ministry of Justice and Youth Justice Board, 2019, p. 14), but without injecting more staff and other resources into custodial units it is unclear how such standards can ever be achieved.

CIVIL ORDERS

Civil orders against young people

As noted in the introduction, the state has always dealt with the safety and accommodation of children through civil orders, but prior to 1998 and the introduction of the Crime and Disorder Act it had rarely used them to tackle offending behaviour. One reason for this change was due to a surge of interest in anti-social behaviour (ASB), and in particular how to deal with children behaving in this way. In this context ASB is defined as either conduct that has caused, or is likely to cause, harassment, alarm or distress; conduct capable of causing nuisance or annoyance to a person in relation to that person's occupation or residential premises; or, conduct capable of causing housing-related nuisance or annoyance to any person (s. 2 Anti-Social Behaviour, Crime and Policing Act 2014). In an attempt not to clog up the YJS and to keep young people out of the criminal courts, the government decided to use civil orders.

The main civil response to ASB was originally the anti-social behaviour order (ASBO) which was introduced by the Crime and Disorder Act 1998 although this has now been replaced by the injunction. One of the reasons the ASBO was replaced is because the injunction can be sought more quickly and is therefore a better response to ASB. This is largely because the standard of proof for an injunction is on the balance of probabilities while the standard for the ASBO was beyond all reasonable doubt. This criminal standard was required because any breach of an ASBO would lead to a criminal offence and a penalty of up to five years imprisonment. ASBOs were also heavily criticised, because they were used on such a grand scale with young people. While for some children this led to restrictions on their lives, for others having an ASBO was viewed as a badge of honour which enhanced street credibility. Research carried out for the YJB in 2006 further stated that ASBOs were ineffective, overused, had very little positive impact on behaviour and were readily breached (Solanki, et al., 2006).

Civil orders for young people

Injunctions: used for those aged 10 and over when the person has engaged or threatened to engage in ASB and it will prevent reoffending. It can prohibit and compel activity including rehabilitation and educational courses. Can last for 12 months with a power of arrest attached if behaviour was violent. Breach can result in a supervision order or a DTO.

Criminal Behaviour Orders: applicable with a criminal conviction and can be given when ASB has occurred and the order will help prevent reoffending. Can last 12–36 months. Breach is likely to result in a youth caution (see Chapter 5).

Dispersal powers: allows a uniformed constable to direct a person to leave a location and to not return for a maximum period of 48 hours if the person has contributed or is likely to contribute to ASB, crime or disorder and the constable believes that the dispersal removes or reduces the likelihood of this behaviour occurring.

Community Protection Orders: can be used on those 16 or over where conduct is having a detrimental effect of a persistent or continuing nature of an individual's quality of life and the conduct in question is unreasonable. The order can prohibit and compel activity. Failure to comply can result in a fine of between £100 and £2500.

Public Space Protection Orders: this is similar to an injunction but relates to a geographically defined area rather than an individual. It can prohibit certain activity and is often targeted at particular activities or groups, including young people. The order can last for up to three years.

Child Safety Orders: for children under 10. Used when a child has either committed a criminal offence or ASB and intervention is needed to prevent reoffending. Can last 12 months and is supervised by the YOT or social services

Acceptable Behaviour Contracts: a non-statutory option where a voluntary contract of behaviour is agreed between the young person and the YOT. Can last for six months and is very similar to the referral order.

Civil orders against parents

In addition to civil orders against children, the court can also make orders against the young people's parents. These include:

- Parenting contracts: a voluntary document where parents promise to comply with requirements outlined by the YOT or local authority. These can relate to truancy, ASB or criminal conduct. Modelled on the acceptable behaviour contract, they can require the parent to attend counselling or guidance sessions. Failure to comply may be the reason to grant a parenting order.

- Parenting orders: available when the child is involved in criminal or ASB or the child has failed to attend school or an attendance centre. They are more formal that the parenting contract and will involve counselling and or guidance programmes. Additional requirements relating to the child's behaviour may also be imposed.
- Parental compensation orders: parents must provide compensation where a child under the age of 10 has damaged or taken property, either in the course of ASB or, where if they were over 10, their behaviour would have been classed as criminal.

Discussion Points

1. What do you think about these civil orders? Are they a credible and better alternative to the criminal options?
2. What do you think about the ability to disperse young people? Does this solve the problem or just move it on elsewhere?
3. Civil orders against parents try to ensure that parents take responsibility for their children's behaviour. What do you think to this and should it be something which is transferred to the YJS?

CONCLUSION

How you are treated within the YJS in England and Wales largely depends on your age, your offending history and whether you plead guilty. Those who do plead guilty and especially those who are first time entrants to the system are likely to be treated fairly and through the use of a referral order have welfare, restorative justice and rehabilitation as the guiding principles. Once a young person crosses the custody threshold, however, the picture changes dramatically. In virtually every way, excepting escapes, the young people's estate is currently failing. Levels of violence are high, education provision is poor and punishment appears to feature much more than rehabilitation and welfare. Such an environment does not prevent reoffending nor keep some of the most vulnerable of our young people safe. In order to do this a radical alternative is needed, such as abolishing the DTO and instead replacing it with FGC. Custody would be available, but only for those who absolutely need to be detained for public protection reasons. Rather than just introducing a list of minimum standards, which have no hope of being achieved without the necessary resources, this would finally place welfare at the heart of the YJS and treat children and young people with humanity and respect. If such change is not realised we will make many of our young people worse, only setting them up for a life of further crime.

Now read:

HM Inspectorate of Prisons (2017a) *Children in Custody 2016–17. An Analysis of 12–18 Year-Olds' Perceptions of their Experiences in Secure Training Centres and Young Offender Institutions.* London: HMIP.

Lappi-Seppala, T. (2011) 'Nordic Youth Justice'. *Crime and Justice: A Review of Research*, 40, 199–265. This offers a detailed account of the juvenile justice system in Denmark, Norway, Finland and Sweden.

Prison Service Journal (2016) *Special Edition Young People in Custody.* July, No 226. Leyhill: Ministry of Justice, available at: https://www.crimeandjustice.org.uk/publications/psj/prison-service-journal-226

 Now watch:

BBC Panorama (2017) *Teenage Prison. Abuse Exposed* (Medway STC), available on YouTube at: https://www.youtube.com/watch?v=0HQuJpiUOGw (this does contain some upsetting scenes).

Open University (2019) *Why we should abolish imprisonment for children*, available on YouTube at: https://www.youtube.com/watch?v=5SygFXPP6ck

RNZ (2018) *Young People Tell Their Stories – Inside a Youth Justice Residence* (New Zealand), available on YouTube at: https://www.youtube.com/watch?v=2uKevUaZQAI

 Now consider:

Moving on from your design of an adult prison, think about an institution for the purposes of securely holding children and young people. For example: what would this institution look like? What sort of regime would it run? What would be its main aims? What would the staff/young person ratios be? What support would you offer on release? What contact would the young person have with their family/community?

12 Social Inequalities in Custody

INTRODUCTION

When looking at the data for those managed by HM Prison and Probation Service (HMPPS) in England and Wales, the vast majority held either on a custodial sentence or supervised in the community are adult, White, men. This has meant that the penal system, in the main, has been designed and run with these characteristics in mind. In October 2010, however, The Equality Act came into force in England, Wales and Scotland. This requires ministers and organisations to 'have regard to the desirability of reducing socio-economic inequalities ... prohibit victimisation ... eliminate discrimination ... increase equality of opportunity [and] ... amend the law relating to rights and responsibilities' (The Equality Act 2010, Preamble). Replacing a number of previous discrimination laws, The Equality Act provides protection for what it refers to as 'protected characteristics' and tries to ensure that no one is discriminated against on any of these grounds. This includes age, disability, gender reassignment, marriage and civil partnership, pregnancy and maternity, race, religion or belief, sex and sexual orientation (s. 4 Equality Act 2010). Space precludes looking at all of these characteristics. Age is considered in Chapter 11, with sex (including pregnancy) and race discussed here.

SEX

The problem

On 10 May 2019, there were 82,599 people detained within prison establishments in England and Wales. Of this number 3804 (4.6 per cent) were women (Ministry of Justice, 2019e). While this may be viewed as a positive, the fact that there are so few women in the prison system has its problems, succinctly summed up by Frances Crook of the Howard League:

> Women are a minority at every stage of the justice system. Women in conflict with the law have completely different needs from men. The combination of the small number of women and their strikingly different needs means they are routinely and severely disadvantaged throughout their experience in the criminal justice system, including their safe resettlement. (Epstein, 2017)

This has meant that not only are women being held in a system designed 'by men for men' (Corston, 2007, p. 2), their needs are often ignored, partly because the crisis in the male prison estate (see Chapters 7–9) always appears to be more important and thus more deserving of attention. An example of this was noted by HM Chief Inspector of Prisons in 2017: 'At Peterborough, some important outcomes for women had deteriorated because senior staff had become more focused on difficulties in the male side of the prison' (HM Chief Inspector of Prisons for England and Wales, 2018, p. 56). While social inequality can be felt between a man and a woman in society, with the gender pay gap being an example, this is experienced at a much heightened level when the woman is imprisoned.

To reflect the gender difference between men and women and to abide by Prison Rule 12, which states that 'women prisoners shall normally be kept separate from male prisoners', of the 116 prison establishments across England and Wales, 12 are reserved for women and young females (see Chapter 11 for young people). Unlike the male prison estate, however, these are not equally dispersed across the country, with the most noticeable problem being that there are no establishments for women in Wales or London. Perhaps due to the fact that not all regions have women's prisons, the women prison estate is managed under a separate directorate. This encompasses all women's prisons except HMP Bronzefield and HMP Peterborough which are both contracted out to Sodexo Justice Services. Different from men, women are not assigned to the security classifications of Category B, C or D (see Chapter 7). Rather it is decided whether they need open or closed conditions with there currently being 10 closed and 2 open prisons. Closed prisons are also designated into training and local prisons although this can be rather misleading because most closed prisons fulfil a 'multiplicity of roles' (HM Inspectorate of Prisons, 2010).

When looking at Table 12.1 the scarcity of prisons for women is further highlighted. For example, of the two open prisons, one (Askham Grange) is 135 miles north of Birmingham, and the other (East Sutton Park) 172 miles south. If pregnant and accepted onto a Mother and Baby Unit (MBU) the only option for someone suitable for open conditions is Askham Grange irrelevant of where that woman lives. Furthermore, there is only one therapeutic community and one Psychologically Informed Planned Environment (PIPE) unit (see Chapter 10). Due to the paucity of serious female offenders there are also very few prisons which can accommodate restricted status, life and/or indeterminate sentenced prisoners. Consequentially a large proportion of women prisoners are detained vast distances from their homes and families. While this is an issue for some men, the distances which women are placed away from their homes is starker. In 2009, for example, 753 women held in the penal system were housed over 100 miles from their home (HM Inspectorate of Prisons, 2010).

This problem is also mirrored when looking at the availability of approved premises (APs) for women. These are the residential units which some offenders will live in on their release from prison. While in 2017 there were 94 APs for men across England and Wales, there were only 6 for women, situated in Bedford, Birmingham, Leeds, Liverpool, Preston and Reading. There is again no provision in either London or Wales. This led to the Supreme Court being asked to rule on whether such a lack of availability amounted to unlawful sex discrimination (*Coll v Secretary of State for Justice* [2017] UKSC 40). Coll, the appellant, was a life sentenced prisoner, from London, who had been given a minimum tariff of 11 years

Table 12.1 The women's prison estate.

Prison name	Location	Function	Public or Private	Additional information
Askham Grange	York	Open training	Public	Became the first open prison for women in 1947. Has a mother and baby unit (MBU).
Bronzefield	Middlesex	Closed local	Private	Became the first privately managed purpose-built women's prison in 2004. Has a 12 room MBU.
Downview	Surrey	Closed training	Public	Reopened for women in 2016 and took many prisoners when HMP Holloway was closed.
Drake Hall	Staffordshire	Closed training	Public	Has 15 residential units, accommodating up to 315 women.
East Sutton Park	Kent	Open training	Public	First opened as a Borstal in 1946. Can hold up to 100 women and young offenders.
Eastwood Park	Gloucestershire	Closed local	Public	Catchment area covers Cornwall across to Wolverhampton, across Wales and the South Coast. Has a 12 bed MBU.
Foston Hall	Derbyshire	Closed local	Public	Has a 42 bed unit for women with complex needs and personality disorders.
Low Newton	Durham	Closed training	Public	Covers the Scottish borders, Cumbria and North Yorkshire. Has a PIPE unit (see Chapter 10) and receives restricted status (Category A) prisoners.
New Hall	West Yorkshire	Closed local	Public	Houses a range of women including life and indeterminate sentenced prisoners, those with complex needs, 'normal' offenders, those on remand and a MBU.
Peterborough	Cambridgeshire	Closed local	Private	The only prison purpose built to separately house both men and women. Has a 12 room MBU.
Send	Surrey	Closed training	Public	Has a 20 bed substance misuse unit, a 80 bed resettlement unit and a 40 bed therapeutic community (see Chapter 10).
Styal	Cheshire	Closed training	Public	The largest women's prison with capacity for up to 486 women. Has a MBU.

Source: Ministry of Justice (2017j) 'Prisons in England and Wales'. [Online] Available at: http://www.justice.gov.uk/contacts/prison-finder [Accessed 14 June 2018].

for murder. Knowing that she would be situated in an AP away from her family she had argued in front of the High Court that the current practice of housing women so far from their families was discriminatory. The High Court dismissed the claim as did the Court of Appeal, but in May 2017, the Supreme Court unanimously held that by having so few APs, meaning that women were at a far greater risk of being housed significant distances away from their family, when compared to men, meant that they were being directly discriminated against based on their sex. This was only lawful if the Secretary of State could justify why this discrimination was occurring, something which had not been established. A declaration was therefore made that the provision of APs in England and Wales constitutes direct discrimination against women contrary to section 13(1) of the Equality Act 2010. Despite the ruling and media coverage, very little progress has since been made.

Family ties and pregnancy

One of the reasons why having a fair geographical distribution of both prisons and APs for women is so important is because of the need for them to have contact with their family and in particular with their children. In 2010, 55 per cent of women in prison had children under the age of 18 and 20 per cent were living with dependent children before they were imprisoned. This amounted to more than 17,700 children separated from their mothers due to imprisonment (HM Inspectorate of Prisons, 2010). In 2014, it was thought that 66 per cent of all women in prison were mothers of dependent children, with only 5 per cent of these children being able to remain in their own home when their mothers were incarcerated (Epstein, 2014). The effects on children of having a parent imprisoned have been described as wrecking 'havoc on family stability and children's well-being' with other consequences including long-lasting psychopathology, social and welfare disadvantage, substance abuse, family discord and mental health issues (Epstein, 2014). Many children are not told the truth when their parent is imprisoned, with some believing that their parent has instead died. Some experience stigmatism and are ostracised by their friends and some have to leave their communities (Scharff-Smith & Gampell, 2011). The negative effects of parental imprisonment are also thought to be much more severe when the parent is the mother as this generally means that the child is unable to remain in their own home and may be separated from other family members, sometimes resulting in care and adoption proceedings (Women in Prison, 2017a). Scharff-Smith and Gampell (2011), therefore describe the children of imprisoned parents as the forgotten victims of the punishment system.

Being a mother in prison can also be a traumatic experience for the woman in question. The fact that she is in prison, separated from her children and perhaps the cause of them being in care or with relative strangers can put additional emotional pressures on her. If she does not have any meaningful contact with them and does not feel that she is having any influence on or say in her children's lives this can lead to additional emotional and mental distress. Even on release, some mothers have reported how these feelings have not abated and how their 'good mother' identify is 'forever tarnished' (Baldwin, 2018).

Another gender specific difference between men and women is the fact that women become pregnant and have children and a period of incarceration does not obviate the need to give birth to and then look after this child. On 31 December 2017, for example, there were 93 pregnant women in prison (Prison Reform Trust, 2018e). While some babies will stay with their fathers or extended families in the community, reflecting society's normal assumption that the best place for a young child is with its mother, there are six MBUs within the women's prison estate (see Table 12.1). 1n 2016–17, there were 119 applications for women to be transferred to a MBU. Of this number 61 were approved, 16 were declined and 42 were not proceeded with, either because the woman had changed her mind, was released from custody or due to miscarriage or termination was no longer pregnant (HC Deb, 16 March 2018 cW). All applications are considered by an Admission Board with the best interest of the child being the primary factor for consideration. Other factors taken into account will be the woman's risk and offending behaviour profile, her behaviour whilst she has been imprisoned, family circumstances and release plans (HMPPS, 2008). The length of the woman's sentence will also be a deciding factor with the desirable scenario being one where mother and baby leave prison together. If the mother has more than 18 months left to serve (the maximum period for which a baby can be kept in prison), it is unlikely that her application will be successful. This limit has been tested in the courts (see *R. v Secretary of State for the Home Department ex p. Q* [2001] EWCA Civ 1151) with the Court of Appeal ruling that whilst in the majority of circumstances it is preferable to separate the mother and child before the latter is 18 months, the limit should be applied flexibly depending on individual circumstances, such as the mother's length of time left to serve, alternative placement arrangements for the child and whether the harm caused by the separation is likely to outweigh other considerations. In May 2018, there were 39 babies living in prison (Prison Reform Trust, 2018c).

Over the years, research has focused on those women who reside in MBUs in England and Wales. Birmingham and colleagues, for example, found that many of the mothers were serving sentences for drug offences, many were from Black and Minority Ethnic (BAME) groups and over 60 per cent were exhibiting at least 1 of 5 specific forms of mental disorder (Birmingham, et al., 2006). More recent research discovered that although women were more likely to be accepted onto a MBU if they came from a stable background and showed low levels of mental dysfunction, many on the unit still showed high levels of depression and anxiety (Dolan, et al., 2019). The units can, however, be beneficial for women, with parenting programmes such as New Beginnings having a positive effect on the mother's relationship with her child (Sleed, et al., 2013).

Mental health

Perhaps due to some of the problems highlighted above, women in prison are more likely than men to exhibit higher levels of emotional distress (MacDonald, 2013), often resulting in depression and eating disorders (World Health Organisation, 2009). Self-harm and suicide are also prevalent amongst imprisoned women. For the year ending December 2016, the rate of self-harm per 1000 prisoners was 299 for women and 121 for men, with women carrying out on average 6.65 self-harm incidents as opposed to 3.30 for men (Ministry of Justice, 2017h). Despite the fact that there has been a significant rise in self-harm in men over the last 10 years (see Figure 12.1 and Chapter 8), bearing in mind that women make up only 4.6 per cent of the overall prison population, women still account for a disproportionate number of self-harm incidents. Such figures may be because women in prison are five times more likely than those in the general population to suffer from a mental health concern (Women in Prison, 2017b). This vulnerability often relates to personal histories, with 53 per cent of women in prison having experienced sexual, physical and emotional abuse during childhood; 46 per cent having histories of domestic violence and 31 per cent having spent time in local authority care as a child (Women in Prison, 2017b). This can therefore mean that procedures designed for men such as strip searches may be wholly inappropriate in the case of some women. This is therefore another example of where 'prison is disproportionately harsher for women because prisons and the practices within them have for the most part been designed by men' (Corston, 2007, p. 3).

In terms of suicide, it is estimated that up to 46 per cent of women in prison have attempted suicide at some point in their lifetime. For men this stands at 21 per cent and on average is 6 per cent, for both men and women in the general population (Women in Prison, 2017b). Marzano and colleagues, in their study of 60 women prisoners who had engaged in near-lethal self-harm, found that contributing factors to this behaviour included single cell accommodation, being on remand and having a negative experience of imprisonment. Other contributing factors were childhood abuse, a family history of suicide, high levels of depression and low levels of self-esteem (Marzano, et al., 2011). Liebling also cites a breakdown in family relationships, poor communication, receipt of bad news and fear (Liebling, 1994). In the 10 years between 2007 and 2017 there were 93 deaths of women in prison, 37 of which have been classified as self-inflicted (Bulman, 2018a). One example is

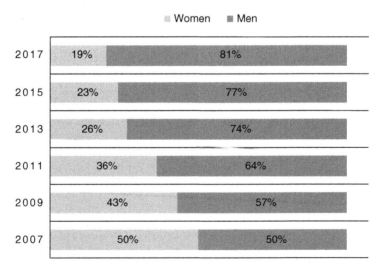

Figure 12.1 Proportion of self-harm incidents between women and men 2007–2017
Source: Prison Reform Trust (2018e) *Prison: The Facts. Bromley Briefings Summer 2018*. London: Prison Reform Trust, p. 4.

Emily Hartley, who hanged herself at HMP New Hall in 2016. She had a history of mental illness and was serving her first custodial sentence, having been convicted of arson: an incident where she had set herself alight. An inquest into the death found that it took prison staff two-and-a-half hours to notice that Ms Hartley had gone missing, despite the fact that she was on 30-minute observations. Furthermore, it held that there had been insufficient assessment of her mental health and that she should have been moved to a therapeutic unit (Bulman, 2018b). Prison is therefore a highly inappropriate and dangerous place to hold such vulnerable women, with Coles arguing that the number of preventable deaths that have occurred in women's prisons displays 'incontrovertible evidence of serious human rights abuses of women prisoners and abject failures in the criminal justice system' (Coles, 2010).

Sentencing statistics

Another issue is the fact that prison is often disproportionately and unnecessarily used when sentencing women. In 2018, for example, 8106 women were sentenced to either immediate custody or held on remand (Prison Reform Trust, 2018c). Of those sentenced to immediate custody, the vast majority were given less than 12 months, with only 23 per cent sentenced to more than 1 year. In fact, the proportion of women serving short-term sentences has increased on an annual basis. In 1993, for example, 33 per cent of women were held for less than 6 months, with this rising to 62 per cent in 2017. Furthermore, the majority of these women were sentenced for offences of theft (39 per cent), summary non-motoring offences (19 per cent) or crimes against society (10 per cent), with 83 per cent of women sentenced to custody in 2017 because of a non-violent offence (Prison Reform Trust, 2018e). Women prisoners therefore generally pose much less of a risk to the public than their male counterparts, both in terms of escape and risk of serious reoffending. Short custodial sentences also do not allow enough time for the prison to do anything meaningful with these women. It therefore has to be questioned whether custody is an appropriate response to this type of offending, especially when all of the above implications are taken into account.

Discussion Questions

1. Should a woman be sentenced to prison if the consequence of that sentence is that her children will not be allowed to stay in their home?
2. What is your view of MBUs? Should babies and young children be kept in prison and how long should they be allowed to stay?
3. Scotland has a presumption against short-term sentences of less than three months, with plans to extend this to less than 12 months. Applied to England and Wales this would reduce the prison population of women by nearly 3000. Is this something which should be brought into England and Wales for both men and women?

Possible solutions

The government has for some time accepted that there are gender differences between men and women and that women should be treated differently, but despite several attempts and much prevarication, the necessary modifications have not been made. One of the first evaluations to call for change was The Corston Report (Corston, 2007). This was the result of a review of vulnerable women in the criminal justice system following the deaths of 6 women at Styal prison in a 12-month period. From visiting and speaking to women in prison and those attending local women's centres, the report highlighted 'the need for a distinct, radically different, visibly-led, strategic, proportionate, holistic, woman-centred, integrated approach' (Corston, 2007). Corston made 43 recommendations and while the government started to make progress on some of these, perhaps one of the most important, which it did not, was the recommendation that prison was 'not the right place for women offenders who pose no risk to the public' (Corston, 2007, p. 11). Corston's vision was that by 2017, the vast majority of women's prisons would be closed and replaced with local secure units.

Ten years on from the Corston Report, Women in Prison, a specialist women's charity, considered what progress had been made on each of the 43 recommendations. While its report praised the development of a network of 'one-stop-shops' (see below) it found that only 2 of the 43 recommendations had been implemented. Moreover, 'The core aim of the Corston report to radically reduce the use of custody for only those few women that pose a danger to others has yet to be achieved' (Women in Prison, 2017a, p. 27). The recommendation from both Corston (2007) and Women in Prison (2017a) is that instead of being detained in a penal system which exacerbates rather than ameliorates the problems of women, the vast majority of women should instead be held in the communities within which they live. This can be achieved through making greater use of community alternatives to imprisonment, which also allows families to be kept together. It is also worth noting that a prison place costs 14 times more than a community order, with it being sensible to use these savings to fund the types of services which will prevent women from reoffending. In those few cases where community sentencing is inappropriate, detainment should take place in geographically dispersed, small, multi-functional custodial centres, located in the woman's local area (Corston, 2007). In either case, women should have access to one-stop-shops where they can access multi-agency services so that the reasons that they offend (drugs, alcohol, mental health, poverty, emotional difficulties) can be dealt with. One way in which this is working already is through the Together Women Project (TWP), which Corston was in favour of expanding. While there was some initial progress on this (see Hedderman & Gunby, 2013), since the privatisation of probation (Chapter 6) funding for these centres has been reduced and currently the TWP only extends to West, South and East Yorkshire with centres based in Bradford, Leeds, HMP New Hall, Sheffield, Rotherham, Barnsley and Hull. Instead of treating women as offenders (in fact the centres work with offenders and non-offenders) the TWP is a woman-only space where women come to help themselves move away from their damaging lifestyles. While the TWP does not provide accommodation, the key to their success is that they tailor support to the individual woman's needs.

One solution for women, therefore, is to have local units, which offer a gradual reduction in the level of support provided. Such a system could incarcerate, in traditional prisons, those few dangerous women who need to be kept separate from society for public protection reasons. Such an establishment may also be needed for those women who refuse to comply with other options. The vast majority of women however would be housed in local secure residential units of no more than 12–15 beds. This would allow key workers to offer intensive support, focusing on the areas which most contribute to that woman's offending behaviour. When it is thought that support can be lessened, the woman would be released but then referred to a non-residential unit (perhaps as a condition of her release) similar to a TWP so that progress and support can be maintained. This would still involve intensive support but would also allow the woman to return to society and start to make her own decisions. Length of time in these units would therefore be determined by the needs of the woman and not the original offence, making the sentence offender rather than offence focused. Evaluations on such centres has been positive with results from the Brighton Women's Centre showing that 'those who received support had a lower frequency of reoffending than those who did not' (Ministry of Justice, 2017k, p. 1).

Another idea is the setting up a number of social enterprises. These would have two purposes: first, to help secure funding for the organisations involved and second to provide work experience for the woman receiving support. For some women who think that it is easier to earn money from sex work rather than working in a shop, it is important to be able to give them the opportunity to allow them to see themselves in a different role. Examples given by a TWP worker was the setting up of a charity shop, which would operate to make money but would also be a retail-training centre; a cleaning organisation with a training framework embedded within it and an enterprise based around catering.

Together Women Projects (TWP)

The TWP works to keep women out of the criminal justice system. Originally, set up as an alternative to prison it now focuses on early intervention work, so works with victims of crime, women involved with probation and those involved with social services due to their need for parenting support. This is because all of these factors are known to increase the likelihood of a woman committing a crime. In general, however, the charity will not turn anyone away and works with any vulnerable woman with complex needs. Support starts with a holistic assessment, which focuses on 13 areas of a woman's behaviour that could lead to offending if left unaddressed. Examples include accommodation, employability, health, alcohol/drug issues, etc., and based on this, a support plan is devised. This may involve counselling and cognitive-behavioural therapy, with support offered on a one-to-one and/or group work basis.

The type of support or programme that is used may change over time depending on the needs of the women. For example, at the time of the interview the charity had just purchased and trained a member of staff to deliver a programme on self-harm and because no suitable programme existed for suicide attempts, had created its own programme of support. Length of support will depend on the woman involved and how she came to be working with TWP. For those referred by probation, for example, it will be the length of the community order or license. The minimum is weekly face-to-face meetings, plus fortnightly telephone contact. In reality, support tends to be much more intensive especially when the woman has either just left prison or received a community order. Usually she will be given a key worker and a volunteer mentor and if appropriate referred to other agencies, such as mental health. Minimum standards will then be reverted to when her life becomes more stable. On average probation will refer 16 women a month, with additional women coming to the charity on a self-referral basis. At any one time, the charity can be working with up to 250 women, 110 of who will come from probation. It is only those who come from probation however, that are funded and so it is only those who receive the 'full service'. The others receive the level of support that the charity can afford to provide.

In general, TWP works with two types of women. The first has a chaotic lifestyle often caused by drugs and/or alcohol. To fund the addiction, petty offences are committed leading to a large number of short prison sentences. The problem therefore is trying to work out how to facilitate change. One way in which TWP is trying to influence this is to work with the significant partner who sometimes contributes to the downward spiral and further offending. Unlike other agencies, TWP is trying to work with the couples together rather than as separate entities, because they are so influential on each other. Often TWP can get the woman housing, but it is the addiction, which is the greater problem. The other type of woman is the one who has made a mistake in life and needs some support in order to get her life back on track. They have often been victims of physical or sexual abuse, and once they receive support, TWP will never see them again.

In addition to the more formal types of support, the charity also offers 'knit and natter', a sewing group, 'soup and a roll' and a poetry club. These were originally set up because many women wanted to stay on with their key worker but did not really need that level of support. This lower level of support means that women can still visit the TWP, use their computers and showers and importantly have some social interaction, with it freeing up the more formal support resources for others who are in greater need. TWP also tries to focus on equipping women with life and employability skills. One such programme, 'building better futures' is based on a self-enterprise programme called 'Make £5 blossom' which encourages women to improve their employment, financial and social skills. It also works to increase self-confidence and self-esteem.

The key point of any TWP is that it is a woman only space; although a common sense, approach is also used. Male professionals are welcomed with the charity believing it important that women encounter positive male role models. It is however, a place of refuge for women, so male partners of the women are not allowed, although this can be more problematic when the partner is of the same sex.

Governmental response

As acknowledged above, the government has been largely supportive of the fact that women in the criminal justice system need to be treated differently, but concrete actions have been less evident. In 2016, the white paper, *Prison Safety and Reform*, acknowledged that for female offenders 'there is evidence that a specific approach is most effective in helping women to address [their] issues' (Ministry of Justice, 2016b, p. 7). To further this, the government spoke about the building of five small community prisons for women, as envisaged by Corston (2007), but in June 2018, through the *Female Offender Strategy* (Ministry of Justice, 2018b), backtracked on this. The strategy instead talks about a re-emphasis on community sentencing and the piloting of residential women's centres in five sites across England and Wales. The strategy also announced £3.5 million of extra support for women. Action under this strategy has still not yet been seen however, indeed when asked about it in January 2019, Lord Keen of Elie, who was the Lords Spokesperson for the Ministry of Justice, stated that the strategy 'will take some years to implement' (HL Deb, 31 January 2019, c1164). When huge savings could be made by these proposals, both in terms of money but also in relation to how imprisonment effects women and their families, it appears nonsensical that this delay is occurring. The government's answer to women offenders therefore appears to be 'promises and postponements' (Booth, et al., 2018) and arguably is in breach of The Equality Act 2010.

Discussion Questions

1. What do you think to the suggestion that women's prisons should be abolished and instead replaced with geographically dispersed, small, multi-functional custodial centres?
2. Another suggestion is to have mixed prisons so that women can be closer to their families. These could have separate residential wings like HMP Peterborough and mixed provision for education, leisure and dining. What are the advantages and disadvantages of this?
3. What other ways could we deal with women offenders?

Population	52,037,856 (Worldometers, 2019c)
Prison population (including remand prisoners)	51,130 (Institute for Criminal Policy Research, 2019f)
Prison population per 100,000 of national population	102 (Institute for Criminal Policy Research, 2019f)
Remand prisoners	48% (Institute for Criminal Policy Research, 2019f)
Number of female prisoners	7.4% (Institute for Criminal Policy Research, 2019f)
Number of establishments	108 (Institute for Criminal Policy Research, 2019f)
Official capacity of prison service	26,837 (Institute for Criminal Policy Research, 2019f)
Occupancy level	190.5% (Institute for Criminal Policy Research, 2019f)

Brief Profile

Kenya is a country in East Africa located on the equator. Similar to Bangladesh (see Chapter 3) it is a former British colony, gaining independence in 1963. Its largest city and capital is Nairobi with English and Swahili being the two main languages spoken. It is a developing country with many of its citizens living in poverty. It is widely known for having an abundance of national parks and wildlife reserves, commonly used for safaris. Tourism and coffee are the country's largest industries (National Geographic, 2018).

Women in Prison

Women in Kenya, make up a very small proportion of the adult prison population, with them often receiving custodial sentences for very different crimes when compared to men. Men, for example, are most likely to be imprisoned for committing property offences, violence against the person and offences against the state. For women, however, 70 per cent are detained because they have breached the Liquor Act (brewing and selling alcohol without a license). Other similarities with women in prison in Kenya and England and Wales, include high levels of depression and that up to 90 per cent of Kenyan inmates are mothers. Women in Kenya, however, are allowed to keep their babies with them until they are four years old. In 2017, there were 18 women's prisons across Kenya with two having maximum-security status (Mungai, 2017). Custodial conditions in Kenya are largely gender-neutral, which have the effect of imposing greater hardships on women (Penal Reform International/Kenya Probation and Aftercare Service, 2016).

Gender-Sensitive Community Sanctions

Acknowledging the fact that many women in the criminal justice system do not pose a risk to the public and that prison can be detrimental to the lives of these women and their children, Kenya has started to look at ways in which it can offer more gender-sensitive community alternatives. This change is largely attributable to the 2016

Sentencing Policy Guidelines (The Judiciary, 2016), which implement the United Nations Rules for the Treatment of Women Prisoners and Non-custodial Measures for Women Offenders (Bangkok Rules). Under part three of the Guidelines women are seen as requiring 'further consideration' and so when sentencing decisions are made 'the best interest of the [woman's] child becomes an important consideration' (The Judiciary, 2016).

There are currently three main alternatives to custody: a fine, a probation order or a community service order. Even though, in theory, a fine is deemed to be less punitive than either probation or community service, it is rarely used as the courts realise that in many instances a woman will not be able to pay. A probation order can require young offenders to stay in a probation hostel for the length of their order, which will usually be for one year. There are currently four of these hostels in Kenya with their aim being to provide rehabilitation and educational services for those aged from 12 to 22 (Penal Reform International/Kenya Probation and Aftercare Service, 2016). Community Service Orders can last for up to three years, but, interestingly, they can also be made for as little as one day, with women receiving the sentence in the morning and then expected to spend the rest of that day in unpaid public work (Penal Reform International/Kenya Probation and Aftercare Service, 2016). This allows women to complete their sentence in the quickest time possible so that the impact on their families and children is kept to a minimum. There are a number of workstations set up across the country so that women can complete the order without having to leave their local area. This makes it more financially viable for the women and means that they do not spend too long away from the family home. Projects endeavour to take into consideration the skills and health of the woman, ensuring too that they are kept safe from sexual harassment (Penal Reform International, 2016).

The Probation and Aftercare Service in Kenya has also initiated some economic empowerment projects, where women are trained in entrepreneurial skills and given the opportunity to set up small businesses. One example is the Uwezo Initiative where women receive training to help them identify business opportunities and then receive resources to get them set up. For example, if a woman wants to establish a second hand clothing shop the organisation will provide her with the second-hand clothes (Penal Reform International/Kenya Probation and Aftercare Service, 2016). Across the board, probation officers and workstation supervisors are trained in this gender-sensitive approach, where the best interests of the woman and her children are paramount and rehabilitation is the key driving force.

Discussion Points

1. What similarities are there between women offenders in England and Wales and Kenya?
2. What is your view of the Sentencing Policy Guidelines? Should England and Wales be working towards implementing the Bangkok Rules in this way?
3. Are there any other aspects of the system in Kenya, which you think should be implemented into England and Wales?

RACE

The problem

Race, for the purposes of this book, will be defined as it is under the Equality Act 2010. This means that race can relate to the colour of someone's skin, the country in which either they or their ancestors were born or the ethnic grouping with which they identify. Common ethnic groups in England and Wales include White, Asian and Black, but others encompass Travellers, Gypsies, the Roma, Chinese and Mixed categories. According to the 2011 Census, the population in England and Wales is 86 per cent White, 7.5 per cent Asian, 3.3 per cent Black and the remainder classified as either mixed or from another ethnic group (Office for National Statistics, 2011).

Policing practices

For quite some time, race has been identified as a determining factor in policing and the early stages of the criminal justice system, with this apparent in all manner of police contact ranging from stop and searches to fatal shootings (El-Enany & Bruce-Jones, 2015). In 2017/18, for example, there were 3 stop and searches for every 1000 White people, compared with a staggering 29 stop and searches for every 1000 Black people. This means that Black people are nine times more likely to be stopped and searched than White people, with this disparity growing over recent years: in 2016/17 it was eight times more likely and four times more likely in 2014/15 (Home Office, 2018b). In the same time period, Black people were over 3 times as likely to be arrested when compared to White people, with there being 11 arrests for every 1000 White people and 35 arrests for every 1000 Black people (Home Office, 2018b). In terms of the gender split, Black women are more than twice as likely to be arrested when compared to White women (Home Office, 2018b). Furthermore, in terms of age (see Chapter 11), in 2016, BAME children accounted for 60 per cent of all child arrests by the Metropolitan Police (Howard League for Penal Reform, 2017a). Black children also received 11.4 per cent of all youth cautions issued in 2017/18 which is again a disproportionate amount when you take into account that Black children only make up 4.4 per cent of the general population (Youth Justice Board and Ministry of Justice, 2019).

Judicial decision making

It should come as no surprise therefore, that race is also a factor in decision making in Magistrates' and Crown Courts in England and Wales (see Chapter 4 for a discussion on the lack of diversity in both Magistrates' and Crown Courts). For example, Black defendants at the Crown Court are 23 per cent more likely to be remanded in custody than White or Asian defendants (Ministry of Justice, 2017h). Furthermore, where ethnicity was known, the proportion of all defendants prosecuted for an indictable offence was 79 per cent for Whites, 11 per cent for Blacks and 6 per cent for Asians (Cabinet Office, 2018). When looked at in the context of how the general population in England and Wales is made up, with there being 86 per cent Whites, 3.3 per cent Blacks and 7.5 per cent Asian, it is clear that once again Black people are over-represented in these figures. This disparity is also evident in custodial remands, with Black defendants more likely to be remanded in custody than White or Asian ethnic groups (Ministry of Justice, 2018a).

Further discrepancy is also seen in imprisonment rates, with Black and Asians being 11 per cent more likely to be sent to immediate custody than Whites. This is also true for young people (see Chapter 11), with the Black ethnic group having the highest percentage of offenders sent to young offender institutions in 2017/18 (Ministry of Justice, 2018a). While in general the prison population of young people has rapidly decreased over the last 10 years, the percentage of Black, Asian and Other ethnic groups has doubled (Youth Justice Board and Ministry of Justice, 2019). Black and Asian offenders also serve longer sentences than White offenders (Cabinet Office, 2018) and are less likely to be released. In the year ending March 2017, for example, 50 per cent of Whites were released by the Parole Board, but for all other ethnic groups this ranged from 40 per cent to 48 per cent (Ministry of Justice, 2017l). The inequalities witnessed in our prisons have thus been summarised by David Lammy MP:

> Despite making up just 14% of the population, BAME men and women make up 25% of prisoners, while over 40% of young people in custody are from BAME backgrounds. If our prison population reflected the make-up of England and Wales, we would have over 9,000 fewer people in prison, the equivalent of 12 average-sized prisons. There is greater disproportionality in the number of Black people in prisons here than in the United States. (Lammy, 2017, p. 3)

The ethnic makeup of the prison population in England and Wales, in March 2019, can be seen in Table 12.2, although perhaps this should be put into some sort of context. In the United States of America (US) for example, Blacks make up 12 per cent of the general population but 37.6 per cent of the prison population (Kaiser Family Foundation, 2019; Federal Bureau of Prisons, 2019). Disproportionate numbers of ethnic minorities, particularly indigenous groups are also seen in Australia and Canada (Carr, 2017). The mass imprisonment of Black people is a phenomenon which is largely associated with the US, but as shown above there are strong parallels in England and Wales and a number of other countries. Wacquant maintains that this came about due to restrictions in social welfare and the 'rolling out of the gargantuan penal state ... fuelled by a politics of resentment towards categories deemed undeserving and unruly' (Wacquant, 2010, p. 74). He further argues that policies and practices of the police, the criminal courts and the prisons themselves have all had targeted policies in place which have ensured that custodial sentences are determined by class, race and place. This he states has led not just to mass incarceration but to the 'hyperincarceration of (sub)proletarian African American men from the imploding ghetto' (Wacquant, 2010, p. 74). Race and class are also cited by Pettit and Western, but they also looked at levels of educational achievement. Looking at a population of Black men, born between 1965

Table 12.2 Prison population by ethnic group, 31 March 2019.

Ethnic Category	Amount in numbers	Amount in %
White	59,911	72.5
Asian or Asian British	6617	8
Black or Black British	10,460	12.7
Mixed	3830	4.6
Other ethnic group	1320	1.6
Unrecorded	279	0.3
Unstated	217	0.3

Source: Ministry of Justice (2018i) *Offender Management Statistics Quarterly: October to December 2018*. London: Ministry of Justice.

and 1969 they found that 60 per cent of those who had dropped out of high school and 30 per cent of those who did not have a college education had been to prison by 1999. They therefore contend that imprisonment has become 'a new stage in the life course of young low-skill Black men' (Pettit & Western, 2004) (see also Garland, 2001).

The prison experience

In addition to the disparity in the numbers of BAME people in the penal system, there is also the problem of how they are treated once they are within it. One issue is whether rehabilitative programmes are as effective with BAME offenders as they are with White offenders. This is an issue, which the government has been aware of for quite some time. In 1998 when the 'What Works?' policy was introduced, the initial idea was to introduce a core curriculum of accredited offending behaviour programmes (OBPs) across both prison and probation. The aim was that these programmes would cater for different offences (general offending, anger management, domestic violence, sex offending) and different offender groups such as those based on age, sex and race. While this aspiration was partly achieved in terms of offence, it has never been sufficiently realised in terms of offender groups. Research has therefore been conducted to answer how well BAME people respond to rehabilitative services currently being delivered by both prison and probation staff (Shingler & Pope, 2018). While some aspects of the standard OBPs were found to be relevant to BAME offenders, better results were found where the programmes were:

> culturally aware, sensitive and inclusive; that is delivered by culturally aware and sensitive staff; and delivered by staff from similar ethnic backgrounds to their clients ... [this, it was found] is more likely to reduce the chances that potential BAME participants will experience any fear or resistance associated with feeling isolated or misunderstood. (Shingler & Pope, 2018, p. 2)

Another important issue, found by the report, were the barriers to treatment that some BAME offenders experienced, including racism and other forms of discrimination, including the fact that the treatment was not culturally relevant. One example given is the fact that 'a strong sense of cultural identity and pride is associated with greater reductions in substance misuse among juveniles' (Shingler & Pope, 2018, p. 2), so acknowledging this cultural identity is imperative.

Another issue is the general racism that some BAME prisoners face in prison. One recent study, based on 13 interviews with BAME prisoners in an English Northern prison, noted experiences of racial harassment, racial abuse and intimidation (Chistyakova, et al., 2018). One prisoner explained how "On F wing, on the pad on the wall, it says: "All Pakis should be killed. All blacks should be killed"" (Chistyakova, et al., 2018, p. 12). Worryingly, while the prison staff in this study were aware of such incidents they did not appear to view them as problematic. Another interesting finding in relation to an Irish Traveller was a feeling of discrimination because he was unable to read and so could not understand the information placed on the noticeboards or understand the complaints process (Chistyakova, et al., 2018).

Another study found overwhelming racism in the way that Muslim and BAME prisoners experience day-to-day prison life (Jolliffe & Haque, 2017). Examples included time out of cell, with 60 per cent of non-Muslim boys saying they had daily association time when compared to only 36 per cent of Muslim boys. Furthermore Kimmett and Tsintsadze found that not only were Black prisoners over-represented in the segregation unit, they were more likely to have force used against them, and more likely to be on the basic regime (see Chapter 8). Black prisoners were also less likely than their white counterparts to believe that the prison officers treated them with respect (Kimmett & Tsintsadze, 2017). BAME prisoners are also less likely to be released on temporary license, less likely to be housed on the favourable wings and more likely to face adjudications (Jolliffe & Haque, 2017).

If a prisoner feels that they have been subject to discrimination, irrelevant of which protected characteristic is in question, they can complain through the completion of a Discrimination Incident Reporting Form (DIRF). Research carried out by the Prison Reform Trust and The Zahid Mubarek Trust (named after a 19 year old Asian man who was murdered in HMYOI Feltham in 2000 by a known racist) has looked at the handling of DIRFs in prison. Using data from 8 prisons in 2014, they found that of the DIRFs submitted, 70 per cent were from prisoners and 30 per cent from staff. In terms of subject matter, the majority of DIRFs were about race (62 per cent) with incidents relating to religion (15 per cent) and disability (10 per cent) also noted. Verbal abuse was the most common form of abuse, but there were also incidences of unfair treatment, where prisoners, for example, reported being given 'a behaviour warning for taking a shower when a white prisoner did the same' and 'not allowed to remain out while white prisoners were' (Kimmett & Tsintsadze, 2017, p. vi). Such findings are not news to the government and in 2016 it commissioned David Lammy, MP for Tottenham North, to undertake a review into the treatment of, and outcomes for BAME individuals in the Criminal Justice System (Lammy, 2017). The findings of the review (see Figure 12.2) were stark, highlighting, as noted above, a disproportionate amount of BAME and in particular Black men in custody.

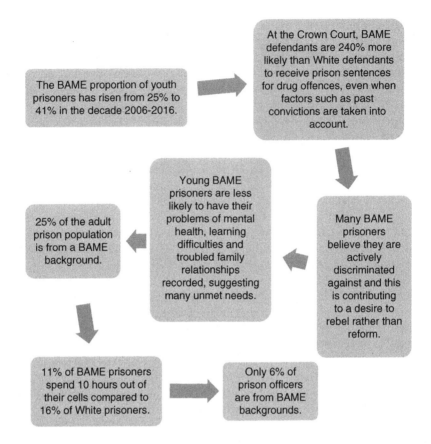

Figure 12.2 Findings from the Lammy Review

Source: Lammy, D. (2017) *The Lammy Review. An Independent Review into the Treatment of, and Outcomes for, Black, Asian and Minority Ethnic Individuals in the Criminal Justice System.* London: Home Office.

Possible solutions

The Lammy Review argues that there are three core principles that must be embedded into the entire criminal justice system if there is any hope that the current disproportionate representation of BAME people is ever reversed. These are focused on fair treatment, including ensuring that decision making is more transparent and accountable; trust, with there being a higher representation of BAME professionals in the criminal justice system; and responsibility, where greater partnerships exist between the criminal justice system and local communities (Lammy, 2017). The report also makes 35 recommendations including:

1. Improvements needed in data collection.
2. Redacting ethnic information from case files so that charge decisions are race-blind.
3. Recording sentencing remarks in audio form for those who cannot read.
4. The setting of national targets to ensure that the judiciary and magistracy are more diverse.

5. Ensuring prison committees have BAME representatives on them.
6. Renaming youth offender panels as local justice panel, emphasising the involvement of parents and local communities.
7. Introducing national targets to ensure BAME prison staff enter into leadership positions (Lammy, 2017).

For some, however, the findings of the Review were 'not as hard hitting as so many had hoped' (Bridges, 2017), largely due to the government's terms of reference which excluded any analysis of the police. There have also been criticisms based on which statistics were used, how these statistics were analysed and claims of general misunderstanding (Bridges, 2017). Fekete also argues that in addition to a list of recommendations, there was a lost opportunity to also include 'an analysis and diagnosis of the causes of disproportionality' (Fekete, 2017), that is institutional racism. Until this is addressed, focusing on issues such as single parent families, poverty and school exclusion, she argues, will never be sufficient.

Another possible solution is to ensure that OBPs are more culturally relevant. This includes increasing the number of BAME staff trained to deliver such pro-grammes, ensuring that the treatment material is relevant to BAME groups and actively engaging with and respecting the cultural experiences and differences of BAME people (Shingler & Pope, 2018). This is not an easy task, because each BAME grouping will be different, but with time, consultation and will this must be achieved if the government want to abide by its obligations under the Equality Act 2010.

Governmental response

The Government's response to the Lammy Review took three months (Ministry of Justice, 2017e). In a 32 page document, endorsed by the then Justice Secretary, David Liddington, it agreed with the main principles as set out by Lammy and outlined what it intended to do. Each recommendation is individually commented on. The Government has pledged to embrace the challenge that the Review has presented and are 'committed to taking data-driven, practical steps to address disparity wherever it may be found' (Ministry of Justice, 2017e, p. 28). To date, changes include the Race Disparity Audit which shows a better commitment to the collection and publication of race related data and the adoption of the principle 'explain [the racial disparity] or change'. In addition to the 35 recommendations, the Government has also set up a Race and Ethnicity Board, tasked with moni-toring the government's progress (Liddington, 2017b). While this may all sound encouraging, there are no key targets or dates by which time any of these actions need to be completed. In November 2018, for example, the Government was asked what conclusions the Race and Ethnicity Board had reached on how best to engage the Gypsy, Roma and Traveller communities. Its reply cannot fill anyone with con-fidence that real change will occur anytime soon.

> Following the publication of the Lammy Review last year, we are making efforts to explore and address specific disparities among the Gypsy, Roma and Traveller (GRT) communities in the justice system, overseen by the Race and Ethnicity Board. Our

ability to design and assess effective policies will be strengthened by engagement with representatives of GRT communities with direct experience of the justice system. To this end, we are establishing a dedicated stakeholder forum to inform, review and partner with on emerging work. (HL Deb, 2 November 2018, cW)

CONCLUSION

The criminal justice system and within it the penal system is one which is designed, in the main, by White adult men, for White adult men. Our society and more to the point those who encounter the criminal justice system are, however, much more varied than this and so it is essential that the system can accommodate this diversity. While this used to be an aspiration, since the Equality Act 2010, it is now mandatory, with this chapter using sex and race to assess how well the government is guarding against discrimination for those with protected characteristics. The task of the government is therefore to ensure that there are no more BAME people in the criminal justice system than is proportionate to their population in society, and that when in the system such people are treated with humanity and respect. With reference to women they need to ensure that they are dealt with appropriately and that custody is used only if it is absolutely necessary. In both cases, the government needs to acknowledge not just that everyone is not the same but it must also make real changes in the system in order to properly accommodate these variations. This includes culturally relevant OBPs, gender-sensitive policies and of prime importance ensuring that these policies, assurances and recommendations are turned into actual practice. A lack of action appears, however, to be its biggest problem, with promises, procrastination and inertia being better ways of describing what the government has actually achieved. While the government want to look as if they are tackling these inequalities, in truthfulness they are not and it is questionable whether even in the future they really have any intention of doing so.

Now read:

Brennan, I., Green, S. and Sturgeon-Adams, L. (2018) 'Early diversion and empowerment policing: evaluating an adult female offender triage project', *Policing and Society*, 28(5), 570–586.

Pina-Sanchez, J., Roberts, J. and Sferopoulos, D. (2019) 'Does the Crown Court discriminate against Muslim-named offenders? A novel investigation based on text mining techniques', *British Journal of Criminolgy*, 59(3), 718–736.

Poso, T., Enroos, R. and Vierula, T. (2010) 'Children residing in prison with their parents: An example of institutional invisibility', *The Prison Journal*, 90(4), 516–533. This looks at Finland where children are allowed to live with their parents in prison.

For annual statistics on all of the protected characteristics, see the *Annual Offender Equalities Report*, published by the Ministry of Justice in November each year.

Now watch:

BBC Scotland (2016) *Women Prisoners: Throw Away the Key?* Available at: https://learningonscreen.ac.uk/ondemand/playlists/190. This considers whether women prisons should be closed and replaced with community projects.

Global News (2014) *Babies Behind Bars*, available on YouTube at: https://www.youtube.com/watch?v=Jcv6dT40Fvo&t=17s. This looks at MBUs and questions the human rights aspects involved.

 Now consider:

So far you have designed a custodial institution for men (Chapters 7–9) and thought about how young people should be detained (Chapter 11). Taking into consideration the protected characteristics of sex, pregnancy and race, how would you ensure that people with these characteristics are not discriminated against in the penal system of England and Wales?

Bibliography

Adams, K. & Ferrandino, J. (2008) "Managing mentally ill inmates in prisons", *Criminal Justice and Behavior*, 35(8), pp. 913–927.

Alcoholics Anonymous, 2016. "The Twelve Steps of Alcoholics Anonymous". [Online] Available at: http://www.alcoholics-anonymous.org.uk/About-AA/The-12-Steps-of-AA [Accessed 10 November 2016].

Allen, F. (1998) "The decline of the rehabilitative ideal". In: A. von Hirsch & A. Ashworth (eds.) *Principled Sentencing. Readings on Theory & Policy*. Oxford: Hart Publishing, pp. 14–19.

Allen, R. (2016) *Reflections on Prison Overcrowding*. [Online] Available at: http://reformingprisons.blogspot.co.uk/2016/08/reflections-on-prison-overcrowding.html [Accessed 9 August 2017].

Allen, R. (2017) *Less is More – The Case for Dealing with Offences Out of Court*. London: Transform Justice.

Allison, E. & Hattenstone, S. (2016) "Approved restraint techniques can kill children, MoJ found", *The Guardian*, (5 December 2016). [Online] Available at: https://www.theguardian.com/uk-news/2016/dec/05/approved-restraint-techniques-can-kill-children-moj-found [Accessed 29 July 2019].

Allison, E. (2017) "Thousands of IPP prisoners are trapped in a shameful limbo. They must be freed", *The Guardian*, (15 September 2017). [Online] Available at: https://www.theguardian.com/commentisfree/2017/sep/15/ipp-prisoners-james-ward-jail-sentences-parole?utm_source=dlvr.it&utm_medium=twitter [Accessed 29 July 2019].

Ambort, G. (2018) *Solitary. Alone We Are Nothing*. Hook: Waterside Press.

American Friends Service Committee (1972) *Struggle for Justice*. New York: Hill and Wang.

Amnesty International (2017) *The State of the Worlds's Human Rights – Report 2016/17*. London: Amnesty International.

Antillano, A. (2017) "When prisoners make the prison. Self-rule in Venezuelan prisons", *Prison Service Journal*, Volume 229, pp. 26–34.

Ashworth, A. & Roberts, J. (2012) "Sentencing: Theory, principle and practice". In: R. Morgan, M. Maguire & R. Reiner (eds.) *The Oxford Handbook of Criminology*. Oxford University Press, p. 866.

Ashworth, A. (1998) "Deterrence". In: A. von Hirsch & A. Ashworth (eds.) *Principled Sentencing. Readings on Theory & Policy*. Oxford: Hart Publishing, pp. 44–52.

Ashworth, A. (2010) *Sentencing and Criminal Justice*. 5th edition Cambridge University Press.

Ashworth, A. (2015) *Sentencing and Criminal Justice*. 6th edition Cambridge University Press.

Ayer, U. (2017) *The Effects of Spice Use*. [Online] Available at: http://drugabuse.com/library/the-effects-of-spice-use/ [Accessed 17 August 2017].

Bachmaier, L. & Garcia, A. (2010) *Criminal Law in Spain*. Kluwer Law International.

Baldwin, L. (2018) "Motherhood disrupted: Reflections of post-prison mothers". *Emotion, Space and Society*, Volume 26, pp. 49–56.

Bales, W. & Piquero, A. (2012) "Assessing the impact of imprisonment on recidivism". *Journal of Experimental Criminology*, 8(1), pp. 71–101.

Barnardo's (2014) *Just Visiting. Experiences of Children Visiting Prisons*. London: Barnardo's.

Barnett, R. E. (1977) "Restitution: A new paradigm for criminal justice". *Ethics*, 87(4), pp. 279–301.

Bates, A., Macrae, R., Williams, D. & Webb, C. (2012) "Ever-increasing circles: A descriptive study of Hampshire and Thames Valley circles of support and accountability 2002–09". *Journal of Sexual Aggression*, 18(3), pp. 355–373.

Bazemore, G. & Griffiths, C. T. (2003) "Conferences, circles, boards, and mediations: the 'new wave' of community justice decisionmaking". In: E. McLaughlin, R. Fergusson, G. Hughes & L. Westmarland, (eds.) *Restorative Justice Critical Issues*. London: Sage Publications, pp. 76–93.

BBC News (2011a) "England riots: maps and timeline". [Online] Available at: http://www.bbc.co.uk/news/uk-14436499 [Accessed 11 December 2017].

BBC News (2011b) "Some England riot sentences 'too severe'". [Online] Available at: http://www.bbc.co.uk/news/uk-14553330 [Accessed 11 December 2017].

Beard, J. & Dent, J. (2018) *Contracting Out Probation Services, Briefing Paper Number 06894*. London: House of Commons Library.

Beard, J., Sturge, G., Lalic, M. & Holland, S. (2019) *Recall of Women to Prisons*. London: House of Commons Library.

Beckford, M. (2012) "London riots: Almost 1,000 jailed as judges give tougher sentences". [Online] Available at: http://www.telegraph.co.uk/news/uknews/crime/9101436/London-riots-Almost-1000-jailed-as-judges-give-tougher-sentences.html [Accessed 11 December 2017].

Beech, A., Fisher, D., Beckett, R. & Scott-Fordham, A. (1998) *An evaluation of the prison sex offender treatment programme* London: Home Office.

Benezra, J. (2013) "On the inside: Venezuela's most dangerous prison". *Time Magazine*, (6 June 2013). [Online] Available at: http://time.com/3800088/on-the-inside-venezuelas-most-dangerous-prison/ [Accessed 29 July 2019].

Bennett, A. (2014) "Service users' initial hopes, expectations and experiences of a high security psychologically informed planned environment". *Journal of Forensic Practice*, 16(3), pp. 216–227.

Bennett, C. (2008) *The Apology Ritual. A Philosophical Theory of Punishment*. Cambridge University Press.

Bennett, J. & Shuker, R. (2017) "The potential of prison-based democratic therapeutic communities". *International Journal of Prisoner Health*, 13(1), pp. 19–24.

Bentham, J. (1781) *An Introduction to the Principles of Morals and Legislation*. London: Batoche Books.

Bentham, J. (1998) "Punishment and deterrence". In: A. von Hirsch & A. Ashworth, (eds.) *Principled Sentencing. Readings on Theory & Policy*. Oxford: Hart Publishing, pp. 53–57.

Bilton, A. & Bottomley, K. (2012) "About Parole". *Prison Service Journal*, Volume 200, pp. 15–17.

Bindman, G. & Monaghan, K. (2014) *Judicial Diversity: Accelerating Change.* London: Courts and Tribunals Judiciary.

Birmingham, L. et al. (2006) "The mental health of women in prison mother and baby units". *Journal of Forensic Psychiatry and Psychology*, 17(3), pp. 393–404.

Blagden, N. & Wilson, K. (2019) "We're all the same here – investigating the rehabilitative climate of a re-rolled sexual offender prison: A qualitative longitudinal study", *Sexual Abuse*, pp. 1–24.

Bochel, D. (1976) *Probation and After-Care: Its Development in England and Wales.* Edinburgh: Scottish Academic Press.

Booth, N., Masson, I. & Baldwin, L. (2018) "Promises, promises: Can the Female Offender Strategy deliver?" *Probation Journal*, 65(4), pp. 429–438.

Bosworth, M. & Kellezi, B. (2015) *Quality of Life in Detention: Results from the MQLD Questionnaire Data Collected in IRC Campsfield House, IRC Yarl's Wood, IRC Colnbrook and IRC Dover, September 2013–August 2014.* Oxford: Centre for Criminology.

Bosworth, M. & Vannier, M. (2016) "Comparing Immigration Detention in Britain and France: A Matter of Time?" *European Journal of Migration and Law*, 18(3), pp. 1–16.

Bottoms, A. & McWilliams, W. (1979) "A non-treatment paradigm for probation practice". *British Journal of Social Work*, 9(2), pp. 160–201.

Bottoms, A. & Shapland, J. (2011) "Steps towards desistance among male young adult recidivists". In: S. Farrall, M. Hough, S. Maruna & R. Sparks, (eds.) Escape Routes: Contemporary Perspectives on Life after Punishment. Abingdon: Routledge, pp. 43–80.

Bottoms, A.E. (1995) "The philosophy and politics of punishment and sentencing. In: C. Clarkson & R. Morgan, (eds.) *The Politics of Sentencing Reform.* Oxford: Clarendon Press, pp. 17–49.

Bowcott, O. (2016) "Crisis in morale blamed for resignation of 842 magistrates since April". *The Guardian*, (12 December 2016). [Online] Available at: https://www.theguardian.com/law/2016/dec/12/crisis-in-morale-blamed-for-resignation-of-842-magistrates-since-april [Accessed 29 July 2019].

Braithwaite, J. (1989) *Crime, Shame and Reintegration.* Cambridge University Press.

Braithwaite, J. (2013) "Restorative Justice and a better future". In: G. Johnstone, (ed.) *A Restorative Justice Reader.* London: Routledge, pp. 57–69.

Branston, G. (2015) "A reprehensible use of cautions as bad character evidence?" *Criminal Law Review*, Volume 8, pp. 594–610.

Brennan, I., Green, S. & Sturgeon-Adams, L. (2018) "Early diversion and empowerment policing: evaluating an adult female offender triage project", *Policing and Society*, 28(5), 570–586.

Bridges, L. (2017) "Lammy Review: will it change outcomes in the criminal justice system?" *Race & Class*, 59(3), pp. 80–90.

Brody, S. R. (1976) *The Effectiveness of Sentencing Home Office Research Study No. 35*, London: HMSO.

Brooks, T. (2015) "A Precis of Punishment", *Philosophy and Public Issues*, 5(1), pp. 3–23.

Brown, M. & Pratt, J. (2000) *Dangerous Offenders. Punishment and Social Control*. Abingdon: Routledge.

Brown, S. (2010) *Treating Sex Offenders: An Introduction to Sex Offender Treatment Programmes*. Cullompton: Willan Publishing.

Bulman, M. (2018a) "Nearly 100 women die in prison over 11-year period due to 'glaring failures' by government says report". [Online] Available at: https://www.independent.co.uk/news/uk/home-news/women-inmates-deaths-prison-uk-government-failure-protection-police-figures-a8330576.html [Accessed 23 September 2018].

Bulman, M. (2018b) "Prison Staff failing contributed to death of 21-year-old woman who took her own life behind bars". [Online] Available at: https://www.independent.co.uk/news/uk/home-news/prison-woman-suicide-death-emily-hartley-21-hmp-new-hall-inquest-a8189686.html [Accessed 23 September 2018].

Burke, L. & Collett, S. (2016) "Transforming Rehabilitation: Organisational bifurcation and the end of probation as we knew it?" *Probation Journal*, 63(2), pp. 120–135.

Burke, L. (2017) "Transforming Rehabilitation and Through the Gate: Research from a resettlement prison". Cardiff: Paper given at the European Society of Criminology 13th–16th September 2017.

Butler, M. & Maruna, S. (2016) "Rethinking prison disciplinary processes: A potential future for restorative justice". *Victims & Offenders*, 11(1), pp. 126–148.

The Butler Trust (2019) *The Good Book of Prisons*. [Online] Available at: http://www.goodbookofprisons.com/ [Accessed 29 July 2019].

Cabinet Office (2018) *Race Disparity Audit*. London: Cabinet Office.

Calverley, A. (2012) *Cultures of Desistance: Rehabilitation, Reintegration and Ethnic Minorities*. London: Routledge.

Canton, R. (2017) *Why Punish? An Introduction to the Philosophy of Punishment*. London: Palgrave Macmillan.

Carlile, A. (2006) *An Independent Inquiry into the use of Physical Restraint, Solitary Confinement and Forcible Strip Searching of Children in Prisons, Secure Training Centres and Local Authority Secure Children's Homes*. London: Howard League for Penal Reform.

Carr, N. (2017) "The Lammy Review and race and bias in the criminal justice system". *Probation Journal*, 64(4), pp. 333–336.

Carr, N. (2018) "Transforming Rehabilitation? Destination unknown". *Probation Journal*, 65(1), pp. 3–6.

Case, S. et al. (2017) *Criminology*. Oxford: Oxford University Press.

Cavadino, M. & Dignan, J. (2006) *Penal Systems. A Comparative Approach*. London: Sage Publications.

Centre for Justice Innovation (2017) *Community Sentences Across Borders*. London: Centre for Justice Innovation.

Chapman, T. & Hough, M. (1998) *Evidence Based Practice – A Guide to Effective Practice*. London: Home Office Publications Unit.

Child Rights International Network (2018) *Minimum Ages of Criminal Responsibility Around the World.* [Online] Available at: https://www.crin.org/en/home/ages [Accessed 29 July 2019].

Chistyakova, Y., Cole, B. & Johnstone, J. (2018) "Diversity and vulnerability in prisons in the context of the Equality Act 2010: the experiences of Black, Asian, Minority Ethnic (BAME), and Foreign National Prisoners (FNPs) in a Northern Jail", *Prison Service Journal*, Volume 235, pp. 10–16.

Christie, N. (1977) "Conflicts as property". *British Journal of Criminology*, 17(1), pp. 1–15.

Cid, J. & Tebar, B. (2010) "Spain". In: N. Padfield, D. van Zyl Smit & F. Dunkel, (eds.) *Release from Prison. European Policy and Practice.* Cullompton: Willan Publishing, pp. 358–394.

Cid, J. & Tebar, B. (2012) "Revoking early conditional release measures in Spain". *European Journal of Probation*, 4(1), pp. 112–124.

Cieslak, R., Korczynska, J., Strelau, J. & Kaczmarek, M. (2008) "Burnout predictors among prison officers: The moderating effect of temperamental endurance". *Personality and Individual Differences*, Volume 45, pp. 666–672.

Clark, A. (2013) "Criminogenic needs". In: R. Canton & D. Hancock, (eds.) *Dictionary of Probation and Offender Management.* Cullompton: Willan Publishing, pp. 74–76.

Clinks (2015) *Early Doors. The Voluntary Sector's Role in Transforming Rehabilitation.* London: Clinks.

Clinks (2016) *Change & Challenge. The Voluntary Sector's Role in Transforming Rehabilitation.* London: Clinks.

Cockburn, H. (2019) "Blow to privatisation of probation services as three companies collapse into administration". *Independent,* (15 February 2019), [Online] Available at: https://www.independent.co.uk/news/uk/home-news/government-privatisation-probation-services-working-links-administration-collapse-a8781426.html [Accessed 29 July 2019].

Codd, H. (2008) *In the Shadow of Prison. Families, Imprisonment and Criminal Justice.* Cullompton: Willan Publishing.

Coles, D. (2010) "Protecting the human rights of vulnerable women: A spotlight on deaths of women in prison". *Probation Journal*, 57(1), pp. 75–82.

Comfort, M. (2007) *Doing Time Together: Love and Family in the Shadow of Prison.* Chicago: University of Chicago Press.

The Consortium of Therapeutic Communities (2013) "What is a TC". [Online] Available at: https://www.therapeuticcommunities.org/what-is-a-tc/ [Accessed 18 June 2018].

Conway, Z. (2014) "David Blunkett 'regrets injustices' of indeterminate sentences". [Online] Available at: http://www.bbc.co.uk/news/uk-26561380 [Accessed 29 July 2019].

Corston, J. (2007) *The Cortson Report.* London: Home Office.

Council of Europe (2016) *White Paper on Prison Overcrowding,* Strasbourg: Council of Europe.

Council of Europe (2017) *Report to the Government of the United Kingdom on the Visit to the United Kingdom Carried Out by the European Committee for the Prevention of Torture and Inhuman or Degrading Treatment or Punishment from 30 March to 12 April 2016.* Strasbourg: Council of Europe.

Courts and Tribunals Judiciary (2017a) *Crown Court*. [Online] Available at: https://www.judiciary.gov.uk/you-and-the-judiciary/going-to-court/crown-court/ [Accessed 13 February 2017].

Courts and Tribunals Judiciary (2017b) *Magistrates' Court*. [Online] Available at: https://www.judiciary.gov.uk/you-and-the-judiciary/going-to-court/magistrates-court/ [Accessed 13 February 2017].

Coyle, A. (2005) *Understanding Prisons. Key Issues in Policy and Practice*. Maidenhead: Open University Press.

Crawford, A. (1997) *The Local Governance of Crime: Appeals to Community and Partnerships*. London: Clarendon Press.

Crawley, E. (2004) "Emotion and performance: Prison officers and the presentation of self in prisons". *Punishment & Society*, 6(4), pp. 411–427.

Crewe, B. (2011) "Depth, weight, tightness: Revisiting the pains of imprisonment". *Punishment & Society*, 13(5), pp. 509–529.

Crewe, B. (2015) "Open prisons: A governor's perspective". *Prison Service Journal*, pp. 12–13.

Crewe, B. & Bennett, J. (2011) *The Prisoner*. London: Routledge.

Crewe, B. & Liebling, A. (2018) Quality, Professionalism and the Distribution of Power in Public and Private Sector Prisons. In: A. Hucklesby & S. Lister, (eds.) *The Private Sector and Criminal Justice*. Oxford: Blackwell Limited, pp. 161–194.

Crewe, B., Hulley, S. & Wright, S. (2017a) "Swimming with the tide: adapting to long-term imprisonment". *Justice Quarterly*, 34(3), pp. 517–541.

Crewe, B., Hulley, S. & Wright, S. (2017b) "The gendered pains of life imprisonment". *British Journal of Criminology*, 57(6), pp. 1359–1378.

Crewe, B., Warr, J., Bennett, P. & Smith, A. (2014) "The emotional geography of prison life". *Theoretical Criminology*, 18(1), pp. 56–74.

Crook, F. (2018) "Reinventing different ways of locking up children – a cautionary tale". [Online] Available at: https://howardleague.org/blog/reinventing-different-ways-of-locking-up-children-a-cautionary-tale/ [Accessed 1 August 2018].

Crossman, A. (2018) "Understanding functionalist theory". [Online] Available at: https://www.thoughtco.com/functionalist-perspective-3026625 [Accessed 6 March 2018].

Crown Prosecution Service (2017) *Youth Offenders*. [Online] Available at: https://www.cps.gov.uk/legal-guidance/youth-offenders [Accessed 27 July 2018].

Crown Prosecution Service (2018a) *Key Measures 2017/18*. London: Crown Prosecution Service.

Crown Prosecution Service (2018b) *Youth Crime*. [Online] Available at: https://www.cps.gov.uk/youth-crime [Accessed 29 July 2019].

Cullen, F. T. & Gilbert, K. E. (1982) *Reaffirming Rehabilitation*. Cincinnati: Anderson Publishing Co.

Daley, S. (2015) "Speeding in Finland can cost a fortune, if you already have one". *The New York Times*. [Online] Available at: https://www.nytimes.com/2015/04/26/world/europe/speeding-in-finland-can-cost-a-fortune-if-you-already-have-one.html [Accessed 26 January 2017].

Daly, K. (2006) "The limits of restorative justice". In: D. Sullivan & L. Tifft, (eds.) *Handbook of Restorative Justice*. New York: Routledge, pp. 134–145.

Daly, K. (2013) "The punishment debate in restorative justice". In: J. Simon & R. Sparks, (eds.) *The Sage Handbook of Punishment and Society*. London: Sage, pp. 356–374.

Daly, K. (2016) "What is restorative justice? Fresh answers to a vexed question". *Victims & Offenders*, 11(1), pp. 9–29.

Darke, S. & Garces, C. (2017) (eds.) "Informal dynamics of survival in Latin American prisons – Special Edition", *Prison Service Journal*, 229.

Davies, P. (2015) "Fines". UK Parliament: Written question, 24 June 2015, HC 4023. [Online] Available at: http://www.parliament.uk/business/publications/written-questions-answers-statements/written-question/Commons/2015-06-24/4023/ [Accessed 24 January 2017].

Department for Education/National Statistics (2018) *Children Accommodated in Secure Children's Homes at 31 March 2018: England and Wales*. Sheffield: Department for Education.

Department of Corrections (2018) *Young People Who Offender*. [Online] Available at: http://www.corrections.govt.nz/resources/newsletters_and_brochures/young_people_who_offend.html [Accessed 29 July 2018].

Department of Corrections (2019) *Prison Facts and Statistics – March 2019*. [Online] Available at: https://www.corrections.govt.nz/resources/research_and_statistics/quarterly_prison_statistics/prison_stats_march_2019.html [Accessed 9 May 2019].

Dingwall, R. (1989) "Some problems about predicting child abuse and neglect". In: O. Stevenson, (ed.) Child abuse policy and professional practice. Hemel Hempstead: Harvester Wheatsheaf.

Dodgson, K. et al. (2001) *Electronic Monitoring of Released Prisoners: An Evaluation of the Home Detention Curfew Scheme*. London: Home Office.

Dolan, R., Hann, M., Edge, D. & Shaw, J. (2019) "Pregnancy in prison, mental health and admission to prison mother and baby units", *Journal of Forensic Psychiatry and Psychology*, 30(4), pp. 551–569.

Duff, A. (1998) "Desert and penance". In: A. von Hirsch & A. Ashworth, (eds.) *Principled Sentencing Readings on Theory and Policy*. Oxford: Oxford University Press, pp. 161–167.

Duff, R. A. (1986) Trials and Punishments. Cambridge University Press.

Durkheim, E. (2002) *Suicide: A Study in Sociology*. 2nd edition London: Routledge.

Earle, R., Newburn, T. & Crawford, A. (2002) "Referral orders: Some reflections on policy transfer and what works". *Youth Justice*, 2(3), pp. 141–150.

The Economist (2013) "What price justice?" *The Economist*, (29 June 2013). [Online] Available at: http://www.economist.com/news/britain/21580184-better-ways-cut-states-justice-bill-what-price-justice [Accessed 29 July 2019].

Edgar, K. (2016) "Restorative segregation", *Prison Service Journal*, November (228), pp. 30–34.

Edgar, K. & Newell, T. (2013) "Restorative justice and prisons". In: G. Johnstone, (ed.) *A Restorative Justice Reader*. London: Routledge, pp. 129–133.

Edwards, I. (2011) "Referral Orders after the Criminal Justice and Immigration Act 2008". *The Journal of Criminal Law*, Volume 75, pp. 45–69.

Eglash, A. (1957) "Creative restitution. A broader meaning for an old term", *The Journal of Criminal Law, Criminology, and Police Science*, 48(6), pp. 619–622.

Eglash, A. (1959). "Creative restitution: Its roots in psychiatry, religion and law", *The British Journal of Delinquency*, 10(2), pp. 114–119.

Eglash, A. (1977) "Beyond restitution – creative restitution". In: J. Hudson and B. Galaway, (eds.) *Restitution in Criminal Justice*. Lexington, Massachusetts: Lexington Books, pp. 91–99.

El-Enany, N. & Bruce-Jones, E. (2015) *Justice, Resistance and Solidarity. Race and Policing in England and Wales*. London: Runnymede Trust.

Encyclopaedia Britannica (2019) "Penology". [Online] Available at: https://www.britannica.com/topic/penology [Accessed 18 May 2019].

Epstein, R. (2010) "Where now for the Parole Board". *Criminal Law & Justice Weekly*, 174, p. 9.

Epstein, R. (2014) *Mothers in Prison: The Sentencing of Mothers and the Rights of the Child*. London: Howard League for Penal Reform.

Epstein, R. (2017) "Hostels for women leaving prison: The Coll Case". *Criminal Law & Justice Weekly*, 181(24), p. 422.

Evans, M. & Willgress, L. (2016) "240 prisoners moved out of HMP Birmingham after worst riot since Strangeways". [Online] Available at: http://www.telegraph.co.uk/news/2016/12/16/prison-riot-breaks-hmp-birmingham/ [Accessed 14 August 2017].

The FACTfile, 2018. 61 Interesting Facts About Finland. [Online] Available at: http://thefactfile.org/finland-facts/ [Accessed 2 October 2018].

Farmer, B. (2017) "Riot squad officers sent to regain control of The Mount prison after inmates take over wing". [Online] Available at: http://www.telegraph.co.uk/news/2017/07/31/riot-squad-officers-sent-regain-control-hmp-mount-prison/ [Accessed 14 August 2017].

Farrall, S. & Calverley, A. (2006) *Understanding Desistance from Crime: Emerging Theoretical Directions in Resettlement and Rehabilitation*. Maidenhead: Open University Press.

Fazel, S., Ramesh, T. & Hawton, K. (2017) "Suicide in prisons: an international study of prevalence and contributory factors", *Lancet Psychiatry*, Volume 4, pp. 946–952.

Federal Bureau of Prisons (2019) *Inmate Race*. [Online] Available at: https://www.bop.gov/about/statistics/statistics_inmate_race.jsp [Accessed 12 May 2019].

Feeley, M. & Simon, J. (1992) "The new penology: Notes on the emerging strategy of corrections and its implications", *Criminology*, 30(4), pp. 449–474.

Fekete, L. (2017) "Lammy Review: without racial justice, can there be trust?", *Race & Class*, 59(3), pp. 75–79.

Fitzalan Howard, F. & Pope, L. (2019) *Learning to Cope: An Exploratory Qualitative Study of the Experience of Men Who Have Desisted from Self-harm in Prison*. London: Ministry of Justice.

Fitzalan Howard, F., Travers, R., Wakeling, H., Webster, C. & Mann R. (2018) *Understanding the Process and Experience of Recall to Prison*. Analytical Summary 2018. London: HMPPS.

Fitz-Gibbon, K. & Walklate, S. (2017) "The efficacy of Clare's Law in domestic violence reform in England and Wales". *Criminology & Criminal Justice*, 17(3), pp. 284–300.

Fitzpatrick, M. (2017) "Keep out of jail order cuts re-offending rates". [Online] Available at: http://www.bbc.co.uk/news/amp/uk-northern-ireland-40808086 [Accessed 8 August 2017].

Flanagan, T. (1980) "The pains of long-term imprisonment: A comparison of British and American perspectives", *British Journal of Criminology*, Volume 20, pp. 148–56.

Floud, J. & Young, W. (1981) *Dangerousness and Criminal Justice*. London: Heinemann.

Foucault, M. (1977) *Discipline and Punish. The Birth of the Prison*. London: Penguin Books.

Fox, K. (2015) "Theorising community integration as desistance-promotion", *Criminal Justice and Behavior*, 42(1), pp. 82–94.

France 24 International News (2016) "Turkey to release 38,000 from prison, frees space for coup plotters". [Online] Available at: http://www.france24.com/en/20160817-turkey-mass-parole-pre-coup-crimes-prison-overcrowding [Accessed 9 August 2017].

Frankel, M. (1972) "Lawlessness in sentencing", *University of Cincinnati Law Review*, Volume 41, pp. 1–54.

Frase, R. S. (2012) "Theories of proportionality and desert". In: J. Petersilia and K. R. Reitz (eds.) *The Oxford Handbook of Sentencing and Corrections*. New York: Oxford University Press, pp. 131–149.

G4S (2016) *HMP & YOI Parc Family Interventions*. London: G4S.

Gannon, T., Wood, J., Pina, A., Vasquez, E. & Fraser, I. (2012) *The Evaluation of the Mandatory Polygraph Pilot*. London: Ministry of Justice.

Garland, D. (1986) "Foucault's Discipline and Punish – An exposition and critique". *American Bar Foundation Research Journal*, 11(4), pp. 847–880.

Garland, D. (1996) "The limits of the sovereign state". *The British Journal of Criminology*, 36(4), pp. 445–471.

Garland, D. (2000) "The culture of high crime societies: Some precondition of recent law and order policies". *British Journal of Criminology*, 40(3), pp. 347–375.

Garland, D. (2001) *Mass Imprisonment: Social Causes and Consequences*. London: Sage Publications.

Garland, D. (2018) *Punishment and Welfare: A History of Penal Strategies*. New Orleans: Quid Pro Books.

Garnier, E. (2017) "There's an obvious way out of the prison crisis – New Statesman". [Online] Available at: http://www.newstatesman.com/politics/staggers/2017/08/theres-obvious-way-out-prisons-crisis?amp [Accessed 16 August 2017].

Garside, R. (2019) *Centre for Crime and Justice Studies - Bulletin*. [Online] Available at: https://www.crimeandjustice.org.uk/civicrm/mailing/view?reset=1&id=1970 [Accessed 17 May 2019].

Gavrielides, T. (2011) "Restorative practices: From the early societies to the 1970s", *Internet Journal of Criminology*, Volume November, pp. 1–20.

Gavrielides, T. (2016) "Repositioning restorative justice in Europe", *Victims & Offenders*, 11(1), pp. 71–86.

Geis, G., Mobley, A. & Schichor, D. (1999) "Private prisons, criminological research and conflict of interest: A case study", *Crime & Delinquency*, 45(3), pp. 372–388.

Goffman, E. (1959) *The Presentation of Self in Everyday Life*. New York: Anchor Books.

Gooch, K. (2015) "Who needs restraining? Re-examining the use of physical restraint in an English young offender institution". *Journal of Social Welfare and Family Law*, 37(1), pp. 3–20.

Gooch, K. & Treadwell, J. (2019) "The illicit economy and recovery. What we need to understand". *Prison Service Journal*, Volume 242, pp. 56–63.

Gov.UK (2016) "Become a magistrate". [Online] Available at: https://www.gov.uk/become-magistrate/can-you-be-a-magistrate [Accessed 10 February 2017].

Greene, D. (2013) "Repeat performance: Is restorative justice another good reform gone bad?", *Contemporary Justice Review*, 16(3), pp. 359–390.

Grubin, D. & Wingate, S. (1996) "Sexual offence recidivism: prediction versus understanding". *Criminal Behaviour and Mental Health*, 6(4), pp. 349–59.

Grubin, G., Kamenskov, M., Dwyer, G. & Stephenson, T. (2019) "Post-conviction polygraph testing of sex offenders", *International Review of Psychiatry*, 31(2), pp. 141–148.

Guidoni, O. (2003) "The ambivalences of restorative justice: Some reflections on an Italian prison project", *Contemporary Justice Review*, 6(1), pp. 55–68.

The Guardian (1993) "Clarke bows to criticism of unit fine 'straitjacket'", *The Guardian*.

The Guardian (2017) "HMP Hewell unrest brought under control by prison riot squads". [Online] Available at: https://www.theguardian.com/society/2017/jul/23/ongoing-incident-security-specialists-called-to-english-jail [Accessed 14 August 2017].

Gyimah, S. (2017) "Reoffenders". Written question 107703. [Online] Available at: http://www.parliament.uk/business/publications/written-questions-answers-statements/written-question/Commons/2017-10-13/107703/ [Accessed 20 October 2017].

Haney, C. (2009) "The social psychology of isolation: why solitary confinement is psychologically harmful", *Prison Service Journal*, Volume 181, p. 12.

Hanson, K. et al. (2002) "First report of the collaborative outcome data project on the effectiveness of psychological treatment for sex offenders", *Sexual Abuse: A Journal of Research and Treatment*, 14(2), pp. 169–194.

Hanvey, S. & Hoing, M. (2013) "A more ethical way of working: circles of support and accountability". In: K. Harrison & B. Rainey, (eds.) *The Wiley-Blackwell Handbook of Legal and Ethical Aspects of Sex Offender Treatment and Management*. Chichester: John Wiley & Sons, pp. 372–387.

Harding, J., Davies, P. & Marir, G. (2017) *An Introduction to Criminal Justice*. London: Sage.

Hardwick, N. (2018) "Letter of resignation from Nick Hardwick to the Secretary of State for Justice". [Online] Available at: https://www.gov.uk/government/news/letter-of-resignation-from-nick-hardwick-to-the-secretary-of-state-for-justice [Accessed 10 October 2018].

Hardwick, N. & Jones, M. (2017) "Evidence given by Nick Hardwick and Martin Jones to the Justice Committee" [Interview] (18 October 2017).

Harris, T. (2015) *Changing Prisons, Shaping Lives. Report of the Independent Review into Self-inflicted Deaths in Custody of 18–24 year olds*. London: HMSO.

Harrison, K. (2007) "The High Risk Sex Offender Strategy in England and Wales: Is chemical castration an option?", *The Howard Journal*, 46(1), pp. 16–31.

Harrison, K. (2011) *Dangerousness, Risk and the Governance of Serious Sexual and Violent Offenders*. Abingdon: Routledge.

Harrison, K. & Rainey, B. (2009) "Suppressing human rights? A rights-based approach to the use of pharmacotherapy with sex offenders", *Legal Studies*, 29(1), 47–74.

Harrison, K. & Tamony, A. (2010) "Death row phenomenon, death row syndrome and their affect on capital cases in the US". *Internet Journal of Criminology*, pp. 1–16. [Online] Available at: https://www.internetjournalofcriminology.com/peer-reviewed-articles [Accessed 29 July 2019].

Hedderman, C. & Gunby, C. (2013) "Diverting women from custody: The importance of understanding sentencers' perspectives", *Probation Journal*, 60(4), pp. 425–438.

Hedderman, C. & Sugg, D. (1996) *Does Treating Sex Offenders Reduce Reoffending? Home Office Research Findings No 45*. London: Home Office.

Hegel, G. (1991) *Hegel: Elements of the Philosophy of Right*. Cambridge University Press.

Henning, K. & Frueh, B. (1996) "Cognitive-behavioural treatment of incarcerated offenders. An evaluation of the Vermont Department Corrections' cognitive self change program", *Criminal Justice and Behavior*, 23(4), pp. 523–541.

Henriques, U. (1972) "The rise and decline of the separate system of prison discipline", *Past and Present*, 54(1), pp. 61–93.

Hillier, J. & Mews, A. (2018) *The Reoffending Impact of Increased Release of Prisoners on Temporary Licence*. London: Ministry of Justice.

HM Chief Inspector of Prisons (2010) *Report on an Announced Inspection of HMYOI Feltham*. London: HMIP.

HM Chief Inspector of Prison (2013) *Report on an Unannounced Inspection of HMP/ YOI Feltham A*. London: HMIP.

HM Chief Inspector of Prisons (2016a) *Report on an Unannounced Inspection of HMP Full Sutton 11–22 January 2016*. London: HMIP.

HM Chief Inspector of Prisons (2016b) *Report on an Unannounced Inspection of HMP/YOI Parc 30 November – 1 December 2015 and 18–22 January 2016*. London: HMIP.

HM Chief Inspector of Prisons (2017a) *Annual Report 2016–17*. London: HMIP.

HM Chief Inspector of Prisons (2017b) *Report on an Announced Inspection of HMP Lindholme 2–6 October 2017*. London: HMIP.

HM Chief Inspector of Prisons (2017c) *Report on an Unannounced Inspection of HMP Grendon 8–18 May 2017*. London: HMIP.

HM Chief Inspector of Prisons (2017d) *Report on an Unannounced Inspection of HMP Whatton 15–26 August 2016*. London: HMIP.

HM Chief Inspector of Prisons (2018a) *Annual Report 2017–18*. London: HMIP.

HM Chief Inspector of Prisons (2018b) *Report on an Unannounced Inspection of HMP Springhill 4–15 December 2017*. London: HMIP.

HM Chief Inspector of Prisons (2018c) *Report on an Unannounced Inspection of HMP Wandsworth 26 February - 9 March 2018*. London: HMIP.

HM Chief Inspector of Prisons (2018d) *Report on an Unannounced Inspection of HMYOI Feltham*. London: HMIP.

HM Courts & Tribunals Service (2014) *Freedom of Information Request 90585*. London: HM Courts & Tribunals Service.

HM Government and College of Policing (2013) *Consultation on Out of Court Disposals*. London: Ministry of Justice.

HM Government and College of Policing (2014) *Out of Court Disposals Consultation Response*. London: Ministry of Justice.

HM Inspectorate of Prisons (2010) *Women in Prison*. London: HMIP.

HM Inspectorate of Prisons (2014) *Release on Temporary Licence (ROTL) failures*. London: HMIP.

HM Inspectorate of Prisons (2015) *People in Prison: Immigration Detainees*. London: HMIP.

HM Inspectorate of Prisons (2016a) *Life in Prison: Contact with Families and Friends*. London: HMIP.

HM Inspectorate of Prisons (2016b) *Unintended Consequences: Finding a Way Forward for Prisoners Serving Sentence of Imprisonment for Public Protection*. London: HMIP.

HM Inspectorate of Prisons (2017b) *Expectations Criteria for Assessing the Treatment of and Conditions for Men in Prisons, Version 5*. London: HMIP.

HM Inspectorate of Prisons (2019) "HMYOI Feltham A Children's Unit – new approach needed after 'extraordinary' collapse in safety and care, says Chief Inspector". Press Release, 24 July 2019. [Online] Available at: https://www.justiceinspectorates.gov.uk/hmiprisons/media/press-releases/2019/07/hmyoi-feltham-a-childrens-unit-new-approach-needed-after-extraordinary-collapse-in-safety-and-care-says-chief-inspector/ [Accessed 29 July 2019].

HM Inspectorate of Probation (2006) *An Independent Review of a Serious Further Offence Case: Anthony Rice*. London: HMIP.

HM Inspectorate of Probation (2011) *Putting the Pieces Together: An Inspection of Multi-agency Public Protection Arrangements*. London: HMIP.

HM Inspectorate of Probation (2014) *Transforming Rehabilitation Early Implementation*. London: HMIP.

HM Inspectorate of Probation (2015a) *A Follow Up Inspection of Multi-Agency Public Protection Arrangements*. London: HMIP.

HM Inspectorate of Probation (2015b) *Transforming Rehabilitation Early Implementation 2*. London: HMIP.

HM Inspectorate of Probation (2015c) *Transforming Rehabilitation Early Implementation 3*. London: HMIP.

HM Inspectorate of Probation (2016a) *Quality & Impact Inspection. The Effectiveness of Probation Work in North London*. London: HMIP.

HM Inspectorate of Probation (2016b) *Referral Orders, Do They Achieve Their Potential?* London: HMIP.

HM Inspectorate of Probation (2016c) *Transforming Rehabilitation Early Implementation 4*. London: HMIP.

HM Inspectorate of Probation (2016d) *Transforming Rehabilitation Early Implementation 5*. London: HMIP.

HM Inspectorate of Probation (2017a) *Annual Report 2017*. London: HMIP.

HM Inspectorate of Probation (2017b) *Quality & Impact inspection. The effectiveness of probation work in Gloucestershire*. London: HMIP.

HM Inspectorate of Probation (2017c) *Quality & Impact Inspection. The effectiveness of probation work in Gwent*. London: HMIP.

HM Inspectorate of Probation (2017d) *An Inspection of Through the Gate Resettlement Services for Prisoners Serving 12 Months or More*. London: HMIP.

HM Inspectorate of Probation/Criminal Justice Joint Inspection (2016) *An Inspection of Through the Gate Resettlement Services for Short-Term Prisoners*. London: HMIP.

HMPPS (2008) *Women Prisoners, Prison Service Order 4800*. London: Ministry of Justice.

HM Prison and Probation Service (2018a) *Enforcement of Community Orders and Suspended Sentence Orders, Probation Instruction 06/2014*. London: HM Prison & Probation Service.

HM Prison and Probation Service (2018b) *Breakdown of the Prison Estate and CPAs*. [Online] Available at: https://www.gov.uk/government/publications/prisons-and-their-resettlement-providers [Accessed 19 April 2019].

HM Prison and Probation Service (2019) *Youth Custody Data: February 2019*. London: HMPPS.

HM Prison Service (2005) *Use of Force – Prison Service Order 1600*. London: Ministry of Justice.

HM Prison Service (2012) *Parole, Release and Recall. Prison Service Order 6000*. London: Ministry of Justice.

Hollin, C. (2004) "To treat or not to treat? An historical perspective". In: C. Hollin, (ed.) *The Essential Handbook of Offender Assessment and Treatment*. Chichester: John Wiley & Sons, pp. 1–16.

Home Office (1970) *Report of the Advisory Council on the Penal System, Non-custodial and Semi-custodial Penalties*. London: Home Office.

Home Office (1984) *Probation Service in England and Wales: Statement of National Objectives and Priorities*. London: Home Office.

Home Office (1988) *Punishment, Custody and the Community*. London: HMSO.

Home Office (1998) *Effective Practice Initiative, a National Implementation Plan for the Effective Supervision of Offenders, Probation Circular 35/1998*. London: Home Office.

Home Office (1999) *Draft Guidance on the Disclosure of Information About Sex Offenders Who May Present a Risk to Children and Vulnerable Adults*. London: Police Science and Technology Unit.

Home Office (2010) *Protecting Children*. [Online] Available at: http://webarchive.nationalarchives.gov.uk/20100412124519/http://www.homeoffice.gov.uk/about-us/news/child-sex-offenders-disclosure.html [Accessed 16 July 2018].

Home Office (2014) *Crime Outcomes in England and Wales 2013/14, Home Office Statistical Bulletin 01/1.* London: Home Office.

Home Office (2017) *Freedom of Information Request Reference Number 42373.* London: Home Office .

Home Office (2018a) *Crime Outcomes in England and Wales: Year Ending March 2018 Statistical Bulletin 10/18.* London: Home Office.

Home Office (2018b) *Police Powers and Procedures, England and Wales, Year Ending 31 March 2018.* London: Home Office.

Hornle, T. (2013) "Moderate and non-arbitrary sentencing without guidelines: The German experience", *Law & Contemporary Problems,* 76(1), 189–210.

House of Commons Committee of Public Accounts (2016) *Transforming Rehabilitation HC 484.* London: House of Commons.

House of Commons Committee of Public Accounts (2018) *Government Contracts for Community Rehabilitation Companies.* London: House of Commons.

House of Commons Home Affairs Committee (2015) *Out Of Court Disposals. Fourteenth Report of Session 2014–15.* London: The Stationery Office Ltd.

House of Commons Justice Committee (2016) *Restorative Justice.* London: House of Commons.

House of Lords, Select Committee on the Constitution (2012) *Judicial Appointments, 25th Report of Session 2010–12.* London: The Stationery Office Ltd.

Howard League for Penal Reform (2011) *Twisted: The Use of Force on Children in Custody.* London: The Howard league for Penal Reform.

Howard League for Penal Reform (2016a) *A Million Days.* London: Howard League for Penal Reform.

Howard League for Penal Reform (2016b) *Preventing Prison Suicide: Perspectives from the Inside.* London: The Howard League for Penal Reform.

Howard League for Penal Reform (2017a) *Child Arrests in England and Wales 2016.* London: Howard League for Penal Reform.

Howard League for Penal Reform (2017b) *The 3 Rs of Prison Reform: Recall to Prison.* [Online] Available at: http://howardleague.org/what-you-can-do/the-3-rs-of-prison-reform/recall-to-prison/ [Accessed 18 October 2017].

Howard League for Penal Reform (2019) *Most Overcrowded Prisons in England and Wales.* [Online] Available at: http://howardleague.org/prisons-information/ [Accessed 2 May 2019].

Hoyle, C. & Rosenblatt, F. F. (2016) "Looking back to the future: Threats to the success of restorative justice in the United Kingdom". *Victims & Offenders,* 11(1), pp. 30–49.

Hudson, B. (2003) *Understanding Justice: An Introduction to Ideas, Perspectives and Controversies in Modern Penal Theory.* Buckingham: Open University Press.

Hulley, S., Crewe, B. & Wright, S. (2016) "Re-examining the problems of long-term imprisonment", *British Journal of Criminology,* Volume 56, pp. 769–792.

Hutton, M. (2016) "Visiting time: A tale of two prisons". *Probation Journal,* pp. 347–361.

Hutton, N. (2005) "Beyond populist punitiveness", *Punishment & Society,* 7(3), pp. 243–258.

Improvement of the Real Situation of Overcrowding in Prisons in Bangladesh (2016) *Key Statistics*. Dhkar: Improvement of the Real Situation of Overcrowding in Prisons in Bangladesh.

Independent (1993) "Earnings-related fines scrapped: Second government U-turn as Clarke abolished key parts of 1991 Act and Cabinet sets law and order programme". [Online] Available at: http://www.independent.co.uk/news/earnings-related-fines-scrapped-second-government-u-turn-as-clarke-abolishes-key-parts-of-1991-act-2322699.html [Accessed 06 January 2016].

Independent Monitoring Board (2016a) *Her Majesty's Prison and Young Offender Institution, PARC, Bridgend. Annual Report 2015–2016*. London: IMB.

Independent Monitoring Board (2016b) *Independent Monitoring Board HMP Lindholme Cat C Working prison, Annual Report 2015–2016*. London: IMB.

Independent Monitoring Board (2017a) "About us". [Online] Available at: https://www.imb.org.uk [Accessed 17 August 2017].

Independent Monitoring Board (2017b) *Annual Report HMP Wandsworth*. London: IMB.

Independent Monitoring Board (2017c) *Annual Report of the IMB at HMP Full Sutton*. London: IMB.

Independent Monitoring Board (2017d) *Annual Report of the IMB at HMP Whatton*. London: IMB.

Independent Monitoring Board (2017e) *Annual report of the Independent monitoring Board at HMP Springhill*. London: IMB.

Independent Monitoring Board (2018a) *Annual Report of the IMB at HMYOI Feltham*. London: IMB.

Independent Monitoring Board (2018b) *Annual Report of the Independent Monitoring Board at HMP Grendon*. London: IMB.

Insidetime (2017) "Get a grip!" [Online] Available at: https://insidetime.org/get-a-grip-2/ [Accessed 29 July 2019].

Institute for Criminal Policy Research (2016) *World Prison Brief Data – United States of America*. [Online] Available at: http://www.prisonstudies.org/country/united-states-america [Accessed 14 May 2019].

Institute for Criminal Policy Research, 2018. *World Prison Brief Data – Finland*. [Online] Available at: http://www.prisonstudies.org/country/finland [Accessed 15 May 2019].

Institute for Criminal Policy Research (2019a) *Bangladesh*. [Online] Available at: http://www.prisonstudies.org/country/bangladesh [Accessed 29 July 2019].

Institute for Criminal Policy Research (2019b) *New Zealand*. [Online] Available at: http://www.prisonstudies.org/country/new-zealand [Accessed 9 May 2019].

Institute for Criminal Policy Research (2019c) *United Kingdom: Scotland*. [Online] Available at: http://www.prisonstudies.org/country/united-kingdom-scotland [Accessed 15 May 2019].

Institute of Criminal Policy Research (2019d) *World Prison Brief Data – Spain*. [Online] Available at: http://www.prisonstudies.org/country/spain [Accessed 5 May 2019].

Institute for Criminal Policy Research (2019e) *World Prison Brief Data – Venezuela*. [Online] Available at: http://www.prisonstudies.org/country/venezuela [Accessed 2 May 2019].

Institute for Criminal Policy Research (2019f) *World Prison Brief – Kenya*. [Online] Available at: http://www.prisonstudies.org/country/kenya [Accessed 11 May 2019].

Institute of Race Relations (2017) "Death in immigration detention 1989–2017". [Online] Available at: http://www.irr.org.uk/news/deaths-in-immigration-detention-1989-2017/ [Accessed 29 July 2019].

Jack, A. (2017) A low benchmark? *New Law Journal*, Issue 7729.

James, A., Bottomly, A., Liebling, A. & Clare, E. (1997) *Privatising Prisons; Rhetoric and Reality*. London: Sage.

James, E. (2003) *A Life Inside: A Prisoner's Notebook*. London: Atlantic.

Jameson, N. & Allison, E. (1995) *Strangeways 1990: A Serious Disturbance*. London: Larkin.

Jewkes, Y. (2005) "Men behind bars 'doing' masculinity as an adaption to imprisonment". *Men and Masculinities*, 8(1), pp. 44–63.

Jewkes, Y. (2008) Local Prisons. In: *Dictionary of Prisons and Punishment*. Cullompton: Willan Publishing, pp. 156–157.

Jewkes, Y. (2018) "Just design: Healthy prisons and the architecture of hope". *Australian & New Zealand Journal of Criminology*, 51(3), pp. 319–338.

Jewkes, Y. & Gooch, K. (2019) "How lessons in Scandinavian design could help prisons with rehabilitation". *The Conversation*. [Online] Available at: https://theconversation.com/how-lessons-in-scandinavian-design-could-help-prisons-with-rehabilitation-106554 [Accessed 6 January 2019].

Jewkes, Y. & Johnston, H. (2006) *Prison Readings*. Cullompton: Willan Publishing.

Jewkes, Y., Crewe, B. & Bennett, J. (2016). *Handbook on Prisons*. 2nd edition. London: Routledge.

Johnson, B. (2011) "Sentencing". In: M. Tonry, (ed.) *The Oxford Handbook of Crime and Criminal Justice*. New York: Oxford University Press, pp. 696–729.

Johnston, H. (2016) "Prison histories, 1770s–1950s. Continuities and contradictions". In: Y. Jewkes, B. Crewe & J. Bennett (eds.) *Handbook on Prisons*. 2nd edition. London: Routledge, pp. 24–38.

Johnstone, G. (2008) "The agendas of the restorative justice movement". In: H. V. Miller, (ed.) *Restorative Justice From Theory to Practice*. Bingley, UK: JAI Press, pp. 59–79.

Johnstone, G. (2011) *Restorative Justice. Ideas, Values, Debates*. 2nd edition Abingdon, Oxon: Routledge.

Johnstone, G. (2014) *Restorative Justice in Prisons: Methods, Approaches and Effectiveness*. Strasbourg: Council of Europe.

Johnstone, G. (2016) "Restorative justice in prisons", *Prison Service Journal*, November (228), pp. 9–14.

Johnstone, G. & Van Ness, D. W. (2011) "The meaning of Restorative Justice". In: G. Johnstone and D. W. Van Ness, (eds.) *Handbook of Restorative Justice*. Abingdon, Oxon: Routledge, pp. 5–23.

Jolliffe, D. & Haque, Z. (2017) *Have Prisons Become a Dangerous Place? Disproportionality, Safety and Mental Health in British Prisons*. London: Runnymede and University of Greenwich.

Jones, H. (1981) "Old and new ways in probation". In: *Society Against Crime – Penal Practice in Modern Britain*. Harmandsworth: Penguin.

Jones, M. (2017a). "IPPs, recalls and the future of parole". [Online] Available at: http://www.russellwebster.com/martin-jones2/ [Accessed 25 October 2017].

Jones, M. (2017b) "The parole board faces up to new challenges". [Online] Available at: http://www.russellwebster.com/parole-board-50/ [Accessed 29 July 2019].

The Judiciary (2016) *Sentencing Policy Guidelines*. Nairobi: The Judiciary.

Justice (2017a) *Increasing Judicial Diversity*. London: Justice.

Justice (2017b) "Judicial diversity". [Online] Available at: https://justice.org.uk/our-work/areas-of-work/judicial-diversity/ [Accessed 5 May 2017].

Justice (2017c) "The parole system of England and Wales". [Online] Available at: https://justice.org.uk/parole-system-england-wales/ [Accessed 11 September 2017].

Kaiser Family Foundation (2019) "Population distribution by race/ethnicity". [Online] Available at: https://www.kff.org/other/state-indicator/distribution-by-raceethnicity/?currentTimeframe=0&sortModel=%7B%22colId%22:%22 Location%22,%22sort%22:%22asc%22%7D [Accessed 12 May 2019].

Kantorowicz-Reznichenko, E. (2018) "Day fines: Reviving the idea and reversing the (Costly) punitive trend", *American Criminal Law review*, 55, 333–372.

Kemshall, H. (2002) *Risk Assessment and Management of Serious Violent and Sexual Offenders: A Review of Current Issues*. Edinburgh: Scottish Executive Social Research.

Kemshall, H. & Weaver, B. (2012) "The sex offender public disclosure pilots in England and Scotland: Lessons for 'marketing strategies' and risk communication with the public". *Criminology & Criminal Justice*, 12(5), pp. 549–565.

Kemshall, H. & Wood, J. (2007) *The Operation and Experience of Multi-Agency Public Protection Arrangements*. London: Home Office.

Kemshall, H., McKenzie, G. & Wood, J. (2005) *Strengthening Multi-Agency Public Protection Arrangements*. London: Home Office.

Khan, O., Ferriter, M., Huband, N., Powney, M.J., Dennis, J.A. & Duggan, C. (2015) Pharmacological interventions for those who have sexually offended or are at risk of. *The Cochrane Database of Systematic Reviews*, 18(2), p. Feb.

Kimmett, E. & Tsintsadze, K. (2017) *Tackling Discrimination in Prison: Still not a Fair Response*. London: Prison Reform Trust/Zahid Mubarek Trust.

King, R. & McDermott, K. (1990) "'My geranium is subversive': some notes on the management of trouble in prisons", *British Journal of Sociology*, Volume 41, pp. 445–71.

King, R. & McDermott, K. (1995) *The State of Our Prisons*. Oxford: Clarendon Press.

Kitson-Boyce, R., Blagden, N. & Winder, B. (2018) "'This time it is different'. Preparing for release through a prison-model of CoSA: A Phenomenological and repertory grid analysis", *Sexual Abuse*, pp. 1–22.

Kitson-Boyce, R., Blagden, N., Winder, B. & Dillon, G. (2019) "Ambiguous practice or additional accountability: What can be learnt from the first prison-based model of CoSA in England and Wales?" *Journal of Forensic Psychology Research and Practice*, 19(2), pp. 186–209.

Lammy, D. (2017) *The Lammy Review. An Independent Review into the Treatment of, and Outcomes for, Black, Asian and Minority Ethnic Individuals in the Criminal Justice System*. London: Home Office.

Lappi-Seppala, T. (2009) "Imprisonment and penal policy in Finland". In: P. Wahlgren, (ed.) *Scandinavian Studies in Law*. Stockholm: Stockholm Institute for Scandinavian Law, pp. 334-379.

Lappi-Seppala, T. (2011) "Nordic youth justice", *Crime and Justice: A Review of Research*, Volume 40, pp. 199–265.

Lappi-Seppala, T. (2012) "Criminology, crime and criminal justice in Finland", *European Journal of Criminology*, 9(2), pp. 206–222.

Laws, B. (2014) *Fronting, Masking and Emotion Release: An Exploration of Prisoners' Emotional Management Strategies*. London: Howard league.

Laws, B. & Crewe, B. (2016) "Emotion regulation among male prisoners". *Theoretical Criminology*, 20(4), pp. 529–547.

Leese, M., Thomas, S. & Snow, L. (2006) "An ecological study of factors associated with rates of self-inflicted death in prisons in England and Wales". *International Journal of Law and Psychiatry*, 29(5), pp. 355–360.

Lewis, S. (2014) Exploring positive working relationships in light of the aims of probation, using a collaborative approach. *Probation Journal*, 61(4), pp. 334–345.

Liddington, D. (2017a) "Prison reform must also factor in a new focus on rehabilitation". [Online] Available at: https://www.standard.co.uk/comment/comment/prison-reform-must-also-factor-in-a-new-focus-on-rehabilitation-a3611251.html?amp [Accessed 16 August 2017].

Liddington, D. (2017b) *Written Statement to the House of Lords – HLWS365*. London: Ministry of Justice.

Liebling, A. (1994) "Suicide amongst women prisoners", *The Howard Journal*, 33(1), pp. 1–9.

Liebling, A. (1999) "Doing research in prison: Breaking the silence", *Theoretical Criminology*, 3(2), pp. 147–73.

Liebling, A. (2000) "Prison officers, policing and discretion". *Theoretical Criminology*, 4(3), pp. 333–357.

Liebling, A. (2011) "Moral performance, inhuman and degrading treatment and prison pain", *Punishment & Society*, 13(5), pp. 530–550.

Liebling, A. & Arnold, H. (2002) *Measuring the Quality of Prison Life (Research Findings No. 174)*. London: Home Office Research, Development and Statistics Development.

Liebling, A. & Williams, R. (2018) "The new subversive geranium: some notes on the management of additional troubles in maximum security prisons". *The British Journal of Sociology*, 69(4), pp. 1194–1219.

Liebling, A., Armstrong, R., Bramwell, R. & Williams, R. (2015) "Locating trust in a climate of fear: Religion, moral status, prisoner leadership, and risk in maximum security prisons". [Online] Available at: https://www.prc.crim.cam.ac.uk/publications/trust-report [Accessed 15 April 2019].

Liem, M. & Kunst, K. (2013) "Is there a recognizable post-incarceration syndrome among released lifers?", *International Journal of Law and Psychiatry*, Volume 36, pp. 333–337.

Light, R. & Campbell, B. (2007) "Prisoners' families: Still forgotten victims?", *Journal of Social Welfare and Family Law*, 28(3–4), pp. 297–308.

Lipscombe, S. & Beard, J. (2015) *Mandatory Life Sentences for Murder, House of Commons Briefing Paper Number 3626*. London: House of Commons Library.

Lloyd, C. et al. (2017) *The Evaluation of the Drug Recovery Wing Pilots – Final Report*. London: Department of Health.

Lombroso, C. (2006) *Criminal Man*. Durham: Duke University Press.

Lord Chief Justice of England and Wales (2018) *Judicial Diversity Statistics 2018*. London: Judicial Office.

Losel, F. & Schmucker, M. (2005) "The effectiveness of treatment for sexual offenders: A comprehensive meta-analysis". *Journal of Experimental Criminology*, Volume 1, pp. 117–146.

Loucks, N. (2000) *Prison Rules: A Working Guide*. London: Prison Reform Trust.

MacDonald, M. (2013) "Women prisoners, mental health, violence and abuse". *International Journal of Law and Psychiatry*, Volume 36, pp. 293–303.

Mackie, A., Raine, J., Burrows, J., Hopkins, M. and Dunstan, E. (2003) *Clearing the Debts: The Enforcement of Financial Penalties in Magistrates' Courts. Home Office Online Report 09/03*. London: Home Office.

MacRae, A. & Zehr, H. (2004) *The Little Book of Family Group Conferences New Zealand Style*. Intercourse, PA: Good Books.

Madsen, L., Parsons, S. & Grubin, D. (2004) "A preliminary study of the contribution of periodic polygraph testing to the treatment and supervision of sex offenders". *The Journal of Forensic Psychiatry & Psychology*, 15(4), pp. 682–695.

Maguire, M. et al. (2001) *Risk Management of Sexual and Violent Offenders: The Work of Public Protection Panels*. London: Home Office.

Mair, G. (1997) "Community penalties and the probation service". In: R. Morgan, M. Maguire & R. Reiner (eds.) *The Oxford Handbook of Criminology*. Oxford: Oxford University Press.

Mair, G. & Rumgay, J. (2014) *Probation Key Readings*. Abingdon: Routledge.

Mantle, G. (2006) "Probation: Dead, dying or poorly". *The Howard Journal*, 45(3), pp. 321–324.

Marshall, P. (1997) *Reconviction Study of HMP Grendon Therapeutic Community, Research Finding No 53*. London: Home Office.

Marshall, T. (1999) *Restorative Justice: An Overview*. London: Home Office Research Development and Statistics Directorate.

Martinson, R. (1974) "What works? Questions and answers about prison reform", *The Public Interest*, Volume 35, pp. 22–54.

Maruna, S. (2001) *Making Good. How Ex-Convicts Reform and Rebuild their Lives*. Washington, DC: American Psychological Association.

Maruna, S. (2014) "The role of wounded healing in restorative justice: An appreciation of Albert Eglash", *Restorative Justice: An International Journal*, 2(1), pp. 9–23.

Marzano, L., Hawton, K., Rivlin, A. & Fazel, S. (2011) "Psychosocial influences on prisoner suicide: A case-control study of near-lethal self-harm in women prisoners", *Social Science & Medicine*, Volume 72, pp. 874–883.

McCartan, K., Hoggett, J. & O'Sullivan, J. (2018) "Police officer attitudes to the practicalities of the sex offenders' register, ViSOR and Child Sexual Abuse Disclosure Scheme in England and Wales", *Journal of Sexual Aggression*, 24(1), pp. 37–50.

McConville, S. (1998) "The Victorian prison England, 1865–1965". In: N. Morris & D. J. Rothman (eds.) *The Oxford History of the Prison The practice of punishment in Western Society*. Oxford: Oxford University Press, pp. 117–150.

McEwan, A. W. (1986) "A typology of dispersal prisoners", *Personality and Individual Differences*, pp. 73–80.

McGowen, R. (1998) "The well ordered prison England, 1780–1865". In: *The Oxford History of the Prison*. Oxford: Oxford University Press, pp. 71–99.

McLaughlin, E. & Muncie, J. (2001) *Controlling Crime*. London: Sage.

McNeill, F. (2006) "A desistance paradigm for offender management". *Criminology & Criminal Justice*, 6(1), pp. 39–62.

McNeill, F., Farrall, S., Lightowler, C. & Maruna, S. (2012) "How and why people stop offending: Discovering desistance". *Insight*, (4 April 2012). [Online] Available at: https://www.iriss.org.uk/resources/insights/how-why-people-stop-offending-discovering-desistance [Accessed 29 July 2019].

McWilliams, W. (1983) "The mission to the English police courts 1876–1936". *The Howard Journal*, 22(1–3), pp. 129–147.

Merton, R. (1968) *Social Theory and Social Structure*. New York: The Free Press.

Mews, A., Di Bella, L. & Purver, M. (2017) *Impact Evaluation of the Prison-based Core Sex Offender Treatment Programme*. London: Ministry of Justice.

Mews, A., Hillier, J., McHugh, M. & Coxon, C. (2015) *The Impact of Short Custodial Sentences, Community Orders and Suspended Sentence Orders on Re-offending*. London: Ministry of Justice.

Ministry for Children (2018) *Youth Justice Residences*. [Online] Available at: https://www.orangatamariki.govt.nz/youth-justice/residences/ [Accessed 29 July 2018].

Ministry of Justice (2009) *The Future of the Parole Board, Consultation Paper 14/09*. London: Ministry of Justice.

Ministry of Justice (2010) *Controlling Anger and Learning to Manage It*. London: Ministry of Justice.

Ministry of Justice (2012a) *Certified Prisoner Accommodation Prison Service Instruction 17/2012*. London: Ministry of Justice.

Ministry of Justice (2012b) *The Legal Aid, Sentencing and Punishment of Offenders Act 2012 – General Summary of Release and Recall Provisions*. London: Ministry of Justice.

Ministry of Justice (2013a) *Code of Practice for Adult Conditional Cautions*. London: The Stationery Office.

Ministry of Justice (2013b) *Code of Practice for Youth Conditional Cautions*. London: Ministry of Justice.

Ministry of Justice (2013c) *Criminal Justice Statistics September 2012*. London: Ministry of Justice.

Ministry of Justice (2013d) *Quick Reference Guides to Out of Court Disposals*. London: Ministry of Justice.

Ministry of Justice (2013e) *Transforming Rehabilitation. A Revolution in the Way we Manage Offenders, Cm 8517*. London: HMSO.

Ministry of Justice (2013f) *Transforming Rehabilitation. A Strategy for Reform, Cm 8619*. London: HMSO.

Ministry of Justice (2014) *Penalty Notices for Disorder (PNDs)*. London: Ministry of Justice.

Ministry of Justice (2015) *Simple Cautions of Adult Offenders*. London: Ministry of Justice.

Ministry of Justice (2016a) *Freedom of Information Request 108509*. London: Ministry of Justice.

Ministry of Justice (2016b) *Prison Safety and Reform, Cm 935*. London: Ministry of Justice.

Ministry of Justice (2016c) *Prison Safety and Reform*. London: Ministry of Justice.

Ministry of Justice (2017a) *Annual NOMS Digest 2016/17*. London: Ministry of Justice.

Ministry of Justice (2017b) *Freedom of Information Request*. [Online] Available at: https://www.whatdotheyknow.com/request/363599/response/1003511/attach/3/108001%20Mick%20Geen.pdf?cookie_passthrough=1 [Accessed 31 July 2017].

Ministry of Justice (2017c) *Freedom of Information Act Request – 110785*. London: Ministry of Justice .

Ministry of Justice (2017d) *Freedom of Information Act Request 113134*. London: Ministry of Justice.

Ministry of Justice (2017e) *Government Response to the Lammy Review on the Treatment of, and Outcomes for, Black, Asian and Minority Ethnic Individuals in the Criminal Justice System*. London: Ministry of Justice.

Ministry of Justice (2017f) "Grendon prison Information". [Online] Available at: http://www.justice.gov.uk/contacts/prison-finder/grendon [Accessed 14 June 2018].

Ministry of Justice (2017g) "Home detention curfew". [Online] Available at: https://www.justice.gov.uk/offenders/before-after-release/home-detention-curfew [Accessed 6 October 2017].

Ministry of Justice (2017h) *National Offender Management Service Offender Equalities Annual Report*. London: Ministry of Justice.

Ministry of Justice (2017i) *NOMS Annual Workforce Statistics Bulletin 31 March 2017*. London: Ministry of Justice.

Ministry of Justice (2017j) "Prisons in England and Wales". [Online] Available at: https://www.justice.gov.uk/contacts/prison-finder [Accessed 14 June 2018].

Ministry of Justice (2017k) *Re-offending Behaviour After Participation in the Brighton Women's Centre Inspire programme*. London: Ministry of Justice.

Ministry of Justice (2017l) *Statistics on Race and the Criminal Justice System 2016*. London: Ministry of Justice.

Ministry of Justice (2017m) *The Urgent Notification process: Overview*. London: Ministry of Justice.

Ministry of Justice (2018a) *Criminal Justice System Statistics (December 2017)*. London: Ministry of Justice.

Ministry of Justice (2018b) *Female Offender Strategy, Cm 9642*. London: Ministry of Justice.

Ministry of Justice (2018c) *Female Offender Strategy*. London: HMSO.

Ministry of Justice (2018d) *HMPPS Annual Digest 2017/18*. London: Ministry of Justice.

Ministry of Justice (2018e) *HMPPS Annual Digest 2017/18 Official Statistics Bulletin*. London: Ministry of Justice.

Ministry of Justice (2018f) *HMPPS Workforce Statistics Bulletin, as at 30 June 2018*. London: Ministry of Justice.

Ministry of Justice (2018g) *Multi-Agency Public Protection Arrangements Annual Report 2017/18*. London: Ministry of Justice.

Ministry of Justice (2018h) *Offender Management Statistics Quarterly: January to March 2018*. London: Ministry of Justice.

Ministry of Justice (2018i) *Offender Management Statistics Quarterly: October to December 2018*. London: Ministry of Justice.

Ministry of Justice (2018j) *Our Secure Schools Vision*. London: Ministry of Justice.

Ministry of Justice (2018k) "Press release". [Online] Available at: https://www.gov.uk/government/news/justice-secretary-outlines-future-vision-for-probation [Accessed 4 October 2018].

Ministry of Justice (2018l) "Press release: Ministry of Justice takes over running of HMP Birmingham". [Online] Available at: https://www.gov.uk/government/news/ministry-of-justice-takes-over-running-of-hmp-birmingham [Accessed 8 October 2018].

Ministry of Justice (2018m) *Review of the Law, Policy and Procedure Relating to Parole Board Decisions*. London: Ministry of Justice.

Ministry of Justice (2019a) "Agreement reached on construction of new Wellingborough prison". [Online] Available at: https://www.gov.uk/government/news/agreement-reached-on-construction-of-new-wellingborough-prison?utm_source=2ac503e2-87a4-4d50-a191-a64c9013beb1&utm_medium=email&utm_campaign=govuk-notifications&utm_content=weekly [Accessed 4 May 2019].

Ministry of Justice (2019b) "Justice Secretary announces new model for probation". [Online] Available at: https://www.gov.uk/government/news/justice-secretary-announces-new-model-for-probation [Accessed 16 May 2019].

Ministry of Justice (2019c) "New prison anti-corruption taskforce unveiled". [Online] Available at: https://www.gov.uk/government/news/new-prison-anti-corruption-taskforce-unveiled?utm_source=ccf4693d-2662-4f06-ad83-13f47afaa01f&utm_medium=email&utm_campaign=govuk-notifications&utm_content=weekly [Accessed 4 May 2019].

Ministry of Justice (2019d) *Population and Capacity Briefing for Friday 10th May 2019*. London: Ministry of Justice.

Ministry of Justice (2019e) *Population Bulletin: Weekly 10 May 2019*. London: Ministry of Justice.

Ministry of Justice (2019f) "Prisons map". [Online] Available at: https://www.justice.gov.uk/downloads/contacts/hmps/prison-finder/prisons-map-2019-v1.pdf [Accessed 15 April 2019].

Ministry of Justice & Ipsos MORI (2013) *The Strengths and Skills of the Judiciary in the Magistrates' Court*. London: Ministry of Justice.

Ministry of Justice and National Statistics (2016) *Criminal Court Statistics Quarterly, England and Wales July to September 2016*. London: Ministry of Justice.

Ministry of Justice and National Statistics (2017) *Offender Management Statistics Quarterly, England and Wales*. London: Ministry of Justice and National Statistics.

Ministry of Justice and National Statistics (2019a) *Criminal Justice Statistics Quarterly Update to September 2018 England and Wales*. London: Ministry of Justice.

Ministry of Justice and National Statistics (2019b) *Offender Management Statistics Bulletin, England and Wales October to December 2018, Annual 2018, Prison population 31 March 2019*. London: Ministry of Justice.

Ministry of Justice and National Statistics (2019c) *Proven Reoffending Statistics Quarterly Bulletin April 2017 to June 2017*. London: Ministry of Justice.

Ministry of Justice and Youth Justice Board (2013) *Youth Cautions Guidance for Police and Youth Offending Teams*. London: Ministry of Justice.

Ministry of Justice and Youth Justice Board (2019) *Standards for Children in the Youth Justice System 2019*. London: Ministry of Justice.

Moore, M. (1998) The Moral Worth of Retribution. In: Principled Sentencing Readings of Theory & Policy. Oxford: Hart Publishing, pp. 150–155.

Morris, N. (1976) *Punishment, Desert and Rehabilitation*. Washington DC: US Government Printing Office.

Morris, N. & Rotham, D. (1998) *The Oxford History of the Prison*. Oxford: Oxford University Press.

Mountbatten Report (1966) *Report of the Inquiry into Prison Escapes and Security. Cmd 3175*. London: HMSO.

Moxon, D., Sutton, M. & Hedderman, C. (1990) *Unit Fines: Experiments in Four Courts. Research and Planning Unit Paper 59*. London: Home Office.

Moyle, P. & Tauri, J. M. (2016) "Māori, Family Group Conferencing and the mystifications of restorative justice", *Victims & Offenders*, 11(1), pp. 87–106.

Mungai, C. (2017) "The notorious law: This is what has landed many Kenyan women in Jail". [Online] Available at: https://www.sde.co.ke/article/2001249715/the-notorious-law-this-is-what-has-landed-many-kenyan-women-in-jail [Accessed 29 July 2019].

Nathan, S. (2003) "Prison privatization in the United Kingdom". In: R. Neufeld, A. Coyle & A. Campbell (eds.) *Capitalist Punishment. Prison Privatization & Human Rights*. London: Zed Books, pp. 162–178.

National Audit Office (2016) *Transforming Rehabilitation*. London: House of Commons.

National Debtline (2016) "Magistrates' court fines". [Online] Available at: https://www.nationaldebtline.org/EW/factsheets/Pages/magistratescourtfines/magistratescourtdebt.aspx# [Accessed 17 January 2017].

National Geographic (2018) "Kenya Travel Guide". [Online] Available at: https://www.nationalgeographic.com/travel/destinations/africa/kenya/ [Accessed 29 July 2019].

National Offender Management Service (2015a) *Minimising and Managing Physical Restraint*. London: National Offender Management Service.

National Offender Management Service (2015b) *Notification and Review Procedures for Serious Further Offences*. London: Ministry of Justice.

National Offender Management Service (2015c) *Sentence Calculation – Determinate Sentenced Prisoners*. London: National Offender Management Service.

National Offender Management Service (2016) *Providing Visits and Services to Visitors. Prison Service Instruction 16/2011*. London: Ministry of Justice.

National Offender Management Service (2017) *Recall Review & Re-release of Recall Offenders*. London: National Offender Management Service.

National Records of Scotland (2018) "Scotland's population – key statistics". [Online] Available at: https://www.nrscotland.gov.uk/statistics-and-data/statistics/stats-at-a-glance/scotlands-population-key-statistics [Accessed 9 May 2018].

National Statistics (2018) *Criminal Justice Statistics: September 2017*. London: National Statistics.

National Statistics and Ministry of Justice (2019a) *Safety in Custody Statistics Bulletin, England and Wales, Deaths in Prison Custody to March 2019, Assaults and Self-Harm to December 2019*. London: Ministry of Justice.

National Statistics and Ministry of Justice (2019b) *Offender Management Statistics Bulletin England and Wales July to September 2018*. Newport/London: National Statistics and Ministry of Justice.

Neese, B. (2017) "Classifying crime: major schools of criminology". [Online] Available at: https://online.seu.edu/schools-of-criminology/ [Accessed 6 March 2018].

Nellis, M. (1995) "Probation values for the 1990s", *The Howard Journal*, 34(1), pp. 19–44.

O'Donnell, I. (2014) *Prisoners, Solitude and Time*. Oxford: Oxford University Press.

Office for National Statistics (2011) *2011 Census*. London: ONS.

Oxford Dictionaries Online (2015) *Oxford Dictionary of English*. 3rd edition Oxford: Oxford University Press.

Padfield, N. (2012) "Reflection on 'About Parole'", *Prison Service Journal*, Volume 200, pp. 18–23.

Padfield, N. (2016) "A new chapter for the Parole Board", *Criminal Law Review*, pp. 379–380.

Padfield, N., Morgan, R. & Maguire, M. (2012) "Out of court, out of sight? Criminal sanctions and non-judicial decision-making". In: M. Maguire, R. Morgan & R. Reiner, (eds.) *Oxford Handbook of Criminology*. Oxford University Press, pp. 955–985.

Panchamia, N. (2012) *Competition in Prisons*. London: Institute for Government. Available at: https://www.instituteforgovernment.org.uk/publications/competition-prisons [Accessed 29 July 2019].

Parker, P. (2016) "Restorative justice in prison: A contradiction in terms or a challenge and a reality?", *Prison Service Journal*, November (228), pp. 15–20.

Parole Board for England and Wales (2018) *Annual Report and Accounts 2017/18*. London: The Parole Board.

The Parole Board (2017a) *Parole Board for England and Wales Annual Report and Accounts 2016/17*. London: The Parole Board.

The Parole Board (2017b) *Parole Board for England and Wales Business Plan April 2017 to March 2018*. London: The Parole Board.

Parsons, T. (2013) *The Social System*. London: Routledge.

Pedder, K. (2017) *Out for Good Lessons for the Future*. London: Prison Reform Trust.

Penal Reform International (2016) "Equal justice: Making community sanctions work for women in Kenya". [Online] Available at: https://www.penalreform.org/resource/equal-justice-making-community-sanctions-work-women-kenya/ [Accessed 18 September 2018].

Penal Reform International/Kenya Probation and Aftercare Service (2016) *Community Service and Probation for Women. A Study in Kenya*. London: Penal Reform International.

Peters, E. (1998) "Prison before the prison. The ancient and medieval worlds". In: *The Oxford History of the Prison. The Practice of Punishment in Western Society*. Oxford: Oxford University Press, pp. 3–43.

Pettit, B. & Western, B. (2004) "Mass imprisonment and the life course: Race and class inequality in US incarceration", *American Sociological review*, 69(2), pp. 151–169.

Pina-Sanchez, J., Roberts, J. & Sferopoulos, D. (2019) "Does the Crown Court discriminate against Muslim-named offenders? A novel investigation based on text mining techniques", *British Journal of Criminology*, 59(3), 718–736.

Pinsker, J. (2015) "Finland, home of the $103,000 speeding ticket". [Online] Available at: http://www.theatlantic.com/business/archive/2015/finland-home-of-the-103000-speeding-ticket/387484/ [Accessed 26 January 2017].

Polasckek, D. (2006) "Violent offender programmes: concept, theory and practice". In: C. Hollin & E. Palmer, (eds.) *Offending Behaviour Programmes: Development, Application and Controversies*. Chichester: John Wiley & Sons.

Police Officer (2017) "Interview with police officer" [Interview] (20 January 2017).

politics.co.uk (2017) "Immigration removal/detention centres". [Online] Available at: http://www.politics.co.uk/reference/immigration-removal-detention-centres [Accessed 29 July 2019].

Pollock, N., McBain, I. & Webster, C. (1989) "Clinical decision making the assessment of dangerousness". In: K. Howells & C. Hollin, (eds.) *Clinical Approaches to Violence*. Chichester: John Wiley & Sons.

Posner, R. (1985) "An economic theory of criminal law". *Columbia Law Review*, Volume 85, p. 1193.

Poso, T., Enroos, R. & Vierula, T. (2010) "Children residing in prison with their parents: An example of institutional invisibility", *The Prison Journal*, 90(4), 516–533.

Prison Insider (2015) "Venezuela". [Online] Available at: https://www.prison-insider.com/countryprofile/prisonsinvzla [Accessed 2 August 2017].

Prison Reform Trust (1991) *The Woolf Report. A Summary of the Main Findings and Recommendations of the Inquiry into Prison Disturbances*. London: Prison Reform Trust.

Prison Reform Trust (2005) *Private Punishment: Who Profits?* London: Prison Reform Trust.

Prison Reform Trust (2017) *Prison: The Facts. Bromley Briefings Summer 2017* London: Prison Reform Trust.

Prison Reform Trust (2018a) *Broken Trust. The Rising Number of Women Recalled to Prison*. London: Prison Reform Trust.

Prison Reform Trust (2018b) *Bromley Briefing Autumn 2018*. London: Prison Reform Trust.

Prison Reform Trust (2018c) *Bromley Briefings Prison Factfile Autumn 2018*. London: Prison Reform Trust.

Prison Reform Trust (2018d) *More Carrot, Less Stick. Proposals for a Radical Reassessment of the use of Release on Temporary Licence in Prisons to Support Work, Training and Resettlement*. London: Prison Reform Trust.

Prison Reform Trust (2018e) *Prison: The Facts. Bromley Briefings Summer 2018*. London: Prison Reform Trust.

Prison Service Journal (2016) *Special Edition Young People in Custody*. July, No 226. Leyhill: Ministry of Justice. [Online] Available at: https://www.crimeandjustice.org.uk/publications/psj/prison-service-journal-226 [Accessed 29 July 2019].

Prison Service Journal (2018) *Special Edition 50 Years of the Parole System for England and Wales*. May, No. 237.

Prisons Research Centre (2019) "Comparative Penology". [Online] Available at: https://www.prc.crim.cam.ac.uk/directory/research-themes/comparative-penology [Accessed 19 April 2019].

Probation Journal (2019) "Special edition: Five years of Transforming Rehabilitation: Markets, management and vales", *Probation Journal*, 66(1).

Raine, J. & Dunstan, E. (2009) "How well do sentencing guidelines work? Equity, proportionality and consistency in the determination of fine levels in the Magistrates' Courts of England and Wales", *The Howard Journal*, 48(1), pp. 13–36.

Raynor, P. (1998) "Attitudes, social problems and reconvictions in the 'STOP' probation experiment", *The Howard Journal*, 37(1), pp. 1–15.

Raynor, P. & Vanstone, M. (1997) *Straight Thinking On Probation (STOP) The Mid-Glamorgan Experiment*. Oxford: Centre for Criminological Research: University of Oxford.

Remedi, P. (2016) [Interview] (22 November 2016).

Rex, S. (1998) "A new form of rehabilitation". In: A. von Hirsch & A. Ashworth, (eds.) *Principled Sentencing, Readings on Theory and Policy*. Oxford: Hart Publishing.

Richards, B. (1978) "The experience of long-term imprisonment", *British Journal of Criminology*, Volume 18, pp. 162–9.

Roberts, J. (2013) "Sentencing Guidelines in England and Wales: Recent developments and emerging issues", *Law & Contemporary problems*, 76(1), pp. 1–25.

Roberts, J. & Harris, L. (2017) "Addressing the problems of the prison estate. The role of sentencing policy", *The Prison Service Journal*, 231, 8–14.

Roberts, R. & Garside, R. (2005) *Punishment before justice? Understanding Penalty Notices for Disorder*, London: Crime and Society Foundation.

Robinson, G. (2008) "Late-modern rehabilitation. The evolution of a penal strategy". *Punishment & Society*, 10(4), pp. 429–445.

Robjant, K., Robbins, I. & Senior, V. (2009) "Psychological distress amongst immigration detainees: A cross-sectional questionnaire study", *British Journal of Clinical Psychology*, 48(3), pp. 275–286.

Rocque, M., Jennings, W., Ozkan, T. & Piquero, A. (2017) "Forcing the plant. Desistance from crime and crime prevention". In: N. Tilley (ed.) *Handbook of Crime Prevention and Community Safety*. London: Routledge, pp. 183–204.

Romania-insider.com (2017) "Romania could introduce electronic monitoring to reduce prison overcrowding". [Online] Available at: https://www.romania-insider.com/electronic-monitoring-prison-overcrowding/amp/ [Accessed 8 August 2017].

Rusche, G. & Kirchheimer, O. (1939) *Punishment and Social Structure*. New York: Columbia University Press.

Sanders, A., Young, R. & Burton, M. (2010) *Criminal Justice*. 4th edition Oxford: Oxford University Press.

Scharff-Smith, P. & Gampell, L. (2011) *Children of Imprisoned Parents*. Denmark: The Danish Institute for Human Rights.

Schmucker, M. & Losel, F. (2015) "The effects of sexual offender treatment on recidivism: An international meta-analysis of sound quality evaluations". *Journal of Experimental Criminology*, Volume 11, pp. 597–630.

Schwartz, M. & Nurge, D. (2004) "Capitalist punishment: ethics and private prisons". *Critical Criminology*, Volume 12, pp. 133–156.

Scott, D. (2011) "'That's not my name': prisoner deference and disciplinarian prison officers", *Criminal Justice Matters*, Volume 84, pp. 8–9.

Scott, D. (2017) *Against Imprisonment. An Anthology of Abolitionist Essays*. Hook: Waterside Press.

Scottish Executive (2003) *Scotland in Short*. Edinburgh: Scottish Executive.

Scottish Parliament (2013) *Inquiry into Purposeful Activity in Prisons*. Edinburgh: Scottish Parliament.

Sentencing Council (2016a) *Out of Court Disposals*. [Online] Available at: https://www.sentencingcouncil.org.uk/explanatory-material/item/out-of-court-disposals/ [Accessed 05 January 2016].

Sentencing Council (2016b) *Reduction in Sentence for a Guilty Plea Guideline – Consultation*. London: Sentencing Council.

Sentencing Council (2016c) *Robbery Definitive Guideline*. London: Sentencing Council.

Sentencing Council (2017a) "Council Members". [Online] Available at: https://www.sentencingcouncil.org.uk/about-us/council-members/ [Accessed 14 February 2017].

Sentencing Council (2017b) "Fine calculator". [Online] Available at: http://www.sentencingcouncil.org.uk/fine-calculator/ [Accessed 17 January 2017].

Sentencing Council (2017c) *Imposition of Community and Custodial Sentences Definitive Guideline*. London: Sentencing Council.

Sentencing Council (2017d) "Prosecution costs". [Online] Available at: https://www.sentencingcouncil.org.uk/explanatory-material/item/fines-and-financial-orders/prosecution-costs/ [Accessed 5 May 2017].

Sentencing Council (2017e) *Reduction in Sentence for a Guilty Plea*. London: Sentencing Council.

Sentencing Council (2017f) *Reduction in Sentence for a Guilty Plea Guideline: Consultation*. [Online] Available at: https://www.sentencingcouncil.org.uk/publications/item/reduction-in-sentence-for-a-guilty-plea-guideline-consultation/ [Accessed 14 February 2017].

Sentencing Council (2017g) *Sentencing Children and Young People. Overarching Principles and Offence Specific Guidelines for Sexual Offences and Robbery – Definitive Guideline*. London: Sentencing Council .

Sentencing Council (2018) *Breach Offences Definitive Guideline*. London: Sentencing Council.

Sentencing Guidelines Council (2004) *Overarching Principles: Seriousness*. London: Sentencing Guidelines Secretariat.

Sentencing Guidelines Council (2007) *Reduction in Sentence for a Guilty Plea*. London: Sentencing Guidelines Council.

Sentencing Guidelines Council (2008) *Magistrate's Court Sentencing Guidelines, Definitive Guideline*. London: Sentencing Guidelines Council.

Shammas, V. (2015) "A prison without walls: Alternative incarceration in the late age of social democracy", *Prison Service Journal*, pp. 3–9.

Sharrock, D. (1993) "Judges try to 'preserve public confidence'", *The Guardian*.

Shaw, D. (2019) "Feltham YOI: Prison officers attacked by teenage inmates", *BBC News*, (9 April 2019), [Online] Available at: https://www.bbc.co.uk/news/uk-england-london-47862354 [Accessed 29 July 2019].

Sherman, L. & Strang, H. (2007) *Restorative Justice: The Evidence*. London: Smith Institute.

Sherman, L., Strang, H., Mayo-Wilson, E., Woods, D. J. & Ariel, B. (2015) "Are restorative justice conferences effective in reducing repeat offending? Findings from a Campbell systematic review", *Journal of Quantitative Criminology*, Volume 31, pp. 1–24.

Shichor, J. (1998) "Private prisons in perspective: Some conceptual issues", *The Howard Journal*, 37(1), pp. 82–100.

Shingler, J. & Pope, L. (2018) *The Effectiveness of Rehabilitative Services for Black, Asian and Minority Ethnic People: A Rapid Evidence Assessment*. London: Ministry of Justice.

Silvestri, A. (2013) *Prison Conditions in the United Kingdom*. Rome: European Prison Observatory.

Sleed, M., Baradon, T. & Fonagy, P. (2013) "New beginnings for mother and babies in prison: A cluster randomized controlled trial", *Attachment & Human Development*, 15(4), pp. 349–367.

Smith, K. (2016) [Interview] (21 November 2016).

Smith, P. (2016) "Prisoner's diaries reveal what it's really like to be inside as the crisis deepens". [Online] Available at: https://www.buzzfeed.com/patricksmith/prison-diaries?utm_term=.apj3vRLkEl#.sydonPzrgq [Accessed 29 July 2019].

Smith, R. (2014) "Re-inventing diversion", *Youth Justice*, 14(2), pp. 109–121.

Solanki, A.-R., Bateman, T., Boswell, G. & Hill, E. (2006) *Antisocial Behaviour Orders for Young People*. London: Youth Justice Board.

Sommers, I., Baskin, D. & Fagan, J. (1994) "Getting out of the life: crime desistance by female street offenders". *Deviant Behaviour*, Volume 15, pp. 125–149.

Spicer, G. H.-D. a. K. (2004) *Piloting "On the Spot Penalties" for Disorder: Final Results from a One-year Pilot, Home Office Findings 257*. London: Home Office.

Spierenburg, P. (1998) "The Body and the State". In: N. Morris & D. J. Rothman (eds.) *The Oxford History of the Prison. The Practice of Punishments in Western Society*. Oxford: Oxford University Press, pp. 44–70.

Stafford, M. & Warr, M. (1993) "A reconceptualization of general and specific deterrence", *Journal of Research in Crime and Delinquency*, 30(2), pp. 123–135.

Strang, H. (2002) *Repair or Revenge: Victims and Restorative Justice*. Oxford: Oxford University Press.

Strickland, P. (2016) *Contracting Out Probation Services 2013–2016*. London: House of Commons.

Strickland, P. (2017) *The Prisons and Courts Bill – Prison Aspects. Briefing Paper Number 7907*. London: House of Commons Library.

Strong, K. & Van Ness, D. (2015) *Restoring Justice. An Introduction to Restorative Justice*. 5th edition Abingdon, Oxon: Routledge.

Suzuki, M. & Hayes, H. (2016) "Current debates over restorative justice: Concept, definition and practice", *Prison Service Journal*, November (228), pp. 4–8.

Sykes, G. (1958) *The Society of Captives: A Study of a Maximum-Security Prison*. Princeton, NJ: Princeton University Press.

Tanner, W. (2013) *The Case for Private Prisons*. London: Reform.

Taylor, C. (2016) *Review of the Youth Justice System in England and Wales*. London: Ministry of Justice.

Taylor, R. (2000) *Seven-Year Reconviction Study of HMP Grendon Therapeutic Community, Research Finding No 115*. London: Home Office.

Taylor, S., Burke, L., Millings, M. & Ragonese, E. (2017) "Transforming Rehabilitation during a penal crisis: A case study of Through the Gate services in a resettlement prison in England and Wales", *European Journal of Probation*, 9(2), pp. 115–131.

The Telegraph (2013) "Use of police cautions has 'got out of hand', magistrates warn". [Online] Available at: http://www.telegraph.co.uk/news/uknews/law-and-order/9830254/Use-of-police-cautions-has-got-out-of-hand-magistrates-warn.html [Accessed 06 January 2016].

The Telegraph (2017) "British prison is first to use 'disruptor' to create drone-proof 'shield' around jail". [Online] Available at: http://www.telegraph.co.uk/news/2017/05/16/british-prison-first-use-disruptor-create-drone-proof-shield/ [Accessed 14 August 2017].

The Times (1993a) "Justice in unit fines", *The Times*.

The Times (1993b) "Magistrates meet Clarke to urge reform of unit fine", *The Times*.

Thomas, C. (2017) *2016 UK Judicial Attitude Survey*. London: UCL Judicial Institute.

Thomas, T. (2003) "Sex offender community notification: Experiences from America", *Howard Journal*, 42(3), 217–228.

Thompson, D. & Thomas, T. (2017) *The Resettlement of Sex Offenders after Custody: Circles of Support and Accountability*. Abingdon: Routledge.

Tomlinson, K. (2016) "An examination of Deterrence Theory: Where do we stand". *Federal Probation*, 80(3), pp. 33–38.

Tonry, M. (1996) *Sentencing Matters*. New York: Oxford University Press.

TrackTR partnership (2018) *Under Represented, Under Pressure, Under Resourced. The Voluntary Sector in Transforming Rehabilitation*. London: Clinks.

Transform Justice (2016) *The Role of the Magistrates?* London: Transform Justice.

Turley, C., Payne, C. & Webster, S. (2013) *Enabling Features of Psychologically Informed Planned Environments*. London: Ministry of Justice.

United States Department of State (2016) *Country Reports on Human Rights Practices for 2016 – Venezuela*. Washington: United States Department of State – Bureau of Democracy, Human Rights and Labor.

United States Sentencing Commission (2016) *Guidelines Manual 2016*. Washington: United States Sentencing Commission.

van Ginneken, E., Sutherland, A. & Molleman, T. (2017) "An ecological analysis of prison overcrowding and suicide rates in England and Wales, 2000–2014". *International Journal of Law and Psychiatry*, Volume 50, pp. 76–82.

Van Ness, D. & Strong, K. (2010) *Restoring Justice: An Introduction to Restorative Justice*. 4th edition New Providence NJ: Matthew Bender & Co Inc.

von Hirsch, A. (1976) *Doing Justice*. New York: Hill and Wang.

von Hirsch, A. (1998) "Rehabilitation". In: A. von Hirsch & A. Ashworth, (eds.) *Principled Sentencing Readings on Theory & Policy*. Oxford: Hart Publishing, pp. 1–6.

von Hirsch, A. (2017) *Deserved Criminal Sentences*. Oxford: Hart Publishing.

von Hirsch, A. & Jareborg, N. (1991) "Gauging criminal harm: A living standard analysis", *Oxford Journal of Legal Studies*, Volume 11, p. 1.

von Hirsch, A. & Maher, L. (1998) "Should penal rehabilitation be revived". In: A. von Hirsch & A. Ashworth, (eds.) *Principled Sentencing. Readings on Theory & Policy*. Oxford: Hart Publishing, pp. 26–33.

Wacquant, L. (2009) *Punishing the Poor: The Neoliberal Government of Social Insecurity*. Durham: Duke University Press.

Wacquant, L. (2010) "Class, race & hyperincarceration in revanchist America", *Daedalus*, 139(3), pp. 74–90.

Waiton, S. (2006) *Amoral Panic: The Construction of "Antisocial Behaviour" and the Institutionalisation of Vulnerability*. Glasgow: University of Glasgow.

Walgrave, L. (2008) *Restorative Justice, Self Interest and Responsible Citizenship*. Cullompton: Willan Publishing.

Walmsley, R. (2018) *World Prison Population List*. 12th edition. London: Institute for Criminal Policy Research.

Walters, M. (2015) "I thought he's a monster … [but] he was just … normal: Examining the therapeutic benefits of restorative justice for homicide", *British Journal of Criminology*, 55(6), pp. 1207–1225.

Ward, T. (2002) "Good lives and the rehabilitation of sexual offenders: promises and problems", *Aggression and Violent Behaviour*, Volume 7, pp. 513–528.

Ward, T. & Brown, M. (2004) "The good lives model and conceptual issues in offender rehabilitation", *Psychology, Crime & Law*, 10(3), pp. 243–257.

Ward, T. & Maruna, S. (2007) *Rehabilitation*. Abingdon: Routledge.

Ward, T., Fox, K. & Garber, M. (2014) "Restorative justice, offender rehabilitation and desistance", *Restorative Justice: An International Journal*, 2(1), 24–42.

Warner, K. (2012) "Equality before the ale and equal impact of sanctions: Doing justice to differences in wealth and employment status". In: L. Zedner & J. V. Roberts, (eds.) *Principles and Values in Criminal Law and Criminal Justice: Essays in Honour of Andrew Ashworth*. Oxford University Press, pp. 225–243.

Warrell, H. & Plimmer, G. (2015) "Wrexham jail to be run by public sector". *Financial Times*, (24 February 2015) [Online] Available at: https://www.ft.com/content/ea817594-bc37-11e4-a6d7-00144feab7de [Accessed 29 July 2019].

Weaver, M. (2016) "Prison riot ends after 60 inmates take over a wing at HMP Swaleside". [Online] Available at: https://www.theguardian.com/society/2016/

dec/23/prison-riot-ends-60-inmates-hmp-swaleside-isle-of-sheppey   [Accessed 14 August 2017].

Webster, C. M. & Doob, A. N. (2012) "Searching for sasquatch: Deterrence of crime through sentence severity". In: J. Petersilia & K. Reitz, (eds.) *The Oxford Handbook of Sentencing and Corrections*. New York: Oxford University Press, pp. 173–195.

Webster, R. (2017) "Why are offenders recalled to prison". [Online] Available at: http://www.russellwebster.com/recalls/ [Accessed 19 October 2017].

Whittaker, C. & Mackie, A. (1997) *Enforcing Financial Penalties Home Office Research Study 165*. London: Home Office.

Wilcox, D. & Sosnowski, D. (2005) "Polygraph examination of British sexual offenders: A pilot study on sexual history disclosure testing", *Journal of Sexual Aggression*, 11(1), pp. 3–25.

Wilcox, D., Sosnowski, D. & Middleton, D. (1999) "The use of the polygraph in the community supervision of sex offenders", *Probation Journal*, Volume 46, pp. 234–240.

Williams, K. (2001) *Textbook on Criminology*. Oxford: Oxford University Press.

Williams, K. (2012) *Textbook on Criminology*. 7th edition. Oxford: Oxford University Press.

Wilson, R. J., Cortoni, F. & McWhinnie, A. J. (2009) "Circles of support & accountability: A Canadian national replication of outcome findings", *Sexual Abuse: A Journal of Research and Treatment*, 21(4), pp. 412–430.

Wilson, R., McWhinnie, A. & Wilson, C. (2008) "Circles of Support and Accountability: An international partnership in reducing sexual offender recidivism", *The Prison Service Journal*, Volume 178, pp. 26–36.

Winder, B. et al. (2017) "Evaluation of the use of pharmacological treatment with prisoners experiencing high levels of hypersexual disorder", *The Journal of Forensic Psychiatry & Psychology*, 29(1), pp. 53–71.

Women in Prison (2017a) *Corston 10+. The Cosrton Report 10 Years on*. London: Women in Prison.

Women in Prison (2017b) "Key Facts". [Online] Available at: http://www. womeninprison.org.uk/research/key-facts.php [Accessed 23 September 2018].

Wood, J. & Kemshall, H. (2010) "Effective multi-agency public protection: Learning from the research". In: K. Harrison, (ed.) *Managing High Risk Sex Offenders in the Community: Risk Management, Treatment and Social Responsibility*. Cullompton: Willan Publishing, pp. 39–60.

Wood, W. (2016) "Editor's introduction: The future of restorative justice?", *Victims & Offenders. An International Journal of Evidence-Based Research, Policy and Practice*, 11(1), pp. 1–8.

Wood, W. & Suzuki, M. (2016) "Four challenges in the future of restorative justice", *Victims & Offenders*, 11(1), pp. 149–172.

Woodall, J., Dixey, R., Green, J. & Newell, C. (2009) "Healthier prisons: The role of a prison visitors' centre", *International Journal of Health Promotion & Education*, 47(1), pp. 12–18.

World Health Organisation (2009) *Women's Health in Prison: Correcting Gender Inequity in Prison Health*. Copenhagen: World Health Organisation.

World Prison Brief (2019a) "Highest to lowest – occupancy level (based on official capacity)". [Online] Available at: http://www.prisonstudies.org/highest-to-lowest/occupancy-level?field_region_taxonomy_tid=All [Accessed 2 May 2019].

World Prison Brief (2019b) "Highest to lowest – prison population total". [Online] Available at: http://www.prisonstudies.org/highest-to-lowest/prison-population-total?field_region_taxonomy_tid=14 [Accessed 15 April 2019].

Worldometers (2019a) "Bangladesh Population". [Online] Available at: http://www.worldometers.info/world-population/bangladesh-population/ [Accessed 13 May 2019].

Worldometers (2019b) "Countries in the world by population". [Online] Available at: http://www.worldometers.info/world-population/population-by-country/ [Accessed 14 May 2019].

Worldometers (2019c) "Kenya population". [Online] Available at: http://www.worldometers.info/world-population/kenya-population/ [Accessed 11 May 2019].

Worldometers (2019d) "New Zealand population". [Online] Available at: http://www.worldometers.info/world-population/new-zealand-population/ [Accessed 9 May 2019].

Worldometers (2019e) "Spain". [Online] Available at: http://www.worldometers.info/world-population/spain-population/ [Accessed 5 May 2019].

Worldometers (2019f) "U.S. Population". [Online] Available at: http://www.worldometers.info/world-population/us-population/ [Accessed 14 May 2019].

Worldometers (2019g) "Venezuela". [Online] Available at: http://www.worldometers.info/world-population/venezuela-population/ [Accessed 2 May 2019].

Wright, V. (2010) *Deterrence in Criminal Justice. Evaluating Certainty vs. Severity of Punishment*. Washington DC: The Sentencing Project.

Young People Tell Their Stories – Inside a Youth Justice Residence (2018) [Film] New Zealand: RNZ.

Youth Justice Board, n/d. *Referral Orders*. London: Youth Justice Board.

Youth Justice Board and Ministry of Justice (2018) *Length of Time Spent in Youth Custody 2016/17*. London: Youth Justice Board.

Youth Justice Board and Ministry of Justice (2019) *Youth Justice Statistics 2017/18, England and Wales*. London: Youth Justice Board/Ministry of Justice.

Zedlewski, E. (2010) *Alternatives to Custodial Supervision: The Day Fine*, NCJ 230401, Washington: U.S. Department of Justice.

Zehr, H. (1985) *Retributive Justice, Restorative Justice, Occasional Paper No. 4*. Ontario: MCC Canada Victim Offender Ministries Program and the MCC U.S. Office of Criminal Justice.

Zehr, H. (2005) *Changing Lenses: A New Focus for Crime and Justice*. 3rd edition Scottdale, PA: Herald Press.

Zehr, H. (2014) *The Little Book of Restorative Justice*. New York: Good Books.

Index

Printed by Printforce, United Kingdom